After King Philip's War

Reencounters with Colonialism: New Perspectives on the Americas

editors (all of Dartmouth College)

Mary C. Kelley, AMERICAN HISTORY
Agnes Lugo-Ortiz, LATIN AMERICAN STUDIES
Donald Pease, AMERICAN LITERATURE
Ivy Schweitzer, AMERICAN LITERATURE
Diana Taylor, LATIN AMERICAN AND LATINO STUDIES

Francis R. Aparicio and Susana Chávez-Silverman, eds.
Tropicalizations: Transcultural Representations of Latinidad

Michelle Burnham
Captivity and Sentiment: Cultural Exchange in American Literature, 1682–1861

Colin G. Calloway, ed.
After King Philip's War: Presence and Persistence in Indian New England

After King Philip's War

Presence and Persistence in Indian New England

EDITED, WITH AN INTRODUCTION BY

Colin G. Calloway

Dartmouth College

PUBLISHED BY UNIVERSITY PRESS OF NEW ENGLAND

HANOVER AND LONDON

Dartmouth College
Published by University Press of New England, Hanover, NH 03755
© 1997 by the Trustees of Dartmouth College
All rights reserved
Printed in the United States of America

5 4 3 2 1

CIP data appear at the end of the book

Chapter 3, "The 'Disappearance' of the Abenaki in Western Maine," by David L. Ghere, is reprinted from the *American Indian Quarterly*, volume 17, by permission of the University of Nebraska Press. Copyright © 1993 by the University of Nebraska Press.

Chapter 10, "Tribal Network and Migrant Labor," by Harald E. L. Prins, was originally published in Alice Littlefield and Martha C. Knack, eds., *Native Americans and Wage Labor: Ethnohistorical Perspectives* (Norman: University of Oklahoma Press, 1966), pp. 45–66. © 1996 by the University of Oklahoma Press, Norman, Publishing Division of the University. All Rights Reserved.

The royalties from sales of this book are being contributed to a prize fund for Native American students at Dartmouth College.

Contents

Preface

The essays in this book represent a sampling of works in print and in progress that examine the place and persistence of Native Americans in New England between King Philip's War (1675–1676) and the revitalization of Indian societies in the twentieth century. They focus primarily on the eighteenth and nineteenth centuries, a time when Indians were widely assumed to have disappeared from New England and were being made to disappear from the region's history. I am grateful to Philip Pochoda, editorial director of the University Press of New England, for the invitation to do something like this, and to Barry O'Connell, Jean O'Brien, Neal Salisbury, Thomas Doughton, John Moody, Ann Plane, Mary Kelley, and Ivy Schweitzer for suggestions along the way. O'Connell and Doughton each went beyond my initial request and wrote a new essay especially for this collection; O'Brien made revisions to her previously published work.

The essays are reproduced here in essentially their original form, although they have been edited to provide uniformity within the volume. Some authors prefer to use the historical mode of notation; others prefer the anthropological form of brief citations in parenthesis, keyed to a list of references at the end of the chapter. Some authors use the plural form for tribal names—Abenakis, Pequots, and so on—others prefer the singular. Some prefer to capitalize "Native"; others do not. I have retained such styles and preferences within each chapter rather than enforce consistency. I am grateful to Carol Sheehan for her meticulous copyediting.

All of the contributors have agreed to forego royalties from their work; the funds will be used instead to finance an annual prize for the best piece of writing by a Native American student attending Dartmouth College.

Hanover, New Hampshire   C.G.C.
December 1996

After King Philip's War

Colin G. Calloway

I

Introduction

Surviving the Dark Ages

In August 1676, in a swamp near Mount Hope, Rhode Island, Captain Benjamin Church and his soldiers tracked down the Wampanoag chief Metacomet, whom the English called King Philip. An Indian who had led the English to the place shot Metacomet from ambush; the English cut off Metacomet's head and quartered the body, the quarters to be hung on trees as fitting punishment for a traitor.

Metacomet's death marked the end of a brutal war, one of the bloodiest conflicts in American history. In 1675, in the face of increasing pressures and escalating tensions with the English, the Wampanoags and other Indian peoples of southern and central New England initiated a desperate war of resistance. English soldiers and settlers fell to Indian guns and tomahawks, the scorched ruins of English towns and farms dotted the landscape, and Puritan ministers admonished their congregations to mend their sinful ways to appease the wrath of their angry God. By the winter, Puritan New England was on its knees.

But the tide of the war turned with the turn of the year. Disease thinned the ranks of Metacomet's followers. The Mohawks, instigated by Governor Andros of New York, attacked Metacomet's forces in their winter camps. Captain Benjamin Church began to employ Indian allies and Indian tactics to fight Indian enemies. And the English began to win victories. In December, after the Narragansetts of Rhode Island refused to surrender noncombatant refugees from other tribes, a Puritan army stormed and destroyed the main Narragansett village in the Great Swamp Fight. In April, troops from Connecticut captured the Narragansett chief, Canonchet, and handed him over to their Mohegan allies for execution. In May, Captain William Turner and his men attacked an Indian fishing village at Peskeomskut, today called Turner's Falls, Massachusetts, and inflicted terrible slaughter as the inhabitants tried to escape over the falls. In the summer, Benjamin Church captured Metacomet's wife and nine-year-old son and packed them off to Plymouth for trial and probable shipment to the West Indies for a brief living death as slaves in the sugar cane fields. And, finally, Church caught up with Metacomet himself.

The war dragged on in the north and pulled in Abenakis from Maine, but the outcome was sealed. Like the Seventh Cavalry's massacre of Lakota people at Wounded Knee, South Dakota, in 1890, the killing of Metacomet came to symbolize an end to Indian independence, the last gasp of a way of life already battered and broken. For most people and in most history books, Metacomet's death and the dispersal of his followers is the final chapter in the story of Indian peoples in New England.

And it is a short story. Most history books ignore or gloss over the thousands of years of human history in New England that predated the arrival of Europeans. Usually, the action begins when Indian people, already ravaged by a major epidemic on the coast of New England in 1616–1619 — or swept aside to make way for God's chosen people, as the Puritans said — met the Pilgrims in 1620. Squanto, a Patuxet Indian who had been captured, taken to Europe, and made his way home to find his people wiped out by disease, assisted the newcomers, and Indians joined Pilgrims for a meal that grew in the national mythology to become the first Thanksgiving feast. But tensions grew, the English destroyed the Pequots in 1637, and, after a generation of uneasy coexistence during which John Eliot worked to convert Indians in Massachusetts to Christianity, the Puritans broke the power of the Indian tribes of New England in King Philip's War. Before contact and exposure to European epidemic diseases, Indian populations in New England exceeded 100,000;[1] now, survivors huddled in "enclaves." Invisible to outsiders, they became invisible in the history books.

Oral traditions, modern developments, and more closely scrutinized historical documents often suggest different stories. In recent years a new generation of scholars working in and across a variety of disciplines has greatly increased our understanding of New England's Indian history, especially before 1676. These scholars have developed new methodologies and asked new questions of the old sources to create a more richly textured and multidimensional picture of the Indian past and of Indian-white relations. Studies of Indian life in New England before contact are becoming increasingly detailed and sophisticated, providing greater understanding of Native settlement and subsistence patterns, political structures, social and gender relations, cosmology, and ritual.[2] Archaeologists have recovered from the ground material evidence that allows them to better understand Native daily life, and how Indian people incorporated new goods into their world and their world views.[3] Demographers and epidemiologists have produced new estimates of pre-contact Indian populations and greater awareness of the devastating impact of European epidemic diseases on these populations.[4] Scholars have looked beyond the first Thanksgiving to create more complex, and more disturbing, analyses of Indian-white relations during the first generations of contact.[5] They have debated the nature of Puritan-Indian relations and confronted issues of racism and genocide in early New England.[6] They have argued about the origins of the Pequot War and produced a thorough account of that controversial conflict.[7] They have looked at the uneasy coexistence that characterized relations between New England Indians and English settlers between the end of the Pequot War and the outbreak of King Philip's War.[8] They have examined the changing technology and tactics of Indian-white warfare in New England.[9] They have analyzed the cause and told and retold the story of King Philip's War.[10] They have explored Puritan responses to the war,[11] and examined Puritan responses to the Indian as "other" and as threat.[12] They have studied the position and treatment of Indians under English colonial law and, more recently, compared it with the situation in French mission villages around Montreal.[13] They have looked closely at land deeds and examined the processes by which Indian lands passed to non-Indian hands.[14] They have recovered individual lives from the records to produce biographical sketches of real people and reconstruct the experiences of Indian women in colonial New England.[15] Historians, anthropologists, and scholars of religion have re-examined the missionary work of John Eliot in Massachusetts and the Mayhew family on Martha's Vineyard. They have endeavored to reconstruct the motivations of Indian people who converted to Christianity and what they understood by that conversion; considered the impact of Christianity on gender relations in Algonquian societies; pointed out that many Indian people resisted conversion or accepted only limited aspects of Christian teachings; and recognized that Christianity could be a source of community cohesion when adopted and adapted by Indian people.[16] Anthropologists and linguists have explored Native literacy.[17] Scholars of history and literature have reread captivity narratives to recover what those stories can tell us about Indian society and gender relations, as well as what they reveal about the cultural and sexual anxieties of the narrators and their publishers.[18] Historians have examined the impact on Indian societies of the environmental changes generated by the invasion of English people and their animals.[19] They have looked beyond the borders of New England to consider the relations of New England Algonquians with the Iroquois to their west and with Micmac and other peoples to the north.[20] Historians and anthropologists have revised earlier models of tribal organization and demonstrated the inadequacy of old tribal labels for identifying Indian peoples and communities during times of turmoil when individual and band migrations produced frequent ethnic realignments.[21] Native and non-Native scholars have even debated whether early colonists imported the practice of using fish as a fertilizer or learned it from the Indians.[22] Short, popular histories of New England Indian tribes have taken their place alongside those of the Sioux, Cheyennes, Apaches, and Navajos.[23]

But King Philip's War remains the great watershed. Like the Civil War in United States history, it is difficult to escape the shadow it casts: we cannot study Indian New England prior to 1675 without the knowledge of the destruction to come; after the war, things are never the same again. Indian people no longer seemed to play a significant role in the history of southern and central New England. As recently as 1991, the *Historical Atlas of Massachusetts* noted that after King Philip's War disrupted and dislocated the Indian peoples of southern New England "they were no longer important in matters of public policy for the English" and faded into obscurity by the end of the eighteenth century.[24] If one wants to find Indians in New England after 1676, one usually must look to the north, where the Abenakis continued to resist, striking south to raid English settlements and carry off captives. But even these Indians, then and since, were often identified as "French Indians," from Canada rather than New England. As in American history as a whole, it seems that Indians figure in the story only when they offer violent resistance. Indians are "the frontier"; once their armed resistance is overcome, once the "frontier" has passed them by, they no longer seem to count. Many historians and most members of the general public seem to share the not-so-sneaking suspicion that "real Indians" steadfastly resist European expansion and oppose cultural change. Indians who stop fighting stop being Indians, so why bother with Indian history after King Philip's War?

The years between the end of King Philip's War in 1676 and the revitalization of Native communities in the twentieth century constituted a dark time for Indian people in New England. They were confined on tiny reservations, subjected to increasing state regulation, and saw their lands whittled away. Indian converts who inhabited mission towns and Indian students who attended Eleazar Wheelock's schools, first in Lebanon, Connecticut, and later at Dartmouth College, were pressed to abandon their tribal heritage and embrace Anglo-American civilization.[25] Indians worked as servants in white households, many forced into involuntary servitude for nonpayment of debts. South Kingston, Rhode Island, had a population of 935 whites, 333 African Americans, and 223 Indian slaves in 1730; by one estimate, 35.5 percent of all Indians in Rhode Island were living with white families in 1774.[26] Massachusetts and Connecticut imposed guardian systems that were supposed to protect Indian lands and resources, but guardians often abused the system and sold Indian lands. The Indian town of Mashpee on Cape Cod petitioned for relief from its guardians and won a measure of self-government under the British crown in 1763, but Massachusetts reinstituted the guardian system after the Revolution.[27] Where Indians and whites shared the same town—as at Natick, Hassanamisco, and Stockbridge—whites edged Indians out of town offices and off the land. [28]

In Vermont, Ethan and Ira Allen and their cronies laid claim to Abenaki lands and promoted the notion that Abenakis who resisted their efforts were visiting troublemakers from St. Francis in Quebec, not indigenous people trying to protect their homeland.[29] In Maine, Penobscots and Passamaquoddies, who supported the American cause during the Revolution, appealed to Congress for justice as their former allies invaded their hunting territories. But, in defiance of the Indian Trade and Intercourse Act of 1790, which prohibited transfer of Indian lands without congressional approval, first Massachusetts and then, after 1820, the new state of Maine made treaties that gobbled up huge areas of Indian land. In 1794, the Passamaquoddies ceded more than one million acres to Massachusetts. Two years later, the Penobscots ceded almost 200,000 acres in the Penobscot Valley; in 1818 they relinquished all their remaining land except the islands in the Penobscot River above Old Town and four six-mile-square townships. In 1833 the State of Maine bought the four townships for $50,000. By midcentury, the Penobscots were confined to a "ghetto community" on Indian Island at Old Town, and the Passamaquoddies were reduced to two reservations at Pleasant Point and Peter Dana Point.[30]

In Massachusetts, Rhode Island, and Connecticut, individuals sold lands to pay medical bills and other debts.[31] Stephen Badger, minister at the Indian town of Natick, Massachusetts, reported in 1798 that Indians were "generally considered by white people, and placed, as if by common consent, in an inferiour and degraded situation, and treated accordingly." Covetous white neighbors "took every advantage of them that they could, under colour of legal authority . . . to dishearten and depress them." At Stockbridge, Indians were surrounded by "Designing People who aim at Geting Away all that The Indians are Possessed of." Traders would sell Indian people liquor, encourage them to run up debts, then take them to court for nonpayment of the debts. Indians would be compelled to sell their lands "at a very low rate, in order to have their debts discharged." Such schemes left them "impoverished and disheartened," said Badger.[32]

Disease continued to ravage Indian communities and break Indian hearts. Forty-six people died at Natick between 1744 and 1746 during an epidemic that may have been brought back by Indian soldiers returning from King George's War; veterans returning from the Seven Years' War brought disease with them in 1759; "it spread very fast, and carried off some whole families," recalled Stephen Badger.[33] The Indian population on Nantucket—once described as an island "full of Indians"—was halved between 1600 and 1670 and then fell by another 90 percent or so over the next century; an outbreak of yellow fever in 1763 scythed the population from 358 to 136.[34] Just before Christmas 1770, John Shattock, a Narragansett, died of consumption, the eighteenth-century term for tuberculosis. Two years earlier his brother Tobias had died of smallpox in Edinburgh after they had crossed the Atlantic to try to persuade King George III to prohibit sachem Thomas Ninigret from selling tribal lands. Their deaths were the latest in a series of tragedies for their father, John Shattock, Sr. "God has blessed me with Twelve Children, and has called Nine of them out of the World," he wrote to the Reverend Joseph Fish at the end of the year. "I have no reason to think but they are all at rest,—Six of them dying in their Infancy."[35]

The diaspora of New England Indian peoples that began with King Philip's War continued in its aftermath. Indians from New England migrated north and west, mingling with other tribes and building new communities. Refugees from King Philip's War joined Abenaki communities in Maine, Vermont, and New Hampshire; many Abenakis retreated from the English war zone in the eighteenth century and relocated in the northern reaches of their homelands or around French mission villages in Quebec.[36] There were Abenakis living in Indian communities around the Great Lakes by the early eighteenth century, and Spanish records contain references to people they identified as Abenakis as far west as Arkansas and Missouri in the decade after the American Revolution.[37] At the time of the Revolution, many Narragansetts were reported to be leasing what was left of their lands "and moving off to other tribes."[38] Indian people from seven communities—Charlestown, Groton, Stonington, Niantic, Farmington, Mohegan, and Montauk on Long Island—were reduced "to such a small pittance of land that they could no longer remain there" and migrated to Brothertown, New York, the genesis of a new community in the west.[39]

Indian people who had once moved seasonally for subsistence purposes were now compelled to move about by poverty and the search for work or dislocated relatives. White observers concluded that Indians were "addicted to wander from place to place" and "naturally inclined to a roving and unsettled life." Ministers worried that such a "wandering and irregular practice" threatened the morals and the health of Indian women and children, but New England towns often "warned out" needy people to avoid paying poor relief, thereby adding to the numbers of Indian people traveling the roads.[40]

Many Indian men went away to sea. A petition to the state legislature on behalf of the Mashpees in 1788 noted that the young men from the town had gone "into the whaling business and their wives and children and the poor indigent families are about among the white people a beging [sic] for the necessaries of life." John Milton Earle, investigating the conditions of the Indians in Massachusetts, reported in 1861 that, sooner or later, "nearly all the males" in the coastal areas "engage in seafaring as an occupation." They were often absent for years at a time. The women they left behind "seek employment wherever it can be had, usually in the neighboring towns and cities."[41]

Many women married outsiders. Some Mashpee women married Africans, as well as Portuguese sailors and German veterans of the Revolutionary War.[42] Indian people who moved to Boston, New Bedford, Providence, Worcester, and other cities often took up residence among the growing African American urban populations. Such intermarriage and intermingling made it difficult for outsiders who employed categories of racial purity to identify Indians. Stephen Badger was unable to give an accurate head count of Indians at Natick because "they are so frequently shifting their place of residence, and are intermarried with blacks, and some with whites; and the various shades between those, and those descended from them." To observers like Badger, many Indians seemed to "vanish" as Indians among "people of color."[43]

New England Indians did not stop fighting after King Philip's War, and men continued to be called away to war. Abenakis in the north resisted English expansion onto their lands for almost another hundred years. Abenaki warriors waged small-scale guerilla warfare, raiding frontier settlements and slipping away as English troops approached. Abenaki communities dispersed in the face of English assaults and regrouped once the danger had passed.[44] Mohegans and other Indians in the south served in English armies during the so-called French and Indian Wars—sometimes Indian soldiers comprised as much as one-seventh of English colonial armies.[45] New England Indians served alongside their colonial neighbors during the American Revolution, often with tragic consequences. Mashpee furnished twenty-six men for the Patriot cause, all but one of whom "fell martyrs to liberty in the struggle for independence," wrote William Apess. "In this late War we have suffered much, our Blood has been spilled with yours and many of our Young Men have fallen by the Side of your Warriors," Stockbridge Indians reminded the government of Massachusetts in September 1783; "almost all those Places where your Warriors have left their Bones, there our Bones are seen also. Now we who remain are become very poor."[46] Indian soldiers—William Apess was one of them—served the United States in the War of 1812. In 1833, Mashpee Indians openly defied the authority of the State of Massachusetts and staged a "revolt" that, though never violent, did win for them a measure of self-government and a limited victory for Indian rights.[47] In the Civil War, some southern New England Indians fought for the Union in the ranks of the United States Colored Infantry.[48] And men from New England's Indian communities fought in America's wars in the twentieth century.

Historical accounts in the eighteenth and nineteenth centuries portrayed Indians fading from sight as non-Indian settlers edged them off their lands. Hector St. Jean de Crèvecoeur said that the Indians "appear to be a race doomed to recede and disappear before the superior genius of the Europeans."[49] Luigi Castiglioni, an Italian botanist visiting Boston in 1785, said that the Indians "live at a great distance and very rarely come to the city, so that there are many inhabitants who have never seen them." The few poverty-stricken people he encountered at Natick, and the Penobscots in Maine, were the only "miserable remnants" he saw "of so many and such numerous nations that used to inhabit this part of America before the arrival of the Europeans."[50] Three years later, a fellow passenger noted that a young Oneida returning from France caused as much surprise in Boston as he had in Paris, "for Indians are never seen there. They have been gone from Massachusetts for so long that people have forgotten what one looks like."[51] Stephen Badger pronounced that by 1798 Indians in Massachusetts had "dwindled, become wretched, and in some places are almost extinct."[52] Even in Indian towns like Natick and Stockbridge, the story in the eighteenth century was one of dispossession and decline.[53] In the north, the Abenaki strategy of pulling back into the farthest reaches of their territory or maintaining a low profile on the peripheries of the new towns, villages, and farms that sprang up on their homelands reinforced the notion that Indians were fast disappearing from the region.[54]

By the nineteenth century, the prevailing view among white Americans was that Indians were a doomed race—an idea embodied in James Fenimore Cooper's *The Last of the Mohicans* (1826), Catherine Maria Sedgwick's *Hope Leslie; or, Early Times in Massachusetts* (1827), and John Augustus Stone's play *Metamora, or the Last of the Wampanoags* (1829). Nowhere did Indian extinction seem more assured than in New England. John Adams, writing to Thomas Jefferson in 1812, recalled growing up seventy years earlier with Indians for neighbors and as visitors to his father's house. A large Indian family had lived in the town, and Adams remembered nostalgically visiting their wigwam and being treated with blackberries, strawberries, whortle berries, apples, plumbs, and peaches. "But the Girls went out to Service and the Boys to Sea, till not a Soul is left," he wrote. "We scarcely see an Indian in a year."[55] In his *Report on Indian Affairs*, submitted to the secretary of war in 1822, Jedidiah Morse portrayed the Indian communities in New England as a "few feeble remnants" teetering on the brink of extinction.[56] "All the Indian tribes who once inhabited the territory of New England—the Narragansetts, the Mohicans, the Pequots—now live only in men's memories," wrote Alexis de Tocqueville in 1833 after his visit to the United States.[57] Town histories throughout New England often begin with an early reference to an Indian individual or family who frequented the neighborhood for a time but then disappeared as the town grew.

Indian people who did not disappear from view faced racism and persecution. After the Great Swamp Fight, the English forced many of the surviving Narragansetts into servitude to English families. As Rhode Island increased its control over their lives, many Narragansett people migrated to less hostile environments. Others stayed on their ancestral lands and maintained their tribal government and ancestral ways. In the early 1740s, many embraced the New Light religion of the Great Awakening, a revivalist movement that appealed to the poor and the oppressed but that also offered a form of Christianity that in some ways resembled traditional religion. The Narragansett church became a core of the Narragansett tribe "as it became immersed in, and yet remained apart from, Yankee life." But in 1880 the Rhode Island State legislature declared the Narragansett people extinct, took away their tribal status, and authorized the sale at public auction of all tribal land except a two-acre plot containing the church and cemetery.[58] Massachusetts also removed protections from its "Indian wards" and their lands: in 1869 the legislature gave individual Indians citizenship and voting rights and opened the way for unrestricted sales of their lands.[59]

Like their non-Indian neighbors, many Indian people had to change their ways of living and working in areas of New England that were becoming increasingly industrial and urban. Many young women left home to find work in textile mills in Lowell and Worcester, Massachusetts, or in Manchester, New Hampshire. Many men moved to Boston or New York City for work in heavier industry. A mobile Indian labor force developed, as people moved from job to job and city to city and home community to urban slum.[60] Others preferred occupations that more closely resembled traditional patterns of life, work, and movement. Men found employment as seasonal laborers, loggers, trappers, and guides. Women wove baskets—sometimes rebuilding their lives "one basket at a time"—and peddled them door to door in white settlements. Later, they sold baskets to Victorian tourists at summer resorts in the White Mountains of New Hampshire and on the coast of Maine, and they crafted smaller, more elaborate and more colorful "fancy baskets" for the tourist trade.[61]

Indian people who experienced poverty and dislocation as a result of non-Indian assault and dominance often found themselves persecuted as paupers and "delinquents." Indians who maintained more traditional lifestyles found themselves harassed as "vagrants" and "transients." From 1925 to 1936, a privately funded project known as the Eugenics Survey of Vermont sought to "purify" the state by identifying and often institutionalizing mental and moral "defectives" who were deemed to represent a "drain" on the state's finances and a threat to the "character" of its population. In 1931 Vermont became the twenty-seventh state to pass a sterilization law to "prevent the procreation of idiots, imbeciles, feeble-minded or insane persons." At least two hundred people were sterilized in the next twenty years. Employing broad definitions of "degeneracy," the eugenicists focused particular attention on people of Abenaki or French-Canadian heritage who did not match their notion of how Vermonters should look and live. Many Vermont Abenakis maintain that they were the targets of a campaign of genocide that produced broken families and childless marriages.[62]

In such circumstances, generations of Indian people found that survival in New England often required that they *not* draw attention to themselves as Indians. Many people kept their heads down in the racist atmosphere of the times; many families with Indian ancestors suppressed and denied knowledge of that ancestry. Nevertheless, despite erosion of land and language, and changes in dress and appearance — the things that most outsiders regarded as crucial determinants of identity and culture — many people held on to their Indianness through ties of community, family, and kinship. Some community leaders spoke up time and again in defense of their people's lands and rights, and in the early twentieth century many people began to display their Indian identity in public events and ceremonies. After generations of concealing their own traditions from hostile outsiders, Native people often adopted western-style dress as symbols of "Indianness" for these occasions — after all, Plains Indian feather headdresses and buckskins were the things most non-Indians identified as distinctively "Indian." At the same time, Indian people in New England strengthened regional networks to produce a greater regional Native consciousness and form pan-Indian organizations, often with the assistance of white supporters. In 1923 the New England Indian Council formed, adopting for its motto "I still live."[63]

Clearly, the disappearing act of New England's Native peoples was more apparent than real. But, with the exception of anthropologist Frank Speck, Mohegan anthropologist Gladys Tantaquidgeon, and museum collector Rudolf Haffenreffer, few scholars bothered to document the persistence of Indian communities and cultures in New England in the early twentieth century.[64]

In the second half of the century, by contrast, Indian activities and activism meant that Indians in New England could no longer be ignored. Figures from the U.S. censuses from 1900 to 1990 (table 1) graphically illustrate the dramatic "reappearance" of Indian people in the six New England states. All of the figures in the table are almost certainly wrong. In 1900 you were counted as an Indian if the census taker thought you looked like one; in 1990 you were counted as an Indian if you identified yourself as one. Many people of Indian heritage preferred not to be identified as Indian in 1900; many still chose not to be identified in 1990, but most people found it was relatively safe, even prestigious, to claim Indian heritage, and some "wannabees" (people who are not Indian but "wannabee") no doubt got themselves counted. The varied and complex levels of identity in the demographic makeup of Indian New England make it impossible to gather accurate figures, and U.S. census figures are notoriously inaccurate at the best of times. Nevertheless, the figures do reflect a clear trend: by the late twentieth century more and more Indian people were, quite literally, standing up to be counted. Throughout the region, Indian people are visible again; Indian communities are actively asserting their rights and reviving their traditions.

The last twenty years have produced dramatic developments in New

TABLE 1
Indian Populations of the New England States, 1900–1990

State	1900	1910	1920	1930	1940	1950	1960	1970	1980	1990
Conn.	153	152	159	162	201	333	923	2222	4431	6654
Maine	798	892	839	1012	1251	1522	1879	2195	4057	5998
Mass.	587	688	555	874	769	1201	2118	4475	7483	12241
N.H.	22	34	23	64	50	74	135	361	1297	2134
R.I.	35	234	110	318	196	385	932	1390	2872	4071
Vt.	5	26	24	36	16	30	57	229	968	1696

Source: Extracted and updated from Russell Thornton, *American Indian Holocaust and Survival: A Population History since 1492* (Norman: University of Oklahoma Press, 1987), 162–63.

England Indian country. The Penobscots and Passamaquoddies secured federal recognition and then won a landmark victory and national publicity in 1980 when President Jimmy Carter signed into law the Maine Indian Land Claims Settlement Act. The Settlement Act recognized that tribal lands had been taken in direct contravention of the provisions of the Indian Trade and Non-Intercourse Acts of 1790–1834 and awarded $81.5 million in compensation, giving the tribes vital capital for investment in business development.[65] The Narragansetts negotiated the return of 1800 acres of tribal land in 1979, secured federal recognition as an Indian tribe, and are planning to build a casino on tribal land. The Pequots supposedly were destroyed in the Pequot War of 1637 and declared extinct as a tribe at the Treaty of Hartford the following year; but they won federal recognition as an Indian tribe in 1983. Today, the Pequot Tribe is a major economic power in southern New England, generating thousands of jobs and millions of dollars in income from its gaming operations, building a new tribal museum, sponsoring archaeological projects and historical conferences, and exercising considerable political influence. The neighboring Mohegans won federal recognition in the spring of 1994 and opened a casino in the fall of 1996. Other groups continue to pursue recognition of their tribal status. Despite bitter disappointment in their pursuit of land claims and federal recognition in the past, the Wampanoags of Mashpee have not given up: they are still living on lands their ancestors inhabited when the Pilgrims arrived, and they expect to win recognition.[66] Generations of schoolchildren in Vermont were taught that there never were any Indians in the state; but today Abenakis are visible and active, pursuing federal recognition, initiating and administering projects for cultural preservation, and challenging the state to recognize their rights as a sovereign nation.

If we believe what we used to read, we allow the Indian strand in New England's history to be cut short in 1676, and we offend Indian people today who know that their history did not stop there. We perpetuate a distorted and impoverished view of the region's past, and we deprive historic Indian people of the capacity to adapt and to survive by bending rather than breaking.[67] If we ignore the eighteenth and nineteenth centuries, we can make little sense of what is happening in New England in the twentieth century: if Indians disappeared after King Philip's War, how can the people asserting their rights today be "real Indians?"

But the activities of Indian people today have forced Americans to wake up to the continuing presence of Indian communities in New England. More and more scholars recognize the endurance of Indian people, communities, and traditions in New England.[68] Tribal scholars have produced their own histories, which incorporate community oral traditions and family memories as well as documentary evidence.[69] Newspapers and magazines have devoted extensive coverage to the "Return of the Natives."[70] In Maine, where as late as the 1950s state policies were predicated on the assumption that the Penobscot and other tribes would disintegrate and individual Indians be swallowed up in the general population, texts by and about Native Americans have now been introduced into classrooms, and Indians figure prominently in new editions of a history of the state.[71] A university press that specializes in books about Indians has published the remarkable biography of a twentieth-century Penobscot woman who fits almost none of the standard stereotypes about Indians: Molly Spotted Elk starred in movies, danced in Paris nightclubs, and was caught in the upheaval of the German occupation of France during World War II.[72] The current popular interest in all things Indian will no doubt fade, but it seems unlikely that Indians in New England will ever be ignored again.

Nevertheless, the resurgence of tribal pride and power that has occurred in the late twentieth century depended upon survival through the dark ages following King Philip's War. Mohegan tribal historian Melissa Jayne Fawcett relates the perspective of a Sac and Fox Indian from the midwest on what happened to the peoples on the east coast after the flood tide of European invasion engulfed them and swept west: Indians there, he said, "simply learned to live under the water . . . [and] are now rising to the surface."[73] Surviving day to day under the water or on the underside of society rarely makes for a dramatic story—then as now, murder and mayhem, not labor and quiet coexistence, made the news—but it is an essential part of New England's history. The essays in this volume acknowledge the devastation suffered by Indian cultures and communities, but, in one way or another, they all tell stories of change and survival rather than decline and disappearance. These stories are relatively new to most non-Indians, but they are familiar tales in Indian country. Penetrating the gloom of the eighteenth and nineteenth centuries is more difficult for scholars than in other eras where the light is better—for all their biases and blindness, the Puritan chroniclers of the seventeenth century left a substantial body of literature with which to work. But reconstructing the stories of survival and patterns of persistence in those dark times is vital if we are to avoid leaving a huge gap in our understanding of New England's past and perpetuating a notion of New England as a place without Indians during most of its history.

The "disappearing act" attributed to Indians in New England has created problems for Indian groups attempting to win federal recognition from the Bureau of Indian Affairs. Like the philosopher who questions whether a tree falling in a forest makes a noise if no one is there to hear it, the BIA has doubted that a tribe can have existed unless someone was there to document it. New England Indians know that they "have been here all along," but the government looks for a paper trail of uninterrupted presence and tribal organization. The Golden Hill Paugusetts in Connecticut lost their bid for federal recognition in 1996 after they failed to provide "sufficient evidence" documenting their Indian ancestry.[74]

The lack of a clearly marked paper trail also makes more difficult and challenging the job of writing history in the dark ages. Refocusing attention on the eighteenth and nineteenth centuries requires more than a recognition that the historical narrative needs to be carried forward. It requires scholars to apply new methodologies, substantial diligence, and considerable imagination to their study of the past. Often, the historical record reveals only tantalizing glances of Indian people in these times, places, and roles, and of the imprint they left on non-Indian New Englanders through these contacts. Susanna Johnson, who was captured by Abenakis in the 1750s, recalled in her old age traveling as a girl of fourteen from Leominster, Massachusetts, to Charlestown, New Hampshire, which was then "the most northerly settlement on the Connecticut River." Nine or ten pioneer families lived in scattered cabins, surrounded by Indians who "were numerous, and associated in a friendly manner with the whites." In such regions, said Johnson, Indians and settlers mixed so freely "that the state of society cannot be easily described."[75] So she did not describe it, and the historian is left to try and reconstruct the state of such societies and the Indian presence in and around them.

Following the tracks of people who have "disappeared" requires consulting "new" sources of evidence as well as asking new questions of old sources. Some of the "new sources" are actually very old. In the absence of written records, a people's history survives in their oral traditions handed down across generations. Many historians and most ethnohistorians today try to incorporate oral tradition into their work. The remembered past, and sometimes just the common knowledge, of Native families and communities can provide sources of evidence and example and serve as a guide to understanding written records that might otherwise seem "silent" or prove misleading in regard to the history of Indian people. Native folklore, legends, and stories survive in New England in the same places where Indian people survive, reinforcing the continued connections of tellers and listeners to their traditional homelands even where non-Indians now occupy the lands.[76]

Writing the histories of people who are supposed to have disappeared into thin air also involves adopting a "needle in the haystack" approach to the documents, for their traces remain in vital records, petitions, deeds, and wills. They got married, were buried, sued and were sued, sought and were granted or denied poor relief, and, of course, they transferred land. They are in evidence also in the journals of travelers, in state archives, town records, local libraries, and historical societies. Historian Jean O'Brien found that "even a cursory glance at the Natick town records" revealed that Indians were there in the eighteenth century.[77]

But one has to look for them. Often, the search involves tracking Indian people not identified as members of clearly visible "tribes" but as individuals with names that give no immediate clue as to their identity. They might be described as Indian in one source, as "Negro," "mulatto," "gypsy," or poor white in another. It requires gaining familiarity with the names of Indian families in particular communities, piecing together people's lives from the scattered occasions when those individuals appear in the records, tracing lineages and connecting family histories; it demands painstaking and patient detective work, shifting to other sources when one set of records has played out, and poring over reels of microfilm for hours to find one brief reference that might later provide a small piece in a larger but always incomplete puzzle. Not surprisingly, most historians have not bothered to look for Indians in this way; it is much more convenient to have them exit history in 1676.

The contributors in this volume have bothered to look. And what they are beginning to piece together is a fascinating picture of how and where Indian people survived New England's dark ages, struggling to keep family, community, and cultural ties intact amid the turmoil of a changed and changing world. Historians have examined Abenaki relations with French allies and English enemies up through the eighteenth century and have shown how Abenaki families survived in the wake of the imperial wars, often living as members of dispersed communities on the peripheries of their homelands.[78] They have shown that Indian people and Indian communities survived in eighteenth-century Massachusetts, adapting, intermarrying, rebuilding kin connections and communities, and even redefining themselves; and they are piecing together similar pictures of presence and persistence in the nineteenth century.[79] The writings of Christian Indians and preachers like Joseph Johnson, Samson Occom, and William Apess may seem alien to many twentieth-century readers, but they open windows into the experiences of Indian people living in a different era and, certainly in the case of Apess, provide a forceful Native critique of Anglo-American injustice and hypocrisy.[80]

But the history of Indian peoples in New England in the eighteenth and nineteenth centuries is still incomplete. Much of the best literature exists in the form of articles in scholarly journals and collections of essays and is not easily accessible to more general readers. This volume pulls together some of these articles into one book and points out some of the new paths being explored as scholars try to reconstruct the histories of some of New England's "forgotten people." Readers will not find here colorful accounts of "Indian wars"; instead they will encounter Indian people living and working alongside their white neighbors, and tables and charts depicting demographic and economic profiles. They will find scholars, finally, treating Indian people in the past as they have treated others: as real human beings living day to day in uncertain times and hoping that the world they pass on to their children is a little better than the one they inherited.

Evan Haefeli and Kevin Sweeney take as their starting point a famous event, with Indians playing a familiar role — the raid on Deerfield, Massachusetts, in the winter of 1704, by Indian warriors and their French-Canadian allies. But Haefeli and Sweeney go beyond the familiar narratives of the raid and the subsequent experiences of John and Eunice Williams.[81] They place the event in the broader context of a northern New England borderland of interethnic complexity, and they search out the identities of the Abenaki, Mohawk, and Huron Indians involved. They find that many of the Indians had ties to the Deerfield region and even to the colonists they raided, and that all had compelling motives for participating in the infamous attack. They also demonstrate the connections that existed between different Indian communities in northern New England and Quebec in the wake of the diaspora of Indian peoples following King Philip's War.

That diaspora produced refugee communities in Catholic mission villages on the banks of the St. Lawrence and provided sources of manpower for raids like the one against Deerfield. The northward migration of peoples also contributed to the commonly held notion that Indians "disappeared" from many areas of New England and went to Canada. Focusing attention on the little-studied region of western Maine, David L. Ghere explains how and why colonial officials and early historians ignored evidence of the continued Abenaki presence in the area and assumed instead that all the Androscoggin and Pigwacket Indians migrated permanently to Canada in the early eighteenth century and merged into the new communities of St. Francis and Becancour on the St. Lawrence.

Indian people who did remain, and remain visible, in their homelands often became participants in the developing economy of their colonial neighbors. Indian men from Cape Cod, Martha's Vineyard, and Nantucket took to sea in the emerging whaling industry. In "The First Whalemen of Nantucket," Daniel Vickers explains how Nantucket men were coerced into such perilous occupations in an industry controlled by English colonists. As the Indian population of Nantucket plummeted and the survivors struggled to survive in a new and alien world, English owners, argues Vickers, employed credit and coercion to secure an Indian labor force at a time when English labor was in short supply.

Historian Ruth Wallis Herndon and Narragansett ethnohistorian Ella Wilcox Sekatau combine their knowledge of town records and oral tribal history to examine the relationship between Rhode Island officials and those Narragansett people who remained on their ancestral lands in the era of the American Revolution. Town leaders generally regarded Indian people as "the poor," whose lives required official management. The authorities often compiled detailed records of people's lives as they investigated their entitlement to, or found reason to deny them, poor relief. At the same time, they redesignated Native people as "Negro" or "black" in the written record, thereby denying the existence of Indians in the state and preparing the way for tribal "extinction."

In a revised version of her essay "Divorced from the Land," a Native American woman from twentieth-century Minnesota considers how Native American women in eighteenth-century Massachusetts adjusted to colonial domination. Algonquian women in New England traditionally worked the land; as Europeans took over the land, family and kinship practices were disrupted, and English missionaries insisted on a gendered division of labor that made agriculture a predominantly male activity. Jean O'Brien pieces together from fragmentary sources profiles of individual Indian women who developed new ways of living and working that enabled them to survive in the new world of colonial dominance and expectations, while at the same time maintaining ties to their old world and traditional lifeways.

Barry O'Connell's edition of the writings of William Apess has not only made accesssible an important source of New England's Indian history, it has also established Apess as a significant figure in the landscape of early American literature.[82] Apess's life and writings reveal much about the devastation and despair many Indian people faced in early nineteenth-century New England; they also reveal much about Indian resistance and resilience through those same hard times. In this new essay, O'Connell considers Apess the writer as self-consciously an historian seeking to create the grounds for a more inclusive history of New England and ultimately of the United States, and considers Apess's life as itself a crucial piece of historical data for beginning to write the as yet mostly unwritten history of Native Americans in New England. In addition, O'Connell takes up a body of concepts and terms that present problems even in the hands of scholars endeavoring to do justice to the ongoing historical presence of Native people, an issue also addressed by Thomas Doughton.

Ann Marie Plane, an historian, and Gregory Button, an anthropologist, examine the granting of citizenship and voting rights to Indians in Massachusetts in 1869 in the historical context of Reconstruction-era politics and race relations. Their work reveals competing definitions and meanings of Indian identity between, on the one hand, whites who perceived Indians as "nonwhites" who should therefore be treated as blacks, and on the other, Indian people who maintained their own ethnic boundaries and resisted efforts to force them into a biracial society. The Massachusetts Indian Enfranchisement Act demonstrates the inadequacy of "Indian-white policy" as a rubric for understanding what Plane and Button depict as a complicated case of multiethnic negotiation. By dividing Indian lands among individuals and opening the doors for their sale to non-Indians, the act also prefigured the federal government's disastrous General Allotment Act of 1887—introduced into Congress by Senator Henry Dawes of Massachusetts.

Writing as a Native person and a historian, Thomas Doughton takes exception to the notion that Indian people disappeared from sight or even from the records. Tracing and connecting the histories of Indian families in central Massachusetts, he finds plenty of evidence that Indian people, often intermixed with African Americans, survived in the nineteenth century; what's more, they were identified as Indians in the records. Only the Eurocentric assumption that Indians must have disappeared, argues Doughton, could blind scholars to the persistence and presence of Indian people in nineteenth-century Massachusetts.

Harald Prins, a Dutch anthropologist with extensive experience as tribal researcher for the Aroostook Band of Micmacs in northern Maine, discusses the importance of seasonal wage labor in the culture of the Micmac or Mi'kmaq Indians. (The Aroostook Band is the only Mi'kmaq band located in the United States, the other twenty-eight being in Quebec, Nova Scotia, New Brunswick, Prince Edward Island, and Newfoundland.) With the disintegration of traditional subsistence activities of hunting, fishing, gathering, and trapping, Mi'kmaqs turned to crafts and migrant wage labor, especially harvesting blueberries in the summer and potatoes in the fall. Such wage labor often produces dependency and furthers community disintegration. But Prins argues that, by finding temporary wage-earning opportunities that reflected traditional migratory patterns of life and were located within traveling distance of home communities, Mi'kmaq seasonal workers in Maine managed to resist full proletarianization, to maintain a diffuse tribal network, and even to reinforce their identity as a distinct tribal nation.

The essays in this book do not offer complete coverage of Indian experiences in New England, nor do they constitute all the good scholarship of recent years. The authors represent a variety of academic disciplines and include Native and non-Native scholars. They do not speak with one voice or tell one story; it is a safe bet that none of the contributors—including the editor—would agree with all of the interpretations offered by all the others. But taken as a whole, the essays show the many sources and places of Indian presence and persistence in New England long after the catastrophe of King Philip's War. They expose as myth the notion that Indians "disappeared" from New England, refuting the narrative of extinction that has dominated New England's history for so long. As Jean O'Brien found in her study of eighteenth-century Natick, Indian "disappeareance" occurred only in the imaginations of Euro-Americans, "or rather in their failure to imagine how Indians struggled and survived, and how cultural change *is* persistence."[83] These essays give scholarly validation to what Native people have always known: that invisibility, like beauty, is in the eye of the beholder, that Indians have been here all along, and that any portrait of New England's past that omits Indians through the eighteenth, nineteenth, and early twentieth centuries is an incomplete sketch. As Native and non-Native scholars continue to explore the paths marked out here, and to venture down other trails that are perhaps yet to be charted, they will add depth, dimension, and texture to that sketch of the past.

It would be wrong to replace one stereotype with another and suggest that all Indian people waged a heroic and steadfast struggle to preserve their Indian heritage during New England's dark ages. Racism, poverty, broken homes, and alcohol produced despair as often as defiance. Inevitably, some people succumbed to the incremental erosion of their remaining sources of hope and happiness. Some, no doubt, did not care whether they survived as Indians, just so long as they survived. But enough did care so that Indians persisted in a society that denied their presence. The sufferings and survivals of Indian people during these times matter if we are to understand our shared past and present. The stories of their everyday lives are ultimately more illuminating than the "last stands" that usually serve as historical exits for Indians.

NOTES

1. S. F. Cook, *The Indian Population of New England in the Seventeenth Century* (Berkeley: University of California Press, 1976), estimates 72,000 within a range of 60,000 to 80,000; Kathleen J. Bragdon, *Native People of Southern New England, 1500–1650* (Norman: University of Oklahoma Press, 1996), accepts Daniel Gookin's figures for a regional population of more than 90,000; Neal Salisbury, *Manitou and Providence: Indians, Europeans, and the Making of New England, 1500–1643* (New York: Oxford University Press, 1982), 22–30, and Dean R. Snow and Kim M. Lanphear, "European Contact and Indian Depopulation in the Northeast: The Timing of the First Epidemics," *Ethnohistory*, 35 (1988), 15–33, both estimate pre-epidemic populations in New England to have been well over 100,000.

2. Howard S. Russell; *Indian New England Before the Mayflower* (Hanover, N.H.: University Press of New England, 1980); Bragdon, *Native People of Southern New England*. See also the articles on the various tribes of New England in Bruce G. Trigger, ed., *Handbook of North American Indians*, vol. 15: *Northeast* (Washington, D.C.: Smithsonian Institution, 1978).

3. For example, William S. Simmons, *Cautantowwit's House: An Indian Burial*

Ground on the Island of Conanicut in Narragansett Bay (Providence, R.I.: Brown University Press, 1970); Dean Snow, *The Archaeology of New England* (New York: Academic Press, 1980); Susan G. Gibson, ed., *Burr's Hill, a Seventeenth Century Wampanoag Burial Ground in Warren, Rhode Island* (Providence, R.I.: Haffenreffer Museum of Anthropology, 1980); Paul A. Robinson, Marc A. Kelly, and Patricia E. Rubertone, "Preliminary Biocultural Interpretations from a Seventeenth-Century Narragansett Indian Burial Ground in Rhode Island," in William W. Fitzhugh, ed., *Cultures in Contact: The European Impact of Native Cultural Institutions in Eastern North America, A.D. 1000–1800* (Washington, D.C.: Smithsonian Institution Press, 1985), 107–30; Constance A. Crosby, "From Myth to History, or Why King Philip's Ghost Walks Abroad," in Mark P. Leone and Parker B. Potter, Jr., eds., *The Recovery of Meaning in Historical Archaeology* (Washington, D.C.: Smithsonian Institution Press, 1988), 183–209; Kevin A. Mcbride, "The Historical Archaeology of the Mashantucket Pequots, 1637–1900: A Preliminary Analysis," in Laurence M. Hauptman and James D. Wherry, eds., *The Pequots in Southern New England: The Fall and Rise of an American Indian Nation* (Norman: University of Oklahoma Press, 1990), 96–140, and "'Ancient and Crazie': Pequot Lifeways during the Historic Period," in Peter Benes, ed., *Algonkians of New England: Past and Present* (The Dublin Seminar for New England Folklife Annual Proceedings 1991, Boston University, 1993), 63–75. William A. Haviland and Marjory W. Power, *The Original Vermonters: Native Inhabitants, Past and Present*, rev. ed. (Hanover, N.H.: University Press of New England, 1994), trace the whole range of Western Abenaki history, but the bulk of their story, as it should, concentrates on precontact developments.

4. Cook, *The Indian Population of New England in the Seventeenth Century*; Arthur and Bruce D. Speiss, "New England Pandemic of 1616–1620: Cause and Archaeological Implication," *Man in the Northeast*, 34 (1987), 71–83; Timothy L. Bratton, "The Identity of the New England Indian Epidemic of 1616–19," *Bulletin of the History of Medicine*, 62 (1988), 351–83; Snow and Lanphear, "European Contact and Indian Depopulation in the Northeast"; Catherine C. Carlson, George J. Armelagos, and Ann L. Magennis, "Impact of Disease on the Precontact and Early Historic Populations of New England and the Maritimes," in John W. Verano and Douglas H. Ubelaker, eds., *Disease and Demography in the Americas* (Washington, D.C.: Smithsonian Institution Press, 1992), 141–53. See also Virginia Miller, "Aboriginal Micmac Population: A Review of the Evidence," *Ethnohistory*, 23 (1976), 117–27.

5. Salisbury, *Manitou and Providence*; Emerson W. Baker, Edwin A. Churchill, Richard S. D'Abate, Kristine L. Jones, Victor A. Konrad, and Harald E. L. Prins, eds., *American Beginnings: Exploration, Culture, and Cartography in the Land of Norumbega* (Lincoln: University of Nebraska Press, 1994).

6. The polar positions in the debate are Alden T. Vaughan, *New England Frontier: Puritans and Indians 1620–1675*, 3rd. ed. (Norman: University of Oklahoma Press, 1995; orig. pub. 1965), which argues that the first two generations of Puritan settlers pursued generally peaceful and equitable relations with Indians, and Francis Jennings, *The Invasion of America: Indians, Colonialism, and the Cant of Conquest* (New York: W. W. Norton, 1976), which argues that not only did the Puritans have genocidal intentions toward Indians but they also distorted the record. See also Richard Drinnon, *Facing West: The Metaphysics of Indian-Hating and Empire-Building* (New York: New American Library, 1980), part 1, which offers a scathing indictment of Puritan treatment of the Indians; and Charles M. Segal and David C. Stineback, eds., *Puritans, Indians, and Manifest Destiny* (New York: Putnam's Sons, 1977).

7. Alden T. Vaughan, "Pequots and Puritans: The Causes of the War, 1637," *William and Mary Quarterly*, 21 (1969), 256–69; Jennings, *Invasion of America*, chs. 12–13; Stephen T. Katz, "The Pequot War Reconsidered," *New England Quarterly*, 64 (1991), 206–24; Alfred Cave, *The Pequot War* (Amherst: University of Massachusetts Press, 1996).

8. Neal Salisbury, "Social Relationships on a Moving Frontier: Natives and Settlers in Southern New England, 1638–1675," *Man in the Northeast*, 33 (1987), 89–99, and "Indians and Colonists in Southern New England after the Pequot War: An Uneasy Balance," in Hauptman and Wherry, eds., *The Pequots in Southern New England*, 81–95; Peter A. Thomas, "Bridging the Cultural Gap: Indian/White Relations," in John W. Ifkovic and Martin Kaufman, eds., *Early Settlement in the Connecticut Valley* (Deerfield: Historic Deerfield, Inc., 1984), and "Cultural Change on the Southern New England Frontier, 1630–1665," in Fitzhugh, ed., *Cultures in Contact*, 131–11. Peter Thomas's excellent dissertation, "In the Maelstrom of Change: The Indian Trade and Cultural Process in the Middle Connecticut River Valley, 1635–1665" (Ph.D. diss., University of Massachusetts, 1979), has also been published (New York: Garland, 1991). Colin G. Calloway, "Wanalancet and Kancagamus: Indian Strategy and Leadership on the New Hampshire Frontier," *Historical New Hampshire*, 43 (1988), 264–90, traces Pennacook relations with the colonists before and after King Philip's War. See also Joshua Micah Marshall, "'A Melancholy People': Anglo-Indian Relations in Early Warwick, Rhode Island, 1642–1675," *New England Quarterly*, 68 (1995), 402–28.

9. Patrick M. Malone, *The Skulking Way of War: Technology and Tactics among the New England Indians* (Lanham, Md.: Madison Books, 1991); Adam J. Hirsch, "The Collision of Military Cultures in Seventeenth-Century New England," *Journal of American History*, 74 (1988), 1187–1212.

10. Douglas Edward Leach, *Flintlock and Tomahawk: New England in King Philip's War* (New York: W. W. Norton, 1966; orig. pub. 1958); Philip Ranlet, "Another Look at the Causes of King Philip's War," *New England Quarterly*, 61 (1988), 79–100; Russsell Bourne, *The Red King's Rebellion: Racial Politics in New England 1675–1678* (New York: Oxford University Press, 1990); James Drake, "Symbol of a Failed Strategy: The Sassamon Trial, Political Culture, and the Outbreak of King Philip's War," *American Indian Culture and Research Journal*, 19, no. 2 (1995), 111–41. See also Jill Lepore, "Dead Men Tell No Tales: John Sassamon and the Fatal Consequences of Literacy," *American Quarterly*, 46 (1994), 479–512.

11. Richard Slotkin and James K. Folsom, eds., *So Dreadfull a Judgment: Puritan Responses to King Philip's War, 1676–77* (Middletown, Conn.: Wesleyan University Press, 1978).

12. John Canup, *Out of the Wilderness: The Emergence of an American Identity in Colonial New England* (Middletown, Conn.: Wesleyan University Press, 1990); Alden T. Vaughan, "Early English Paradigms for New World Natives," American Antiquarian Society, *Proceedings*, 102 (1992), part 1: 33–67. See also David D. Smits, "'We Are Not to Grow Wild': Seventeenth-Century New England's Repudiation of Anglo-Indian Intermarriage," *American Indian Culture and Research Journal*, 11, no. 4 (1987), 1–32.

13. Lyle Koehler, "Red-White Power Relations and Justice in the Courts of Seventeenth-Century New England," *American Indian Culture and Research Journal*, 3 (1979), 1–32; James P. Ronda, "Red and White at the Bench: Indians and the Law in Plymouth Colony, 1620–1691," *Essex Institute Historical Collections*, 110 (1974), 200–15; Kathleen J. Bragdon, "Crime and Punishment among the Indians of Massachusetts,

1675–1750," *Ethnohistory*, 28 (1981), 23–32; Yasuhide Kawashima, *Puritan Justice and the Indian: White Man's Law in Massachusetts, 1630–1763* (Middletown, Conn.: Wesleyan University Press, 1986); James Warren Springer, "American Indians and the Law of Real Property in Colonial New England," *American Journal of Legal History*, 30 (1986), 25–58. Jan Grabowski, "French Criminal Justice and Indians in Montreal, 1670–1760," *Ethnohistory*, 43 (1996), 405–29.

14. Emerson W. Baker, "'A Scratch with a Bear's Paw': Anglo-Indian Land Deeds in Early Maine," *Ethnohistory*, 36 (1989), 235–56.

15. Neal Salisbury, "Squanto: The Last of the Patuxets," in David G. Sweet and Gary B. Nash, eds., *Struggle and Survival in Colonial America* (Berkeley: University of California Press, 1981), 228–45; Ann Marie Plane, "'The Examination of Sarah Ahaton': The Politics of 'Adultery' in an Indian Town of Seventeenth-Century Massachusetts," in Benes, ed., Algonkians of New England, 14–25. Robert S. Grumet, ed., *Northeastern Indian Lives, 1632–1816* (Amherst: University of Massachusetts Press, 1996), includes essays on Miantonomi (Paul Robinson), Uncas (Eric S. Johnson), Robin Cassacinamon (Kevin McBride), Rawandagon alias Robin Hood (Harald E. L. Prins), Awashunkes (Ann Marie Plane), Thomas Waban (Daniel Mandell), Daniel Spotso (Elizabeth Little), and Molly Ockett (Bunny McBride and Harald Prins). See also Ann Marie Plane, "Childbirth Practices among Native American Women of New England and Canada, 1600–1800," in Peter Benes, ed., *Medicine and Healing* (Dublin Seminar for New England Folklife, Annual Proceedings, Boston: Boston University Press, 1991), 14–25.

16. Francis Jennings, "Goals and Functions of Puritan Missions to the Indians," *Ethnohistory*, 18 (1971), 197–212; Neal Salisbury, "Red Puritans: The 'Praying Indians' of Massachusetts Bay and John Eliot," *William and Mary Quarterly*, 3rd series, 31 (1974), 27–54; Kenneth M. Morrison, "'That Art of Coyning Christians': John Eliot and the Praying Indians of Massachusetts," *Ethnohistory*, 21 (1974), 77–92; James P. Ronda, "'We Are Well as We Are': An Indian Critique of Seventeenth-Century Christian Missions," *William and Mary Quarterly*, 3rd series, 34 (1977), 66–82; William S. Simmons, "Conversion from Indian to Puritan," *New England Quarterly*, 52 (1979), 197–218; Elise Brenner, "To Pray or Be Prey; That Is the Question: Strategies for Cultural Autonomy of Massachusetts Praying Town Indians," *Ethnohistory*, 27 (1980), 135–52; Henry W. Bowden and James P. Ronda, eds., *John Eliot's Indian Dialogues: A Study in Cultural Interaction* (Westport, Conn.: Greenwood Press, 1980); James Axtell, *The Invasion Within: The Contest of Cultures in Colonial North America* (New York: Oxford University Press, 1985), chaps. 7 and 9; James P. Ronda, "Generations of Faith: The Christian Indians of Martha's Vineyard," *William and Mary Quarterly*, 3rd series, 38 (1981), 369–94; Robert James Naeher, "Dialogue in the Wilderness: John Eliot and the Indian Exploration of Puritanism as a Source of Meaning, Comfort, and Ethnic Survival," *New England Quarterly*, 62 (1989), 346–68; Harold W. W. Van Lonkkhuyzen, "A Reappraisal of the Praying Indians: Acculturation, Conversion, and Identity at Natick, Massachusetts, 1646–1730," *New England Quarterly*, 63 (1990), 396–428; Richard W. Cogley, "John Eliot in Recent Scholarship," *American Indian Culture and Research Journal*, 14 (1990), 77–92; Dane Morrison, *A Praying People: Massachusett Acculturation and the Failure of the Puritan Mission, 1600–1690* (New York: Peter Lang, 1995); Kathleen Bragdon, "Gender as a Social Category in Southern New England," *Ethnohistory*, 43, no. 4 (1996), Special Issue on "Native American Women's Responses to Christianity." Kathleen Bragdon has also examined "Native Christianity in Eighteenth-Century Massachusetts: Ritual as Cultural Reaffirmation," in Barry

Gough and Laird Christie, eds., *New Dimensions in Ethnohistory: Papers of the Second Laurier Conference on Ethnohistory and Ethnology* (Ottawa: Canadian Museum of Civilization, 1991), 117–26.

17. Kathleen J. Bragdon, "'Another Tongue Brought In': An Ethnohistorical Study of Native Writings in Massachusset" (Ph.D. diss., Brown University, 1981); idem, "Vernacular Literacy and Massachusett World View, 1650–1750," in Benes, ed., *Algonkians of New England*, 26–34; Ives Goddard and Kathleen J. Bragdon, eds. and trans., *Native Writings in Massachusett*, 2 vols. (Philadelphia: American Philosophical Society, 1988).

18. For collections of captivity narratives, see Alden T. Vaughan and Edward W. Clark, eds., *Puritans among the Indians: Accounts of Captivity and Redemption, 1676–1724* (Cambridge, Mass.: Belknap Press of Harvard University Press, 1981), and Colin G. Calloway, ed., *North Country Captives: Selected Narratives of Indian Captivity from Vermont and New Hampshire* (Hanover, N.H.: University Press of New England, 1992). For broader analysis of such narratives, from New England and beyond, see James Axtell, "The White Indians of Colonial America," in *William and Mary Quarterly*, 3d ser., 32 (1975), 55–88; June Namias, *White Captives: Gender and Ethnicity on the American Frontier* (Chapel Hill: University of North Carolina Press, 1993), and Gary L. Ebersole, *Captured by Texts: Puritan to Post-Modern Images of Indian Captivity* (Charlottesville: University Press of Virginia, 1995). Alden T. Vaughan and Daniel Richter analyze the statistics of Indian captivities in "Crossing the Cultural Divide: Indians and New Englanders, 1605–1765," American Antiquarian Society *Proceedings*, 90 (1980), 23–99. John Demos reconstructs the story of a famous New England captive who stayed with the Indians—Eunice Williams—in *The Unredeemed Captive: A Family Story from Early America* (New York: Knopf, 1994).

19. William Cronon, *Changes in the Land: Indians, Colonists, and the Ecology of New England* (New York: Hill and Wang, 1983); Carolyn Merchant, *Ecological Revolutions: Nature, Gender, and Science in New England* (Chapel Hill: University of North Carolina Press, 1989); Virginia DeJohn Anderson, "King Philip's Herds: Indians, Colonists, and the Problem of Livestock in Early New England," *William and Mary Quarterly*, 3rd ser., 51 (1994), 601–24.

20. Neal Salisbury, "Toward the Covenant Chain: Iroquois and Southern New England Algonquians, 1637–1684," in Daniel K. Richter and James H. Merrell, eds., *Beyond the Covenant Chain: The Iroquois and Their Neighbors in Indian North America, 1600–1800* (Syracuse: Syracuse University Press, 1987), 61–73; Gordon M. Day, "The Ouragie War: A Case History in Iroquois-New England Indian Relations," in Michael K. Foster, Jack Campisi, Marianne Mithun, eds., *Extending the Rafters: Interdisciplinary Approaches to Iroquoian Studies* (Albany: State University of New York Press, 1984), 35–50; Bruce J. Bourque and Ruth H. Whitehead, "Tarrentines and the Introduction of European Trade Goods in the Gulf of Maine," *Ethnohistory*, 32 (1985), 327–41.

21. For example, the model that each Abenaki tribe in Maine occupied a river drainage area, as described in Frank G. Speck, *Penobscot Man: The Life History of a Forest Tribe in Maine* (Philadelphia: University of Pennsylvania Press, 1940), 7–9, and Dean Snow, "Eastern Abenaki," in Trigger, ed., *Handbook of North American Indians*, vol. 15: *Northeast*, 143–46, has given way to a model of interrelated kinship groups. Gordon Day, *The Identity of the Saint Francis Indians* (Ottawa: National Museum of Man, 1981); Evan Haefeli and Kevin Sweeney, "Wattanummon's World: Personal and Tribal Identity in the Algonquian Diaspora, c. 1600–1712," in William Cowan, ed.,

Papers of the Twenty-Fifth Algonquian Conference (Ottawa: Carleton University Press, 1994), 1–13; Bruce J. Bourque, "Ethnicity on the Maritime Peninsula, 1600–1759," *Ethnohistory*, 36 (1989), 257–84; Harald Prins and Bruce Bourque, "Norridgewock: Village Translocation on the New England-Acadian Frontier," *Man in the Northeast*, 33 (1986), 137–58.

22. Lynn Ceci, "Fish Fertilizer: A Native North American Practice?," *Science*, 188 (April 1975), 26–30; Nanepashemet, "It Smells Fishy to Me: An Argument Supporting the Use of Fish Fertilizer by the Native People of Southern New England," in Benes, ed., *Algonkians of New England*, 42–50.

23. For example: Colin G. Calloway, *The Abenaki* (New York: Chelsea House, 1989); Laurie Weinstein-Farson, *The Wampanoag* (New York: Chelsea House, 1989); William Simmons, *The Narragansett* (New York: Chelsea House, 1989).

24. Richard W. Wilkie and Jack Tager, eds., *Historical Atlas of Massachusetts* (Amherst: University of Massachusetts Press, 1991), 15.

25. "List of Indians in the Indian Charity School as prepared by Eleazar Wheelock, 1770," in Stockbridge Town Library Historical Room, "Stockbridge Indians" box; Eric P. Kelly, "The Dartmouth Indians," *Dartmouth Alumni Magazine*, 22 (Dec. 1929), 122–25.

26. Almon Wheeler Lauber, *Indian Slavery in Colonial Times within the Present Limits of the United States* (Williamstown, Mass.: Corner House Publishers, 1979), 110; John A. Sainsbury, "Indian Labor in Early Rhode Island," *New England Quarterly*, 48 (1975), 378–93.

27. Daniel R. Mandell, *Behind the Frontier: Indians in Eighteenth-Century Eastern Massachusetts* (Lincoln: University of Nebraska Press, 1996), 143–58; Jack Campisi, *The Mashpee Indians: Tribe on Trial* (Syracuse: Syracuse University Press, 1991), 85–89.

28. Jean M. O'Brien, *Dispossession by Degrees: Indian Land and Identity in Natick, Massachusetts, 1650–1790* (New York: Cambridge University Press, 1997); Mandell, *Behind the Frontier*, 132; Lion G. Miles, "The Red Man Dispossessed: The Williams Family and the Alienation of Indian Land in Stockbridge, Massachusetts, 1736–1818," *New England Quarterly*, 67 (1994), 46–76; Massachusetts Archives, 32: 61–64, 72–73, 76–78; 33: 115–17, 210–13, 249–52, 265–68, 277–88.

29. Colin G. Calloway, *The Western Abenakis of Vermont, 1600–1800: War, Migration, and the Survival of an Indian People* (Norman: University of Oklahoma Press, 1990), 226–30.

30. Papers of the Continental Congress, 1774–89, National Archives microfilm, reel 71, item 58: 59–63, 67–68, 75–79; reel 163, vol. 149, pt. 2: 561–62; Colin G. Calloway, ed., *Dawnland Encounters: Indians and Europeans in Northern New England* (Hanover, N.H.: University Press of New England, 1991), 128–31; Paul Brodeur, *Restitution: The Land Claims of the Mashpee, Passamaquoddy, and Penobscot Indians of New England* (Boston: Northeastern University Press, 1985), 78.

31. For example, Massachusetts Archives, 33: 543, 545–46, 556–66, 591–92; 144: 460–61; Connecticut State Archives, Hartford: Connecticut Archives, Indian Series, I, vol. 2: 201, 203, 248, 329; II, vol. 1: 41, 86.

32. Stephen Badger, "Historical and Characteristic Traits of the American Indians in General, and those of Natick in particular," Massachusetts Historical Society, *Collections*, 1st ser., 5 (1798), 32–45; quotes at 38–39; Massachusetts Archives, 33: 311–13, 591.

33. Daniel Mandell, "'To Live More Like My Christian Neighbors': Natick Indians in the Eighteenth Century," *William and Mary Quarterly*, 3d ser., 48 (1991), 573; Mandell, *Behind the Frontier*, 129; Badger, "Historical and Characteristic Traits of the American Indians," 41.

34. Elizabeth Little, "The Nantucket Indian Sickness," in William Cowan, ed., *Papers of the Twenty-First Algonquian Conference* (Ottawa: Carleton University Press, 1990), 181–96; Mandell, *Behind the Frontier*, 182; Daniel Vickers, "The First Whalemen of Nantucket," p. 103 this volume, table 2.

35. James Dow McCallum, ed., *The Letters of Eleazar Wheelock's Indians* (Hanover, N.H.: Dartmouth College Publications, 1932), 201, 211–16; William S. Simmons and Cheryl L. Simmons, eds., *Old Light on Separate Ways: The Narragansett Diary of Joseph Fish, 1765–1776* (Hanover, N.H.: University Press of New England, 1982), xxxii–xxxv, 46–47, 49, 70–71.

36. Calloway, *The Western Abenakis of Vermont*; Day, *The Identity of the Saint Francis Indians*.

37. Colin G. Calloway, *The American Revolution in Indian Country: Crisis and Diversity in Native American Communities* (New York: Cambridge University Press, 1995), 288.

38. *Records of the State of Rhode Island*, 10 vols. (Providence, R.I., 1856–65), 8: 573–74.

39. McCallum, ed., *Letters of Eleazar Wheelock's Indians*, 153–99; W. De Loss Love, *Samson Occom and the Christian Indians of New England* (Boston: Pilgrim Press, 1890), 222.

40. Badger, "Historical and Characteristic Traits of the American Indians," 39–40; John Milton Earle, *Report to the Governor and Council concerning the Indians of the Commonwealth* (Boston: State Printer, 1861), 6 (hereafter Earle Report); both quoted in O'Brien, *Dispossession by Degrees*, 160, 163; Mandell, *Behind the Frontier*, 160–63.

41. Campisi, *The Mashpee Indians*, 88; Earle Report, 6–7, quoted in O'Brien, *Dispossession by Degrees*, 163.

42. William S. Simmons, *Spirit of the New England Tribes: Indian History and Folklore, 1620–1984* (Hanover, N.H.: University Press of New England, 1986), 20–21, 25; Carter G. Woodson, "The Relations of Negroes and Indians in Massachusetts," *Journal of Negro History*, 5 (1920), 45–57; "A Letter from Rev. Gideon Hawley of Marshpee, containing an Account of his services among the Indians of Massachusetts and New-York," Mass. Hist. Soc., *Collections*, 1st ser., 40 (1794), 65–66; Gideon Hawley, "An account of the number of Indian houses in Mashpee," July 1, 1793; Harvard University, Houghton Library manuscript.

43. Mandell, *Behind the Frontier*, 163, and ch. 6; O'Brien, *Dispossession by Degrees*, 160; Badger, "Historical and Characteristic Traits," 43.

44. Calloway, *Western Abenakis of Vermont*.

45. Richard R. Johnson, "The Search for a Usable Indian: An Aspect of the Defense of Colonial New England," *Journal of American History*, 64 (1977–78), 623–51.

46. Calloway, *The American Revolution in Indian Country*, 28, 34–36, 85–107; Calloway, "Sentinels of Revolution: Bedel's New Hampshire Rangers and the Abenaki Indians on the Upper Connecticut," *Historical New Hampshire*, 45 (1990), 271–95; Calloway, "New England Algonkians in the American Revolution," in Benes, ed., *Algonkians of New England: Past and Present*, 51–62; "Copy of a Petition from Stockbridge Indians," Sept. 2, 1783, Stockbridge Library Historical Room, "Stockbridge Indians," box m. 73–130 (1).

47. Donald M. Nielsen, "The Mashpee Indian Revolt of 1833," *New England Quarterly*, 88 (1985), 400–20.

48. Laurence M. Hauptman, *Between Two Fires: American Indians in the Civil War* (New York: Free Press, 1995), 145–60.

49. J. Hector St. John de Crèvecouer, *Letters from an American Farmer* (New York: Penguin, 1981; orig. pub. 1782), 123.

50. Antonio Pace, trans. and ed., *Luigi Castiglioni's Viaggio: Travels in the United States of North America, 1785–87* (Syracuse: Syracuse University Press, 1983), 20, 43–44.

51. J. P. Brissot de Warville, *New Travels in the United States of America, 1788* (Cambridge, Mass., 1964), 82n; quoted in James Axtell, *Beyond 1492: Encounters in Colonial North America* (New York: Oxford University Press, 1992), 221. The Oneida was probably Peter Otsiquette, who accompanied the Marquis de Lafayette to France in 1784.

52. Badger, "Historical and Characteristic Traits of the American Indians," 35.

53. Mandell, "'To Live More Like My Christian Neighbors': Natick Indians in the Eighteenth Century"; O'Brien, *Dispossession by Degrees*; Patrick Frazier, *The Mohicans of Stockbridge* (Lincoln: University of Nebraska Press, 1992); Lion G. Miles, "The Red Man Dispossessed: The Williams Family and the Alienation of Indian Land in Stockbridge, Massachusetts, 1736–1818," *New England Quarterly*, 68 (1994), 46–76.

54. Calloway, *The Western Abenakis of Vermont, 1600–1800*. See also David L. Ghere, "The 'Disappearance' of the Abenaki in Western Maine," ch. 3 this volume.

55. Lester J. Cappon, ed., *The Adams-Jefferson Letters: The Complete Correspondence between Thomas Jefferson and Abigail and John Adams*, 2 vols. (Chapel Hill: University of North Carolina Press, 1959), 2: 310–11.

56. Reverend Jedidiah Morse, *A Report to the Secretary of War of the United States, on Indian Affairs* (New Haven: S. Converse, 1822), 64–75.

57. Alexis de Tocqueville, *Democracy in America*, ed. J. P. Mayer (New York: Doubleday, 1969), 321.

58. William S. Simmons, "Red Yankees: Narragansett Conversion in the Great Awakening," *American Ethnologist*, 10 (1983), 253–71; Paul R. Campbell and Glenn W. LaFantasie, "Scattered to the Winds of Heaven—Narragansett Indians 1676–1880," *Rhode Island History*, 37 (Aug. 1978), 67–83; Ethel Boissevain, "The Detribalization of the Narragansett Indians: A Case Study," *Ethnohistory*, 3 (1956), 225–45.

59. Ann Marie Plane and Gregory Button, ch. 8 this volume.

60. Jeanne Guillemin, *Urban Renegades: The Cultural Strategy of American Indians* (New York: Columbia University Press, 1975), examines this phenomenon among Micmac workers in twentieth-century Boston.

61. Trudy Ann Parker, *Aunt Sarah, Woman of the Dawnland* (Lancaster, N.H.: Dawnland Publications, 1994), 261. On Indian basket making in New England see Ann McMullen and Russell G. Handsman, eds., *A Key into the Language of Woodsplint Baskets* (Washington, Conn.: The American Indian Archaeological Institute, 1987), and McMullen, "Native Basketry, Basketry Styles, and Changing Group Identity in Southern New England," in Benes, ed., *Algonkians of New England*, 76–88. See also, Bunny McBride, ed., *Our Lives in Our Hands: Micmac Indian Basketmakers* (Gardiner, Maine: Tilbury House, 1991).

62. Kevin Dann, "From Degeneration to Regeneration: The Eugenics Survey of Vermont, 1925–1936," *Vermont History*, 59 (Winter 1991), 5–29; *Boston Globe*, Sept. 3, 1995; *Sunday Rutland Herald and Times Argus*, April 3, 1995; *News from Indian Country*, Dec. 1988.

63. Ethel Boissevan, "Narragansett Survival: A Study of Group Persistence Through Adopted Traits," *Ethnohistory*, 6 (1959), 347–62; Ann McMullen, "What's Wrong with This Picture? Context, Coversion, Survival, and the Development of Regional Cultures and Pan-Indianism in Southeastern New England," in Laurie

Weinstein, ed., *Enduring Traditions: The Native Peoples of New England* (Westport, Conn.: Bergin and Garvey, 1994), 123–50.

64. Frank G. Speck, "Native Tribes and Dialects of Connecticut: A Mohegan-Pequot Diary," *43rd Annual Report of the Bureau of American Ethnology, 1925–26* (Washington, D.C.: U.S. Gov't Printing Office, 1928), 264–79; *Penobscot Man: The Life History of a Forest Tribe in Maine*; "Reflections Upon the Past and Present of the Massachusetts Indians," *Bulletin of the Massachusetts Archaeological Society*, 4, part 3 (1943), 33–38; Ann McMullen, "'The Heart Interest': Native Americans at Mount Hope and the King Philip Museum," in Shepard Krech, ed., *Passionate Hobby: Rudolf Frederick Haffenreffer and the King Philip Museum* (Bristol, R.I: Haffenreffer Museum of Anthropology, Brown University; distributed by University of Washington Press, 1994), 167–85; Gladys Tantaquidgeon, *Folk Medicine of the Delaware and Related Algonquin Indians* (Harrisburg: Pennsylvania Historical Commission, 1977).

65. Brodeur, *Restitution: The Land Claims of the Mashpee, Passamaquoddy, and Penobscot Indians of New England*. Robert H. White traces postsettlement business developments among the Passamaquoddies in three chapters of his book *Tribal Assets: The Rebirth of Native America* (New York: Henry Holt, 1990).

66. Jack Campisi, *The Mashpee Indians: Tribe on Trial* (Syracuse: Syracuse University Press, 1991); James Clifford, "Identity in Mashpee," in *The Predicament of Culture: Ethnography, Literature and Art* (Cambridge, Mass.: Harvard University Press, 1988), 277–346; Russell Peters, comments at Dartmouth College Symposium "On the Thread of the Speaking Past: Survival and Revival in Native New England," April 25–26, 1996.

67. As James Axtell puts it: "Only if we persist in equating courage with mortal resistance to the forces of change can we condemn the praying Indians as cultural drop-outs or moral cowards. For life is preferable to death, and those who bend are also possessed of courage, the courage to change and to live in the face of overwhelming odds as well as the contempt of their brothers who died with stiff necks." Axtell, *After Columbus: Essays in the Ethnohistory of Colonial North America* (New York: Oxford University Press, 1988), 50.

68. For example, Weinstein, ed., *Enduring Traditions: The Native Peoples of New England*, and "'We're Still Living on Our Traditional Homeland'; The Wampanoag Legacy in New England," in Frank W. Porter III, ed., *Strategies for Survival: American Indians in the Eastern United States* (Westport, Conn.: Greenwood Press, 1986), 85–112. See also Harald E. L. Prins, *The Mi'kmaq: Resistance, Accommodation, and Cultural Survival* (Fort Worth: Harcourt Brace, 1996).

69. Russell M. Peters, *The Wampanoags of Mashpee: An Indian Perspective on American History* (Nimrod Press, 1987); Melissa Jayne Fawcett, *The Lasting of the Mohegans: The Story of the Wolf People* (Uncasville, Conn.: The Mohegan Tribe, 1995); Trudie Lamb Richmond, "A Native Perspective of History: The Schaghticoke Nation, Resistance and Survival," in Weinstein, ed., *Enduring Traditions*, 103–12.

70. "Return of the Natives: The Northeast's Indians Rise Again," *Hartford Courant*, May 22–29, 1994; "Return of the Natives: A Cultural Rebirth for Vermont's Abenakis," *Vermont Life*, 69, no. 1 (autumn 1994), 38–45.

71. David L. Ghere, "Assimilation, Termination, or Tribal Rejuvenation: Maine Indian Affairs in the 1950s," *Maine Historical Society Quarterly*, 24 (1984), 239–61; *The Wabanakis of Maine and the Maritimes: A resource book about Penobscot, Passamaquoddy, Maliseet, Micmac and Abenaki Indians, with lesson plans for grades 4 through 8* (Bath, Maine: American Friends Service Committee, 1989); Richard W.

Judd, Edwin A. Churchill, and Joel W. Eastman, eds., *Maine: The Pine Tree State from Prehistory to the Present* (Orono: University of Maine Press, 1995).

72. Bunny McBride, *Molly Spotted Elk: A Penobscot in Paris* (Norman: University of Oklahoma Press, 1995). McBride provides a personal account of the process by which she came to "know" Molly through her diaries in "The Spider and the WASP: Chronicling the Life of Molly Spotted Elk," in Jennifer S. H. Brown and Elizabeth Vibert, eds., *Reading Beyond Words: Contexts for Native History* (Peterboro, Ontario: Broadview Press, 1996), 403–27.

73. Melissa Jayne Fawcett, *The Lasting of the Mohegans*, 6.

74. *Indian Country Today*, vol. 16, issue 15 (Oct. 7–14, 1996), A6.

75. "A Narrative of the Captivity of Mrs. Johnson," reprinted in Calloway, ed., *North Country Captives*, 48.

76. See, for example, Simmons, *Spirit of the New England Tribes: Indian History and Folklore, 1620–1984*; idem "'The Mystic Voice': Pequot Folklore from the Seventeenth Century to the Present," in Hauptman and Wherry, eds., *The Pequots in Southern New England*, 141–75; Joseph Bruchac, *The Wind Eagle and Other Abenaki Stories* (Greenfield Center, N.Y.: Bowman Books, 1985), and *The Faithful Hunter: Abenaki Stories* (Greenfield Center, N.Y.: Greenfield Review Press, 1988). See also, Russell G. Handsman, "Illuminating History's Silences in the 'Pioneer Valley,'" *Artifacts*, 19 (1991), 14–25.

77. O'Brien quotation from session on "Survival and Persistence in 18th-Century Indian New England" (American Historical Association Annual Meeting, Washington, D.C., 1987). See also Kathleen Bragdon, "Probate Records as a Source of Algonquian Ethnohistory," in William Cowan, ed., *Papers of the Tenth Algonquian Conference* (Ottawa: Carleton University Press, 1979), 136–41, and Elizabeth A. Little, *Probate Records of Nantucket Indians* (Nantucket: Nantucket Historical Association, 1980).

78. Kenneth M. Morrison, *The Embattled Northeast: The Elusive Ideal of Alliance in Abenaki-Euramerican Relations* (Berkeley: University of California Press, 1984); Calloway, *The Western Abenakis of Vermont*; David L. Ghere, "Mistranslations and Misinformation: Diplomacy on the Maine Frontier, 1725 to 1755," *American Indian Culture and Research Journal*, 8, no. 4 (1984), 3–26; and "Eastern Abenaki Autonomy and French Frustrations, 1745–1760," *Maine History*, 34, no. 1 (summer 1994), 2–21.

79. Frazier, *The Mohicans of Stockbridge*; Mandell, *Behind the Frontier*; O'Brien, *Dispossession by Degrees*. Donna Keith Baron, J. Edward Hood, and Holly V. Izard—a curator, a research historian, and an archaeologist—describe the strategy of their research in progress for documenting the continuing presence of Indian peoples in "They Were Here All Along: The Native American Presence in Lower-Central New England in the Eighteenth and Nineteenth Centuries," *William and Mary Quarterly*, 3d ser., 53 (1996), 561–86.

80. Laura Murray, ed., *"To Do Good To My Indian Brethren": The Writings of Joseph Johnson, 1751–1776* (Amherst: University of Massachusetts Press, 1997); Samson Occom, "A Short Narrative of My Life," reprinted in Colin G. Calloway, ed., *The World Turned Upside Down: Indian Voices from Early America* (Boston: Bedford Books, 1994), 55–61; Harold Blodgett, *Samson Occom* (Hanover, N.H.: Dartmouth College Publications, 1935); Bernd Peyer, "Samson Occom: Mohegan Missionary and Writer of the 18th Century," *American Indian Quarterly*, 6 (1982), 208–17; Margaret Connell Szasz, "Samson Occom: Mohegan as Spiritual Intermediary," in Szasz, ed., *Between Indian and White Worlds: The Cultural Broker* (Norman: University of Oklahoma Press, 1994), 61–78; Laurie Weinstein, "Samson Occom: A Charismatic

Eighteenth-Century Mohegan Leader," in Weinstein, ed., *Enduring Traditions*, 91–102; Barry O'Connell, ed., *On Our Own Ground: The Complete Writings of William Apess, a Pequot* (Amherst: University of Massachusetts Press, 1992); David Murray, *Forked Tongues: Speech Writing and Representation in North American Indian Texts* (Bloomington: Indiana University Press, 1991), ch. 4; Peyer, ed., *The Elders Wrote: An Anthology of Early Prose by North American Indians 1768–1931* (Berlin: Dietrich Reiner, 1982), 12–24, 44–50.

81. The saga of the Reverend John Williams and his daughter Eunice, who married a Caughnawaga Indian, converted to Catholicism, and refused to return home, is well told in Demos, *The Unredeemed Captive*.

82. O'Connell, ed., *On Our Own Ground*. See also O'Connell, "William Apess and the Survival of the Pequot People," in Benes, ed., *Algonkians of New England*, 89–100.

83. O'Brien, *Dispossession by Degrees*, 3.

Evan Haefeli and Kevin Sweeney

2

Revisiting *The Redeemed Captive*

New Perspectives on the 1704 Attack on Deerfield

On May 24, 1718, the Reverend John Williams of Deerfield, Massachusetts, dashed off a brief letter to his son Stephen informing him that "My Indian Master has been to visit me several times. [He] is here about [.] He proposes next week for Canada."[1] Fourteen years after taking Williams prisoner and marching him overland to Canada during the winter of 1704, one of Williams's two Indian captors had come back to Deerfield in a time of peace. While staying in the area, the warrior visited the minister several times before returning to his home in Canada.

This apparently amiable reunion of old enemies was as characteristic of the colonial New England frontier as their violent meeting on February 29, 1704, when a party of French and Indians had captured and sacked Deerfield.[2] The northwesternmost village in New England for most of the colonial period, Deerfield has become a symbol of the region's frontier experience, and the story of this place as a point of contact between cultures has been dominated by Williams's account of the 1704 raid. The minister's relation of the attack and his captivity, *The Redeemed Captive Returning to Zion*, has been called "the masterpiece" of the captivity narrative genre.[3] More than any other text, this book etched in the memory of later generations the image of the New England frontier as a zone of constant conflict where English colonists fought off the French and their native allies.

Williams's depictions of his French and Indian enemies are classic portraits of ethnic Others that reinforced cultural norms espoused by the clerical leaders of New England. These representations locate the Deerfield raid in a confrontation between Puritan New England and Catholic New France, casting the natives as either willing or reluctant minions of the French.[4] Here and in subsequent retellings of the attack, such as Francis Parkman's well-known account, much space is devoted to recounting the outrages committed by the "savages," and little is said of the motivations that brought the Indians in arms to Deerfield.[5] Williams reported hearing that "many of the Indians much lamented their making a war against the English, at the instigation of the French."[6] Nineteenth-century New England authors likewise assumed that the persuasions of the French or "an insatiate desire for scalps" sufficed to explain the participation of the Indians in the attack.[7] Later scholars have been content to focus on the meanings of Williams's representations of Frenchmen and Indians and have tended to view the struggle in terms of a confrontation between cultures and ideologies.[8] They have not demonstrated much interest in identifying the native attackers, reconstructing their understandings of the event, or recovering their voices, which can be heard even in Williams's narrative.

To discover who these natives were and to attempt to understand why they went to Deerfield, this article situates the 1704 attack and Williams's narrative in several established patterns of interaction between Indians and colonists. Using the raid as a window into the histories of native homelands and villages, it identifies more precisely than any previous study the Indians who took part, examining in succession the actions and possible motivations of four distinct groups of attackers. By employing this approach we shift the story of Deerfield from accounts such as those of Williams and Parkman that place it solely within "a half-century of conflict" between England and France and relocate it in the histories of the region's native peoples. Long-standing native associations with and claims upon the region, the bitter legacy of King Philip's War, and more peaceable and commonplace kinds of intercultural exchange, as well as French policy, all played roles in determining the composition of the attacking party and the fate of Deerfield's residents.

This broader context also furthers our understanding of Williams's perspective as author and participant. The Indians about whom Williams the author wrote in his public role as a minister were, like the French, ethnic Others. At the same time, however, the received images of mutual isolation and cultural antagonism between the English and the Indians do not tell the entire story of New England's frontier. The region's natives were an integral part of Williams's life, a fact not obvious from *The Redeemed Captive*, subsequent discussions of it, or even some recent histories of New England's borderlands.[9] Not just an isolated frontier outpost, Deerfield also served as a way station for native peoples who moved through the middle ground lying between the

French and English empires.[10] Any historical or literary analysis of Williams's narrative needs to take into account the character of this terrain and the identities and motives of its native as well as its English inhabitants.

The attack on Deerfield was one of a series of joint military expeditions carried out by French and Indians during the War of the Spanish Succession (1702–1713) or Queen Anne's War, as it was known in the English colonies. These raids required much planning and long overland marches, often under arduous conditions. The party that attacked Deerfield had covered approximately 300 miles before launching its assault just before dawn on February 29. The assailants breached the palisade without detection and stormed the houses. Some occupants resisted, but most were overpowered. After killing 42 residents and 5 garrisoned militiamen and capturing 109 persons, the raiders withdrew, leaving the southern end of the village largely untouched.[11] Eleven of the attackers died and a score were wounded.[12] Reinforcements from towns downriver joined men of the village in counterattacking the retreating party. The raiders beat them back, killing nine and wounding others. Although they suffered additional casualties of their own, they succeeded in forestalling further pursuit and returned to Canada unmolested.[13]

Reckonings of the size and composition of the raiding party have been based largely on interpretations and misinterpretations of English estimates. Contemporary English reports put the number of raiders at between 300 and 400 men; Williams said about 300.[14] The numbers commonly cited by historians are 200 French soldiers and 142 Indians.[15] In actuality, the attack was carried out by approximately 250 men: 200 Indians and 48 French. The reports of French officials who were in a position to know are consistent. Philippe de Rigaud de Vaudreuil, governor general of New France, wrote that there were 250 attackers. In a separate letter, Claude de Ramezay, governor of Montreal, broke the figure down into 48 French and approximately 200 Indians.[16]

The 48 Frenchmen appear to have been *canadiens*, and it is likely that only a few of them were regular soldiers. The three we know by name, Jean-Baptiste Hertel de Rouville, François-Marie Margane de Batilly, and René Boucher de la Perrière, were all Canadian-born officers in the Troupes de la Marine, regulars who guarded French ports and served in the colonies under the command of the minister of the Marine.[17] Sons of upper-class Canadian seigneurial families, these officers had proved themselves by participation in previous frontier raids. Their leader, Hertel de Rouville, came from a family with ties to the St. Francis Abenakis; Perrière apparently had ties to the French Mohawks. The men these officers led to Deerfield were probably Canadian militia, not regular soldiers. The rank-and-file Troupes de la Marine, who were recruited in France, did not have the skills to survive winter campaigning in North America and were usually relegated to garrison duty. Rather, those Canadians who were accustomed to hunting, fishing, and Indian warfare had the requisite experience for raids against the New England frontier.[18] Three Canadians, Ensign de Batilly among them, died in the attack on Deerfield; twenty others, including de Rouville and Perrière, were wounded.[19]

Despite the high proportion of casualties, the use of Canadian officers and militiamen on this kind of expedition furthered the strategic goals of Governor Vaudreuil. By deploying fewer than fifty men, officials in Canada helped spread fear throughout New England. The commitment of these men demonstrated French willingness and ability to stand by their native allies and helped insure that these allies would carry the war to the English.[20] The Deerfield raid forced the English colonies to disperse their forces and employ most of them in passive and expensive frontier defenses instead of offensive operations.[21] Subsequent raids that usually had similarly modest contingents of *canadiens* kept up the pressure.

Williams also reported that the attack on Deerfield and his capture gave the Canadian governor a desirable bargaining chip. On his arrival in Montreal, Williams learned from the governor that he would "be sent home as soon as Captain Battis was returned, and not before; and that I was taken in order to [secure] his redemption."[22] The nineteenth-century historian George Sheldon embroidered this observation into a secret plan in which Deerfield was targeted to obtain a suitable captive to exchange for an imprisoned Acadian corsair, identified as Jean Baptiste or Jean-Baptiste Guyon.[23] It is clear that Vaudreuil did link Williams's treatment and ultimate repatriation to the fate of privateer Pierre Maisonnat, whose nom de guerre was "Baptiste."[24] The explanation of the raid as a design to seize the then obscure Deerfield minister most likely represents a post hoc justification by the governor and the confusion of an effect with a cause by some historians.[25] Even Sheldon acknowledged that "neither Mr. Williams, nor any of his readers, took seriously the statement of Vaudreuil."[26]

It is relatively easy to establish the size of the French forces and to recover and assess the Canadian governor's purposes; it is difficult to determine the identities of the native participants and to reconstruct their motives. William's narrative provides the first clues, delineating three groups of natives: "Indians," "Indians belonging to the eastern parts," and "Macquas."[27] Twenty "Indians and Macquas" entered his house; he was seized by "three Indians."[28] One of his captors, "a captain," did not survive the attack; the two other "Indians" took him eventually to "the fort called St. François," indicating that they were natives whom the English and the French called "Abenakis."[29]

Period sources and recent ethnohistorical studies enable us to explicate and refine Williams's categories and locate the groups geographically and culturally with some precision. Setting forth the results, table 1 presents variations in contemporary and present-day nomenclature and identifies homelands and principal villages. Three of the groups named—the St. Francis

TABLE 1
Identities of the Indians in John Williams's *The Redeemed Captive*

Williams's Term	"Indians"	"Eastern Indians"			"Maquas"	
Likely identity	St. Francis Abenakis	Cowassucks	Pennacooks	Pigwackets	French Mohawks	Hurons
Alternative period names	Arsikantegouk, Alsikantegouk, Canada Indians	Cohass, Coos, Cohassiac, Koes	Penacook, Penikoke, Openango	Pequawket, Pequaki	Caughnawagas, Kahnawakes	"French Mohawks"
Modern cultural and linguistic categories	Algonquian, mostly Western Abenakis	Algonquian, Western Abenakis	Algonquian, Western Abenakis	Algonquian, Western Abenakis	Iroquoian, Iroquois	Iroquoian, Huron
Location	St. Francis River	Upper Connecticut Valley	Merrimack Valley	Saco River, White Mts.	St. Lawrence Valley near Montreal	Near Quebec
Principal villages	Odanak	Cowass (Newbury, Vt.)	Pennacook (Concord, N.H.)	Pigwacket (Fryeburg, Maine)	Kahnawake, La Montagne, Kanesatake	Lorette

Source: Adapted from Colin G. Calloway, *The Western Abenakis of Vermont, 1600–1800* (Norman, Okla., 1990), 8–9.

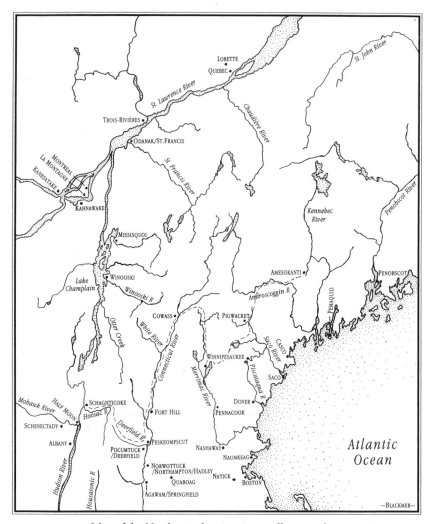

FIGURE 1. Map of the Northeast, showing rivers, villages, and east–west route.

Abenakis, the French Mohawks from Kahnawake and La Montagne, and the Hurons of Lorette—were *sauvages domiciliés*, praying Indians living in mission villages in New France, while the Western Abenakis categorized by Williams as "Eastern Indians" lived in villages such as Cowass, Pennacook, Pigwacket, and Winnipesauke situated in the middle ground between English and French settlements (see figure 1). Indians from all of these groups allied with the French to attack Deerfield, but they did so for different reasons. Insights into their motivations can be obtained only by examining in turn the particular histories of the St. Francis Abenakis, the Eastern Indians, the French Mohawks, and the Hurons. Although they lived in different places and had different histories, all had reasons, arising from their involvement in wars with the Five Nations of the Iroquois or in King Philip's War, to join the Deerfield raid.

Historians have long recognized that Abenakis from St. Francis took part in the Deerfield raid. Usually, their participation has been viewed exclusively from the perspective of the strategic calculations of the French involving the Eastern Abenakis who lived in Maine. The *sauvages domiciliés* living at St. Francis in 1704 were primarily Western Abenakis, however, and had closer ties to the Connecticut Valley than to Maine. Many St. Francis Abenakis were descended from natives who had been driven from western and southern New England by the Iroquois in the 1660s and the English in the 1670s. Their expulsion from New England had pushed them into close alliance with the French. Their participation in the attack on Deerfield had its roots in this relationship and in older conflicts with the English.

In letters to his superiors in France, Vaudreuil repeatedly emphasized the Abenakis when explaining why he had sent men to Deerfield in the middle of the winter. In the fall of 1703, he wrote, Abenakis had come to him, saying that the English had killed some of their people and asking the French to join them in a raid of retribution.[30] Afterward, Vaudreuil felt French participation in the Deerfield raid had been justified when a group of Abenakis came in the spring of 1704 to thank him for his support. To his superiors in France, he explained that the winter expedition had shown the Abenakis that they could "count on us."[31] Such a demonstration, he believed, was essential to his wartime policy of keeping the English and the Abenakis "irreconcilable enemies," for he assumed that if the Abenakis were not enemies of the English, they would be friends of the English and a threat to the French.[32] This assumption, however, failed to take into account the variety and complexity of the military, diplomatic, religious, commercial, and personal motivations of the peoples the French and the English categorized as Abenakis.

Abenaki motivations are difficult to uncover, in part because it is difficult to discover who the Abenakis in question were. The blanket categorization "Abenaki" suggests a cohesion and identity that did not exist in the 1600s and early 1700s. The Abenaki homeland stretched from Lake Champlain to the coast of Maine and from the southern bank of the St. Lawrence River to the northern Massachusetts border (see figure 2).[33] Within this area lived several linguistically related peoples grouped primarily in family bands. Most scholarly studies of the Abenakis have focused on the Eastern Abenakis of Maine, especially Penobscots and Kennebecs, and emphasis on Eastern Abenakis has led historians to conclude that the Abenaki attackers of Deerfield came directly or originally from eastern Maine.[34] The evidence instead indicates that the natives Williams categorized as "Indians" were Western Abenakis from St. Francis and related bands in parts of Canada and Vermont.[35] We do not

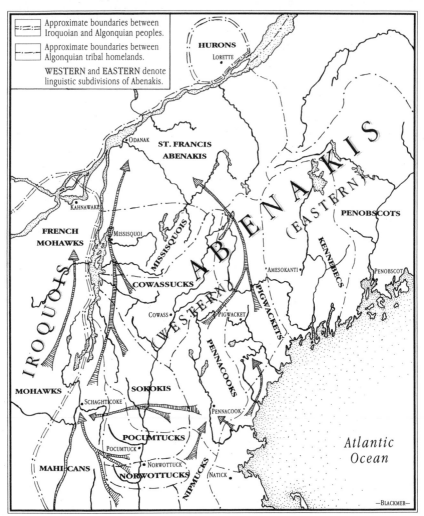

FIGURE 2. Map of the Northeast, showing tribal homelands and movements circa 1675–1704.

suggest that Western Abenakis acted as a cohesive group, but the correct identification of the Abenaki attackers reveals relationships between struggles in the Connecticut Valley and struggles along the southern coast of Maine and New Hampshire that otherwise remain obscure.

The presumption that the two Indians who took Williams to the fort called St. François were Western Abenakis is a strong one, for few Eastern Abenakis lived at the Indian village associated with the St. Francis mission in 1704.[36] The tribal or ethnic origins of this Canadian community were, however, complex; not all its residents were Western Abenaki-speakers by birth. St. Francis, founded in the turmoil of seventeenth-century wars, was about the same age as Deerfield. Then called Arsikantegouk, known today as Odanak, the village had been established in the 1660s, when Sokokis, who were Western Abenakis, moved there after a 1663 Mohawk attack on their village at Fort Hill (today Hinsdale, New Hampshire).[37] The Sokokis were joined by other Western Abenakis, including some Pennacooks, who were also at war with the Mohawks and other members of the Five Nations.

The number of refugees trekking to Odanak increased in the 1670s after the outbreak of general fighting between natives in southern New England and English colonists. The discontent of the Wampanoags in southeastern New England escalated into a war in July 1675 as Metacom, called King Philip by the English, led a series of hit-and-run raids on villages in Plymouth Colony. The fighting spread to central Massachusetts and the Connecticut Valley during the late summer and fall as Nipmucks, Norwottucks, and Pocumtucks joined in. Despite numerous victories, the Indians' offensive waned in the spring of 1676 as dwindling supplies of food and munitions sapped their strength. On May 19, 1676, 140 colonists fell on a large encampment of sleeping natives at Peskeompscut, the "Great Falls" of the Connecticut River (today, Turner's Falls, Massachusetts), killing between 200 and 300, most of them "old men and women." The slaughter shocked and demoralized the natives.[38] Although some fighting in the Connecticut Valley and in Maine continued into 1677, most of the natives in western Massachusetts had been killed, captured, or driven from their homes by the end of 1676. The resulting diaspora created new refugee villages, such as Schaghticoke in New York, and increased the population of existing ones such as Odanak.[39]

Members of twenty nations eventually settled at Odanak, among them refugees from Pocumtuck (Deerfield) who fled north after King Philip's War.[40] Speakers of Western Abenaki, however, remained the core of Odanak's population, and the others, regardless of their original ethnic identity, learned Western Abenaki.[41] The Jesuit mission of St. Francis, originally located on the Chaudière River near Quebec, moved in 1701 to the St. Francis River and became the mission for Odanak. Gradually a distinctive community of Western Abenaki-speaking, praying Indians emerged from the coalescence of Norwottucks, Pocumtucks, Sokokis, Pennacooks, and others who made Odanak their new home. The French referred to them as Abenakis or "our Indians." Williams called them "Indians." They identified themselves as Arsikantegouks. In 1704, there were about 200 warriors at Odanak, including those who had moved in with the new mission.[42]

Since 1690, the village's warriors had participated in military expeditions against New England in association with French forces under the command of members of the Hertel family. Headed by Joseph-François Hertel de la Fresnière, a Canadian born in Trois-Rivières, the family had become involved with the nearby community of Abenakis at Odanak. In addition to negotiating issues of land use and tenancy, the Hertels and the Abenakis fought together in the intercolonial wars, beginning with the March 27, 1690, attack on Salmon Falls, New Hampshire.[43] In all the expeditions the majority of fighters were natives, not French. Joseph-François Hertel's sons also entered the French military and often accompanied him, learning skills that they would put into practice on their own. Of these sons, Jean-Baptiste Hertel de Rouville, who commanded the French at Deerfield, gained the most recognition as a fighter and carried the family tradition of leading colonial troops and native allies into the next generation. Thus the Indian warriors of Odanak and de Rouville's family had lived and fought together for many years. The closeness of the relationship was captured in Cotton Mather's unsympathetic characterization of the party that attacked Salmon Falls as "half Indianized French and half Frenchified Indians."[44]

In part, the St. Francis Abenakis' participation in the Deerfield raid was based on this personal relationship, which counted for more among the natives than the desires of distant French officials.[45] Both the St. Francis Abenakis and the Hertel family benefited from their wartime cooperation, though in different ways. For Joseph-François and Hertel de Rouville, military distinction brought ennoblement and landed estates in a colony where both were highly esteemed and difficult to obtain.[46] The Abenakis of St. Francis gained captives: 54 at Salmon Falls in 1690 and a share of the 109 taken at Deerfield in 1704.[47]

Among the Abenakis as among the Iroquois, live captives had more value than scalps, the other proof of a warrior's deeds. Consequently, the division of captives was a matter of symbolic and material significance. Soon after the Deerfield attack, the party paused "to make a more equal distribution" of the captives, because "some were disturbed, for some had five or six captives, and others had none."[48] Captives had great value; depending on their age and condition, they were used as slaves, retained as hostages, or displayed as status symbols.[49] Occasionally, the Abenakis adopted captives, but, unlike the Iroquois, they do not appear to have waged war specifically to obtain captives to replace dead kin.[50] John Williams did see several English children at Odanak who had become "in habit very much like Indians, and in manners very much symbolizing with them," though John's eleven-year-old son, Stephen, learned that "when alone they would talk familiarly . . . in English, about their own country."[51] Most (probably all) of the Deerfield captives taken by the St. Francis Abenakis were ransomed to the French, affirming the French-Abenaki alliance and providing a source of income.[52]

Captivity among the St. Francis Abenakis at Odanak had a religious dimension that the Deerfield pastor made much of. Personal ties forged by Jesuit missionaries influenced the actions of the Abenakis and gave a religious coloration to some of their motivations. Williams experienced firsthand this religiosity soon after his arrival at the mission village. "One day" in the spring of 1704, while he sat in his master's home, "a certain savagess taken prisoner in

Philip's war, who had lived at Mr. Buckley's at Weathersfield [Connecticut], called Ruth, who could speak English very well and who had been often at my house, being now proselyted to the Romish faith, came into the wigwam, and with her an English maid who was taken in the last war."[53] Throughout his stay at Odanak, Williams was under pressure to convert, both from the Jesuit priests of the St. Francis mission and from one of his Abenaki masters. On this day Ruth joined the efforts of this master to convert the determined Protestant minister, quoting scripture to persuade Williams to obey his master's commands to cross himself and kiss a crucifix. Eventually, Williams's master gave up in frustration exclaiming, "No good minister, no love God, as bad as the Devil."[54]

Such concern for the outward forms of Catholicism highlights another bond some natives shared with the French. To varying degrees, St. Francis Abenakis embraced Catholicism. This acceptance strengthened their ties to the French and heightened their animosity toward the English, whom they sometimes referred to as "hereticks" by the early 1700s.[55] This embrace of Catholicism was conditioned by native traditions, needs, and expectations and did not involve uncritical acceptance of French teachings or renunciation of native beliefs.[56] Throughout New France, native beliefs and practices persisted among peoples who had been nominally Catholic for some time. To this day, services at the Catholic Church at Odanak draw from both Catholic and native traditions.[57]

Even more suggestive of the sources of the St. Francis Abenakis' hostility toward the English was the ability of many of them to speak English, a fact little commented upon by most scholars who have studied Williams's account. On the journey north, one of Williams's two Indian masters showed him how to use snowshoes, assuring him that "you cannot possibly travel without, the snow being knee-deep."[58] At another point in the journey, this master gave Williams a Bible and enjoined him to "arise, pray to God, and eat your breakfast, for we must go a great way to-day."[59] This seemingly more tolerant attitude, as well as his greater fluency in English, distinguished this master from the other who denounced Williams as "No good minister, no love God, as bad as the Devil." Still, both Indian masters could communicate in English, as could Ruth and apparently others at Odanak.[60] Like Ruth, a number were probably refugees from southern New England who had fled to Canada in the years after King Philip's War, journeying north either directly or after living for a while in a refugee village such as Schaghticoke or among the English—perhaps involuntary as servants as Ruth had.

Some of these refugees returned to the Deerfield area as early as 1677, when a raiding party led by Ashpalon, a former resident of the area who had fled to Canada, attacked Hatfield and Deerfield and took prisoners back to their new village in Canada.[61] Norwottucks and Pocumtucks made up most of this party, though it included at least one Narragansett who had been driven all the way to Canada by King Philip's War. Groups of natives who had previously lived in the Connecticut Valley continued to return during the late 1680s and the 1690s, on some occasions to fight with the English and on others to trade with them. For these former residents of the valley and for the descendants of the Norwottucks, Pocumtucks, and Sokokis who lived at Odanak, the 1704 raid on Deerfield was a battle in a contest that had started in the 1670s. Most notable among these earlier battles had been the "Falls Fight" at Peskeompscut, not more than six miles from Deerfield. Because of the involvement of the St. Francis Abenakis, it is likely that Deerfield historian Sheldon erred when he claimed that "not a Pocumtuck, nor the son of a Pocumtuck, wagged a finger in the affair. The expedition was purely a stroke of French policy."[62]

Strokes of French policy provide an even less complete explanation for the presence of those Western Abenakis whom Williams distinguished as "the Indians belonging to the eastern parts."[63] The natives, called "eastward Indians" or "Eastern Indians" by Massachusetts authorities and residents, lived in the lands now constituting Maine and New Hampshire. Williams's contemporaries were often referring specifically to the Eastern Abenakis of Maine when they spoke of "Eastern Indians." They were not consistent, however, and their use of the term does not instantly and easily translate into the linguistic category Eastern Abenakis. A number of the natives whom Massachusetts officials called "Eastern Indians" were *Western* Abenakis according to present-day linguistic classification.[64] The eastward Indians who attacked Deerfield in 1704 were primarily Western Abenakis: Pennacooks, Pigwackets, and Cowassucks who lived along the upper reaches of the Merrimack, Saco, and Connecticut rivers (see figure 2).[65] In all, these bands probably mustered 125 to 200 warriors in the late 1600s and early 1700s.[66]

These natives were involved in the struggles along the coast in the lands of the Eastern Indians as well as in events in the mid-Connecticut River Valley. Unlike their kinsmen who joined the community at St. Francis, these Western Abenakis categorized as Eastern Indians were not *sauvages domiciliés*, though some of them used Odanak as a temporary refuge. Far from being dependent allies of the French, the Eastern Indians who attacked Deerfield endeavored to maintain a middle way between the French and the English. These Eastern Indians had, in fact, initiated the enterprise by calling upon Vaudreuil to join them in attacking the New England frontier,[67] and it is likely that these Western Abenakis and those at St. Francis provided 120 to 140 of the native attackers. Participation in the Deerfield raid represented a measured response on their part to English aggression against their villages in southwestern Maine and New Hampshire.[68] Behind this action lay a complicated history shaped by seventeenth-century wars against the Iroquois and the English that brought the retaliating Eastern Indians to Deerfield in 1704.

Prominent among these Eastern Indians was a Pennacook sachem, Wattanummon, the first native attacker who can be identified by name.[69] Wattanummon took John Williams's eleven-year-old son, Stephen, captive. After the raid, he and his prisoner did not travel directly north to Odanak but remained in the lands lying between New France and New England that were under the control of neither colony, belonging with certainty only to the natives themselves. They spent the winter and spring of 1704 with Wattanummon's family, hunting in lands northwest of Cowass (Newbury, Vermont). In the spring the family took Stephen down to "Cowass, where was their rendezvous."[70] They never got there. A group of natives from Cowass met them on their way and told them that all the Indians were leaving because a family living just south of the village had been ambushed and killed by an Anglo-Mohegan war party. Stephen's party stayed where they were for several weeks and then went north to Odanak.[71]

Despite the presence of kin and former comrades in arms, Wattanummon felt himself a stranger at Odanak. According to Stephen, "he could not comply with their rites and customs, whereupon [in 1704] he went to Albany," presumably Schaghticoke.[72] Wattanummon may have been at Odanak in the 1680s; it was apparently the new mission that alienated him in 1704.[73] Even those Pennacooks and Pigwackets who accepted Catholic teachings "were not as zealous as the Macquas," in Stephen Williams's opinion.[74] Like Cowass, Schaghticoke had not been established as a mission village, and Wattanummon evidently preferred the absence of a Christian orientation. When he departed for "Albany," he did not take Stephen with him but left him with "his kinsman, Sagamore George [George Tohanto]," who had recently arrived from Cowass and who was identified as a Pennacook.[75]

The Pennacooks' involvement in the Deerfield raid had roots in personal animosities and strategic calculations dating from the 1670s. The Pennacooks, Pigwackets, and other "Indians belonging to the eastern parts" who accompanied Wattanummon attempted to keep free of complete dependence on the French, English, or Five Nations Iroquois, all of whom alternately wooed and threatened them.[76] From the 1640s to the 1670s, the Pennacooks' leaders, Passaconaway and his son Wanalancet, had managed to remain on reasonably good terms with the English while fighting a desultory war with the Iroquois. Only in 1676, as King Philip's War was drawing to a close, did the Pennacooks' native alliances bring them into confrontation with the English. That spring, several hundred Nipmucks, Pocumtucks, and other southern New England natives who were fleeing the English moved north to live among the Pennacooks and Pigwackets.[77]

In September 1676, Major Richard Waldron, who had come to know the Pennacooks by trading with them for years, called a meeting at Dover, New Hampshire. Some 400 natives arrived. Waldron had orders to seize all Indians suspected of fighting against the English. Realizing that he could not capture so many Indians by force, he resorted to trickery. He proposed that the English and Indians stage a sham fight, with both sides firing harmless volleys as a sign of mutual respect. After the Indians had fired first, the English turned their loaded guns on the now defenseless natives, disarmed them, and seized them. Waldron then singled out all the refugee Nipmucks and other "strange Indians," as he called them, whom he suspected of having fought in King Philip's War. They were sold into slavery in New England and the West Indies. The others, including Wanalancet, were allowed to return to their homes.[78] Fearing further trouble, some of the Pennacooks moved to the refugee village at Schaghticoke. A number, including Wanalancet's band, headed north to Canada, and another group resettled along the Androscoggin River in Maine.[79]

Some thirty years later, in March 1704, on the day John Williams arrived at Odanak, a Jesuit came into the wigwam where he sat and invited him to supper. Over the meal, as Williams later wrote, the priest "justified the Indians in what they did against us, rehearsing some things done by Major Waldron above thirty years ago, and how justly God retaliated them in the last war, and inveighed against us for beginning this war with the Indians, and said we had before the last winter and in the winter been very barbarous and cruel in burning and killing Indians."[80] Here, in Williams's own narrative, is the best contemporary explanation of what motivated some of the natives to attack Deerfield; it highlights the lingering effects of English treachery. In tracing the problem back to Waldron in 1676, the priest indicated that Pennacooks and probably their Pigwacket neighbors played an important role in promoting and carrying out the 1704 assault on Deerfield. The priest's reference to English counterattacks in the fall of 1703 and early winter of 1704 and the presence of children at Odanak, who had been captured in the summer of 1703 during fighting in southwestern Maine, underscore the conclusion that the Pennacooks, together with the Pigwackets, had a hand in planning the attack on Deerfield.

Even given this evidence, it is not immediately clear why the Pennacooks and their allies would choose to attack in the Connecticut Valley, when their grievances, according to the Jesuit, resulted from actions by Englishmen living along the coast. Part of the answer is that, by 1704, the natives had already had their revenge on the colonists in the latter area. Some of the natives whom Waldron took away had subsequently escaped from servitude, joined with Pennacooks and Pigwackets, attacked Dover, and captured Waldron in June 1689. Then they tortured him to death.[81]

The memory of Waldron's treachery continued to influence events long after his death and well beyond the confines of Pennacook country. Even before the Pennacooks and their allies had taken their revenge on Waldron, their war against the English that his actions had inspired had expanded into the Connecticut Valley. Pennacook raiding parties had been drawn to the west by refugee Nipmuck and Pocumtuck allies who had brought to Pennacook country ties to their western Massachusetts homelands as well as their own grievances against the English. At the same time, war and threats of war during the 1670s and early 1680s had driven some Pennacooks west to the refugee village of Schaghticoke. These movements, from the Connecticut Valley to Pennacook and from Pennacook to Schaghticoke and back again, strengthened connections to the west, creating bonds that influenced the actions of Pennacooks and other Eastern Indians during the later 1600s and early 1700s. New Englanders faced more than just a French-led Indian alliance. Native alliances running east and west played an often overlooked role in shaping the composition of raiding parties moving from north to south during King William's War (1688–1697) and later during Queen Anne's War.

A report from July 1688 provides an unusually detailed example of the ways in which the hybrid identities found in refugee communities influenced a group's actions. A raiding party of "Eleven Indians that formerly lived in New England, and now in Canada" killed several English colonists and Indians who lived in the Connecticut Valley. An Indian, who referred to himself as a Schaghticoke (revealing that he had experienced some transformation of his own identity), was able to point out for the English the former tribal affiliation of each of the raiders. Five were Pennacooks, including Wallamaqueet who had "lived formerly in the Halfe Moone," a Mahican-Schaghticoke village on the Hudson River; one was a "Nimenaet [Naumkeag?] from Penacooke"; two were originally from Quaboag, a village in "Nipmuck Country" (Worcester County, Massachusetts); one was a "Nassawach" (Nashua?), who also would have come from Nipmuck country; another was from "Patrantecooke [sic: probably Patramtecooke]" meaning Pocumtuck; and the last was a Wappinger who originally would have lived along the lower Hudson River.[82] The large number of Pennacooks in the party, one of whom was the leader, suggests the role of the Pennacooks in providing a refuge and an organizational base for natives who had fled western and southern New England. With the exception of the Wappinger, the other warriors had originally come from communities in central and western Massachusetts. One English resident, Micah Mudge, subsequently recognized several as "formerly belonging to these parts."[83] The war party embodied the merging of old associations with new bonds forged in the heterogeneous refugee communities north, east, and west of Deerfield.

These new bonds also helped fashion new allegiances and identities that transformed and transcended previous tribal affiliations. Situated near a junction of the major east-west line of communication and the Connecticut River, Deerfield served as an important site where natives could test and develop their new identities through relations with New Englanders. In the summer of 1690, three Indians claiming to be from Albany, that is, Schaghticoke, were arrested for molesting a Deerfield resident. One of them, Chepasson, was shot trying to escape. Another, John Humpfries (also Humphry, Umphry), took sick and in his illness told the English that his party had been "to the East-ward" and that they had been present at the 1689 taking of Dover, when Waldron was killed. Both Humpfries and Chepasson spoke English quite well. Humpfries had been a "servant" to a New Englander and may have been a Nipmuck or Wampanoag taken prisoner during King Philip's War.[84] Their fluency in English indicates extended, close association with English colonists in some capacity or other. Though a party of Schaghticokes supported Humpfries's claim to be a Schaghticoke, an Indian then living at Hatfield, who was trusted by the English and who had lived for a time at Schaghticoke, did not recognize him as being from there. Instead, the Hatfield Indian identified Humpfries by the cut of his hair as an Eastern Indian.[85] Given the fluid nature of the native communities along the New England frontier, Humpfries and his compatriots may well have had associations with both the Schaghticokes and the Eastern Indians.[86]

Throughout the late 1680s and the early 1690s, New England natives migrated back and forth across the triangle of territory formed by Schaghticoke, Pennacook, and Odanak.[87] Glimpses of passing individuals and groups suggest the extent of the movement throughout the borderlands that embraced Deerfield. "North Indians" from Odanak moved to Schaghticoke, and some Schaghticokes headed north and settled for a time on Lake Champlain. In 1691, approximately 150 Schaghticokes removed to western Massachusetts claiming that a scarcity of food in New York colony forced them to relocate.[88] Most of these natives were probably Norwottucks and Pocumtucks who had fled from the Connecticut Valley to Schaghticoke during King Philip's War. Three years later, another group relocated from Schaghticoke to Amesokanti in Maine.[89] Also in the 1690s, Ashpalon, the Norwottuck or Pocumtuck who had led the 1677 raid on Deerfield from Canada, reappeared at Deerfield as a Schaghticoke sachem who attempted to mediate a dispute between colonists and Indians hunting in the area.[90]

English colonists saw potential danger in these movements and in the contacts thus maintained. In the early 1690s they were unable to prevent Schaghticokes from settling at Hatfield, and by 1698 the English of the Connecticut Valley believed that the Schaghticokes and Hatfield Indians were responsible for virtually all of the local killings of colonists during King William's War. In a letter to the New York governor, the region's military commanders complained that the Indians at Hatfield "in contempt of all commands . . . have not only intruded themselves into our towns, but have shed the blood of war in peace." Neither New York nor New England could control their movements, for "sometimes they dwell at Stratuburk [Schaghticoke], sometime at the eastward and make marriages with the Eastern Indians, and sometimes at Canada."[91] The governor of New York recognized the ties that Schaghticokes had to communities in New England and Canada and, though he considered them allies of New York, realized that they were not necessarily friends of the New Englanders.[92] The Massachusetts governor, Lord Bellomont, also worried about the Schaghticokes' loyalty because he understood that they were "still acknowledged by the Eastern Indians as part of themselves."[93] In 1697 or 1698, English pressure forced the Schaghticokes to abandon their village in the Connecticut Valley, though at least one "friend Indian" named Kindness was still living near Hatfield Mill where he was killed in 1704.[94]

The suspicions of the English—which had a real basis in the unresolved animosities and disruptions caused by King Philip's War—seemed confirmed when, during the winter of 1699, a large number of natives gathered in Pennacook country near Lake Winnipesaukee.[95] These talks were probably a part of preliminary discussions leading to the Montreal Treaty or Grand Settlement of 1701 by which the French and their Algonquian-speaking allies made peace with the Iroquois. The English, however, saw themselves as the target of a conspiracy among the natives.[96] At the meeting a Pennacook leader spoke of a defensive alliance that reached from the Penobscots to the Mohawks; if any of the allies were attacked, all would join together in retaliating. This alliance even boasted of French backing if the common enemy turned out to be English. Mohawks and other Indians from the Canadian mission villages visited the gathering at Winnipesaukee. A few Indians from Natick reportedly visited in 1700, and forty Nipmuck families left their homes in northwestern Connecticut to resettle at Pennacook, adding to the diaspora and increasing English fears of a general conspiracy.[97] But native leaders such as Captain Tom, an Eastern Abenaki, assured the English that his people remained friendly even though the Pennacooks felt disaffected.[98]

In reality, there was no united front of implacable hostility toward the English or unquestioning support for the French. The flexibility of native polities meant that no leader could speak for all of his people, and the groups seem rarely to have reached consensus on a single course of action. At the same time that sachems from various tribes gathered at Winnipesaukee at the urging of some Pennacooks, two Pennacook sachems, George Tohanto (Sagamore George) and his kinsman Wattanummon, met with the Massachusetts governor and informed him that they were not involved in the negotiations and that they desired peace and friendship with the English.[99] In 1702, some Pennacooks accepted an English invitation to settle at Schaghticoke while rejecting a French invitation to move to Canada.[100] The French had to negotiate for Western Abenaki cooperation, which was never guaranteed, for some Eastern Indians, like Wattanummon, sought to maintain a middle way between the English and the French.[101]

Intensifying imperial pressures rendered a Western Abenaki search for a middle way increasingly difficult, as war between England and France broke out in 1702. In March 1703, wary English authorities attempted to limit the movement of Pennacook hunters and prohibited their coming "to any of the

English towns or settlements."[102] Though Wattanummon promised the Massachusetts governor that he would carefully observe these restrictions, he had previously objected to such efforts to control his people.[103] He therefore asserted his independence by removing his people to "Paquasset," where some French Indians joined them.[104] Subsequently, Wattanummon appears to have found refuge at Pigwacket, the home of his sister and a village closely allied to Pennacook.[105] The other Pennacook leader, Tohanto, journeyed north to Quebec. By May, some natives had returned to Pennacook, and the English hoped that these Pennacooks would be "kept in good order."[106]

The strain in relations between the Pennacooks and the English persisted into the summer of 1703 and added to the tension at a June meeting between Eastern Indians and Massachusetts officials held in Casco, Maine. The conference was called by Massachusetts governor Joseph Dudley, who feared retaliation after some Englishmen had killed a Penobscot relative of the baron de St. Castine, a French officer married to a Penobscot woman. Wattanummon attended as a sachem of Pigwacket. Samuel Penhallow, who also attended and later wrote about the meeting, accused Wattanummon "of delaying the negotiations in the hope of detaining the English at Casco" until a force of French and Indians, then on its way, arrived to "seize the Governour, Council and gentlemen and then . . . sacrifice the inhabitants at pleasure."[107] This would have been a powerful coup for the Abenakis, but the English left just a few days too soon. If such had indeed been the plan, it would have paralleled Waldron's deceitful actions in 1676, repaying his truce-breaking in kind.

When the conference ended, Governor Dudley believed that he had persuaded the Eastern Indians to keep the peace. Many of them, especially Eastern Abenakis, needed no persuasion. Their experience of King William's War had been a harsh one, and they repeatedly expressed their desire to remain "Neuters" in any future conflicts between the French and the English.[108] The Kennebecs had refused to join the confederacy at Pennacook, and a Kennebec sachem warned Dudley shortly after the 1703 meeting that a French ship was near Penobscot. Dudley thanked the Kennebecs and gave them presents but took little heed of the warning, believing his peace would hold firm.[109]

What Dudley did not know, John Williams learned a year later, as the missionary at St. Francis explained how the war that occasioned Williams's captivity began. The priest informed Williams that when St. Castine's relative was killed, the Penobscots sought support in the Pennacook confederacy and sent a messenger to Canada to inform the "Macquas and Indians that the English had begun a war." Warriors from the Canadian villages then joined a French force that Vaudreuil was sending to Acadia to draw the "Abenakis" into the war against the English as part of his policy of keeping the two "irreconcilable enemies."[110] When the expedition arrived on the Maine coast, "several of the

Eastern Indians told them of the peace made with the English [the June 1703 meeting at Casco], and the satisfaction given them from the English for that murder." The French certainly did not want the Abenakis to resolve their problems with the English peacefully while there was a dynastic war going on, but it was the Macquas who brought the Abenakis to war. Upon learning of the treaty, the Macquas replied that "it was now too late, for they were sent for and were now come, and would fall on them [the Eastern Indians] if without their consent they made a peace with the English." Then the French showed the Indians a letter that had been taken from an English ship, wherein Queen Anne endorsed Dudley's "designs to ensnare and deceitfully seize upon the Indians." Williams told the priest that the "letter was a lie, forged by the French."[111]

What the Eastern Indians thought of the letter is uncertain. They were, however, already well acquainted with English treachery and land hunger, and, as Kenneth Morrison has concluded, "reminding the Abenaki of English transgressions . . . could move them as presents could not."[112] Whether or not the letter was genuine, the French were playing on fears validated by past experience. Paraphrasing the French priest, Williams reported that the Eastern Indians, "being enraged by that letter, and being forced, as it were, . . . began the present war."[113] The Eastern Indians in this instance included both Western and Eastern Abenakis, who joined a French and Indian expedition that raided the Maine settlements of Casco and Wells in August 1703.

The English counterattacked in the fall, sending two expeditions to Pigwacket, which the colonists believed was "the settlement of the Indian rebels."[114] The raiders killed six Indians and took a similar number prisoner. These were the "barbarous" and "cruel" attacks that the priest at St. Francis considered the immediate cause and justification for the foray on Deerfield. Williams defended the English, claiming that "the Indians, in a very perfidious manner, had committed murders on many of our inhabitants after the signing articles of peace; and as to what they spake of cruelties, they were undoubtedly falsehoods, for I well knew the English were not approvers of any inhumanity or barbarity towards enemies."[115] Each man of the cloth was convinced of the righteousness of his side. For Wattanummon, who undoubtedly knew the Pigwacket victims, such a debate was probably irrelevant; he had joined the expedition to Deerfield.

Accompanying Wattanummon were the "Abenakis of Cowasscuk," who later thanked Vaudreuil for sending the winter expedition to Deerfield to help them avenge themselves on the English.[116] Cowass has been considered the home village of a distinct Western Abenaki people or, alternatively, a refugee village that included Mahican and Sokoki refugees.[117] In 1690, John Humpfries, one of the self-proclaimed Schaghticokes who had been with the Eastern Indians, had informed John Pynchon that a number of Indians with English captives were in a fort at Cowass and that the Indians were

"Pennacooks."[118] By 1704, Cowass was apparently a refugee village consisting primarily of Pennacooks who followed Sagamore George Tohanto and Pennacooks and Pigwackets who followed Wattanummon. All the evidence suggests that there was probably little difference between the Abenakis of Cowassuck, who had called on the French to join them in a raid of retribution, and the Pennacooks and Pigwackets who participated in the attack on Deerfield.

The English may have been aware of this fact at the time. While the delegation of Cowassucks met to thank Vaudreuil in June 1704, a party of English and Mohegan allies retaliated by attacking a family of Cowassucks living just south of the main village.[119] The Cowassucks had intended to remain at Cowass the better to wage war against the English, but the killing of the family shocked them into heading north to Odanak, a more secure location. Cowass's days as a refuge had ended, at least for the time being. Wattanummon's party, which included Stephen Williams, joined the trek to Canada.[120]

Wattanummon's movements did not end with his retreat from Cowass to Odanak and subsequent departure to Schaghticoke. By April 1712 Wattanummon, eleven other men, and their families were back in Pennacook country, living at the confluence of the Pemigewasset and Baker rivers in New Hampshire. Here they were ambushed by Captain Thomas Baker of Northampton, Lieutenant Samuel Williams (Stephen's brother), and twenty-nine militiamen from the Connecticut Valley. Nine of the natives, one of whom was apparently Wattanummon, were killed; the rest escaped. As the English looked over the encampment, they found a "small quantity of plunder," including, as they judged, about two or three years' worth of furs. Wattanummon and his people had been storing the furs for trading and had apparently withdrawn from the fighting, suggesting that their war with the English did not last as long as Queen Anne's War, of which it was a part, though the Pennacooks and Pigwackets did not formally make peace with the English until 1713.[121]

With the conclusion of Queen Anne's War, the Eastern Indians returned to their villages in the borderlands between New England and New France. For these Western Abenakis the Deerfield raid had represented an opportunity to strike back when their aims converged with those of the French and native allies. Later, in the 1720s, Western Abenakis as well as Eastern Abenakis again fought to resist English territorial expansion and exact vengeance. In that struggle, known variously as Dummer's War, Father Rasle's War, or Grey Lock's War, the Eastern Indians fought without direct military support from the French and with only occasional assistance from the St. Francis Abenakis, French Mohawks, and Hurons.[122] That war did not produce for the Pennacooks and Pigwackets a victory comparable to that obtained at Deerfield in 1704.

Most of the natives whom John Williams called "Macquas" were French Mohawks from the mission villages of Kahnawake (Caughnawaga) and La

Montagne, located in the St. Lawrence Valley near Montreal.[123] Often uniformly identified as Caughnawagas or Kahnawakes, the Mohawk allies of the French who attacked Deerfield definitely included Indians from the mission at La Montagne as well.[124] Natives from both villages had been (some quite recently so) members of one of the Five Nations of the Iroquois League—Mohawks, Oneidas, Onondagas, Cayugas, and Senecas—who lived in what is today the western part of New York state. Beginning in the late 1660s, they had moved north to Canada to escape the devastation resulting from a series of wars pitting the Five Nations against the French and their native allies and New England natives. Despite their settlement in mission villages and their status as *sauvages domiciliés*, these Canadian Mohawks maintained ties with Mohawks who continued to live in their traditional homeland. Iroquoian cultural attitudes and history continued to influence the behavior of the French Mohawks. The participation of French Mohawks in the Deerfield attack owed at least as much to motives grounded in their Iroquoian identity as to their situation as mission Indian allies of the French.

Kahnawake, the older of the two mission villages, traced its origins to a native community and Jesuit mission established opposite Montreal in the late 1660s, at the same time English colonists were settling Deerfield. Its founders were christianized Five Nations Iroquois, some native-born but many adopted Eries, Hurons, Susquehannocks, and others who had been captured in wars with the Iroquois. In all, natives from twenty nations, including apparently some Pocumtucks, joined the community.[125] Although many of the founders had come from Oneida, a majority of the members had lived in the central and eastern Mohawk villages, and a Mohawk identity therefore prevailed. In 1676, the village moved to a new site known as Sault Saint Louis or simply the Sault to the French and Kahnawake to the Iroquois. By 1682, the village contained approximately 600 residents. The growing population and the demands placed on the available agricultural land prompted a relocation in 1696. Twelve years after the Deerfield raid, the village moved once again to a location higher up the St. Lawrence opposite La Chine.[126]

A second Iroquoian village and accompanying mission had been established in 1676 on the island of Montreal. These people came to be known as Les Iroquois de la Montagne, though the community included Hurons and Algonquian-speaking peoples as well as Iroquois. In 1696, the mission at La Montagne relocated to the north side of Montreal at Sault au Recollect, though some natives stayed at the old site until 1704. The village moved in 1721 to Lac des Deux Montagnes on land granted for that purpose to the Sulpicians. This village, known today as Kanesatake (or Oka), developed and retains a Mohawk identity despite the diverse backgrounds of its founders.[127]

The French Mohawks initially desired to remain neutral in the wars between the French and the Five Nations that lasted from the mid-1680s until 1701 but were drawn into the conflict. Warriors from Kahnawake accompanied

French troops and their other native allies who invaded the Senecas' homeland in 1687. When war broke out between the French and the English in 1688, members of the mission villages attacked English targets. A number of Kahnawake warriors participated in the February 9, 1690, assault on Schenectady.[128] Others joined small raiding parties that headed for New England. One such party of French Mohawks struck Deerfield in July 1696 and carried off John Gillet and three members of the Belding family.[129] Mohawks from Canada may also have been members of the parties that hit Deerfield in June 1693 and August 1695.[130]

Though these raids in the Connecticut Valley took place during the imperial conflict known as King William's War, they may have been prompted more by Iroquoian traditions than by French policy. Kahnawake and La Montagne were part of the Mohawk nation that had long-standing and still actively asserted interests in the valley. Mohawks living in the Canadian mission villages had most likely carried north with them a long-established interest in Pocumtuck and later in Deerfield. It was a site that had special meaning for Mohawks, who used it as a meeting place from the 1640s until the 1730s.[131] Native traditions and later documentary sources suggest that the Iroquois interest—particularly that of the Mohawks—in the Connecticut Valley dated back to at least the 1630s.[132] This interest appears to have involved more than trade and was viewed by the Mohawks and some Eastern Abenakis as the basis for later claims made by the Five Nations Iroquois upon the native peoples living in western New England.[133] From the 1620s to the 1650s, the Mohawks actively asserted their influence in the region by following up initial military victories, which probably came during the Mohawk-Mahican War of the 1620s, with marriage alliances with the Norwottucks, demands for tribute, and active support for the Norwottucks and the Pocumtucks in their conflicts with the Mohegans of Connecticut. In 1648, 400 Mohawk and other Iroquois warriors traveled to Pocumtuck to join with New England natives in a planned assault on the Mohegans that was only abandoned when opposed by colonial governments.[134]

By the 1660s, maintenance of Mohawk influence in the Connecticut Valley led to conflict with erstwhile allies. In the early 1650s, the Sokokis drew closer to northern Algonquian allies of the French who were then at war with the Iroquois. These ties and the Sokokis' growing resistance to payment of tribute led first to skirmishing and then, in 1663, to a full-scale attack by Mohawks and Senecas on the Sokoki village at Fort Hill. Though victorious, the Sokokis abandoned the village, some finding refuge with the Pocumtucks and others heading north to Odanak. Then in 1664, the killing of a Mohawk peace emissary who traveled to Pocumtuck provoked a retaliatory raid that destroyed the village, scattered the remaining Pocumtucks, and expanded the war. Before the fighting ended in the early 1670s, natives throughout Massachusetts, New Hampshire, and Maine had joined an offensive alliance against the

Iroquois. This war does not appear to have produced a clear victor.[135] The next war did.

King Philip's War strengthened the hand of the Mohawks over the native peoples of the Connecticut Valley. Soon after the outbreak of hostilities in southeastern New England, the Norwottucks, the Pocumtucks, and the Sokokis joined the fighting on the side of Metacom.[136] Metacom and his warriors passed through the valley on their way to New York to enlist the Mohawks in their cause. Governor Edmund Andros of New York countered by offering the Mohawks alliance in exchange for assistance against Metacom. The Mohawks accepted Andros's offer and drove Metacom and his allies back to New England, pursuing them relentlessly and contributing materially to their defeat. By war's end, some of the defeated natives moved west and resettled at Schaghticoke, putting themselves under the protection of the Mohawks and New York province.[137]

At the conclusion of King Philip's War, the Mohawks of the Five Nations emerged as the preeminent native power in western New England. The English had consolidated control over lands along the Connecticut River, while the Mohawks held sway over the interior and its native residents. They reestablished marriage alliances with natives remaining in the region such as the Mahicans, who continued to live along the Westfield River.[138] Hunting parties and war parties of Mohawks and Schaghticokes ranged over the hills and frequented English towns, especially Deerfield. Some bands stopped briefly to trade while others remained in the area for months or even years.[139] The best documented of these groups, from Schaghticoke, established a village just south of Deerfield in northern Hatfield.[140]

The Mohawks asserted jurisdiction over these Schaghticokes and other resident natives as well as over any Mohawks and allied Indians who passed through western Massachusetts by protecting those who became embroiled in disputes with the English. When the colonists imprisoned Humpfries and Chepasson in 1690, the Mohawks were "grieved," claimed that the two "belonged" to their "government," and demanded an explanation.[141] On June 6, 1693, an unidentified group of natives broke into the Deerfield homes of Thomas Broughton and Hepzibah Wells, killed Broughton, his wife, and three children, and scalped three of the widow Wells's daughters. A nearby party of Schaghticokes and Mohawks—referred to as "hunting Indians" or "trading Indians"—was suspected, and one of each was taken into custody. In July, several Mohawk emissaries and Johannes Schuyler of Albany arrived in Springfield to discuss the case with John Pynchon, a magistrate and military commander in western Massachusetts, but the issue became moot when the two natives escaped with the aid of some "Dutchmen."[142] In 1696, Massachusetts authorities sought to avoid offending the Mohawks by sparing the lives of two of four Hatfield Schaghticokes who were charged with the murder of Richard Church of Haldey.[143]

The Mohawks' interest in western Massachusetts increased during the 1680s and 1690s because of the area's strategic importance in the Five Nations' ongoing war against the French and their native allies. The valley provided a return route for raiding parties that went north to attack French and native communities in the St. Lawrence Valley. Despite this advantage and others, including the alliance with New York and the addition of refugees as a result of King Philip's War, the toll exacted by the long war with the French (1684–1701) bled the Five Nations and divided their people, some of whom began moving north in large numbers during the 1680s and 1690s to the Canadian mission villages of Kahnawake and La Montagne.[144]

Peace among the Iroquois and between the Five Nations and their French and Abenaki enemies came four years later with the Grand Settlement of 1701. Though the treaties with the English at Albany and the French at Montreal did not settle the differences dividing anglophile, francophile, and neutralist factions among the Iroquois, they did create a fragile balance upon which a neutralist policy would eventually be built.[145] Related agreements made with the Abenakis in October 1700 ended decades of fighting between the Five Nations and the Eastern Indians.[146] These were the negotiations between the Mohawks and the Abenakis that raised English fears of a pan-Indian conspiracy in 1699 and 1700. And while these negotiations and the Grand Settlement of 1701 were not overtly directed at the English, the agreements did create among the natives obligations that would bring the Eastern Indians into conflict with the English in alliance with the French Mohawks.

When war between France and England resumed in 1702, Mohawk warriors from Kahnawake and La Montagne returned to the New England frontier. The number of Mohawks from these villages who participated in the 1704 attack on Deerfield remains unknown. Estimates from the period suggest that the Mohawk communities in Canada could put 200 to 300 warriors into the field during the late 1600s and early 1700s.[147] In 1703 and 1704, however, the Kahnawakes went out in relatively small raiding parties, suggesting a contribution to the Deerfield raid of fewer than 100 warriors, possibly in the range of 50 to 60.[148] Still, Williams's Macquas, who included Hurons from another mission village, suffered a larger proportion of confirmed casualties among the natives.[149] Judging from the number of prisoners they adopted—eleven—the band of Mohawks appears to have been much larger than the band of Hurons, who retained only three captives.

The majority of the Deerfield captives who stayed with natives lived in one of the two communities of French Mohawks. Of the twenty-eight or thirty former Deerfield residents who appear to have remained in Canada, thirteen settled in French communities, three were at Lorette with the Hurons, four lived with the Mohawks of La Montagne, and seven remained at Kahnawake. At least another seven captives are believed to have been prisoners of the Mohawks before they were ransomed. The residences of three captives who lived out their lives in Canada are unknown.[150] It appears that none of the Deerfield captives (with the possible exception of Mary Field, who joined a native community that cannot now be identified) remained with the Abenakis for any extended period of time.[151]

According to a tradition passed down in one Kahnawake family, at least two members of the Mohawk party came to Deerfield with the goal of obtaining captives to replace family members who had died. Both of these participants were female, and one of them became the adoptive Mohawk mother of Eunice Williams, John's seven-year-old daughter.[152] She came to obtain a child to replace a daughter, her only child, who had died two years earlier, possibly during the smallpox epidemic that ravaged the St. Lawrence Valley in 1701. The other woman obtained a young boy, perhaps six-year-old William Brooks, whose fate is uncertain.[153] The presence of women with war parties or hunting parties was unusual but not unknown.[154] The reported mission of Eunice's Mohawk mother was in keeping with the Iroquoian practice of replacing family members whose death had produced inconsolable grief.[155] In 1704, this practice appears to have distinguished Iroquoian peoples from New England natives.

The Iroquoian practice of waging war to restore the individual emotionally and the community spiritually by replacing lost members created a cultural pattern that anthropologists and historians call the "mourning-war." If the established rites that channeled the grief of mourners failed to assuage the sense of loss resulting from the death of a relative, the women of the mourning household could demand a raid or even a war to obtain captives who, if worthy, could ease their pain by either replacing the deceased through adoption or by suffering ritual execution. Members of the immediate family usually did not undertake such a raid, which was entrusted to kinsmen of the grieving females. The expeditions were usually directed at traditional enemies who may or may not have been responsible for the death that inspired the mourning-war.[156]

The actions of the Mohawks from Kahnawake and La Montagne indicate that a mourning-war motivated some of the Deerfield attackers. As described by Eunice Williams's descendants, the grieving adoptive Mohawk mother exhibited classic signs of the behavior that launched mourning-wars. Since the death of her daughter, she had been "inconsolable" and "so much borne down with, that some of her relations predicted that she could not survive long."[157] "It was visible in her countenance that she was on the decline, she had lost the vivacity which was a peculiar trait in her character before she was bereft of her child."[158] Eunice Williams replaced the child: "the relations of her adopted mother took much notice of her, and the children were instructed to treat her as one of the family."[159] Other young captives taken at Deerfield very likely fulfilled similar needs in other Mohawk families.

The integration of Eunice and other captives into the Kahnawake community was not based entirely on Iroquoian traditions of adoption. For Eunice and for many natives who had come to the village before her, Catholicism played an important role in shaping a new identity. Women adoptees had often taken the lead in establishing the Canadian mission villages, and female sodalities and the stories of saintly native women helped perpetuate the association between Catholic piety and Mohawk community.[160] The life of Kateri Tekakwitha, the daughter of a christianized Algonquian captive of the Mohawks who had fled from New York to Kahnawake and there gained a reputation for great piety, "was held up to her [Eunice's] view."[161] Abandoning her Protestant upbringing, Eunice converted to Catholicism and soon acquired a reputation for "great piety and strictness."[162]

Immediate strategic considerations and possible economic calculations as well as long-established interests and traditional claims in the region led the French Mohawks to look toward Deerfield for captives such as Eunice. Preservation of the peace concluded in 1701 between the Five Nations and the French was an overriding aim for both the Canadian Mohawks and the French. To avoid angering the Five Nations, Vaudreuil resolved against "carrying on any war which might make them unfriendly." New England, however, was "not the same situation," and the governor directed raiding parties against New England in an effort to retain the loyalty of mission Indians.[163] He hoped that in addition to gaining captives, raids would secure plunder that would be an alternative to English goods obtained by force or trade from New Yorkers. Such goods appear to have been highly prized by the Kahnawakes, who later stated flatly "that they would rather be dead than deprived of English goods."[164] Like the other attackers, the Mohawks at Deerfield, including even Eunice's Kahnawake mother, evidently took time to loot.[165]

The Mohawks in Canada had other reasons for directing their military efforts toward New England and away from the New York frontier. Even though they had fought against members of the Five Nations during the 1680s and 1690s, they preferred to avoid such conflicts. In the 1690 raid on Schenectady, French Mohawks had spared thirty Five Nations Mohawks who were found in the village.[166] Still, it is likely that considerations in addition to sentiment and kinship underlay the Kahnawakes' aversion to spilling the blood of Five Nations Mohawks. During the 1690s, a profitable illegal trade had grown up that involved Albany merchants, natives nominally allied to the French, French-Canadian *coureurs de bois*, and Montreal merchants. The Kahnawakes were well situated to facilitate this trade, and they wanted to avoid jeopardizing it by new fighting on the New York-Canadian frontier. Even Vaudreuil took the illicit trade and the Kahnawakes' stake in it into account in his military planning, for disrupting the trade would ruin Montreal merchants and might alienate the Canadian Mohawks.[167]

Deerfield, in fact, may have presented a threat to the illegal trade from which the Kahnawakes profited. This consideration is conjectural, for it involves the possible existence of trade that all parties wanted to obscure. Since the early 1690s, Frenchmen had lived in Deerfield. One, John "Butcher" (probably Boucher), was taken to court for breach of the sabbath in 1692, and another, "Captain John German" (probably Germain), was tried for assault.[168] "Trading Indians" visited Deerfield in the 1690s.[169] At the time of the 1704 attack, a Jacques de Noyon or Denieur, who married Abigail Stebbins of Deerfield, and two other Frenchmen from Canada "had lived in Deerfield some time."[170] The early-twentieth-century researcher Emma Coleman suggested that de Noyon or Denieur may have been involved in the illicit fur trade.[171] Such activity may have represented undesirable competition to which the raid put an end when the three Frenchmen were carried back to Canada by the attackers.

Diverse motives—a mixture of personal, familial, spiritual, strategic, and possibly commercial considerations—probably inspired the French Mohawk attackers in 1704.[172] A similar variety of motivations drew Five Nations Mohawks back to Deerfield in the later 1710s and 1720s after Queen Anne's War ended. Until at least the late 1730s, they used Deerfield as a site for recruiting native allies, for making alliances with Massachusetts authorities, and as a rest stop on hunting expeditions to western New England. Because of the 1704 attack, Mohawks in Canada also came to visit former captives who had returned, and captives who had not returned made their own visits, as Eunice Williams apparently did in 1744 on the fortieth anniversary of the attack.[173]

Huron participation in the Deerfield raid has been overlooked in most published accounts and histories of the event. This omission is somewhat ironic since the Huron presence can be attributed almost entirely to motivations usually uncritically accorded to all the Indians: alliance with and dependence on the French. The Hurons of Lorette, descendants of the nation of the Rope of the Huron Confederacy, had been *sauvages domiciliés* since the 1650s.[174] Still, the actions of particular Hurons make clear the complexity of individual natives' behavior even among the closest allies of the French. A desire to obtain captives for adoption remained an integral part of warfare for Hurons, who were, like the Mohawks, Iroquoian in language and culture.

The Huron role in the attack has been obscured by the imprecise use of "Macqua." Under this term, Williams appears to have lumped the Hurons of Lorette together with the French Mohawks of Kahnawake and La Montagne, and most historians have accordingly assumed that all the Macquas who attacked Deerfield were Mohawks. But other evidence suggests that a native leader Williams identified in his narrative as "one of chief note among the Macquas" was in all likelihood a "great chief of the Lorette Hurons."[175] To understand how a man of "chief note among the Macquas" could be a Huron and not a Mohawk, as most histories and annotated editions of Williams's narrative assume, one must realize that there is no consistent correspondence between the term Macqua and the people known as Mohawks.[176]

Macqua (or Maqua or Magua) was an English rendering of various Algonquian words signifying man-eater.[177] The Algonquian-speaking natives of New England used the word to refer to the Mohawks of the Five Nations. By Macqua, English colonists initially meant Mohawks, but the term became less precise over time and could encompass other peoples, such as Hurons, who were linguistically and culturally Iroquoian. The incorporation of Huron captives into the nations of the Iroquois League, and the migration of Five Nations Iroquois to Canada, where they resided in ethnically mixed villages, blurred distinctions. The French unintentionally compounded the New Englanders' confusion by grouping together their Iroquois and Huron allies for military expeditions.[178] As a result, New Englanders came to categorize both Mohawk raiders from Kahnawake and Hurons from Lorette as French Mohawks or simply Macquas.[179]

The Hurons' participation in the Deerfield raid is recorded in the *Jesuit Relations*, which states that their "great chief" was killed during an attack on the English that, although not identified, was clearly at Deerfield.[180] The Hurons of Lorette descended from people who fled the Five Nations' assaults on Huronia around 1650 to find refuge with the French at Quebec. The Jesuits took some of the Hurons under their care at the mission village founded in 1673 at Lorette, just north of Quebec City.[181] From this village the Hurons and their chief went to Deerfield. The small Huron population at Lorette, which numbered between 100 and 150 persons, and the tiny share of captives claimed by the Hurons—only three—suggest that the contingent at Deerfield was most likely between twenty and thirty men, a conclusion seconded by its low profile in contemporary documents and subsequent histories of the raid.[182]

The Jesuit source indicates that the Hurons' lives in a mission community near the capital of New France were more strongly influenced by European culture than were those of any of the other native attackers and that their motives for joining the expedition lay in their relationship to the French and had little to do with Deerfield itself. The Jesuit missionary at Lorette wrote his account of the great chief's death to assure his audience that Christianity was gaining ground at his mission; he claimed that the Hurons' changed behavior showed its growing influence. According to the priest, their faith in the strength of the Christian God and their pious avoidance of liquor did "not at all diminish the warlike Spirit which these savages commonly possess; it merely impose[d] moderation and certain limits upon their Martial ardor." He portrayed the Lorettans as ideal converts, possessing a Christian discipline that harnessed their ardor for the French cause. He stated that the Hurons "never [took] up arms unless at the Governor's pleasure," but that when they did so, they were eagerly enlisted by French captains, who knew "that in the fray they will never desert the standard, or yield before the enemy's attack."[183] In other words, the Lorette Hurons would fight more like "Christian" French soldiers than "traditional" Huron warriors. It was a blending of native and European cultures most welcome to the embattled French.

In his account of the Hurons, the Jesuit highlights the actions of Thaovenhosen, who is the second native participant in the Deerfield raid known by name. A young man not yet prominent among his people, Thaovenhosen impressed the priest with his charitable and Christian behavior at the village and by his dramatic demonstration of Christian values in a confrontation with other Hurons over the fate of a Deerfield captive. The Hurons had fought well at Deerfield, standing with the French soldiers and repelling the English counterattack, but their bravery cost them their great chief, who was buried with ceremony, as Williams recorded. On the return journey to Canada, the Hurons gathered in council to discuss the fate of their English captives. The nephew of the great chief demanded that a prisoner be turned over to him as "expiation and consolation" for the loss of his uncle. The captive probably would have been tortured and burned to death at the stake. Before the request could be granted, Thaovenhosen rose in the council, evidently out of turn, for he was "not yet honored with the dignity or the title of chief," and "boldly plead[ed] for the life of the Captive." He reminded his fellow Hurons that "they are Christians and citizens of the village of Lorette; that dire cruelty is unbecoming to the Christian name; that this injury cannot be branded upon the reputation of the Lorettans without the greatest disgrace." When the Hurons did not respond to this appeal, Thaovenhosen pointed out that he was also a relative of the fallen chief and claimed the captive as his own, threatening that "If any one lay hands on him against my will, let him look to me for chastisement." The council was reportedly "astounded," and no ritual harm came to any of the Deerfielders captured by the Hurons.[184]

Thaovenhosen had taken advantage of a gloss of Christian morality to justify his violation of Huron tradition and customary authority. He maintained his position with a confidence in outside support that was borne out by the priest's subsequent endorsement of his actions after the party returned to Lorette. The Hurons had participated in the raid to support their French allies and protectors. The French, however, demanded more and expected the Hurons to submit to French moral as well as military authority. Thaovenhosen attempted to exploit these expectations to enhance his position in the councils of the Lorette Hurons, but he only succeeded when he invoked traditional claims based on kinship.

Just which one of the English captives Thaovenhosen rescued is uncertain. Probably it was sixteen-year-old Jonathan Hoyt.[185] Hoyt did not stay long at Lorette, but family tradition suggests that the experience was of great importance not only to him but to his Huron master as well. In 1706, William Dudley, son of the Massachusetts governor, and John Sheldon, a militia officer from Deerfield, went to Quebec to negotiate a truce and prisoner exchange with Vaudreuil on behalf of Dudley's father. There the younger Dudley saw Hoyt selling vegetables with his Huron master in the marketplace. Dudley redeemed Hoyt for twenty "shining silver dollars" and hustled him on board the English ship. The master returned, wanting to cancel the deal, but the English kept Hoyt on the ship and took him back to England, where he resettled in Deerfield and married.[186]

In spite of this rebuff, the Huron did not end his association with Hoyt, nor did Hoyt sever all ties to his former master. When the war ended and travel between New France and New England was no longer hazardous, the Huron returned to Deerfield, sometimes bringing his sister, to visit Hoyt, who treated them with kindness and respect. Hoyt had learned Huron during his two years at Lorette, and it was said that he could speak it till the day he died. The two men evidently enjoyed each other's company, for the Huron visited Hoyt so often that Hoyt allegedly petitioned the General Court of Massachusetts for reimbursement for expenses incurred while hosting him.[187] Such persistence suggests that the man had grown attached to Hoyt, and no Huron had more interest in a Deerfield captive than Thaovenhosen. If Thaovenhosen was in fact the man who visited Jonathan Hoyt, then this represented a singularly personal involvement in Deerfield's middle ground that was formed in the heat of battle in 1704.

The Deerfield that Thaovenhosen, Wattanummon, and John Williams's Indian masters knew was not the isolated outpost that historians have long supposed. On the contrary, Deerfield stood near the center of a web of political, commercial, and familial interests that stretched from Mohawk country in the west to the Canadian mission villages in the north and to Pennacook-Pigwacket country in the east. The men from Dedham, Massachusetts, who planned the English village of Deerfield, selected the site in 1665, a year after a devastating Iroquois attack on Pocumtuck had caused its native residents to scatter to the Norwottucks, Pennacooks, and others for safety. What seemed to the Englishmen to be fertile and empty land was a country with a deeper and more complicated history than the colonists would ever know.[188]

The patterns created by this history continued to shape the lives of English and native residents. King Philip's War, combined with renewed fighting with the Iroquois of the Five Nations, added to the diaspora of southern New England natives in the 1670s, increasing Deerfield's importance as a stopping point for people moving north and south as well as east and west. Pocumtucks, Norwottucks, and Sokokis driven from their homes in the Connecticut Valley returned as Schaghticokes and St. Francis Abenakis; Pennacooks and other Eastern Indians came from the north and the east to trade and raid; and Mohawks from New York and Canada hunted and traveled through these lands to which they laid claim. These older patterns and the new relationships that grew from them combined with immediate familial, strategic, and economic considerations and the calculations of French policy to bring native and Canadian attackers to Deerfield in 1704. Even the attack itself did not destroy native ties to the region; to a degree, indeed, it strengthened them, in the short term, by forging new bonds.

As a frontier village, Deerfield remained a place whose significance was defined by native interests and actions as well as by those of its English inhabitants. During the years of peace in the late 1710s and the early 1720s, natives often visited Deerfield. The first party came in 1714, when young Aaron Denio, son of Jacques Denieur and Abigail Stebbins, journeyed south with a group of Canadian Indians to visit his grandfather Stebbins and decided to remain.[189] In 1716, the Five Nations Iroquois used the site as a gathering place for Algonquian-speaking and possibly French Iroquoian recruits to fight against the Catawbas in the Carolinas.[190] The return of one of John Williams's Western Abenaki masters in 1718, allegedly motivated because he "was so deeply impressed . . . that Mr. Williams was more than a common man," was in retrospect a part of a pattern.[191] Both Williams and his captors had apparently been affected by their journey across the middle ground. When fighting resumed in 1722 between the New Englanders and the Eastern Indians, the Deerfield minister confessed to his son Stephen that he was "Greatly concerned because of the war—he is fearful whether it is just on our side."[192]

The resumption of hostilities during Dummer's War (1722–1727) did not end Deerfield's role as a place of contact between natives and English colonists. The Huron captor of Jonathan Hoyt and the Kahnawake captors of Ebenezer Sheldon and his sister Mary (Sheldon) Clapp came to visit. The Kahnawake visitors made such demands that Sheldon petitioned the government for reimbursement.[193] In the 1730s, other Deerfield residents petitioned for reimbursement for time and money spent caring for sick Five Nations Iroquois.[194] By this time, Massachusetts authorities had lit a council fire at Deerfield, designating it as a place to negotiate with Mohawk representatives of the Five Nations in 1723 and with Kahnawakes, Schaghticokes, and St. Francis Abenakis in 1735.[195] The latter gathering most likely included natives who had participated in the 1704 attack.

After 1740, Deerfield became less central to the trade, diplomacy, and wars of New England's frontier. English settlers pushed farther up the Connecticut River. Others moved along the Merrimack River to Pennacook, which they renamed Concord. Most of the surviving Pennacooks retreated north to Canada, though small groups remained in and around their homelands.[196] To the west, the Schaghticokes drifted north to St. Francis, the last residents leaving in 1754. After an abortive effort to move east to the Mahican mission village at Stockbridge, Massachusetts, Mohawks of the Five Nations retreated farther west or lived uneasily in ever closer proximity to encroaching New Yorkers. As these people, both native and English, moved, the frontier shifted north and west, leaving Deerfield an isolated English village. It was now a community that approached the imagined Puritan ideal evoked by John

Williams in *The Redeemed Captive*, but one that bore less resemblance to the world in which the Redeemed Captive himself had lived.

N O T E S

Acknowledgments: We wish to thank Geoffrey E. Buerger, Colin Calloway, John Demos, Clark Dougan, Donald R. Friary, Ignacio Gallup-Diaz, Richard Melvoin, John Murrin, Neal Salisbury, Nathaniel Sheidley, Margaret Sweeney, members of the Five College Social History Seminar, fellows of the Charles Warren Center Seminar at Harvard, and reviewers of the journal for their comments on versions of this article. We also thank Alice Nash, Harald Prins, and James Spady for sharing their research with us and Kate Blackmer for drawing the maps of the Northeast. We are indebted to Suzanne Flynt, curator of Memorial Hall, and David Proper, librarian of the Memorial Libraries, Deerfield, Mass., for drawing our attention to relevant illustrations and sources.

1. John Williams to Stephen Williams, May 24, 1718, Fisher Howe Miscellaneous Letters, Folder 1, Williams College Archives, Williamstown, Mass.

2. The raid took place on Feb. 29, 1703/4 Old Style, which would have been Mar. 10, 1704 New Style.

3. Perry Miller, *The New England Mind: From Colony to Province* (Cambridge, Mass., 1953), 367. Interest in Williams's captivity narrative remains strong. See Richard Slotkin, *Regeneration through Violence: The Mythology of the American Frontier, 1600–1860* (Middletown, Conn., 1973), 94–145; Greg Sieminski, "The Puritan Captivity Narrative and the Politics of the American Revolution," *American Quarterly*, 42 (1990), 35–56; June Namias, *White Captives: Gender and Ethnicity on the American Frontier* (Chapel Hill, 1993), 53–58; Rosalie Murphy Baum, "John Williams's Captivity Narrative: A Consideration of Normative Ethnicity," in Frank Shuffelton, ed., *A Mixed Race Ethnicity in Early America* (New York, 1993), 56–76; and John Demos, *The Unredeemed Captive: A Family Story from Early America* (New York, 1994).

4. Baum, "John Williams's Captivity Narrative," 56–76.

5. Francis Parkman, *A Half-Century of Conflict*, 2 vols. (Boston, 1909; orig. pub. 1892), 1:55–93, quotation on 58.

6. John Williams, *The Redeemed Captive Returning to Zion* (1707), ed. Stephen W. Williams (Bedford, Mass., n.d. [1987]; orig. pub. 1853), 54.

7. George Sheldon, *History of Deerfield, Massachusetts, . . . with a special study of the Indian Wars in the Connecticut Valley*, 2 vols. (Deerfield, Mass., 1895–1896), 1:672.

8. Slotkin, *Regeneration through Violence*, 94–145; Baum, "John Williams's Captivity Narrative," 56–76; Kenneth M. Morrison, "The Wonders of Divine Mercy: A Review of John Williams' *The Redeemed Captive*," *American Review of Canadian Studies*, 9, no. 1 (1979), 56–62; Richard VanDerBeets, *The Indian Captivity Narrative: An American Genre* (Lanham, Md., 1984), 13–23.

9. Two recent discussions of the borderlands of western New England — Richard I. Melvoin, *New England Outpost: War and Society in Colonial Deerfield* (New York, 1989), and Colin G. Calloway, *The Western Abenakis of Vermont, 1600–1800: War,*

Migration, and the Survival of an Indian People (Norman, Okla., 1990)—have considered interactions peaceful and violent between natives and colonists, though neither considers in depth the identities and motives of those natives who attacked Deerfield in 1704.

10. The "middle ground" suggests a geographic place that was a nonstate world of villages lying between colonial empires, a native diplomatic stance that sought to avoid dependency on a single colonial power, and a series of shared meanings and practices that arose out of creative misunderstandings as native and European cultures met in situations where both sides needed each other and neither could control the other. See Morrison, *The Embattled Northeast: The Elusive Ideal of Alliance in Abenaki-Euramerican Relations* (Berkeley, Calif., 1984), esp. 135, 163, and Richard White, *The Middle Ground: Indians, Empires, and Republics in the Great Lakes Region, 1650–1815* (Cambridge, 1991), esp. ix–xi.

11. For the number of English casualties and captives we follow Melvoin, *New England Outpost*, 220–21. Some accounts use the figure 112 captives, which includes 3 Frenchmen who resided in Deerfield and were taken back to Canada by the raiders.

12. Williams, *Redeemed Captive*, 13–14.

13. Melvoin, *New England Outpost*, 215–26. Williams heard in Canada that the raiders "lost above forty, and that many were wounded"; Williams, *Redeemed Captive*, 13. Massachusetts Governor Dudley writing to Lord——on Apr. 21 claimed that thirty enemy bodies were found in the village and the meadow. See Parkman, *Half-Century of Conflict*, 1:69 n. 1.

14. A contemporary Connecticut source put the number of attackers at "between 3 or 4 hundred, the one halfe or more being French"; William Whiting to Fitz-John Winthrop, Mar. 4, 1704, Winthrop Papers, Massachusetts Historical Society, *Collections*, 6th ser., 3 (1889), 176.

15. The estimate of 200 French soldiers and 142 Indians was first used by Epaphras Hoyt, then picked up by Sheldon, and subsequently repeated by other historians. Hoyt, *Antiquarian Researches: Comprising a History of the Indian Wars . . .* (Greenfield, Mass., 1824), 186; Sheldon, *History of Deerfield*, 1:294; Howard Peckham, *The Colonial Wars, 1689–1762* (Chicago, 1964), 63; Calloway, *Western Abenakis*, 103. For a good review of the issue see the discussion in Melvoin, *New England Outpost*, 336 n. 30, 338–39 n. 52. The figure of 50 Canadians and 200 Abenakis and Caughnawagas was used by Parkman, *Half-Century of Conflict*, 1:56.

16. Ramezay to the Ministry, Nov. 14, 1704, Archives Nationales, Paris (hereafter cited as AN) C11A 22, f. 77, and Vaudreuil to the Ministry, Apr. 3, 1704, ibid., f. 32v. See also Pierre F. X. de Charlevoix, *History and General Description of New France by the Reverend P.F.X. de Charlevoix, S. J.*, ed. and trans. John Gilmary Shea, 6 vols. (Chicago, 1962; orig. pub. 1744), 5:161.

17. Vaudreuil to the Ministry, Apr. 3, 1704, AN, C11A f. 32–33r; Vaudreuil to Louis Phélypeaux de Ponchartrain, Nov. 4, 1706, AN, C11A f. 214; *Dictionary of Canadian Biography*, 13 vols. to date (Toronto, 1966–), 2:455–56, 284–86, 3:81–82; Geoffrey E. Buerger, "Pavillion'd Upon Chaos: The History and Historiography of the Deerfield Massacre" (M.A. thesis, Dartmouth College, 1985), 13–15. It is also possible that three or four of de Rouville's eight brothers, who are not known by name, participated in the attack. See Charlevoix, *History and General Description of New France*, 5:161, and C. Alice Baker, *True Stories of New England Captives, Carried to Canada during the Old French and Indian Wars* (Cambridge, Mass., 1897), 313–14.

18. W. J. Eccles, *The Canadian Frontier, 1534–1760* (New York, 1969), 89, 122, and *France in America* (New York, 1972), 110–12, 115–17.

19. French officials gave their casualties as three French killed and about twenty wounded. See Vaudreuil to the Ministry, Apr. 3, 1704, AN, C11A f. 33r; Vaudreuil and Charles de la Bolsche Beauharnois to the Ministry, Sept. 17, 1704, AN, C11A 22, f. 12v. Williams confirmed the three French deaths, noting de Batilly's death as that of "the lieutenant of the army," in *Redeemed Captive*, 13.

20. Melvoin, *New England Outpost*, 223–25; Buerger, "Pavillion'd Upon Chaos," 11.

21. Melvoin, *New England Outpost*, 227–30.

22. Williams, *Redeemed Captive*, 38.

23. Sheldon, "New Tracks in an Old Trail," *History and Proceedings of the Pocumtuck Valley Memorial Association, 1899–1904* (Deerfield, Mass., 1905), 4:11–28; Baker, "The Adventures of Baptiste," ibid., 342–60, 450–77. See also Demos, *Unredeemed Captive*, 16–17.

24. Williams, *Redeemed Captive*, 87; *Dictionary of Canadian Biography*, 2:449–50.

25. The most critical examination of the "Battis" story is Buerger, "Pavillion'd Upon Chaos," 33–34. Melvoin, *New England Outpost*, 241–43, 339 n. 62, is also skeptical of the story. We share their skepticism.

26. Sheldon, "New Tracks in an Old Trail," 28.

27. Williams, *Redeemed Captive*, 11, 12, 13, 17, 19, 20, 21.

28. Ibid., 11. The most recent editor of Williams's narrative assumes that Williams's captors were all Caughnawaga (Kahnawake) Mohawks. See Edward W. Clark, ed., *The Redeemed Captive, John Williams* (Amherst, Mass., 1976), 11, 12, 125–26 n. 31.

29. Williams, *Redeemed Captive*, 27.

30. Vaudreuil and Beauharnois to the Ministry, Sept. 17, 1704, AN, C11A 22—Marines et Colonies, f. 12, and Vaudreuil to the Ministry, Apr. 3, 1704, ibid., f. 32v.

31. Vaudreuil to the Ministry, Nov. 16, 1704, ibid., Marines et Colonies, f. 34r.

32. Vaudreuil to the Ministry, Oct. 19, 1705, ibid., f. 195–96, 231–32, explains the strategic importance of the Abenakis to both the French and the English at this time. For a discussion of French and English efforts to secure the Abenakis during the 1699–1703 interwar period see Morrison, *Embattled Northeast*, 153–59.

33. Calloway, *Dawnland Encounters: Indians and Europeans in Northern New England* (Hanover, N. H., 1991), 3–7.

34. Morrison's excellent *Embattled Northeast* is one of the better studies of the "Abenaki" that nevertheless maintains its focus on the Eastern Abenaki. Melvoin in *New England Outpost* follows this lead in his otherwise well-informed discussion of Deerfield's attackers, conflating Western and Eastern Abenakis in his assertion that "until the 1670s the Abenaki had lived throughout Maine" (225).

35. Closely related bands of refugee Western Abenakis lived in the Champlain Valley at Winooskeek (Winooski, Vt.) and Missisquoi. Buerger suggests that natives from Missisquoi participated in the Deerfield raid, and although we have not been able to confirm this surmise, it is a reasonable one; Buerger, "Pavillion'd Upon Chaos," 18. See also Calloway, *Western Abenakis*, 97–98, and Gordon M. Day, *The Identity of the Saint Francis Indians*, Canadian Ethnology Service Paper no. 71 (Ottawa, 1981), 23–24, 30, 38–40, 64.

36. Day, *Identity of the Saint Francis Indians*, 31–33.

37. J[oseph] A. Marault, *Histoire des Abenakis, depuis 1605 jusqu'à nos jours* (Sorel, Que., 1866; New York, 1969), vii; Day, *Identity of the Saint Francis Indians*, 1–5.

38. William Hubbard, *The History of the Indian Wars in New England . . .* (1677), ed. Samuel G. Drake, 2 vols. (New York, 1971; orig. pub. 1865), 1:229–34; Sheldon, *History of Deerfield*, 1:152–69; Douglas Edward Leach, *Flintlock and Tomahawk: New*

England in King Philip's War (New York, 1958), 200–205; Melvoin, *New England Outpost*, 113–15, quotation on 115.

39. Day, *Identity of the Saint Francis Indians*, 16–21, traces these movements in more detail and discusses the founding of Schaghticoke.

40. Calloway, *Western Abenakis*, 87–88.

41. The peopling of Odanak is the subject of Day's excellent *Identity of the Saint Francis Indians*. See also Calloway, *Western Abenakis*, 87–88.

42. Day, *Identity of the Saint Francis Indians*, 31–33.

43. *Dictionary of Canadian Biography*, 2:282–86; Baker, *True Stories of Captives*, 309–18; Thomas Charland, *Les Abenakis d'Odanak* (Montreal, 1964), 32–36, 50.

44. Mather, "New Assaults from the Indians," in Alden T. Vaughan and Clark, eds., *Puritans among the Indians: Accounts of Captivity and Redemption, 1676–1724* (Cambridge, Mass., 1981), 137.

45. For the importance to the Abenakis of personal ties see Morrison, *Embattled Northeast*, 31, 70–71, 102, 127, 136.

46. Eccles, "The Social, Economic, and Political Significance of the Military Establishment in New France," *Canadian Historical Review*, 52, no. 1 (1971), 9–10.

47. Emma Lewis Coleman, *New England Captives Carried to Canada: Between 1677 and 1760 during the French and Indian Wars*, 2 vols. (Portland, Me., 1926) 1:183.

48. [Stephen Williams], "What Befell Stephen Williams in his Captivity," published with John Williams, *The Redeemed Captive Returning to Zion* (1707), ed. Stephen W. Williams (Bedford, Mass., n.d. [1987]; orig. pub. 1853), 145. With five critical exceptions, all the citations to "What Befell Stephen Williams" are to this edition.

49. Alice Nash, "Captives among the Abenakis, 1605–1763" (paper presented at McGill University, Feb. 15, 1992), 5–8, 8–12, 12–13.

50. During the 1600s and early 1700s, the Abenakis and other current and former residents of New England do not appear to have waged war to adopt captives specifically to replace deceased relatives, although captive taking was an integral part of their way of war. See Patrick M. Malone, *The Skulking Way of War: Technology and Tactics among the New England Indians* (Baltimore, 1991), 130 n. 3, and Nash, "Captives among the Abenakis," 2. By the mid-1700s, the Abenakis do appear to have adopted captives specifically to replace relatives as warfare and adoption customs grew more alike among the native allies of the French who lived in ethnically mixed mission villages. See Vaughan and Daniel Richter, "Crossing the Cultural Divide: Indians and New Englanders, 1605–1763," *American Antiquarian Society, Proceedings*, 90, pt. 1 (1980), 77, and Calloway, *Western Abenakis*, 27–31.

51. Williams, *Redeemed Captive*, 27; "What Befell Stephen Williams," 150.

52. For a similar conclusion see Sheldon, "New Tracks in an Old Trail," 21.

53. Williams, *Redeemed Captive*, 31–32.

54. Ibid., 32.

55. Jeremy Belknap, *The History of New-Hampshire* . . . , 2d ed., 3 vols. (Boston, 1813), 1:254. See also Coleman, *New England Captives*, 1:168.

56. Here we follow closely Morrison, *Embattled Northeast*, esp. 72–101.

57. Calloway, *Western Abenakis*, 51–52.

58. Williams, *Redeemed Captive*, 23.

59. Ibid., 24.

60. "What Befell Stephen Williams," 150.

61. Increase Mather, "Quenton Stockwell's Relation of His Captivity and Redemption," in Vaughan and Clark, eds., *Puritans among the Indians*, 79–89; John Pynchon

to Sylvester Salisbury, Oct. 5, 1677, *The Pynchon Papers*, ed. Carl Bridenbaugh, with Juliette Tomlinson (Boston, 1982), 1:172–76; Sheldon, *History of Deerfield*, 1:181. This refugee village appears to have been a temporary community of Connecticut Valley natives just outside Sorel, near but not at the site of Odanak.

62. Sheldon, *History of Deerfield*, 1:672.

63. Williams, *Redeemed Captive*, 17, 20.

64. The Pennacooks and Pigwackets are treated as Eastern Indians in Samuel Penhallow, *The History of the Wars of New-England with the Eastern Indians* (New York, 1969; orig. pub. 1726), 16, 17, 22. The 1713 "Treaty for the Submission and Pacification of the Eastern Indians . . . " included the Pennacooks and Pigwackets. See Cecil Headlam, ed., *Calendar of State Papers, Colonial Series: American and West Indies*, vol. 27: 1712–1714 (London, 1910), 229–31.

65. The designation of Pigwackets as Western Abenakis is uncertain, and they have occasionally been categorized as speakers of Eastern Abenaki, as in Dean Snow, "Eastern Abenaki," *Handbook of North American Indians*, vol. 15: *Northeast*, ed. Bruce Trigger (Washington, D.C., 1978), 138–47. Day, "Western Abenakis," ibid., 148, treats them as speakers of Western Abenaki, and this is supported by the Pigwackets' close association with the Pennacooks and other Western Abenakis. Calloway also considers them Western Abenakis in *Western Abenakis*, 7, 15, as does Gary Hume, "Joseph Laurent's Intervale Camp: Post-Colonial Abenaki Adaptation and Revitalization in New Hampshire," in Peter Benes, ed., *Algonkians of New England: Past and Present*, Dublin Seminar for New England Folklife, *Annual Proceedings*, 1991 (Boston, 1993), 101.

66. The following estimates are contained in contemporary documents: "Pennacook tribe," 90 men, and "Pegwacket tribe," 100 men; "Penecook said to be about 100 men," and "Pagwatit," 14 men. See Day, *Identity of the Saint Francis Indians*, 30–31.

67. "Conseil entre les Sauvages Abenaki de Roessek [sic] et Monsieur le Marquis de Vaudreuil, 13 juin 1704," *Collection de Manuscrits Contenant Lettres, Mémoires, et Autres Documents Historiques Rélatifs à La Nouvelle-France . . .* , 4 vols. (Quebec, 1883–1885), 2:414–16.

68. Parkman recognized this fact, mentioning it in a footnote in *Half-Century of Conflict*, 1:56 n. 1. Western Abenakis from Winnipesaukee, another target of English attacks during the fall and winter of 1703, may have participated in the Deerfield raid though there is no specific documentation of their presence. See Drake, *The Border Wars of New England* (Williamstown, Mass., 1973; orig. pub. 1897), 167.

69. Williams, *Redeemed Captive*, 20; Stephen Williams, "What Befell Stephen Williams in his Captivity," ed. George Sheldon (Deerfield, Mass., 1889), 24–25. Stephen W. Williams did not include in his 1853 edition the account of Baker's fight in which Wattanummon was killed and identified by Stephen as his master: "Capt. Baker & my Brother's expedition to Cowass & over to Merrimack, where they killed my old master Wottanammon in April, 1712." Because of the omission, it is necessary here and in four other notes to cite this less accessible version of Stephen Williams's writings. Several Massachusetts documents from the early 1700s identify Wattanummon as one of the two "Sachems of Pennacook" or one of the "two principal Indians of Pennacook." See Headlam, ed., *Calendar of State Papers, Colonial Series: American and West Indies*, vol. 18: 1700 (London, 1910), 171, 425.

70. Williams, *Redeemed Captive*, 147. For a more detailed reconstruction of Wattanummon's life see Evan Haefeli and Kevin Sweeney, "Wattanummon's World: Personal and Tribal Identity in the Algonquian Diaspora, c. 1660–1712," in William Cowan, ed., *Papers of the Twenty-Fifth Algonquian Conference* (Ottawa, 1994), 1–13.

71. Penhallow, *Wars of New-England with the Eastern Indians*, 31–33.

72. Ibid., 149.

73. Calloway, "Wanalancet and Kancagamus: Indian Strategy and Leadership on the New Hampshire Frontier," *Historical New Hampshire*, no. 43 (1988), 285.

74. "What Befell Stephen Williams," 150. See also Morrison, *Embattled Northeast*, 148, and Calloway, "Wanalancet and Kancagamus," 273, and *Western Abenakis*, 48, 109.

75. Williams, *Redeemed Captive*, 35.

76. On the Eastern Abenakis' desire for independence see Morrison, *Embattled Northeast*, 5–6, 128, 134–36, 153–63.

77. Hubbard, *History of the Indian Wars in New England*, 1:248; Calloway, *Western Abenakis*, 81. See also Beth Klopott, "The History of Schaghticoke, New York, 1676–1855" (Ph.D. diss., State University of New York at Albany, 1981), 11.

78. Hubbard, *History of the Indian Wars in New England*, 11, 131–33; Belknap, *History of New Hampshire*, 1:140–45, quotation on 143; Calloway, "Wanalancet and Kancagamus," 275; Drake, *Border Wars of New England*, 17–20.

79. Calloway, "Wanalancet and Kancagamus," 276, and *Western Abenakis*, 81; Harald E. L. Prins, "Amesokanti: Abortive Tribe Formation on the Colonial Frontier" (paper for the Annual Conference of the American Society for Ethnohistory, Williamsburg, Va., 1988), 4.

80. Williams, *Redeemed Captive*, 28.

81. Belknap, *History of New Hampshire*, 1:245:53; Drake, *Border Wars of New England*, 17–20; Calloway, "Wanalancet and Kancagamus," 282–83.

82. E. B. O'Callaghan, ed., *Documents Relative to the Colonial History of the State of New York*, 15 vols. (Albany, N.Y., 1853–1887), 3:562 (hereafter cited as *NY Col. Docs.*).

83. "Examination of Micah Mudge of Northfield aged 38 . . . taken 15th October 1688," Massachusetts Archives (microfilm ed.), 129:243. See also Josiah H. Temple and George Sheldon, *A History of the Town of Northfield, Massachusetts* (Albany, N. Y., 1875), 111–16.

84. Quoted in James Spady, "'As If in a Great Darkness': Ancestral Homelands, Diaspora, and the Schaghticokes of Hatfield, Massachusetts: 1677–1697" (seminar paper, University of Massachusetts, Amherst, 1994), 7.

85. John Pynchon to Robert Treat, June 19, 1690, Judd Manuscripts, Miscellaneous Massachusetts and Long Island, 8:219–24, Forbes Library, Northampton, Mass. We are indebted to James Spady for this reference. The haircut was probably "one side long and the other short," as was Stephen Williams's hair after his fourteen months with the Pennacooks. See "What Befell Stephen Williams," 152.

86. For additional evidence of Schaghticokes fighting in Maine against the English as the allies of the Eastern Indians see Prins, "Amesokanti," 5–6.

87. Tracing these movements and attempting to interpret them is a daunting task. No one has yet surpassed Day's achievement in *Identity of the Saint Francis Indians*, 21–25. Although examining the events for their relevance to Odanak's history, he realizes that Odanak's history is very much intertwined with those of Schaghticoke and Pennacook at this time. See also Klopott, "History of the Town of Schaghticoke," 15–16.

88. John Pynchon to Simon Bradstreet, Dec. 2, 1691, in *Pynchon Papers*, ed. Bridenbaugh, 1:236–38.

89. Prins, "Amesokanti," 7–8.

90. Sheldon, *History of Deerfield*, 1:231–32.

91. John Pynchon and Samuel Partridge to the earl of Bellomont, July 6, 1698, in *Pynchon Papers*, ed. Bridenbaugh, 1:305–307; Mass. Arch., 30:408a.

92. *NY Col. Docs.*, 4:249.

93. Bellomont to the Council of Trade, Sept. 1, 1698, quoted in Morrison, *Embattled Northeast*, 142.

94. John Pynchon to Simon Bradstreet, Dec. 2, 1691, Pynchon to Isaac Addington, May 20, 1692, Pynchon and Samuel Partridge to Bellomont, July 6, 1698, and Pynchon to William Stoughton, July 18, 1698, in *Pynchon Papers*, ed. Bridenbaugh, 1:236–37; 255–56, 305–306, 307–309; "What Befell Stephen Williams," 156–57.

95. See Calloway, *Western Abenakis*, 99–100, for a more detailed description of these events.

96. E[dward] M. Ruttenber, *History of the Indian Tribes of Hudson's River; Their Origin, Manners and Customs, Tribal and Sub-Tribal Organization; Wars, Treaties . . .* (Albany, N.Y., 1872), 183; Calloway, *Western Abenakis*, 98–101.

97. Calloway, assuming that the confederates planned to fight the English in 1700, claims that the "conspiracy proved abortive and the Indian gathering was probably never as large nor as hostile as the rumors suggested," in "Wanalancet and Kancagamus," 287. In principle, he is probably right, but three years later the confederacy played a role in pulling its members into Queen Anne's War. See also Morrison, *Embattled Northeast*, 147–48.

98. Morrison, *Embattled Northeast*, 147–48.

99. Headlam, ed., *Calendar of State Papers, Colonial Series: America and West Indies*, vol. 21: *Dec. 1, 1702–1703* (London, 1913), 171–72. See also Mass. Arch., 30:459, and Calloway, "Wanalancet and Kancagamus," 287.

100. Calloway, *Western Abenakis*, 101.

101. Morrison, *Embattled Northeast*, 125–27; "Memorial of Watanomon and Cadanouokas, two Indian Sagamores of Penacock," n. d., Mass. Arch., 30:459.

102. Headlam, ed., *Calendar of State Papers*, 21:246.

103. Mass. Arch., 30:459.

104. Headlam, ed., *Calendar of State Papers*, 21:385.

105. Ibid., 583.

106. Ibid., 421.

107. Penhallow, *Wars of New-England with the Eastern Indians*, 17–18.

108. Morrison, *Embattled Northeast*, 152, 157–58; Yves F. Zoltvany, *Philippe De Rigaud De Vaudreuil: Governor of New France 1703–1725* (Toronto, 1974), 42.

109. For the warning see Morrison, *Embattled Northeast*, 157–58.; for refusal to join see Calloway, *Western Abenakis*, 99–100.

110. "Lettre de Messieurs de Beauharnois et Vaudreuil au Ministre, 15 Novembre, 1703," *Collection de Manuscrits . . . Rélatifs à La Nouvelle-France*, 2:405–406.

111. Williams, *Redeemed Captive*, 28–29.

112. Morrison, *Embattled Northeast*, 129.

113. Williams, *Redeemed Captive*, 28–29. See also Morrison, *Embattled Northeast*, 157–58.

114. Headlam, ed., *Calendar of State Papers*, 21:726.

115. Williams, *Redeemed Captive*, 28.

116. "Conseil entre les Sauvages Abenaki de Roessek [sic] et Monsieur le Marquis de Vaudreuil, 13 juin 1704," *Collection de Manuscrits . . . Rélatifs à La Nouvelle-France*, 2:414–16.

117. Day, *Identity of the Saint Francis Indians*, 49–52, gives the best existing account

of the Cowassucks before they moved to Odanak in the late 1700s. See also Calloway, *Western Abenakis*, 12, 14, 84.

118. John Pynchon to Robert Treat, June 27, 1690, Judd Manuscripts, Miscellaneous Massachusetts and Long Island, 8:225–26. We are indebted to James Spady for bringing this letter to our attention.

119. Penhallow, *Wars of New-England with the Eastern Indians*, 31–33.

120. Day, *Identity of the Saint Francis Indians*, 50; Calloway, *Western Abenakis*, 109.

121. Sheldon, ed., "What Befell Stephen Williams," 24–25. There is some confusion about the fate of Wattanummon. Concord, N.H., historian Nathaniel Bouton claimed that a chief named Wattanummon greeted the first English settlers of Concord. We tend to discount this story as folklore intended to justify the English occupation of the site. See Bouton, *The History of Concord: From Its First Grant in 1725 . . .* (Concord, N.H., 1856), 40–42, and Haefeli and Sweeney, "Wattanummon's World," 13–14. For more evidence on the war weariness of the Abenakis see Morrison, *Embattled Northeast*, 159–61.

122. Parkman, *Half-Century of Conflict*, 1:212–71; Calloway, *Western Abenakis*, 113–42.

123. The spelling "Caughnawagas" was used by English during the period and in many histories. Most recent histories use the alternative "Kahnawakes."

124. At least four Deerfield residents were taken to Sault au Recollect by Les Iroquois de la Montagne. See Baker, *True Stories of New England Captives*, 223–58, and Coleman, *New England Captives*, 2:92–96, 103–12.

125. Sheldon, *History of Deerfield*, 1:161.

126. William N. Fenton and Elisabeth Tooker, "Mohawk," in Trigger, ed., *Northeast*, 469–71; Daniel K. Richter, *The Ordeal of the Longhouse: The Peoples of the Iroquois League in the Era of European Colonization* (Chapel Hill, 1992), 119–29. See also Demos, *Unredeemed Captive*, 120–66.

127. Fenton and Tooker, "Mohawk," 472–73; Coleman, *New England Captives*, 1:17–21; M. Jean Black, "A Tale of Two Ethnicities: Identity and Ethnicity at Lake of Two Mountains, 1721–1850," in Cowan, ed., *Papers of the Twenty-Fourth Algonquian Conference* (Ottawa, 1993), 1–7.

128. Fenton and Tooker, "Mohawk," 470; Richter, *Ordeal of the Longhouse*, 167–69.

129. "What Befell Stephen Williams," 153–56; Coleman, *New England Captives*, 2:36–38.

130. Melvoin, *New England Outpost*, 197–200.

131. Deerfield gatherings that Mohawks attended occurred in 1648 for an abortive attack on the Mohegans, in 1716 to recruit other natives to fight the "Flat-head Indians," and in 1723 and 1735 for peace conferences with Massachusetts authorities. See Peter Allen Thomas, "In the Maelstrom of Change: The Indian Trade and Cultural Process in the Middle Connecticut River Valley, 1635–1665" (Ph.D. diss., University of Massachusetts, 1979), 76–77; Richter, *Ordeal of the Longhouse*, 239–40; Francis Jennings, *The Ambiguous Iroquois Empire: The Covenant Chain Confederation of Indian Tribes with English Colonies from Its Beginnings to the Lancaster Treaty of 1744* (New York, 1984), 316; and "Indian Treaties," *Collections of the Maine Historical Society*, 1st ser., 4 (1856), 123–44.

132. Calloway, *Western Abenakis*, 59; Day, "The Ouragie War: A Case History in Iroquois-New England Indian Relations," in *Extending the Rafters: Interdisciplinary Approaches to Iroquoian Studies*, ed. Michael K. Foster, Jack Campisi, and Marianne Mithun (Albany, N.Y., 1984), 37–40. See also Jere R. Daniell, *Colonial New Hampshire: A History* (Millwood, N.Y., 1981), 7–8.

133. Eastern Indians to the Governor, July 27, 1721, Mass. Hist. Soc., Collections, 2d ser., 8 (1826), 260.

134. J[osiah] H. Temple, *History of North Brookfield, Massachusetts* (Boston, 1887), 37–38; Thomas, "In the Maelstrom of Change," 51–52, 77, 239–60; Neal Salisbury, "Toward the Covenant Chain: Iroquois and Southern New England Algonquians, 1637–1684," in Richter and James H. Merrell, eds., *Beyond the Covenant Chain: The Iroquois and Their Neighbors in Indian North America, 1600–1800* (Syracuse, 1987), 63.

135. Thomas, "In the Maelstrom of Change," 204–60; Day, "Ouragie War," 39–50; Salisbury, "Toward the Covenant Chain," 65–70; Melvoin, *New England Outpost*, 39–47. See also Grace Greylock Niles, *The Hoosac Valley: Its Legends and Its History* (New York, 1912), 34–39.

136. Leach, *Flintlock and Tomahawk*, 73–102.

137. Jennings, *The Invasion of America: Indians, Colonialism, and the Cant of Conquest* (Chapel Hill, 1975), 315–23; Day, *Identity of the Saint Francis Indians*, 19–20; Salisbury, "Toward the Covenant Chain," 70–73; Melvoin, *New England Outpost*, 92–123; Richter, *Ordeal of the Longhouse*, 135–37.

138. Hendrick, the Mohawk sachem, was born in the Westfield, Mass., area sometime between 1680 and 1690. His father was a Mahican chief and his mother was a Mohawk. See William L. Stone, "King Hendrick," New York State Historical Association, *Proceedings of the Second Annual Meeting* (Albany, N.Y., 1901), 28, and Patrick Frazier, *The Mohicans of Stockbridge* (Lincoln, Neb., 1992), 9.

139. John Pynchon to Robert Treat, June 19, 1690, Judd Manuscripts, Miscellaneous Massachusetts and Long Island, 8:219–24. Stephen W. Williams's edition of Stephen Williams's writings also omits his revealing account of an attack on Deerfield residents that occurred in 1693. See Sheldon, ed., "What Befell Stephen Williams," 13–14.

140. James Russell Trumbull, *History of Northampton, Massachusetts, From Its Settlement in 1654*, 2 vols. (Northampton, Mass., 1898–1902), 1:431–34, 441–43.

141. John Pynchon to Robert Treat, June 19, 1690.

142. Sheldon, ed., "What Befell Stephen Williams," 13–14; John Pynchon to Benjamin Fletcher, June 21, 1693, Pynchon to Isaac Addington, June 28, 1693, Pynchon to Sir William Phips, July 2, 1693, Pynchon to Phips, July 12, 1693, Pynchon to Phips, July 29, 1693, in *Pynchon Papers*, ed. Bridenbaugh, 1:268–78; NY *Col. Docs.*, 4:38–39; Sheldon, *History of Deerfield*, 1:213.

143. John Pynchon and Samuel Partridge to Bellomont, July 6, 1698, in *Pynchon Papers*, ed. Bridenbaugh, 1:305–306; Mass. Arch., 30:378, 381–98, 400–17.

144. Richter, *Ordeal of the Longhouse*, 105–213.

145. Ibid., 216–54.

146. Ruttenber, *History of the Indian Tribes of Hudson's River*, 183; Calloway, *Western Abenakis*, 98–101.

147. Richter, *Ordeal of the Longhouse*, 197; Fenton and Tooker, "Mohawk," 471. See also Zoltvany, *Philippe De Vaudreuil*, 79.

148. For references to Kahnawake complaints that French officials had limited their participation to small groups see Vaudreuil to Ponchartrain, Apr. 3, 1704, AN, C11A 22 f. 32.

149. Five "Macquas" were killed and only three "Indians"; Williams, *Redeemed Captive*, 13.

150. Coleman, *New England Captives*, 2:44. The three at Lorette were Sarah and Jonathan Hoyt and Ebenezer Nims; ibid., 91, 103. The four at Sault au Recollect were Hannah and Thomas Hurst, Abigail Nims, and Jacob Rising; ibid., 92–96, 103–12. The

seven at Kahnawake were William Brooks (possibly), Mercy Carter, Abigail French, Mary Harris, Joanna Kellogg, Waitstill Warner (possibly), and Eunice Williams; ibid., 70, 87, 100–101, 128, 54–63. Other Deerfield residents who appear to have been Mohawk captives were Martha French, Joseph Kellogg, Martin Kellogg, Junior, Rebecca Kellogg, Ebenezer Sheldon, Mary Sheldon, and Warham Williams; ibid., 83, 97–101, 116–18, 63–64. Samuel Carter and Daniel Crowfoot are the other two whose locations are undetermined; ibid., 70, 77, 78. Crowfoot may have been at Kahnawake. See Demos, *Unredeemed Captive*, 283 n. 9.

151. Coleman, *New England Captives*, 2:79. For a similar conclusion see Sheldon, "New Tracks in an Old Trail," 21.

152. Charles B. De Saileville, "A History of the Life and Captivity of Miss Eunice Williams, Alias, Madam De Roguers, Who Was Styled 'The Fair Captive'" (ms., [1842]), 8–9, 14, 27–29 (Neville Public Museum, on deposit in the State Historical Society of Wisconsin, Area Research Center, Green Bay [microfilm edition, reel 7]). The date of the manuscript is established by the following letter: Charles De Saileville to the Reverend Eleazer Williams, Addressed to Samuel G. Drake, Burlington, Vt., June 12, 1842, Eleazer Williams Collection, Missouri Historical Society, St. Louis (microfilm, Memorial Libraries, Deerfield, Mass.). This unpublished biography of Eunice Williams is a combination of facts, family and Kahnawake folklore, and romantic fiction. It must be used with care. For a similar assessment see Demos, *Unredeemed Captive*, 299–300 n. 20.

153. Coleman believes that if Brooks "survived the journey he may have lived at Caughnawaga"; *New England Captives*, 2:68.

154. Mather, "Quentin Stockwell's Relation of His Captivity and Redemption," 82. See also Cornelius J. Jaenen, *Friend and Foe: Aspects of French-Amerindian Cultural Contact in the Sixteenth and Seventeenth Centuries* (New York, 1976), 129.

155. De Saileville, "Life and Captivity of Eunice Williams," 18–19.

156. Richter, "War and Culture: The Iroquois Experience," *William and Mary Quarterly*, 3d ser., 40 (1983), 528–59.

157. De Saileville, "Life and Captivity of Eunice Williams," 28.

158. Ibid.

159. Ibid., 26.

160. Richter, *Ordeal of the Longhouse*, 124–28.

161. De Saileville, "Life and Captivity of Eunice Williams," 57. For a more detailed discussion of the role of Catholicism in this process see Demos, *Unredeemed Captive*, 151–54.

162. De Saileville, "Life and Captivity of Eunice Williams," 56–57, 65, 97–98.

163. Vaudreuil to Ponchartrain, Apr. 3, 1704, AN, C11A 22 f. 32. See also Zoltvany, *Philippe De Vaudreuil*, 48, 76–77, and Richter, *Ordeal of the Longhouse*, 218.

164. La Jonquière to the Ministry, Quebec, Oct. 19, 1751, AN, C11A 97, p. 139, translated and paraphrased in Jean Lunn, "The Illegal Fur Trade Out of New France, 1713–60," *Canadian Historical Association Report* 10 (1939), 65.

165. De Saileville, "Life and Captivity of Eunice Williams," 9, 12.

166. Richter, *Ordeal of the Longhouse*, 168. See also Jennings, *Ambiguous Iroquois Empire*, 176.

167. Lunn, "Illegal Fur Trade Out of New France," 61–76; Thomas Elliot Norton, *The Fur Trade in Colonial New York, 1686–1776* (Madison, Wis., 1974), 121–35; Jennings, *Ambiguous Iroquois Empire*, 284–85, 298; Zoltvany, *Philippe De Vaudreuil*, 75–77.

168. Melvoin, *New England Outpost*, 154.

169. Sheldon, ed., "What Befell Stephen Williams," 13–14.

170. Williams, *Redeemed Captive*, "Appendix and Notes," 142.

171. Coleman, *New England Captives*, 2:118–19. See also Melvoin, *New England Outpost*, 154, and Sheldon, *History of Deerfield*, 2:138.

172. Like Parkman, we have discounted the romantic nineteenth-century story of the Bell of St. Regis first published in Hoyt, *Antiquarian Researches*, 193–94. The story, which is a living tradition at Kahnawake, maintains that the "Kahnawake warriors went to Deerfield to get their bell," which had been captured en route to Canada by the English and subsequently purchased by John Williams for the meetinghouse in Deerfield. During the attack the "Kahnawake fought as a group. They went directly to the church and secured the bell. They then withdrew through the village with the bell and retired from the fight." Quotations from David Blanchard, *Seven Generations: A History of the Kanienkehaka* (Kahnawake, Can., 1980), 208–209. The story does not accord with known facts in too many instances. For the most thorough review see Buerger, "Out of Whole Cloth: The Tradition of the St. Regis Bell" (paper presented at the Mid-Atlantic Conference for Canadian Studies, Bucknell University, 1986; copy in the Pocumtuck Valley Memorial Association Library, Deerfield, Mass.).

173. De Saileville, "Life and Captivity of Eunice Williams," 203–14. This citation of De Saileville's manuscript comes from the second half, which is in the possession of the De Pere (Wis.) Historical Society, Eleazer Williams Papers, 1704–1929 (microfilm edition, 1979), State Historical Society of Wisconsin. Eunice Williams was in Deerfield from Dec. 20, 1743, until Mar. 1, 1744. De Saileville's account of the visit is based in part on excerpts from a volume of Stephen Williams's diary that was destroyed by fire in 1846.

174. Leon Gerin, "The Hurons of Lorette," in "Report on the Ethnology Survey of Canada," *Report of the Seventieth Meeting of the British Association for the Advancement of Science*, held at Bradford in Sept. 1900 (London, 1900), 550–67; Christian Morissonneau, "Huron of Lorette," in Trigger, ed., *Northeast*, 389–92.

175. Williams, *Redeemed Captive*, 13; Reuben Gold Thwaites, ed., *The Jesuit Relations and Allied Documents: Travels and Explorations of the Jesuit Missionaries in New France, 1610–1791*, 73 vols. (Cleveland, 1896–1901), 66:169.

176. Vaughan and Clark, eds., *Puritans among the Indians*, 173, and Clark, ed., *Redeemed Captive, John Williams*, 45, 47, 50, 51, 53, mistakenly make the leap from Macqua to Mohawk. Buerger "Pavillion'd Upon Chaos," 20–21, also connects Williams' Macqua captain and the Huron chief.

177. Fenton, "Northern Iroquoian Cultural Patterns," in Trigger, ed., *Northeast*, 320–21; Fenton and Tooker, "Mohawk," 478.

178. For the grouping together of Mohawks and Hurons see Ian K. Steele, *Betrayals: Fort William Henry and the "Massacre"* (New York, 1990), 83.

179. For the characterization of raiders from Lorette as "French Mohawks" see "Alexander Hamilton's Journal [1722]" in James Phinney Baxter, *The Pioneers of New France in New England* (Albany, N.Y., 1894), 320.

180. Thwaites identifies the location of the fight as Deerfield in the index to the series. See *Jesuit Relations*, 72:194.

181. Morissonneau, "Huron of Lorette," 389–92. The Lorette of 1704 was the last in a series of village sites occupied by the refugee Hurons around Quebec in the late 1600s. It was settled in 1697 and known as Jeune-Lorette, in recognition of the former village of Lorette, now known as Ancienne-Lorette, which had been located a few miles away

and had been the village site from 1673 to 1696. The village exists today as Village-des-Hurons to separate it from the neighboring French-Canadian town of Loretteville.

182. *Jesuit Relations*, 66:159–61, discusses the company of warriors from Lorette. The population of Lorette in 1685 was 146. See G. F. G. Stanley, "The First Indian 'Reserves' in Canada," *Revue d'Histoire de l'Amérique Française*, 4, no. 2 (1950), 195.

183. *Jesuit Relations*, 66:159–61.

184. Ibid., 167–71.

185. A recent account of the raid suggests that John Williams was the intended victim. See Demos, *Unredeemed Captive*, 30–32. Williams, however, was under the control of St. Francis Abenakis, not Hurons, from the time of his capture until his arrival in Canada, and the native leader who threatened him on the march to Canada was "an Indian captain from the eastward," a Western Abenaki, not a Huron. Sheldon also identifies the "Indian captain from the eastward" as Abenaki. See Sheldon, "New Tracks in an Old Trail," 20, and Williams, *Redeemed Captive*, 17.

186. Coleman, *New England Captives*, 2:91.

187. Williams, *Redeemed Captive*, 122–23. Coleman, *New England Captives*, 2:91, mentions the petition, which cannot be located at present.

188. Melvoin, *New England Outpost*, 48–64, describes the beginnings of the English settlement at Pocumtuck.

189. Sheldon, *History of Deerfield*, 2:139.

190. Richter, *Ordeal of the Longhouse*, 239–40.

191. Annotation to handwritten copy of "The Redeemed Captive Returning to Zion," p. 25, in Eleazer Williams Papers, 1634–1964, State Hist. Soc. Wis., Area Research Center, Green Bay.

192. Stephen Williams, Diary, Aug. 10, 1722, microfilm edition of typescript transcription, 1:371, Storrs Library, Longmeadow, Mass.

193. For Hoyt see Sheldon, ed., "What Befell Stephen Williams," 33 n. 38. For the Sheldons see *The Acts and Resolves, Public and Private, of the Province of the Massachusetts Bay . . .* , 21 vols. (Boston, 1869–1922), 12:324–25, 504.

194. Sheldon, *History of Deerfield*, 1:527.

195. Jennings, *Ambiguous Iroquois Empire*, 316; *Collections of the Maine Historical Society*, 4 (1856), 123–44.

196. Calloway, "Wanalancet and Kancagamus," 289.

David L. Ghere

3

The "Disappearance" of the Abenaki in Western Maine

Political Organization and Ethnocentric Assumptions

Prior to the 1980s, most historians of New England had long assumed that the Abenakis in western Maine permanently migrated to the Jesuit missions of Saint Francis and Becancour during Dummer's War (1722–1727). Some explicitly stated that no Indians lived in the area after that time, somehow ignoring such famous examples as Pierpole and Molly Ocket. Others related frontier encounters with raiding or hunting parties, but always identified the Indians as members of the Saint Francis tribe. Most simply mentioned the migrations during Dummer's War and then neglected to make any further reference to Indian inhabitants.[1] The widespread acceptance of permanent Indian emigration from these areas in both historical literature and popular myth resulted from what appeared to be compelling evidence. However, there is overwhelming evidence that many Abenakis remained in western Maine until the end of the century, and some descendants still inhabit the area today. Their "disappearance" from history resulted more from the ethnocentric views of colonial observers and the misunderstandings of early historians than from an absence of Indian inhabitants.

This assertion of continued Indian inhabitation of western Maine will not come as a great surprise to most current scholars of the Abenaki. The works of

Gordon Day and Colin Calloway, while focusing on an adjacent area, have certainly provided some evidence for the Abenakis in western Maine.[2] However, no works have been published detailing their presence in the area after the 1720s or systematically refuting the assumption of permanent emigration during Dummer's War. As a result, popular writers, amateur historians, and scholars unfamiliar with the Abenakis or western Maine continue to assume the accuracy of statements by colonial officials and early historians.[3] An examination of this issue will not only provide a more accurate understanding of the Abenakis but will reveal the extent to which colonial leaders and early historians were blinded by their ethnocentric assumptions.

Our understanding of Abenaki political organization has gone through an important transformation in recent years. Colonial observers and early historians had assumed a tribal organization for the Abenaki, with each tribe occupying a river drainage area. This riverine tribal model was accepted by most modern scholars despite the efforts of some to point out its limitations and inconsistencies.[4] Then, in 1988 and 1989, Harald Prins and Bruce Bourque, utilizing primarily French sources, refuted the riverine tribal model and identified several large interrelated kinship groups. This model provides a much more accurate and useful understanding of Abenaki political organization and migration patterns and accounts for the prevalent intermarriage and intermixing between the Abenaki groups.[5]

The evidence and conclusions in this article support this new model of political organization, but I have chosen to use the English tribal labels in my discussion for a variety of reasons. First, English confusion over Abenaki political organization is particularly apparent in several instances in which the English identify any group of Abenaki (even family bands) as a tribe. Secondly, using the tribal designations found in English sources reveals the overwhelming evidence of continued Abenaki inhabitation of western Maine that was ignored by English colonial officials and early historians. Finally, while distorting Abenaki political organization, English sources do provide accurate locations for various groups of Abenaki in western Maine as well as some information about the arrival or departure of migrants to or from Canada. Unfortunately, after 1730 French government records generally identify all migrants from northern New England as Abenaki without any indication of their original village or area of inhabitation. When referring to Indians still residing in northern New England, French records specify only those associated with the villages of Norridgewalk, Penawabskik, and Missiquoi, while all others are identified only by the general term, Abenaki.

A second point of confusion has been the use of the same tribal name for Indians at the Saint Francis mission village (present day Odanak) and the Abenaki living along the Androscoggin River. This confusion prompted colonial observers, and later historians, to believe that the principal component of the Saint Francis tribe consisted of migrants from western Maine. Early

historians began using the term "Arosaguntacook," the name of the Indian village at Saint Francis, to identify the Indians living along the Androscoggin
River. Their indiscriminate use of the name included periods of the seventeenth century, long before the establishment of Saint Francis or the supposed migration. Gordon Day has shown in *The Identity of the Saint Francis
Indians* that the principal component of the Saint Francis village during the
1700s was Western Abenaki Indians, particularly Sokokis, from New Hampshire and Vermont and that no major influx of Eastern Abenaki residents from
Maine occurred until the middle 1700s.[6]

This confusion over the names and interrelationship of the Saint Francis
Indians and those inhabiting western Maine has continued almost to the present. In the *Handbook of North American Indians*, Dean Snow used Arosaguntacook as the name for the Indians living along the Androscoggin River in
the text and on the map showing tribal areas. He also provided a list of syn-
onyms for Arosaguntacook that intermixed names of both groups of Indians.
In the next *Handbook* chapter, Gordon Day lamented the persistence of this
mistaken association between the two groups.[7] To avoid this confusion, I have
used the name Androscoggin to refer to those Abenakis living along the Androscoggin River. For the Indians living along the Saco and Presumpscot
Rivers, I have used the commonly accepted name of Pigwacket. In both cases,
I am not attempting to establish tribal names for these Abenakis or implying
that they were organized into tribes, only that the English consistently referred to them as tribes.

It should be noted that tribal identifications during this time are suspect
even when the Indians seem to provide the information. Indeed, in 1740, Saint
Francis leaders complained to militia Captain John Gyles that Indians living
closer to the English were claiming to be from Saint Francis. This may not
have been a result of deception, but simply an example of the confusion inher-
ent in cross-cultural communication. The scattered Abenaki family bands in
western Maine had numerous kinsmen at Saint Francis or Becancour, and individuals or family bands frequently journeyed to the mission villages for a variety of social and cultural functions, to trade, or simply to visit relatives. Since
the Abenakis perceived their relationship to other groups in terms of kinship
and social affiliation, Saint Francis may have been the most accurate answer
to English questions. However, the English would have asked questions and
interpreted responses within the context of their own concepts of political relationships and diplomacy. Abenaki responses about their social relations with
Saint Francis would have been interpreted by the English to have political
and diplomatic implications that the Indians had not intended.[8]

In the midst of this, the primary foundation for the belief in permanent
emigration was the disappearance of references to the Pigwacket and Androscoggin Indians in the colonial records and the corresponding emergence
of the Saint Francis and Becancour Indians as diplomatic and military powers

on the New England frontier. During King William's War (1689–1699) and Queen Anne's War (1703–1713),[9] the Pigwackets and Androscoggins were reported to have suffered severe losses and ultimately to have migrated to Canada. Massachusetts officials became aware of the existence of the village at Saint Francis near the end of the latter conflict. Some Pigwacket and Androscoggin Indians returned to their homelands, participating in conferences in 1714 and 1717, but reports during Dummer's War indicated that they had again migrated to Canada.[10] Pigwacket and Androscoggin spokesmen failed to appear at any subsequent major conference, and their presence at minor conferences escaped the notice of early historians. Saint Francis and Becancour representatives appeared at treaty conferences for the first time in the early 1720s and participated in the major conferences for the next three decades. At these meetings, they voiced many of the complaints and concerns of Abenakis from western Maine.[11]

The assumption of a large Pigwacket and Androscoggin migration to Saint Francis seemed to be confirmed by other evidence as well. At one of the Indian conferences in 1720, Massachusetts officials reported that "the Indians of the Amriscoggin River are much lesned there being at present but a very few."[12] In June 1726, militia Colonel Jacob Wendall estimated warrior strengths of only eleven Pigwackets and ten Androscoggins. Five months later, militia Captain John Gyles indicated there were twenty-four Pigwacket fighting men, but only five Androscoggins.[13] These two estimates, Gyles's in particular, have been used repeatedly by historians during the past two centuries as population figures for the Abenakis throughout the mid-1700s. These historians ignored both Gyles's indication that there were numerous uncounted migrants at the Canadian missions and the fluid nature of Abenaki social organization and residence. As we shall see, many of these Indians returned to western Maine shortly after Gyles and Wendall made their estimates.[14]

English colonial officials and frontier settlers actually knew very little about the area in New Hampshire and western Maine beyond English settlement until the 1750s. An effort to survey the Massachusetts (Maine)/New Hampshire border was begun in 1741 but was abandoned when the party encountered Abenakis near the Indian village of Pigwacket. The first exploration and mapping of Winnipesaukee Pond was not performed until 1747, and the area north of that point was unknown even to the most experienced militia leaders. A sketch map of Maine done during this period only shows the coastal area from Saco to the Kennebec River.[15]

The extent of English knowledge of the interior of northern New England is indicated by a map made by Samuel Langdon in 1756. The Connecticut River was depicted reasonably accurately up to the turn east at Great Cowass Intervales, but the river was shown continuing in that direction rather than returning to its actual northerly course. The Saco and lower Androscoggin Rivers were reasonably accurate while the Little Androscoggin was distorted.

The upper Connecticut, upper Androscoggin, and Sandy Rivers were not shown, and a large area in western Maine was marked "Wilderness Unknown." There were also a number of notes indicating that certain items depicted were matters of conjecture.[16]

As a result of all the factors discussed above, colonial officials and later historians concluded that the Pigwackets and Androscoggins had migrated permanently to Canada where they merged with others to become the new villages of Saint Francis and Becancour. The assumption of tribal organization, the confusion over tribal names, the absence of Pigwacket and Androscoggin spokesmen at major conferences, the declining population estimates, and the limited geographical knowledge of the English all played a role in promoting the conclusion of permanent emigration. Yet, a thorough review of official documents and local histories provides overwhelming evidence of Indian residence in western Maine for seven decades after Dummer's War.

Militia Captain Joseph Heath informed Massachusetts Lieutenant Governor Dummer in April 1727 (five months after Gyles's estimate) that many Androscoggin and Pigwacket family bands were returning to their homelands in northern New England. Furthermore, in the letter he specifically refers to the Saint Francis, Becancour, Androscoggin, and Pigwacket Indians as separate political entities. The presence of some Pigwacket family bands along the Saco River was confirmed in June 1727 when these Indians complained that the settlers' fishing nets prevented fish from ascending the river.[17] In 1730, an Androscoggin named Sabattus requested that a truckhouse be established near the mouth of the Androscoggin River, and several references to these Abenakis occurred in 1735 and 1736.[18] In 1742, the Massachusetts House of Representatives directed Diminicus Jordan "to Notifie ye Pigwacott Tribe of Indians in & about Saco" of a conference. Spokesmen from both the Androscoggins and the Pigwackets ultimately attended this meeting.[19]

Supporting evidence also comes from the oral traditions preserved by the families of early settlers in western Maine that were finally recorded a century later in town histories. These sources indicate that the Pigwackets and Androscoggins lived in family band camps and small villages after Dummer's War without ever congregating into tribal villages. George and Henry Wheeler related the story of Phineas Jones surveying the area around Brunswick during the winter of 1731 because fewer Indians were nearby at that time of year. Josiah Pierce indicated that just prior to King George's War "there were more Indians than whites residing in" Gorham, Maine. Hugh McLellan confirmed this assertion, explaining that Indian and white children frequently played together before 1745. Finally, there were numerous reports during King George's War of settlers recognizing members of Indian raiding parties who had been their neighbors before the conflict.[20]

The Pigwackets who had returned to their homeland after Dummer's War separated into distinct factions, each residing in small villages or family band camps. Jacob Wendall's estimate indicated that two of these family bands had already returned by the summer of 1726, with seven warriors living at Pigwacket village and four others at a location further down the Saco River. By November 1726 Gyles reported twenty-four Pigwacket warriors under Adiawando, and local history sources have indicated they inhabited the Presumpscot River area. Joseph Heath's letter the following April indicated a migration by families, and in June the two family bands along the Saco were protesting the blockage of fish on the river.[21]

These Pigwacket factions in separate encampments continued throughout the next decade. Waroonmanood from the Saco River area and Adiawando from the Presumpscot River area were identified as Pigwacket representatives at the 1732 conference at Falmouth. Four years later, the latter group was vigorously protesting a severe shortage of fish in Sebago Lake as a result of dams and fish nets on the Presumpscot River.[22] Frontier tensions mounted during the next two years over this issue and the influx of settlers into the area, prompting Adiawando and some others to migrate permanently to Canada. At the 1739 conference, the Pigwackets who remained in the Presumpscot valley repeated their protests concerning these two issues. Two years later, a surveyor named Walter Bryant encountered the third group, reporting that several hunting bands were in the vicinity of Pigwacket village.[23]

The division of the Pigwackets into three distinct political groups was confirmed at conferences in 1739 and 1742. Rather than using their original tribal designation, Massachusetts treaty commissioners considered each of these factions as a tribe and identified them by the location of their encampments. At the 1739 conference, Polin was recognized as the sachem of the "Indians of Presumpscot," who were reported to number about twenty-five warriors.[24] Three years later, the conference journal recorded "Saquent, Chief of the Saco Tribe," and "Waroonmanood, Chief of the Pigwacket Tribe," but failed to give any indication of the size of their bands.[25]

The separate residence of the three Pigwacket groups seems to be based on political factionalism as well as kinship. The two Pigwacket bands living along the Saco River had friendly relations with the settlers and participated in conferences. Those inhabiting the Presumpscot Valley had tense relations with settlers and numerous complaints about English actions, but rarely participated in conferences. When King George's War commenced, Saquent and Waroonmanood led bands to the Saco truckhouse to join the British, while Polin and his followers allied with the French.[26]

Documentary evidence is too limited for a detailed analysis of Androscoggin factionalism, but a similar division into small villages seems to have taken place. Joseph Heath's letter (April 1727) referred to Androscoggin families returning to their homelands. At a conference in 1738, a Kennebec spokesman voiced some complaints for the Indians living along the lower Androscoggin River. In the journal of the conference proceedings, this group of Androscoggins was identified as a separate tribe named Pejepscots after the section of river they inhabited.[27] Historian John McKeen claimed that three villages existed along the Androscoggin River during this period. One of these villages was depicted as Merocamegog (Naracomecook or Canton Point) on a 1741 scout map drawn by militia captain Joseph Bean, and, in 1755, it was reported to contain several hundred residents.[28]

The scattered residence patterns of both the Pigwackets and Androscoggins were revealed in the 1732 conference dialogue of the Massachusetts governor, Jonathan Belcher. Curiously, Belcher observed that "the Amerescoggins and Pigwackets are all one Tribe, that the Pigwackets are seated near the Truck-House on Saco River, and the Amerescoggins are near Richmond Truck-House."[29] His conclusion that the two "tribes" had merged is contrary to all other evidence and seems to be contradicted by the reference to separate, distant trading locations. The various Abenaki groups frequently asserted that they were all one people. Since the family bands inhabiting western Maine no longer congregated in large villages or represented themselves at conferences, Burnet must have been referring to the absence of any apparent tribal distinctions rather than the actual unification of the two Abenaki groups. This confusion over tribal organization was apparent a decade later when the Indians attending a conference were listed as "Penobscott, Norridgewock, Pigwaket or Amiscogging or Saco, St. Johns, Bescommonconty or Amerescogging, and St. Francis Tribes."[30]

The outbreak of King George's War created a dramatic change in the circumstances faced by all the Abenakis. Nearly two decades of peaceful coexistence were followed by fifteen years of warfare and frontier tension. Sandwiched between King George's War (1745–1749) and the French and Indian War (1754–1760)[31] were five years of official peace. However, random murders of Indians visiting the English settlements and Abenaki retaliatory attacks continued to exacerbate the mutual hostility and mistrust that had been generated during King George's War. In fact, 1752 was the only year of relative calm on the frontier in this period.[32]

Historians have assumed that during periods of warfare the Abenakis in northern New England migrated to the safety of the Canadian missions. This conclusion was based primarily upon numerous references in the correspondence of settlers and truckhouse commanders to the Indians' having gone to Canada. In addition, the infrequency of encounters between militia patrols and Abenaki warriors led writers to assume that these Indians were only war parties from Canada. However, the usual Abenaki response to frontier tension or an outbreak of hostilities was to move to an alternate village site further from the English settlements.

There is some doubt about what area was being indicated when individuals referred to Indians migrating to Canada. Historians have assumed that "Canada" meant the Saint Lawrence Valley and, particularly, the mission villages of Saint Francis and Becancour. However, the boundaries of Canada were not known by the individuals making the references during the late colonial period. Indeed, the last colonial war was precipitated primarily by disputes over the location of Canada's boundaries. Regardless of the official claims by the English and French crowns, to the general population in northern New England "Canada" was simply somewhere beyond the furthest English settlements. From this perception, the upper drainage areas of the Connecticut, Androscoggin, Kennebec, and Penobscot rivers could be considered part of Canada. This situation continued as late as 1773 when the town of Bethel, Maine, was founded on the upper Androscoggin River and was originally incorporated as Sudbury, Canada.[33]

The references to Indians migrating to Canada are open to question for other reasons as well. A few consist of reports citing Indian informants who indicated that "some" Abenakis had migrated to Canada. These reports obviously imply that "some" Abenakis had remained, including those who provided the information. More often, these statements were the suppositions of English settlers or militia officers, who merely noted that the Indians had stopped coming to the settlements to trade. Since the English conducted trade for diplomatic purposes, a decline in trade was interpreted according to its diplomatic implications: English failure and, conversely, French success in their efforts to secure Abenaki loyalty. Predisposed to consider the Abenakis as natural French allies, observers assumed their absence to be proof that the Indians had gone to Canada to join the French. Despite the frequency of peaceful Abenakis being murdered, the Indians' concern for their safety was never mentioned as an explanation for their reluctance to visit English settlements during periods of frontier tension.[34]

The assumption that the Abenakis in northern New England migrated to Canada during periods of warfare was also based on the infrequency of contacts with militia patrols. This resulted from a misunderstanding of the purpose of these operations. Organized to intercept and destroy Indian raiding parties, these patrols traveled parallel to the frontier to discover tracks left by the passage of war parties. Thus, even the most aggressive patrols were usually conducted along the frontier and rarely penetrated into the interior. The Pigwackets and Androscoggins could have inhabited the White Mountains or the upper Androscoggin Valley without ever being discovered. A survey of all surviving reports or journals of these militia patrols and private scalp-hunting parties confirms these observations. Those few patrols that did penetrate into the interior usually found Indians. However, these incidents were assumed to be only encounters with Abenaki raiding parties and went relatively unnoticed by earlier historians because they occurred randomly in the midst of the mass of uneventful patrols recorded in the documents.[35]

The Pigwacket Indians would have been greatly affected by English militia/scalp-hunting activity. Their usual village and encampment sites were relatively close to the English settlements, making them untenable locations during periods of warfare. Unlike most other Abenakis, major portions of the Pigwacket subsistence area were within the area frequently patrolled by the militia. Threatened by attack and denied access to their food resources, the Pigwacket were forced to abandon their old territory. The infrequency of any reported militia contacts would seem to confirm this conclusion.

While some Pigwackets were recognized accompanying Canadian Abenaki war parties during King George's War, there is evidence that other Pigwackets may not have migrated to Canada, but merely moved up into the White Mountains. The French use of "Abenaki" to identify all the migrants from northern New England precludes our ability to identify the migration or residence of this particular group.[36] Governor Wentworth of New Hampshire showed great concern about "the Indians that Inhabit & hunt on our frontiers." He and the legislature ordered fortifications and militia patrols, which clearly indicated their belief that these Indians were in the White Mountains, not operating out of the village of Saint Francis.[37] Later, a captive from Biddeford was reported to have been taken "up river to the White Mountains and [after an unspecified period of time] ultimately . . . to Canada."[38]

The Pigwackets maintained their political factions after King George's War and reoccupied all three village sites that had been abandoned during the conflict. At the 1749 peace conference, Sayweremet, identified as a Saint Francis Indian, requested a truckhouse at Saco. The distance and geographical barriers between Saco and Saint Francis, coupled with the greater accessibility to Fort Richmond on the Kennebec River, make this request implausible for a resident of Saint Francis. There were numerous reports in local histories of Indians inhabiting the Presumpscot Valley during the interval between wars, and William Douglass reported the other two villages near Pigwacket in 1750 with a total of a dozen warriors.[39]

With the outbreak of hostilities in the French and Indian War, the three Pigwacket bands were again in a precarious position. Saquent and Waroonmanood again chose to ally their family bands with the English while those following Polin supported the French. Once more French records were not specific in their identification of Abenaki migrants, so they fail to confirm or refute the Pigwackets' arrival or residence at the Canadian missions.

Polin's band does not appear to have migrated to the Canadian missions during this conflict, but instead retreated again into the White Mountains. Polin was killed May 14, 1756, when he and his warriors ambushed a militia patrol near New Marblehead. Local traditions indicated that the warriors had descended the Presumpscot River to the settlements and that some of their kinsmen had been left behind. The Presumpscot provides an excellent route from the White Mountains but is of little use to raiders coming from Saint Francis. Also, an individual warrior was killed carrying a quarter side of beef on his shoulder. This action was contrary to normal Abenaki raiding practices where the necessity for swift movement and secrecy precluded carrying heavy burdens or using cooking fires. However, if Pigwacket families were in the nearby White Mountains, this incident would be quite understandable considering the restricted subsistence area and the chronic food shortages incurred during periods of hostilities.[40]

Other sources also indicate a Pigwacket presence in the White Mountains. In early May 1757, a settler "was fired upon by two Indians seventy miles [from Falmouth] back in the woods." This location in the White Mountains, the sighting of only two Indians, and the ease of the settler's escape would seem to indicate that he had stumbled upon a Pigwacket family band rather than a war party. Another incident occurred after the conclusion of the raid on Saint Francis in 1759. When Rogers' Rangers disbanded after recuperating from their ordeal, one man separated from the others to take a more direct route home. He encountered Indians and was killed in the White Mountains.[41]

There is a local legend that supports the conclusion that none of the Pigwackets migrated to the Canadian missions during this war. Bartholomew Thorn was captured near Gorham, Maine, in June 1754 and remained a prisoner at either Saint Francis or Becancour for most of the war. Even though Thorn was reported to have been widely known and hated by the Indians living along the Presumpscot, he was never recognized at the Canadian missions. Since public display of the captives was frequent and both villages were relatively small, it is difficult to understand how he went unnoticed unless the Pigwackets did not migrate to those two villages during this particular war.[42]

There are indications that some Androscoggins also remained near their homes in northern New England. As indicated earlier, when militia patrols penetrated into the interior, they usually encountered Indians. Only three instances have been recorded where scalp-hunting parties ascended the upper Androscoggin River. One ventured only as far as Rumford Falls before turning back without having discovered any Indians. Both of the other two expeditions encountered Abenaki when they ascended the river above Rumford Falls.[43]

A final piece of evidence for both the Pigwackets and the Androscoggins concerns the patterns of Indian raids on the New England frontier. French records indicate that Abenaki war parties from Canada conducted their raids either in the spring (late April to early June) or fall (October and November) so as not to interfere with their service as auxiliaries with the French army during the summer campaigns. Two or three raiding parties consisting of about ten warriors each would travel together for safety but would operate independently while among the New England settlements. These various raids were recorded by the French, who provided supplies for them, and a reasonably accurate correlation can be drawn between specific war parties departing from Canada and subsequent incidents on the New England frontier. However, there were some incidents that occurred randomly (not in the spring/fall pattern), involved only a few warriors and consisted of the destruction of livestock without any apparent effort to kill or capture settlers. The frequent references in the documents to the mutilation of cattle reminds one of the warrior mentioned above who was seen carrying a quarter of beef on his shoulder. These attacks were most likely conducted by Abenaki family bands living in the White Mountains or on the upper Androscoggin River who were in need of food.[44]

After the cessation of hostilities in 1760, Pigwacket and Androscoggin family bands returned to occupy their old camping sites and hunting areas in western Maine. Town histories from this area mention numerous Abenaki inhabitants when the first settlers founded the towns of Fryeburg (1760), Poland (1768), Minot (1772), Leeds (1773), Bethel (1774), and Farmington (1751). Some of these Indians, particularly Pierpole and Molly Ocket, became well known in local folklore.[45] The number of Abenakis in New Hampshire was sufficient in 1769 to prompt Jacob Treadwell to petition for a license to trade with them. During the American Revolution, fourteen Pigwacket warriors from Fryeburg petitioned the Massachusetts General Court to enlist in the Patriot army, while many of the Androscoggins living near Bethel joined the British army.[46]

These Abenakis continued to live in family band camps or small villages and were never recorded to have congregated into tribes. Thomas Stinchfield, the original founder of the town of Leeds, visited the family band encampment of Sabattis near the Androscoggin River and indicated that Pocasset resided in a larger, more permanent encampment on the Dead River. Five small villages were reported in the middle portion of the Androscoggin drainage area, while family band camps were scattered about the area. Another source indicated at least twelve warriors in the village at Roccomeco on the Androscoggin River.[47] In 1772, Henry Tufts was temporarily living in a small Androscoggin village near present-day Bethel, Maine. He claimed that 700 Abenakis inhabited the upper Androscoggin and Connecticut River Valleys with their villages "in a scattering, desultory manner" throughout the area.[48]

If all the Abenakis did not permanently emigrate from western Maine in the 1720s or even temporarily during the warfare from 1745 to 1760, did they ever leave the area? Local histories in western Maine continued to record the Indians' annual subsistence trips to the coast throughout the 1780s and early 1790s. The last trip was noted in the spring of 1796, and the Indians were subsequently reported to have emigrated to Saint Francis or to the Penobscot area. Pierpole's family was reported to have left the Farmington area in 1799.[49] Gordon Day's research on the Saint Francis Abenakis has provided some confirmation, indicating the arrival of approximately 700 migrants during the 1790s from New Hampshire and western Maine. However, a few Abenakis still remained since town histories recorded the deaths of Indian residents as late as 1809 in Fryeburg, Maine, and 1840 in Bethel, Maine.[50] Others continued to live in the area selling Indian crafts but were no longer identified in official records as Indians. Some of their descendants still inhabit western Maine.

The "disappearance" of the Pigwacket and Androscoggin Indians from history is curious when one considers the abundant evidence of their continued residence in western Maine. The belief in migration during the latter fifteen years of warfare may be understandable considering the previous discussion of erroneous assumptions by colonial observers and early historians concerning militia patrols, the fur trade, and the timing or destination of Abenaki emigration. But what of the two decades of peace after Dummer's War when there existed ample documentary evidence that Abenaki were living in western Maine? Even after considering the confusion of tribal names between the Androscoggin and Saint Francis Indians, the misuse of Gyles's and Wendall's warrior estimates, and the limited geographic knowledge of the area, this contradiction is still perplexing. Colonial observers and historians must have been predisposed to accept those assumptions and dismiss the contradictory information.

This apparent dilemma results from the ethnocentric perceptions of colonial leaders and historians concerning Indian residence and occupation of territory. Rather than accepting Indian concepts on these matters, they interpreted Indian culture with Euro-American concepts. Thus, Indian villages, while not permanent sites like Massachusetts towns, were considered the Indians' official residence, providing legitimacy (from this perspective) to Indian claims to the surrounding territory. The small temporary hunting camps used by the family bands did not conform to Euro-American concepts and were not thought of as the residence of the family band despite their year-round occupancy. If no tribal village existed in the area, the English assumed that the residence of the hunters must be at some more distant village,such as Saint Francis.

Similarly, colonial leaders perceived the tribe to be the level of Indian political organization possessing territorial rights and diplomatic authority. Throughout the colonial period, English officials assumed that the Abenakis were organized as tribes and that tribal leaders had the right to sell land. At conferences, these officials repeatedly demanded that Abenaki diplomats negotiate for their entire "tribe" and ensure strict adherence to treaty agreements by all "tribe" members. This ethnocentric need for tribal organization is amply illustrated by Governor Belcher's assumption of a Pigwacket/Androscoggin union in 1732, by the confused listing of alternate tribal names at the 1742 conference, and by the references to family bands or small villages as tribes named for locations in 1738, 1739, and 1742. From this English perception, kinship organization was not a legitimate basis for diplomatic authority or property rights. The family bands in western Maine could not be autonomous so they had to be under the authority of some tribal organization, presumably Saint Francis, or they forfeited their treaty and territorial rights.

These conclusions did not conform to Abenaki society. Leaders had very limited authority, and rights to land were primarily the concern of family bands of kinship groups. Traditionally, the Abenaki had only resided in their villages for about a quarter of the year, while the other nine months were spent in the small family band camps. Furthermore, the Abenakis had a variety of village sites and often moved to an alternate site in response to the outbreak of an epidemic, increased frontier tension, or open warfare. The colonial observers who noted the Indians' failure to attend conferences or to reoccupy previous village sites, assumed the Abenakis had remained in Canada.

Massachusetts officials may have been inclined to ignore the Abenakis' return to western Maine for political and personal economic reasons. An increased awareness of these facts would have diminished public acclaim concerning the successful conduct of Dummer's War and prompted renewed demands for stronger frontier defenses while reducing the flow of new settlers and depressing the value of land in the area. Most militia officers and colonial legislators were either landowners or employees/investors in the large land companies in Maine, so they had personal economic as well as political concerns about these developments. Furthermore, if the Indians had abandoned the area, they forfeited their rights to the land (according to the prevailing English attitude) thus relieving the colonial government and the land companies from concern due to frequent Indian claims that their land deeds were fraudulent. Thus, Massachusetts officials, both as political leaders and as private citizens, would have tended to overlook the presence of Abenakis in western Maine.[51]

The "disappearance" of the Pigwacket and Androscoggin Indians was a result of a series of erroneous assumptions by colonial officials and early historians. In reality, Abenakis in western Maine had merely divided into factions inhabiting family band camps or small villages. This effected only a minor alteration in their residence patterns, from spending three quarters of the year in family band camps to year-round residence in that mode. English observers assumed that the absence of tribal villages meant the abandonment of the area and that the family bands were merely hunters from Saint Francis. A series of faulty assumptions followed that seemed to substantiate this perception, resulting in its widespread adoption. The "disappearance" of these two "tribes" from history actually tells us more about English ethnocentic perceptions and assumptions than it does about the reality of Abenaki residence in western Maine.

NOTES

Reprinted from the *American Indian Quarterly*, volume 17, by permission of the University of Nebraska Press. Copyright © 1993 by the University of Nebraska Press.

1. For early examples see William Douglass, *A Summary, Historical and Political of the First Planting, Progressive Improvements and Present State of the British Settlements*

in North America, 2 vols. (Boston: Rogers and Fowle, 1749–53) 1:183; Jeremy Belknap, *The History of New Hampshire*, 3 vols. (Boston: For the author, 1791–92), 2:186–99, 214–18; George Barstow, *The History of New Hampshire, From Its Discovery, in 1614, to the Passage of the Toleration Act, in 1819* (Boston: Little & Brown, 1853), 147; L'Abbe J. A. Marault, *Histoire des Abenakis, depuis 1605 jusqua nos jours* (Sorel, Que.: Gazette de Sorel, 1866), 404–405; Francis Parkman, *A Half Century of Conflict*, 2 vols. (Boston: Little, Brown and Co., 1892), 1:18.

2. The most important of these works would be Gordon Day, *The Identity of the Saint Francis Indians* (Ottawa: National Museum of Canada, 1981), and Colin Calloway, *The Western Abenakis of Vermont, 1600–1800: War Migration and the Survival of an Indian People* (Norman: University of Oklahoma Press, 1990), 132–83.

3. For recent examples see Sherburne F. Cook, "Interracial Warfare and Population Decline Among the New England Indians," *Ethnohistory*, 20 (winter 1973), 22; Solon B. Colby, *Colby's Indian History: Antiquities of the New Hampshire Indians and Their Neighbors* (Center Conway, N.H.: Walker's Pond Press, 1975), 68, 189; P. Andre Sevigny, *Les Abenaquis; habitat et migrations, 17e et 18e siecles* (Montreal: Bellarmin, 1976), 200–203.

4. This riverine tribal organization has been effectively explained in Frank G. Speck, *Penobscot Man: The Life History of a Forest Tribe in Maine* (Philadelphia: University of Pennsylvania Press, 1940), 7–9; and Dean Snow, "Eastern Abenaki," *Handbook of North American Indians*, 20 vols. (Washington: Smithsonian Institution, 1978–), vol. 15: *Northeast*, Bruce G. Trigger, ed., 143, 146. Problems with this model were revealed by the works of Fannie Hardy Eckstorm, particularly *Old John Neptune and Other Maine Indian Shamans* (Portland: The Southworth-Anthoensen Press, 1945), 73–83; and Alvin Morrison, "Western Wabanaki Studies: Some Comments" in *Actes du Huitieme Congres des Algonquinistes*, William Cowan, ed. (Ottawa: Carleton University, 1977), 230–243. These limitations have also been discussed in conversations between the author and Alvin Morrison, Kenneth Morrison, Bruce Bourque, and Harald Prins during the late 1980s.

5. Harald Prins, "Tribulations of a Border Tribe: A Discourse on the Political Ecology of the Aroostook Band of Micmacs (16th–20th Centuries), (Ph.D. diss., New School for Social Research, 1988); Bruce J. Bourque, "Ethnicity on the Maritime Peninsula, 1600–1759," *Ethnohistory*, 36 (summer 1989), 257–84; see also Harald Prins and Bruce Bourque, "Norridgewock: Village Translocation on the New England-Acadian Frontier," *Man in the Northeast*, 33 (1986), 137–58; and Bruce J. Bourque and Ruth H. Whitehead, "Tarrantines and the Introduction of European Trade Goods in the Gulf of Maine," *Ethnohistory*, 32 (1985), 327–41.

6. Gordon Day has provided a detailed historiography of this mistaken association between the Saint Francis and the Androscoggin in *Identity of the St. Francis*, 59, 65, 103, 107–17. See also Dean Snow, "Eastern Abenaki," *Handbook*, 15:143, 146; Gordon Day, "Western Abenaki," ibid., 159; Gordon Day, "The Eastern Boundary of Iroquoia: Abenaki Evidence," *Man in the Northeast*, 1, no. 1: 7–13; Dean Snow, "The Ethnographic Baseline of the Eastern Abenaki," *Ethnohistory*, 23 (1976), 291–306.

7. Dean Snow, "Eastern Abenaki," *Handbook*, 15:143, 146; Gordon Day, "Western Abenaki," ibid., 159. See also Speck, *Penobscot Man*, 18; and Fannie Hardy Eckstorm, *Indian Place Names of the Penobscot Valley and the Maine Coast* (Orono: University of Maine Press, 1941), 147.

8. John Gyles to Gov. Belcher, Aug. 7, 1740, James P. Baxter, ed., *Baxter Manuscripts, Documentary History of the State of Maine*, 24 vols. (Portland: Maine Historical

Society, 1869–1916), 11:213. For other similar situations, or possible diplomatic deception by the Abenakis, see Captain Isreal Williams to Lieutenant Governor Phips, March 19, 1753, *Journal of the House* (N.H.), April 27, 1753; and Lieutenant Governor Dummer's letter, May 23, 1727, *Bax. Mss.*, 10:395–96.

9. These dates refer to the Anglo-Abenaki portion of these conflicts and do not correspond exactly to the official dates of the broader Anglo-French wars.

10. Indian Conference, July 1714, *Bax. Mss.*, 23:67–73; "Conference . . . with Eastern Indians, 1717," Maine Historical Society, *Collections*, ser. 1, 3 (1853), 359–75.

11. Two Indian Conferences during 1720, *Massachusetts Archives, 1622–1799* (Stoughton, Mass.: Graphic Microfilm Inc.), 29:57–74; "Indian Treaties," Maine Historical Society, *Collections*, 3 (1853), 377–447; ibid., 4 (1856), 119–84; Treaty conference, *Bax. Mss.*, 23:67, 83–129. The Pigwackets and Androscoggins appeared at some minor conferences and were referred to occasionally in official documents, but this evidence seems to have gone unnoticed by early historians.

12. Conference at Falmouth, 1720, ibid., 23:86.

13. John Gyles, "John Gyles' Statement of the Number of Indians," Maine Historical Society, *Collections*, 1st ser., 3 (1853), 355–58; [Jacob Wendall], "An Estimate of the Inhabitants, English and Indian, in the North American Colonies, also their Extent in miles 1726," *New England Historical and Geneological Register*, 20 (1866), 7–9. A very similar set of estimates was provided in 1749 by William Douglass, who cited less than a dozen Pigwackets and claimed that the Androscoggins were "extinct." Douglass, *A Summary of British North America*, 183.

14. The reliance of historians on Gyles's figures without critical evaluation resulted from his impressive credentials as an Indian expert. His background included nine years of captivity with the Micmac as a youth and three decades of service as a militia officer, trading post commander, and conference translator. I do not question the accuracy of Gyles's estimate, despite evidence indicating that as a conference translator Gyles consistently used mistranslations and misinformation to secure Abenaki acceptance of objectionable treaty provisions. I do object to historians who have assumed the continuing accuracy of those figures months, years, and even decades later. For Gyles's role as an interpreter see David L. Ghere, "Mistranslations and Misinformation: Diplomacy on the Maine Frontier, 1725–1755," *American Indian Culture and Research Journal*, 8, no. 4 (1984), 3–26.

15. Bryent's Journal, *New Hampshire Provincial Papers*, 19:508–509; Phineas Stevens to Governor Shirley, Jan. 27, 1747, New Hampshire Historical Society, MSS 17C-17; Timothy Clements to Ebenezer Stevens, March 31, 1747, N.H. Hist. Soc., MSS 17B-16; Pencil Map of Maine, Maine Hist. Soc., Jeremiah Powell Papers, coll. 7, box 1/1.

16. Samuel Langdon, "An accurate Map of his Majesty's Province of New Hampshire in New England, 1756." I have had the pleasure of examining all of the old French and English maps of the area that are in the collections of the Library of Congress and the Newberry Library. The accuracy of the Langdon map compares quite favorably to others from around that date. There is a map (dated between 1674 and probably 1690) found in the *British Public Records Office* (CO700/New England 2) by Alric and Gretchen Faulkner that has a more accurate depiction of the upper Androscoggin and Connecticut Rivers. See also map [1762], Vermont Historical Society, MS 912.74-R659.

17. Joseph Heath to Lieutenant Governor Dummer, April 13, 1727, *Bax. Mss.*, 10:380; Lieutenant Governor Dummer to Colonel Wheelwright [May 1727], ibid., 10:397; Samuel Jordon to Dummer, June 8, 1727, ibid., 400.

18. Fannie Hardy Eckstorm Papers, Fogler Library, University of Maine, box 611, f72, box 616, f51; Georgia Drew Merrill, *History of Androscoggin County, Maine* (Boston: W. A. Fergusson and Co., 1891), 62; Ben Larrabee to Josiah Willard, Sept. 19, 1735, *Bax. Mss.*, 11:143; Letter to Col. Westbrook, Sept. 7, 1736, *Bax. Mss.*, 172–73.

19. Proceedings of the House, July 2, 1742, ibid., 282; Massachusetts Bay Colony, *A Conference Held at St. Georges* [August 1742] (Boston: Draper, 1742), 1.

20. George A. and Henry W. Wheeler, *History of Brunswick, Topsham and Harpswell* (Boston: Alfred Mudge and Son, 1878), 30; Josiah Pierce, "History of Gorham" [written in 1862], Fannie Hardy Eckstorm Papers, box 611, f8B, 41; Hugh D. McLellan, *History of Gorham, Maine* (Portland: Smith and Sale, 1903), 35–38. See also James W. North, *The History of Augusta* (Augusta: Clapp and North, 1870), 25; Merrill, *History of Androscoggin County*, 64.

21. [Jacob Wendall], "Estimate of Inhabitants," 9; John Gyles, "Statement of the Number of Indians," 355–58; Joseph Heath to Lt. Gov. Dummer, April 13, 1727, *Bax. Mss.*, 10:380.

22. Massachusetts Bay Colony, *A Conference at Falmouth in Casco-Bay* [July 1732] (Boston: B. Green, 1732), 3, 20; Ben Larrabee to Josiah Willard, Sept. 19, 1735, *Bax. Mss.*, 11:143; Letter to Col. Westbrook, Sept. 7, 1736, *Bax. Mss.*, 172–73.

23. Deposition of John Coks, Jr., Aug. 4, 1738, ibid.; 186–87; Charles Frost to William Pepperrell, Aug. 15, 1738, ibid., 190–91; Conference with Polin & Indians of Presumpscot, Aug. 10–13, 1739, ibid., 257–61; Bryent's Journal, *NHPP*, 19:508–509.

24. Conference with Polin & Indians of Presumpscot, Aug. 10–13, 1739, *Bax. Mss.*, 237.

25. *Conference at St. Georges* [1742], 4, 10.

26. Ammi Ruhama Cutter to Shirley, June 19, 1744, *Bax. Mss.*, 23:291–92.

27. Joseph Heath to Lt. Gov. Dummer, April 13, 1727, *Bax. Mss.*, 10:380; Conference with the Penobscot & Norridgewalk Indians in July, 1738, ibid., 23:253.

28. John McKeen, "Some of the Early Settlements at Sagadahock and on the Androscoggin River," Maine Hist. Soc., *Collections*, ser. 1, 3 (1853), 321–23; William B. Latham, *History of Bethel, formerly Sudbury, Canada, Oxford County, Maine* (Augusta, Maine.: Press of the Maine Farmer, 1891), 78.

29. *Conference at Falmouth* [1732], 13.

30. *Conference at St. Georges* [1742], 1.

31. These dates refer to the Anglo-Abenaki portion of the conflicts and do not correspond exactly to the official dates of the broader Anglo-French wars.

32. M. Bigot to M. Rouille, Aug. 6, 1750, *Documents Relative to the Colonial History of New York*, E. B. O'Callaghan, ed., 15 vols. (Albany: Weed, Parsons, 1855–1861), 10:218–19; Treaty Conference, July 5, 1752, Vermont Historical Society, MSS25-no. 65; Deposition of James Clark, March 1, 1754, *Bax Mss.*, 24:451–52; *Records of the Council* [N.H.], Sept. 7, 1754.

33. Latham, *History of Bethel, formerly Subury, Canada*.

34. The following is a chronology of peacetime murders of Abenakis and periods of warfare: One Penobscot murdered in 1744, warfare from 1745 to 1749, one Kennebec murdered in 1749, warfare in 1750 and 1751, two Saint Francis murdered in 1753, two Saint Francis and two Penobscots murdered in 1754, fourteen Penobscots murdered in 1755, warfare from 1755 to 1760. See David L. Ghere, "Abenaki Factionalism, Emigration and Social Continuity: Indian Society in Northern New England, 1725 to 1765" (Ph.D. diss., University of Maine, 1988), esp. 184, 199–200, 221–23, 226.

35. Sources researched for militia patrols and scalping parties include *Bax. Mss.*;

NHPP, NY Col. Docs., Mass. Archives, Fannie Hardy Eckstorm Papers, document collections of the Maine, New Hampshire, and Vermont Historical Societies; William D. Williamson, *History of the State of Maine*, 2 vols. (Hallowell, Maine: Glazier, Masters and Col, 1832); Herbert Milton Sylvester, *Indian Wars of New England*, 3 vols. (Boston: W. B. Clarke, 1910); and all the town histories for Maine and New Hampshire. For successful encounters with Indians see William Willis, ed., *Journals of Rev. Thomas Smith and Rev. Samuel Deane* (Portland: Joseph S. Bailey, 1849), 170; and Earnest George Walker, *Embden of Yore* (1932), 637.

36. French sources investigated include Public Archives of Canada, Colonial Archives, C11A, vols. 81–93; Reuben G. Thwaites, ed., *The Jesuit Relations and Allied Documents*, 72 vols. (New York: Pageant, 1959); Archives de Quebec, *Bulletin des recherches historiques*; *Archives des Jesuites Canadians-Francais, Fonds Rochemonteix*; *Collection de documents inedits sur le Canada et l'Amerique publies par le Canada-Francais*, 3 vols. (Quebec: L. J. Demers et Frere, 1888–90); *Collection de documents relatifs a l'histoire de la Nouvelle France*, 4 vols. (Ottawa: Public Archives of Canada, 1970).

37. *Journal of the Assembly* [N.H.], May 26, June 19, 1744 (Quote from June 19); *Journal of the House* [N.H.], April 18, May 24, June 26, July 5, 7, 1744.

38. Dane York, *Stories and Legends of Old Biddeford*, 2 vols. (Biddeford, Me.: The McArthur Library, 1946), 38.

39. Fannie Hardy Eckstorm Papers, box 611, f72, box 616, f51; "Treaty at Falmouth, 1749," Maine Hist. Soc., *Collections*, 4:157–48; Douglass, *A Summary of British North America*, 183.

40. Samuel T. Dole, *Windham in the Past*, 82–85; Willis, *Journals of Smith and Deane*, 165.

41. Ibid., 170; Walker, *Embden of Yore*, 637; Barstow, *History of New Hampshire*, 205; Joseph Wait, "Account of Roger's Raid." Vermont Hist. Soc., B-W134 Wj.

42. McLellan, *History of Gorham*, 61; Names and Lists of Captives, June 8, 1758, *Bax. Mss.*, 24:95.

43. Willis, *Journals of Smith and Deane*, 170; Walker, *Embden of Yore*, 637.

44. Ghere, "Abenaki Factionalism," 58–66, 148–49, 181–92, 238–68; Ghere, "The Twilight of Abenaki Independence: The Maine Abenaki During the 1750s" (M.A. thesis, University of Maine, 1980), 41–44, 101–107.

45. Merrill, *History of Androscoggin County*, 585, 726, 758; J. C. Stinchfield, *History of the Town of Leeds, Androscoggin County, Maine, From Its Settlement, June 10, 1780* (Lewiston, Maine.: Lewiston Journal Press, 1901), 19, 311; Latham, *History of Farmington, Franklin County, Maine, From the Earliest Explorations to the Present Time, 1776–1885* (Farmington, Maine: Press of Knowlton, McLeary and Co., 1885), 18, 32–35; Dr. N. T. True, Bethel Centennial Celebration Address, 1874, Fannie Hardy Eckstorm Papers, box 611, f87; Correspondence from Charlotte E. Hobbs, ibid., box 615, f71.

46. Transcript of License to Jacob Treadwell, Jr., to trade with the Indians, Dec. 20, 1769, N.H. Hist. Soc., MSS Hammond 2:8; Latham, *History of Bethel*, 423; G. T. Ridlon, *Saco Valley Settlements and Families: Historical, Biographical, Geneological, Traditional, and Legendary* (Portland: The Author, 1895), 64.

47. Stinchfield, *History of Leeds*, 14–15, 19, 311–12, 316–17.

48. Edmund Pearson, ed., *The Autobiography of a Criminal, Henry Tufts* (New York: Duffield and Company, 1930), 64.

49. Lapham, *History of Bethel*, 423; Yorke, *Legends of Old Biddeford*, 39; Stinchfield, *History of Leeds*; Butler, *History of Farmington*, 35.

50. Day, *Identity of The Saint Francis*, 111; True, "Bethel," Fannie Hardy Eckstorm Papers, box 611, f87.

51. The political power of the various land companies and the aggressive, and at times violent, competition between land companies have been detailed in a number of studies. For original documents see Pejepscot Proprietors Papers, Essex Institute, Salem, Massachusetts; Kennebeck Proprietors Papers, Maine Hist. Soc., Portland; and *Report of the Committee for the Sale of Eastern Lands* (Boston, 1795). For various historical studies see James Sullivan, *The History of Land Titles in Massachusetts* (Boston, 1801), 23–43, 91–92, 193–94, 132–33; William Ladd, "Annals of Bakerstown, Poland and Minot," Maine Hist. Soc., *Collections*, 2 (1847), 110–12; Robert H. Gardiner, "History of the Kennebeck Purchase," ibid., 276, 286; Robert E. Moody, "The Maine Frontier, 1607 to 1763" (Ph.D. diss., Yale University, 1933), 427–34; Gordon E. Kershaw, *The Kennebec Proprietors, 1749–1775* (Portland, Maine, 1975), 26–30, 150–68, 175–92; Alan Taylor, "'A Kind of War': The Contest for Land on the Northeastern Frontier, 1750–1820," *William and Mary Quarterly*, 46 (January 1989), 3–26.

Daniel Vickers

4

The First Whalemen of Nantucket

In the year 1690, so a Nantucket story goes, several townspeople were standing on a hill watching the whales sporting with one another off the south coast of the island. "There," observed one of them, gesturing toward the ocean, "is a green pasture where our children's grandchildren will go for bread."[1] If the sea was to be their garden, however, these islanders, like other American colonists, were only interested in cultivating it as their own. The thought of purchasing and managing vessels may have ignited their imaginations, but few of them entertained any wish to toil on the deep in the service of other men.

Finding help was therefore no easy task. Free men on Nantucket, as in most corners of early America, had seized upon the easy availability of land to establish themselves as independent producers. Accordingly, those who launched the whale fishery at the end of the seventeenth century, like all colonists who wanted to expand production beyond the limits of the household, found labor hard to procure at any price, let alone one that ensured what they felt was a reasonable rate of return. It was not the gathering of capital that troubled the first whaling merchants, for in the early years the costs of entering the industry were moderate. The demand for whale oil and whalebone was well established and markets were easy to locate, while the sources of supply were clearly visible as they swam along Nantucket's coastline. The real challenge to these early entrepreneurs was to find a few men who understood the techniques of whaling, and above all to recruit a larger group to man the oars. In most parts of the New World the scarcity of obedient and reliable workmen pushed employers to consider the institution of bound labor. Historians of tropical production generally invoke this proposition in their explanations of slavery. But should not the same principle have held true in the thinly populated northern colonies, wherever men were producing for the market? This article investigates how capitalist development in one corner of the New England economy took place without wholesale recourse to slavery or indentured servitude.

Nantucket is a low sandy island of forty-six square miles, half a day's journey by sail off the south coast of Cape Cod. The earliest Europeans to call there at the beginning of the seventeenth century found it an attractive if not especially fertile place, inhabited by 2,500 Wampanoag and Nauset Indians, who supported their numbers, enormous for an island that size, by hunting and farming, and especially by fishing.[2] Although they must have profited by the occasional drift whale that washed up on shore, they never pursued these great creatures on the open sea.

The first white settlers arrived in 1660 and purchased from the Indians both permission to settle at the west end of the island and rights to gather hay, graze cattle after the harvest, and cut timber on the rest of the land.[3] In the decade that followed, over twenty families—Coffins, Colemans, Barnards, Bunkers, Husseys, Starbucks, Swains, Worths, Macys, and Folgers being the most prominent—purchased shares in the propriety and moved to the island. By virtue of their control over the land, reinforced by a tight policy of intermarriage, these few families maintained near-total domination over the Nantucket economy through the next hundred years.

Most of the settlers came to farm, but it was soon evident that the island contained too little room to support the generations to come. Some of the early arrivals were craftsmen whose skills must have enabled the newly planted settlement to provide some goods for itself, but certain items would always have to come from the mainland. To pay for these, the settlers began to cast about for commodities that could find markets in Boston.

Most of the colonists of coastal New England were familiar with the whales that the sea washed up and stranded on their beaches, and with the economic value of blubber and baleen. During the seventeenth century, towns from Plymouth to Long Island passed orders governing the ownership of the great creatures, the organization to cut them up, and the manner in which the first casks of oil were to be shared out.[4] On Nantucket, where most of the beaches and beachcombing privileges remained in Indian hands, these problems were normally settled outside the white community, although in fights over the ownership of the animals the Indians sometimes turned for arbitration to the English courts. As their attention was drawn to the abundance of whales around the island, the settlers began to consider the possibilities of commercial exploitation themselves.[5]

Nantucketers knew that elsewhere in the colonies whales were pursued in boats from the shore. The Englishmen who settled on Cape Cod and the eastern end of Long Island had been hunting these beasts and selling their oil and bone to merchants in Boston and New York since the early 1650s.[6] Naturally enough, the men of Nantucket came to envision these products as commodities that could right their balance of trade with the mainland. The problem was that nobody on the island really knew how whaling was carried on.

In 1672, therefore, the settlers invited a Long Island whaleman named James Loper to practice his trade on Nantucket. If he would "Ingage to carry on a Design of Whale Catching," the town would bear two-thirds of the cost, guarantee Loper a near-monopoly in the fishery, and throw in a house lot and commonage to boot. Financing the venture was clearly not a problem for the islanders, who were chiefly interested in the whaleman not for his capital but for his mastery of technique. Unfortunately, although Loper accepted the offer, he must have changed his mind, for he continued to follow the fishery from Long Island and never moved to Nantucket. Not until 1690, when one Ichabod Paddock arrived from Yarmouth on Cape Cod, did the island manage to attract a competent whaleman.[7] Once the expertise had been acquired, however, whaling from the shore developed rapidly. Almost at once the settlers began to organize their own companies, and we have evidence that, by the turn of the century, Indians were purchasing goods from Nantucket merchants out of their earnings in the hunt. The shore fishery continued to expand into the mid-1720s, when close to thirty boats were engaged in the chase.[8]

The object of their pursuit was the right whale. Every autumn these animals returned along the American coast from a summer of feeding in the far reaches of the North Atlantic. From early November to March or April they wintered between Cape Cod and the Carolinas, usually within thirty miles of the shore. At any time during these months, whales could be spotted from the land. Nantucket was especially favored because of its position off the headland of Cape Cod, around which all whales had to swim. During the months of migration, vast numbers of them passed within a few miles of the island.[9] The oil refined from the blubber of the right whale was of a poor grade, suitable only for outdoor lamps and lubrication. In the animal's head, however, hung hundreds of strips of baleen or whalebone, a hard yet flexible material, which the whale used for straining food from the sea; for Europeans of the time this substance served some of the functions that plastics do today. Both oil and bone found steady markets in England.

Over the course of their lives, right whales varied enormously in size. Paul Dudley, a resident of Massachusetts and America's first cetologist, described their development in these words:

> This fish, when first brought forth, is about twenty Feet long, and of little Worth, but then the Dam is very fat. At a Year old, when they are called Short-heads,

they are very fat, and yield to fifty barrels of Oil, but by that Time the Dam is very poor, and term'd a Dry-skin, and won't yield more than thirty Barrels of Oil, tho' of large Bulk. At two Years old, they are called Stunts, being stunted after weaning, and will then yield generally from twenty four to twenty eight Barrels. After this, they are term'd Scull-fish, their Age not being known, but only guess'd at by the Length of the Bone in their Mouths.[10]

Full-grown adults commonly produced up to 90 barrels of oil, and occasionally as much as 120 or 130, but the average produce of all right whales caught ranged around 60 barrels of oil and 750 pounds of bone.[11]

The pursuit of these creatures from the shores of Nantucket had become a regular seasonal activity by the end of the seventeenth century. The fishery was carried on by companies of six men stationed at various points on the south and east coasts of the island. Crèvecoeur, an early visitor, related that each company "erected a mast, provided with a sufficient number of rounds, and near it they built a temporary hut, where five of the associates lived, whilst the sixth from his high station carefully looked toward the sea, in order to observe the spouting of the whales. As soon as any were discovered, the sentinel descended, the whale-boat was launched, and the company went forth in quest of their game."[12] In these slim, double-ended boats, built of cedar clapboards to a length of twenty feet, the company might row after whales the entire day among the Nantucket shoals. The method of the hunt they borrowed from the British Greenland fishery. If a company managed to draw even with its prey—not too difficult a task since right whales were lazy swimmers—the harpooner, perched in the bow, attempted to "fasten on" by sinking his harpoon, or iron, into its flesh. If the iron, connected by hundreds of feet of line to the whaleboat, stuck fast, the whale usually sounded in terror and attempted to flee, with the vessel and crew in tow. As the boat sped across the waves in the wake of the stricken animal, the company drew near to it at every opportunity, hurling lances and harpoons tied to heavy wooden drogues into the enraged beast, trying to bring its life to a speedy conclusion. The outcome of the chase could vary, as Dudley noted: "The Whale is sometimes killed with a single Stroke, and yet at other Times she will hold the Whale-men in Play, near half a Day together, with their Lances, and sometimes they will get away after they have been lanced and spouted blood, with Irons in them, and Drugs fastened to them."[13]

The skills required in whaling from the shore varied from post to post. The harpooner directed the chase from the bow; he gave the orders, paid out the towline when the whale sounded, and handled the actual harpooning and lancing. He needed both an understanding of whale behavior and the capacity to make rapid, correct judgments, two things that came only with years of experience. Since the success of the hunt hung largely on his ability to make his harpoons stick and to wreak damage with his lance on the poor beast's innards, he also needed strength, agility, and a rudimentary knowledge of cetacean anatomy. The steersman took his place in the stern and managed the large steering oar. Although subordinate to the harpooner under normal circumstances, he too had to make quick, independent decisions, once the heat of the chase and the thrashing of the whale had begun to interrupt the regular chain of command. As accurately as they could, both of these endsmen had to follow the movements of the whale; their judgment on where the creature was headed—not an easy matter since it spent most of its time below the surface—often decided the contest. The three or four oarsmen, by comparison, were relatively unskilled, the chief requirements in this post being a strong back and the ability to row. Since handling an oar was as easy to learn as it was backbreaking to execute, the position attracted, as we shall see, a different class of men.[14]

On occasion, companies entered the chase alone, but more frequently they hunted in groups. Alone they stood the chance, if the whale were captured, of claiming the entire prize for themselves; with a sixty-barrel whale at stake, this could mean the equivalent on land of over half a year's wages for each man.[15] In pairs or threesomes, however, though the animal would have to be shared, companies were far less likely to run into danger or to lose their prey completely. The parties might wrangle over their portions of oil and bone, but in the course of time whalemen worked out equitable methods of sharing the produce.[16]

If the chase succeeded, the whalemen towed the dead leviathan back to shore, where pieces of blubber were cut and stripped from its body with the help of a capstan. The blubber was wheeled off in carts to the tryhouses, where the oil was boiled out, cooled down, and poured into wooden casks. The oil, along with the bundles of scrubbed whalebone, was then hauled over the island and stored in warehouses in preparation for shipment to market.[17]

The whaling industry of Nantucket was blessed throughout most of the later colonial period with extraordinarily healthy markets. Owing in part to the collapse of the Dutch North Atlantic fishery and in part to rising demand in Britain and America, oil prices moved upward from about £8 sterling per barrel in 1725 to £10 in 1730, to £13–14 in the 1750s and 1760s, to almost £30 on the eve of the Revolution.[18] The incentive to carry the chase out onto the deep and exceed the limited range of the shore fishery was therefore enormous. Accordingly, about 1715, when Nantucketers first discovered that another species of whale, the spermaceti, frequented the ocean waters beyond sight of land, they began sending out small sloops and schooners with crews of twelve or thirteen on regular short voyages in pursuit. Hunting from the two whaleboats carried on board, and cutting up the creatures at sea, they packed the blubber into casks and brought it home every two or three weeks to be boiled out in the tryhouses that stood near the town wharf.[19]

The spermaceti was smaller than the right whale; it was also swifter, hence more difficult to catch; and it lacked the strips of whalebone that in its counterpart made up to half the value of the carcass. The oil rendered from its body, however, was of a higher grade than that of other cetaceans, and the pure "headmatter" culled from the case in its skull commanded between double and triple the price of common whale oil. It was this "parmecitys" that excited the islanders' acquisitive instincts and drew them out farther and farther from their native shores. By 1730, Nantucket whalers were carrying copper pots with them and establishing temporary tryworks anywhere on the coast from Newfoundland to the Carolinas that they found convenient. Finally, after 1750, merchants who wished to cut their vessels free from the coastline entirely and thus engage them in voyages of several months' duration began to have the trypots installed in brick housings right on the ship's deck. Such technological advances caused the annual product of each deep-sea whaleman to climb from 8.3 barrels in 1715 to 16.7 barrels by the 1770s. Under this impetus, the total output of Nantucket's ocean-going vessels soared from 600 barrels in 1715, to 3,700 in 1730, to 11,250 in 1748, and finally to 30,000 by 1775.[20]

The radical lengthening of voyages that made such growth possible transformed the character of whaling as an occupation. The shore fishery of course involved brutal and dangerous work. Storms, shoals, and angry whales could pound a whaleboat to pieces in a moment, leaving its crew at the mercy of the deep. Flying loops of towline, paid out from the craft to reduce tension while being hauled along by the fleeing beast, could wrap around a hand or an arm and snap it from the body like a brittle twig. Up the coast in Boston harbor, one extraordinarily trusting young seaman named Jonathan Webb was killed when "in coiling up the line unadvisedly he did it about his middle thinking the whale to be dead, but suddenly she gave a Spring and drew him out of the boat, he being in the midst of the line."[21] Even a safely concluded chase was not necessarily a successful one; more often than not, all that a whaleman gained from his hours of straining at the oars was an aching back. In small doses, however, all of this could be borne easily enough, especially when balanced against the spacious living quarters, the fresh food and water, and the proximity to one's family and friends that the shore fishery allowed.

Whaling at sea, by comparison, admitted none of these possibilities. After three or four months of cruising the Atlantic, the tedious spells of inactivity, the rancid meat and stinking water, the cramped quarters, and, above all, the restrictions on one's freedom wore heavily on most whalemen's nerves. "No whales to be seen," complained young Peleg Folger off the Carolina coast in 1751: "Much toil and Labour Mortal man is forc^d to endure & Little profit to be Got by it."[22] And as the ordinary hardships increased, so did the physical danger. Zaccheus Macy, an eighteenth-century islander, speaking for the English if not the Indians, claimed that in all the years of shore whaling there, not a single man was lost. The annals of the deep-sea fishery, by comparison, record dozens of fatal accidents. On a voyage to the eastward of the Grand

Banks, some crewmates of the same Peleg Folger were in pursuit of a large spermaceti when suddenly "she gave a flank & went down & coming up again, She bolted her head out of the Water almost if not quite down to her fins: And then pitch^d the whole weight of her head on the Boat & Stove the Boat & ruin^d her & kill^d their midshipman, an Indian Named Sam Samson Outwright." A "sad and awful Providence," Folger termed it, but not an uncommon one, at least in the experience of a seasoned deep-sea whaleman.[23] Such a life demanded levels of commitment quite foreign to the shore fishery.

Every hand was paid a share or "lay," expressed as a fraction of the whales his company caught. In the shore fishery, once the owner of the boat had taken one-quarter of the bone and oil to cover his investment, the remainder was divided among the crew; each of the six whalemen, therefore, received a one-eighth lay. On deep-sea voyages, the share of labor was further trimmed by half to defray the cost of keeping the ocean-going vessel afloat.[24] What all this meant in absolute amounts is difficult to tell. Different companies met with varying levels of success: some might kill several whales in the space of a few weeks, while others could pass the entire season without a single capture. The few financial records that pertain to the shore fishery, however, suggest that lays were generally unimpressive. None of the surviving account books that report "oyl & bone got along shore" mention any instances of annual earnings greater than £5 sterling.[25] Ocean voyages paid better over the course of the year because they could be extended through a longer season; but recast on a monthly basis, the lays of Nantucket oarsmen usually ranged no higher than £1–2 sterling per month, about what a common Boston mariner could expect to earn.[26] One might be able to support a household on an income of this size, but not in much comfort. Would the sons of freeborn Englishmen consent to work in the lower ranks of this demanding trade on such terms?

Apparently not, for throughout its first fifty years, the Nantucket whaling industry recruited most of its hands from the Indian community. This was particularly true of the shore fishery. "Nearly every boat," wrote Obed Macy in 1830, "was manned in part, many almost entirely, by natives: some of the most active of them were made steersmen, and some were allowed even to head the boats." My research reveals not a single reference to white men credited with earnings from shore whaling, save occasionally as steersmen.[27] Likewise, the ocean-going fishery depended in its early years mostly upon Indian hands. More than half of the fifty-five oarsmen and steersmen who shipped with Silvanus Hussey, one of the island's wealthiest merchant outfitters, between 1725 and 1733 possessed identifiably Indian names. By midcentury, the balance in recruitment had tipped toward whalemen of English origin drawn mostly from the mainland; but in its early years the fishery relied to an extraordinary extent upon Indian labor.[28]

The ownership of capital, on the other hand, was concentrated entirely in the hands of the English. That Indians could not purchase ocean-going vessels is hardly a surprise, but even the whaleboats and appurtenances of the shore fishery appear to have lain beyond their reach. A list of boat owners compiled in 1726 contains mostly the names of well-established island families. Of the twenty-seven owners mentioned, eighteen were descendants of the first proprietors, the Gardners and the Coffins alone accounting for eleven; four more came from the more prominent families among the later arrivals; only the remaining five had been born off-island. The list contains not a single Indian. On one occasion, in 1758, a native islander named Peter Micah received slightly under £1 sterling for his "1/2 of boats part" from Zaccheus Macy, a whaling merchant with whom he apparently shared its ownership. Otherwise, in neither the probate records nor the account books of outfitters were Indians ever credited with whaling investments.[29] In the early years of the Nantucket whale fishery, therefore, class and ethnicity were contiguous. The English were masters; the Indians were servants; and between the two groups there was no mobility at all.

Can we explain this in strictly economic terms? Were the Indians simply too poor to buy whaleboats and equipment? Judged from probate records of the 1720s, Nantucket men who participated financially in the shore fishery normally had about £4 sterling invested in their establishments. Each company required living quarters and a whaleboat with all its accessories: oars, rigging, harpoons, lances, and hundreds of feet of high-quality line. Tryhouses had to be supplied with large trying pots, knives, spades, barrels, wheelbarrows, and a capstan. Horses, carts, warehousing, and wharfage were also necessary if the oil and bone were to be shipped to markets on the mainland. No single investor owned all of these. George Coffin, a prosperous cooper who died in 1727, owned a "tryhouse and furniture" worth £10.5 sterling and a well-equipped but ancient whaleboat appraised at £3.4. His uncle, Joseph Coffin, whose estate was probated in 1725, owned a newer boat valued with its gear at £5. A mariner named Nathan Skiffe, a newcomer to the island, held shares in two boats at his death in 1725, worth together £1.3. Outfitting a complete whaling station from scratch would probably cost over £20, but, by purchasing equipment secondhand, by sharing it, and by paying others to perform a part of the work (especially trying and carting), Nantucketers succeeded in reducing expenses to a level where most of the propertied white community could participate. In no case did shore whaling capital exceed 4 percent of the inventoried personal estate of any white islander.[30]

Expenses such as these would have placed a far greater strain on an Indian's resources. The natives who made their way into the probate records in the eighteenth century usually owned no more than a small shack, a horse or cow, a few tools, some furniture, and their clothing—an average of only £16.6 in personal wealth. These estates were not impressive by comparison to those of their shore fishery employers, which averaged £170; few Indians could muster the funds for even a modest investment of £4 or £5.[31]

This purely economic explanation, however, tells only part of the story, for in maritime New England capital equipment of this nature was normally bought not with ready funds but on credit. In Essex County, fishermen who were no wealthier than the Nantucket Indians could secure advances in supplies well over £100 if their creditors were in the market for fish.[32] Moreover, the whale fishery was profitable: the returns on a single capture could recompense the boat owner for his entire investment and more. Even a moderately successful season would have freed the Indian investor of the debts incurred in the initial outlay. Why, then, did native Nantucketers never purchase whaleboats? Were they uninterested, or did their English neighbors consider them poor risks? Perhaps allowing Indians to control their own labor did not fit into the white men's plans. But what were their plans? To resolve these problems adequately, we must retrace our steps and examine the history of economic relations between the two groups from their earliest encounters.

Nantucket is such a treeless and barren place today that it is difficult to imagine how it once could have supported 2,500 Indians. Before contact with the Europeans, almost 55 natives were squeezed onto every square mile of soil, a density many times that of mainland New England and the equal of most parts of western Europe.[33] The truth is that at the beginning of the seventeenth century, Nantucket, for all its infertility, possessed in some abundance most of what Indians required for their subsistence. Not only was the island stocked with deer and other game, but its freshwater ponds held great flocks of waterfowl, and the surrounding ocean teemed with fish and shellfish.[34] The Indians sustained themselves by exploiting these resources in a seasonal pattern. Like all coastal Algonkians, they lived in semipermanent villages surrounded by partially cleared fields and large tracts of forest, which they maintained by slash-and-burn techniques as hunting parks. John Brereton, who visisted the islands south of Cape Cod in 1602, reported that the woods were so clear of undergrowth that "in the thickest parts . . . you can see a furlong or more round about."[35] Every spring, the Indians planted corn, beans, and squash among the stumps in the fields near their villages, then departed for temporary camps near the ocean. Although they came back periodically to tend their crops, most of the summer was spent along the shore, fishing from canoes, gathering shellfish, and drying both for winter consumption. That Nantucket and all of seaboard New England could support a population so much greater than that of the interior, testifies to the importance of marine creatures in the diet. The Indians returned from the shore in September for the harvest and spent the remainder of the year based in their villages, venturing out only to hunt.[36]

The English settlers wrought many changes in Indian society, most of them catastrophic. Their agriculture eventually destroyed the fertility of the island, denuding it of trees and exposing its soil to the relentless action of the wind. Their fecundity and their appetite for property crowded the original inhabitants into an ever-shrinking portion of the land. Most important, their diseases eventually wiped out the entire native population. In the beginning, however, the Indians entertained the idea of admitting the English as neighbors with few misgivings. Because their own numbers had been declining since the first European contacts at the beginning of the century, they were willing enough by 1660 to sell the rights to settle on what they saw as functionally surplus land. The newcomers were few in number and seemed prepared to recognize all native rights not specifically restricted by the deed of sale.[37] Best of all, the settlers could provide Indians with European goods.

Both parties were eager to trade, the Indians because they recognized the low cost and technological superiority of English manufacturers, and the settlers because they needed commodities to send to Boston for goods that the island could not produce. The survival of an account book kept by the Starbuck family between 1683 and 1757 allows us to examine the nature of this trade. Until the end of the seventeenth century, almost 90 percent of the goods that Indians bought from the Starbucks consisted of cloth, apparel, and equipment for farming, fishing, and hunting (see table 1). Shoes, coats, woolen cloth, fishhooks, lines, powder and shot, horses, and ploughshares were the most sought-after items; foodstuffs were almost never purchased. In return, they brought in feathers, grain, and fish, each of which the Starbucks probably sent to the mainland. In essence, the natives were employing English technology partly in order to produce a surplus that could be exchanged for manufactured goods and probably also to save labor.[38]

In the seventeenth century, the Indians bargained from a position of strength. Because they provided most of their own food, shelter, and fuel, they rarely had to trade from real desperation. Furthermore, as the native population succumbed to diseases, the supply of Indian goods began a parallel decline, leaving whatever the lucky survivors could produce in considerable demand. Now they could take their business to any of a growing number of white families that kept a stock of goods, playing one off against another, taking advantage of the scarcity of their own labor. Every white trader had to

TABLE 1
Purchases of Selected Indians from Starbuck Family, 1680–1750

	Cloth and Clothing	Food	Productive Equipment	Services, Cash, and Misc.
1680–1700 (n = 12)	60	7	30	3
1701–1720 (n = 13)	35	9	38	19
1721–1750 (n = 9)	38	12	9	41

Note: Indians were selected for the legibility and completeness of their accounts. The figures represent a percentage of the value of total purchases. See Mary and Nathaniel Starbuck Account Book, 1662–1757.

confront this dilemma: how could one maintain the volume of one's trade and keep the costs of native produce down in the face of a decline in supply and an increase in demand? Under the pressures of competition, these traders resorted to a potent commercial weapon: the extension of credit.

Too easily, historians make connections between credit and wealth, debt and poverty. While it is obvious that those who lend money must have wealth to lend, it is less clear that those who borrow are necessarily needy. The decision to extend credit is ultimately the creditor's; the amount of goods and cash he is willing to advance depends on the advantage he sees in the action. Earned interest could be one attraction, but in colonial New England, where interest rates were rarely attached to retail accounts, the primary function of credit was to enable the lender to gain control over the labor and property of the borrower. In Europe, where labor was plentiful and inexpensive, it was land, the scarcest element in the process of production, that the serious moneylender hoped most to acquire. In the New World, as the native population collapsed, land lay increasingly vacant and labor became the dearest factor. Colonial merchants advanced goods in order to assure themselves in the coming year the fruits of their customers' toil.

To virtually every Indian with whom they dealt, the Starbucks advanced enough cloth and other supplies (although never more than £10 worth) to oblige him to continue bringing in his produce. We can follow this process in detail for the Starbuck family; we know that the same techniques were also used by other settlers. Hardly a session passed in the Nantucket courts during the seventeenth century without a Swain, Hussey, or Gardner launching an action against some native debtor who was refusing to continue this exchange.[39]

The courts were essential to the working of the system. Only if defaulting debtors could be apprehended could white traders be assured that Indians would honor their obligations. Under similar conditions in the Canadian west at the end of the eighteenth century, the Hudson's Bay Company attempted to use credit in the fur trade to build up a dependable clientele of native trading partners. The system functioned well enough in the wilderness as long as the company could monopolize trade through a small number of posts, but with the rise in competition from Montreal traders after 1763, the credit system became unmanageable. The Indian to whom goods had been advanced could disappear into the forest and carry his furs in the ensuing year to another trader at a different post. Where there was no legal guarantee that debts could be collected, the extension of credit was impracticable.[40] On Nantucket the collection of debts was, by the standard of the times, remarkably easy. The local courts were close at hand and dominated by magistrates, often traders themselves, who understood the need for strictly enforcing native obligations. More important, the limited and featureless confines of the island left few places to hide; unless the debtor could escape to the mainland (leaving behind his kin, his property, and his rights as a member of the tribe), he could not evade the arm of the law.

The extension of credit soon found a useful adjunct in the liquor trade. Alcohol as an item of exchange had risks: as often as not, drinking encouraged in the Indians precisely the stubborn, unpredictable, and even violent behavior that Englishmen feared most. In strictly economic terms, however, liquor possessed one enormous advantage: the elasticity of its demand. The native economy could absorb only so many blankets and knives, whereas a pot of wine or rum could be consumed in a moment and refilled. In the Canadian west, the trade in strong drink reached its peak in the period 1760–1820, when rivalry between the Hudson's Bay and North West companies was most intense.[41] Likewise, on Nantucket a crowd of aggressive English traders, locked in sharp competition among themselves, employed alcohol as a means of gaining control over Indian labor. "Many of the inhabitants," noted Thomas Macy in 1676, "do frequently purchase it p[re]tending for their own use and sel it to the Indians."[42] The chief offender in this regard was John Gardner, a settler from Salem with merchant connections, who carried on a fishing operation with the help of Indian hands. According to Macy, these merchants "have some Yeares past sent Goods to trade with the Indians upon the accompt of Fishing and otherwise and great quantities of strong Liquor have been sent . . . The agent here [Gardner] that carried on the Trade for the Gentlemen hath bargained with the Indians to give each Man a dram before they go out fishing in the Morning; but under that p[re]tense much Abuse hath bin."[43] Recently, Gardner had delivered a shipment of sixteen gallons to the Indians, but as it was, in the words of Macy, a trader himself, merely "a small Quantity," we can assume that the trade was normally quite vigorous. To the end of the colonial period, in fact, drink remained an important source of native indebtedness.[44]

The practice of advancing credit took hold on the island because the Indians appreciated the *short-term* advantages it afforded and because each English trader wished to build up a dependable circle of customers who would be obliged to supply him with trade goods on a continual basis. As the entire body of traders turned to this system, it became a type of communal labor control, an informal brand of debt peonage. Its purpose was not to force the Indian to trade, for he was anxious to do that on his own accord, but to limit the competition over the fruits of his labor and thereby to control their price.

The white Nantucketers who launched the shore fishery in the 1690s were certain about two things. First, though they participated in the chase as steersmen or harpooners, they refused the menial labor of manning the oars. Partly, they knew that rowing after whales was exhausting and dangerous toil; partly, they thought it demeaning to work for others. After all, they had hardly moved to the island to become servants. Since Nantucket was out of the way and shore whaling was a seasonal occupation, recruiting hands from the mainland was unlikely to meet with success. Under these circumstances, the only viable source of labor was the local Indian population.

Second, the English insisted on retaining complete control of the industry themselves. In Indian-white relations on Nantucket, this was a significant departure. Until the 1690s the settlers had always advanced such capital equipment as fishing lines, powder, and shot to the Indians, interest-free, on the promise of being repaid in local produce. The natives remained independent operators, following traditional pursuits with European technology and selling their surpluses to the English to finance their purchases. Some Indians were accustomed to work on occasion in the white community—ploughing, carting, or harvesting—but almost no one worked for his English neighbors on a regular basis.[45] Now, in the shore fishery, Indians were being asked for the first time to participate not as self-employed men working with their own tools and equipment, but as servants.

Some might argue that the Indians were not interested in investing capital equipment on this scale.[46] Profits and accumulated wealth, it is true, were utterly foreign to the native ethos, but the privilege of working on one's own terms was not. Indifferent to legal ownership though they were, the alternative of toiling at the oars under the command of white steersmen while relinquishing one-quarter of each whale to their employers "for the Boat & Craft" was new and unwelcome. The same point—that ownership equaled control—was driven home even more forcefully when, about 1715, the launching of the more capital-intensive deep-sea fishery resulted in whalemen's lays being slashed in half. Indignantly, the Indians petitioned the General Court and complained of their white neighbors' policy of allowing them "but half Price for their Whaling." When called upon to answer, the Nantucket representative to the court, Joseph Coffin, obviously perplexed that anyone would challenge the right of an employer to determine the terms of employment, replied that the Indians had "no reason to Complain, they being allowed according to the Custom of the Island, one Half . . . which is a proportion as is allowed to white Men." The court, too, was a bit mystified by the petition and the matter was dropped.[47] It is difficult to image that, in the light of this incident, the Indians remained oblivious to the advantages of capital ownership.

The real barrier to investment in the shore fishery by natives was their reputation for unreliability. Although the English were willing, even anxious, to entrust the Indians with debts, they were highly skeptical of the latter's capacity for regular daily work. In the first decades of interracial trade, the Starbucks' native clients delivered their produce at irregular intervals, often only two or three times a year, and the annual volume of business swung up and down erratically. If white Nantucketers were to spend time and money building boats, forging harpoons, and purchasing cordage from the mainland, they wanted men ready to join the chase every day throughout the whaling season. As long as the natives were allowed to own the boats they worked in, they would only hang around the beach watching for whales (the English were perhaps correctly convinced), if it suited their wider economic interests; once these were satisfied, they might well head back to their villages. Such routines of work as these were inconsistent with the levels of return that the English demanded.

Whites perceived this sort of behavior as typical of a people who had "little Regard to their own wellfare."[48] In reality, what they saw as irresponsibility was more often simple independence. For those who preferred to stay on shore and work on their own, there were still ways of supporting themselves within the native economy. The supply of fish and shellfish, always the major source of nutrition for the Nantucket tribe, was almost limitless. Waterfowl were still abundant, and the herds of deer did not diminish for many decades.[49] Of an island that in 1700 was "much commended for goodness of soil," Indians still owned over half in 1690 and about a quarter in 1720.[50]

While the traditional Indian economy remained intact, perhaps in the short run enhanced by the application of European technology, the human demands on their portion of the island diminished. The native population of Nantucket had been declining ever since the initial contact with white men at the beginning of the seventeenth century (see table 2)—so rapidly, indeed, that until well into the eighteenth century, the quantity of land owned by individual survivors probably rose. And since the Indians continued to enjoy free access to the sea, as well as hunting and gathering rights on many parts of the island that they had already sold, the mere fact of ownership underestimates the resources within a native's reach. The admittedly substantial estate of Jeremy Netowa, an Indian whaleman who died at sea in 1728, contained not only the earnings from his voyage but also spinning wheels, livestock, and the produce of his fields.[51] Even Isaac Cododah, whose estate (valued at £5.7 sterling) was the poorest of any recorded on the island in the colonial period, owned at his death in 1721, besides his personal effects, a hog and twenty bushels of grain.[52] As table 1 demonstrates, the natives did grow dependent on their English neighbors for a number of items, above all cloth and clothing; and after 1720, when they began to spend more and more of the spring and

TABLE 2
Indian Population of Nantucket, 1600–1792

Year	Population	Year	Population
1600	2,500	1700	800
1640	2,000	1763	358
1670	1,250	1764	136
1698	830	1792	22

Sources: Cook, Indian Population of New England, 42–43; Z. Macy, "Journal of Nantucket," 158–59; O'Callaghan et al., eds., NY Col. Docs., IV, 787.

summer months in the deep-sea fishery, they had to pay white islanders to look after their fields.[53] Through the first quarter of the eighteenth century, however, they remained remarkably self-sufficient and could afford to be choosy about the terms on which they worked.

The white boat owners were therefore in a quandry: Indian whalemen, because of their shrinking numbers and natural independence, were growing difficult to recruit. As the competition over their labor increased, and the need for discipline became evident, so too did the temptation to draw them into indebtedness and servitude.

The links between indebtedness and the shore fishery in the early eighteenth century can be viewed through the records of probate. Of the eight islanders, all white, who died in possession of whaling gear, whaleboats, or tryhouses between 1700 and 1730, six were credited with Indian debts that ranged from £8.5 to £45.1 sterling. Among the eight (five whites, two Indians, and one free Negro) with no whaling appurtenances to their name, money was owed by natives to only one, Nathaniel Barnard, and he owned a fishing operation.[54] Those who dictated the division of their estates on their deathbeds always grouped the two together. Jonathan Bunker, a farmer who died in 1721, bequeathed to his four sons "all my whaling and fishing Craft with all my Indian debts."[55] In 1725, Stephen Coffin, Jr., left to his sons, Shubael and Zephaniah, "the one half of my fishing and whaling craft with the half of all my Indian debts," and to his wife, Experience, the other half of these debts and half of "Everything used or improved in the Carrying on and Managing the fishing and whaling voyages . . . and all my Shipping Imploy'd in fishing and whaling on Nantucket shoals."[56]

Indebtedness had been important in Indian-white relations since the very beginning, but to the shore fishery it was indispensable. A series of exchanges between native islanders, the English inhabitants, and the General Court in Boston makes this plain. In November 1716, an Indian named John Punker petitioned the General Court on behalf of his tribe, "Complaining of great Injustice and Oppression they suffer from some of their *English* Neighbours," and requesting that Nantucket be annexed to some other county so that, in legal contests with the settlers, they might obtain justice before impartial courts. Why was this becoming an issue in 1716? The petition has been lost, but its content is revealed by the resulting order that a committee of three be sent to Nantucket to "enquire into the Matters of Grievance Complained of; and more especially their Whaling: And Assist the Indians in making a proper Representation thereof to [the] Court."[57] The committee visited the island that winter, spent twelve days in investigation, and presented their report the following June. The report too has disappeared, but it must have testified to the truth of Punker's claims, for the General Court decided to act. Although for reasons of physical convenience it denied the annexation request, the court in effect conceded the Indians' difficulty in obtaining justice from the white islanders when it ordered that two magistrates from the mainland be appointed as "Justices . . . of the Peace, to Hear & Determine, all Causes and Matters of Difference, between the English & Indians, and Indian & Indians on the said Island. And that a Bill be prepared accordingly."[58] In June 1718, this bill, entitled "An Act in Addition to the Act for Preventing Abuses to the Indians," was passed and made law. Its preamble, describing these abuses, was drawn from the experience of Nantucket and its whale fishery: "notwithstanding the care taken and provided by said act, a great wrong and injury happens to said Indians, natives of this country, by reason of their being drawn in by small gifts, or for small debts, when they are in drink, and out of capacity for trade, to sign unreasonable bills or bonds for debts, which are soon sued, and great charge brought upon them, when they have no way to pay the same but by servitude."[59] The act went on to declare that no bond or labor contract could be made with an Indian without the approbation of two local justices of the peace, who would ensure (so the legislators hoped) that the Indian had entered into the agreement out of choice. It was the possibility of coercion in the drawing up of indentures that concerned them; to the idea of servitude they had no objection. Indeed, the purpose of the act was to establish a formal indenting procedure.

With the rise of the deep-sea fishery after 1716, the competition over available hands grew even more acute. Each new voyage required eight to ten oarsmen and steersmen to perform work that was both more tedious and more disruptive to the Indians' domestic economy than the shore fishery had ever been. Coercion became so routine in the recruitment process that by the early 1720s the General Court was flooded with Indian complaints of indebtedness and ill-treatment.[60] In 1725, therefore, it supplemented the 1718 legislation with still another act, the general intent of which was to reinforce the earlier laws against fraudulent indentures and to prohibit the binding of Indian householders. Recognizing the necessity, however, "as well for the English as the Indians . . . that the Indians be employed in the whaling and other fishing voyages," the court agreed to grant an exemption for the whaling towns of Cape Cod, Martha's Vineyard, and Nantucket. Native whalemen might henceforth be bound for up to two years at a time, and their employers could contract to "assist the said Indians in building houses for them on their own lands, and furnish them and their families as well with fuel, as necessary subsistence, during such time."[61] An indebted Indian who entered into such an indenture would be required not only to work for his master but to procure supplies from him as well. The cycle of dependence was thus complete: whaling employers could bind their native seamen to as long as a series of two-year stints as they pleased, provided that they took responsibility for their upkeep. Fraud had been prohibited, but servitude was now institutionalized.

By 1730, few Indian whalemen were working on their own account. Of those hired in both the shore and deep-sea fisheries between 1725 and 1733 by

Silvanus Hussey, probably the greatest whaling merchant of the period, at least three-quarters were indebted clients of white islanders. Listed anonymously as "Indians" or "hands," these men were under obligation to deliver their earnings to their white masters after every voyage.[62]

Some of these agreements were formal indentures. Jonas Cooper, an Indian mariner from Martha's Vineyard, who was living on Nantucket in the early 1720s, fell into debt to a cooper and whaleboat owner named John Clark. Clark eventually forced Cooper to "seal, bind and oblige himself to go whaling for him both winter and summer voyages for the space of three years." Cooper, who was unusual in this period for being an off-islander, fled with his belongings after a year's service, and Clark learned a lesson in the advantages of hiring local help.[63] A more detailed indenture survives from Cape Cod, where in 1737 an Indian named Robin Mesrick, in order to repay a debt of £9 to his creditor, Gideon Holway, agreed to "worke On Shoar and Whale for him Three years." In return, Holway was to pay Mesrick 11s a month for his labor on land and

> when he Goes on the Spring [deep-sea] Whaleing to find him a suitable Berth to Proceed in voiages In and to allow him half an Eighteenth of what is Obtained On Each of Spring voiages after the vessels Parte is first deducted and to finde him his Diat & Liquor on s'd Spring voiage into the Bargaine, and on the Bay [shore] voiages the s'd Robin may find himself Diat house room & wood and have a whole Eighth Clear according to Custom and if s'd Holway finds him Diat half his house room & wood then s'd Robin to Draw but Half an Eighth as according to custom.

The whole of Mesrick's earnings was to go toward repaying the debt after deductions were made for clothing and other current necessities. If he succeeded in amassing the sum before the three years were out, he was to be freed from all further obligations.[64]

The rarity of surviving indentures suggests that many, perhaps most, of these agreements were informal. Certain of the terms were customary and understood; others were probably in a constant state of renegotiation. Insults, threats, sulking, and brute force were all part of a bargaining idiom in which both parties tried to obtain the best terms possible. Indians were anxious to avoid the heavy hand of the island's courts, and as long as the threat of prosecution was present, merchants could usually get what they wanted without recourse to law. Naturally, records of the thrusts and parries of this subtle interchange were never kept, but an account of recruiting practices on Martha's Vineyard in 1806 may help to give an idea of how it operated:

> The business of inviting the Indians is a sort of crimping, in which liquor, goods and fair words are plied, till the Indian gets into debt, and gives his consent. Taking the history from the mouths of white people only, it appears that there is often much to be complained of in the business of the voyage, both in

the Indian and in those with whom he connects himself. On the one hand great advantage is taken of his folly, his credulity and his ignorance. On the other, he torments the ship or share owner with his indecision and demands, till the moment of the sailing of the ship. First, he agrees to go, and accordingly receives some stipulated part of his outfit; then he "thinks he won't go;" and then he is to be coaxed and made drunk. Again he "thinks" he "won't go" unless such and such articles are supplied; and these articles he often names at random for the sake of inducing a refusal. One Indian was mentioned to me that he thought he would not go unless five pounds of soap were given him; and another thought the same unless he received seven hats.[65]

If bargaining along these lines came to nothing, merchants could resort to force. In 1747, Paul Quaab from Sakedan Indian Town at the east end of the island complained to the General Court that a man named James Gase (Chase), with the assistance of the constable and two other men, had forcibly carried him away from his home on the back of a horse and sent him out whaling, although, in his words, "I was no ways obliged to him by any account or bromes [sic] to go whaling so long time [f]or I never bromesth."[66] The Nantucket selectmen denied the truth of Quaab's assertions but did concede the existence of "some Evil minded persons among us that makes a trade of supplying the Indians with Rum and have had the produce of their Land and Labour for little or no value."[67] Another group of Indians objected to being dragged off to whale on the Sabbath. As they argued,

> how can we be any ways be like christians when we should be praying to God on the Sabbath day morning then we must be Rowing after whal or killing whal or cutting up whal on Sabbath day when we should be at rest on that day and do no worly labour only to do sum holy duties to draw near to God and when on land then we have no time to go to the meeting and then we are call to go away again to sea whaling. how can we serve God or to worship him on the Sabbath days or at any time when our masters lead us to darkness and not In light[?][68]

Clearly, the need to spend every hour on the lookout was more obvious to the white men than to their Indian servants. Force was sometimes the only insurance that hands would be in ready supply.

Coercion was indeed the key. In the early years of the whale fishery on Nantucket, capitalism and free labor could never coexist. The continued vitality of the native economy, the declining supply of local whalemen, and the burgeoning demands of the fishery all combined to strengthen the natural bargaining position of the Indian and to leave the labor-hungry whaling merchants no alternative but the use of force. In itself, this does not explain the special importance of Indian labor. If the native islanders were hesitant to ship themselves as oarsmen on the white men's terms, surely the English boat owners could have sent their own sons to sea or procured indentured servants from the mainland.[69] That they chose not to do so suggests that free market forces alone cannot account for the entire story, but that native labor attracted English employers precisely because coercion was necessary and the natives could be coerced.

White Nantucketers, writing at the end of the eighteenth century when the aboriginal population had nearly disappeared, retained a sentimental fondness for their Indian neighbors of earlier years. Zaccheus Macy remembered them as kind and hospitable, always ready, "if the English entered their houses, whilst they were eating . . . to offer them such as they had, which sometimes would be very good."[70] In 1807 an anonymous member of the Massachusetts Historical Society described them in a similar way, adding that the natives were "religiously punctual" in their payments to the English, and that "they made excellent oarsmen, and some of them were good endsmen."[71] Nevertheless, this adulation was bought at a price. Our anonymous contributor concluded, "So useful have men of this class been found in the whale fishery, that the Indians having disappeared, negroes are now substituted in their place. Seamen of colour are more submissive than the whites."[72] The implication was clear: Indians, like blacks, merited praise, but only as long as they bent to the white man's rule. An anecdote related by Macy, a onetime employer of Indian whalemen himself, reveals this attitude in a particularly compelling manner:

> But it happened once, when there were about thirty boats about six miles from the shore, that the wind came round to the northward, and blew with great violence, attended with snow. The men all rowed hard, but made little head way. In one of the boats there were four Indians and two white men. An old Indian in the head of the boat, perceiving that the crew began to be disheartened, spake out loud in his own tongue and said, *Momadichchator auqua sarshkee sarnkee pinchee eyoo sememoochkee chaquanks wihchee pinchee eyoo*: which in English is, "Pull a head with courage: do not be disheartened: we shall not be lost now: there are too many Englishmen to be lost now." His speaking in this manner gave the crew new courage. They soon perceived that they made head way; and after long rowing, they all got safe on shore.[73]

In Macy's conviction of the esteem in which Indian whalemen held the English, so that only the threat of a lost white man could rally them, even in the face of death, the story is almost touching. Men so apparently devoted to their masters were fond memories indeed.

What white Nantucketers perceived as natural submissiveness, however, was rather the product of a long and lively struggle. Macy came of age only in 1734, by which time the years of native independence had passed. The Indians he knew in the 1730s and 1740s, vastly outnumbered, riddled by disease, barred by their ethnicity from the avenues of social mobility, and trapped in the southeast corner of the island, were a defeated people. In truth, only the forcible deprivation of their independence had made the success of the whale fishery possible.

Neither labor scarcity nor coercion in recruitment was unique to Nantucket. The Spanish mines and haciendas of Mexico and Peru, the Portuguese sugar plantations of Brazil, and the British sugar and tobacco colonies of the West Indies and the Chesapeake all demanded a level of commitment to work and submission to discipline that free Europeans were reluctant to provide, and all turned in time to the institution of bondage. Indeed, in the New World of the seventeenth and eighteenth centuries, New England was an anomaly, for it flourished without resorting to widespread formal servitude. Nevertheless, where conditions were appropriate, as the case of the whale fishery illustrates; colonists in Massachusetts felt the same need to restrict labor's freedom as did their southern counterparts. Granted, by comparison to the forms of servitude that prevailed in the plantation colonies, debt peonage as practiced on Nantucket was both a gentler solution and easier to scuttle when it no longer made economic sense. The principle involved, however, was little different. As long as land in the New World remained sufficiently abundant that an ordinary European could entertain real possibilities of obtaining a plot of his own, market-oriented production and free labor would seldom keep company.

NOTES

Acknowledgments: The author wishes to extend particular thanks to Ted Byers for his scholarly aid and criticism. An earlier version of the article was presented at the Boston University Colloquium in Early American History, March 1981, and at the Millersville Conference in Early American History, May 1981.

1. Obed Macy, *The History of Nantucket: Being a Compendious Account of the First Settlement of the Island by English, Together with the Rise of Progress of the Whale Fishery* . . . (Boston, 1835), 33.

2. Sherburne Cooke, *The Indian Population of New England in the Seventeenth Century* (Berkeley, Calif., 1976), 41–45.

3. Alexander Starbuck, *The History of Nantucket: County, Island and Town* . . . (Rutland, Vt., 1969; orig. pub. Boston, 1924), 20–22. On the nature of Indian deeds see Francis Jennings, *The Invasion of America: Indians, Colonialism, and the Cant of Conquest* (Chapel Hill, N.C., 1975), 128–45.

4. Glover M. Allen, "The Whalebone Whales of New England," in Boston Society of Natural History, *Memoires*, VIII (1916), 146–58, hereafter cited as Allen, "Whalebone Whales"; Alexander Starbuck, *History of the American Whale Fishery: From Its Earliest Inception to the Year 1876*, 2 vols. (New York, 1964; orig. pub. Washington, D.C., 1878), 1:7, 9, 10; William B. Weeden, *Economic and Social History of New England, 1620–1789*, 2 vols. (New York, 1963; orig. pub. 1890), 1:432.

5. Starbuck, *Nantucket*, 128–30, 172.

6. Starbuck, *Whale Fishery*, 1:9–13; Allen, "Whalebone Whales," 148; William R.

Palmer, "The Whaling Port of Sag Harbor" (Ph.D. diss., Columbia University, 1959), ch. 1.

7. Starbuck, *Nantucket*, 32–33, 33n.

8. Starbuck, *Whale Fishery*, 1:22.

9. Allen, "Whalebone Whales," 141–43.

10. Paul Dudley, "An Essay upon the Natural History of Whales, with a Particular Account of the Ambergris Found in the *Sperma Ceti* Whale," Royal Society of London, *Philosophical Transactions*, 33 (1725), 257.

11. Allen, "Whalebone Whales," 170–71; William Scoresby, *An Account of the Arctic Regions, with a History and Description of the Nothern Whale-Fishery*, 2 vols. (New York, 1969; orig. pub. Edinburgh, 1820), 2:156–57. One barrel of oil equaled 31½ gallons.

12. J. Hector St. John de Crèvecoeur, *Letters from an American Farmer* (New York, 1957; orig. pub. London, 1782), 110.

13. Dudley, "Natural History of Whales," Royal Soc. London, *Phil. Trans.*, 33 (1725), 263.

14. Ibid.; Crèvecoeur, *Letters*, 110–11; O. Macy, *Nantucket*, 30–31; Felix Christian Spörri, *Americanische Reiss-beschreibung nach den Caribes Insslen und Neu-Engelland* (Zurich, 1677), 44–45, quoted in Carl Bridenbaugh, *Fat Mutton and Liberty of Conscience: Society in Rhode Island, 1636–1690* (Providence, R.I., 1974), 144–45; *Griffin & Co. v. Thomas*, 2 Mass. Vice-Admiralty Court, 27–28 (1718); *Davis v. Sturges*, 2 MVAC 68 (1720); *Cowing v. Cushing*, 2 MVAC 166 (1723).

15. One man's share of a sixty-barrel whale was worth £10–15 sterling, oil and bone included, in the 1720s. For wages on land see Gary B. Nash, *The Urban Crucible: Social Change, Political Consciousness, and the Origins of the American Revolution* (Cambridge, Mass., 1979), 114–15, and Jackson Turner Main, *The Social Structure of Revolutionary America* (Princeton, N.J., 1965), 70. All prices and values in this paper have been converted from Massachusetts currency to British sterling using Table 12: Value of Massachusetts Paper Currency, 1685–1775, in Nash, *Urban Crucible*, 405–406.

16. See, for example, *Davis v. Sturges*, 2 MVAC 68 (1720).

17. O. Macy, *Nantucket*, 31.

18. Zaccheus Macy, "A Short Journal of the First Settlement of the Island of Nantucket . . . ," Massachusetts Historical Society, *Collections*, 1st ser., 3 (1794), 161, hereafter cited as Z. Macy, "Journal of Nantucket"; Silvanus Hussey Account Book, 1725–1734, Peter Foulger Museum Library, Nantucket, Mass.; William Rotch Journal B, 2 vols., 1769–1776, Old Dartmouth Historical Society, New Bedford, Mass.

19. O. Macy, *Nantucket*, 37; Z. Macy, "Journal of Nantucket," 157; Starbuck, *Nantucket*, 355–56; Silvanus Hussey Account Book, 1724–1734.

20. Starbuck, *Nantucket*, 356–58; O. Macy, *Nantucket*, 37–38, 54, 71; Z. Macy, "Journal of Nantucket," 161; Richard C. Kugler, "The Whale Oil Trade, 1750–1775," *Old Dartmouth Historical Sketch Number 79* (New Bedford, Mass., 1980), 3–9; Silvanus Hussey Account Book, 1724–1734; Mary and Nathaniel Starbuck Accounting Book, 1662–1757, Foulger Museum Lib.

21. Samuel Bradstreet, Diary, quoted in Allen, "Whalebone Whales," 154.

22. Sloop *Grampus* (1751), July 8, 1751, Peleg Folger Journal, 1751–1757, Nantucket Atheneum, Nantucket, Mass.

23. Z. Macy, "Journal of Nantucket," 157; Starbuck, *Nantucket*, 356, 356n–357n; Sloop *Phebe* (1957), Aug. 9, 1754, Peleg Folger Journal, 1751–1757.

24. Jo. Micah's Account, 1758, Miscellaneous MSS, Nantucket, Mass., American Antiquarian Society, Worcester, Mass.; Indenture of Robin Mesrick, July 6, 1737,

Miscellaneous Bound Papers, Mass. Hist. Soc., Boston, Mass.; *Clark v. Cooper*, 1 Nantucket Inferior Court of Common Pleas, 35 (1726); William Rotch Journal B, 1769–1776.

25. Mary and Nathaniel Starbuck Account Book, 1662–1757; Silvanus Hussey Account Book, 1724–1734.

26. Daniel Frederick Vickers, "Maritime Labor in Colonial Massachusetts: A Case Study of the Essex County Cod Fishery and the Whaling Industry of Nantucket, 1630–1775" (Ph.D. diss., Princeton University, 1981), 295–96; Nash, *Urban Crucible*, 414.

27. O. Macy, *Nantucket*, 30; Mary and Nathaniel Starbuck Account Book, 1662–1757; Silvanus Hussey Account Book, 1724–1734. This pattern is confirmed by evidence on the composition of crews from the mainland. Of thirty-four whalemen from Barnstable and Eastham on Cape Cod, named in a list dated Jan. 20, 1700/1, twenty-six were Indians. On the assumption that the eight Englishmen served mostly as steersmen and harpooners, we can infer that almost all the oarsmen were Indians. Attachment of Goods, Jan. 20, 1700/1, Miscellaneous Bound Papers, Mass. Hist. Soc. See also James Truslow Adams, *History of the Town of Southampton (East of Canoe Place)* (Bridgehampton, N.Y., 1918), 231, 231n; E. B. O'Callaghan et al., eds., *Documents Relative to the Colonial History of the State of New-York . . .*, 15 vols. (Albany, N.Y., 1856–1887), 14:648, 664, 675, 708–709.

28. Silvanus Hussey Account Book, 1724–1734. In calculating the ethnic composition of Hussey's crews, each whaleman was counted once for every voyage in which he participated. See also Vickers, "Maritime Labor," 283–94.

29. Starbuck, *Nantucket*, 356n; Jo. Micah's Account, 1758; Mary and Nathaniel Starbuck Account Book, 1662–1757; Silvanus Hussey Account Book, 1724–1734; John Barnard Account Book, 1699–1738, Foulger Museum Lib.; Probate Records of Nantucket County, vols. 1–3 (1706–1789), Probate Court Office, Town Hall, Nantucket, Mass., hereafter cited as Nantucket Probates.

30. Nantucket Probates 1:59–62, 70–71, 92–94, 103, 139–41, 146–47, 157, 162. It should be noted at this point that the quantifiable documentation relating to the shore fishery on Nantucket is often slim. The probate records, for example, record the estate inventories of only eight Indians and eight more shore whaling investors for the entire colonial period. I have tried to be explicit about the size of my samples and to avoid drawing distinctions too fine for the data to support.

31. Nantucket Probates, vols. 1–3 (1706–1789).

32. Vickers, "Maritime Labor," 76–77, 110–16.

33. Cook, *Indian Population of New England*, 44–45; T. J. C. Brasser, "The Coastal Algonkians: People of the First Frontiers," in Eleanor Burke Leacock and Nancy Oestreich Lurie, eds., *North American Indians in Historical Perspective* (New York, 1971), 65; Jennings, *Invasion of America*, 28; Geoffrey Barraclough, ed., *The Times Atlas of World History* (London, 1978), 180–81.

34. John Brereton, *A Briefe and True Relation of the Discoverie of the North Part of Virginia . . .* (London, 1602), 5–7; O. Macy, *Nantucket*, 16–17.

35. Brereton, *Discoverie*, 7.

36. Brasser, "Coastal Algonkians," in Leacock and Lurie, eds., *North American Indians*, 64; Dean R. Snow, *The Archaeology of New England* (New York, 1980), 76–79; William A. Ritchie, *The Archaeology of Martha's Vineyard: A Framework for the Prehistory of Southern New England* (Garden City, N.J., 1969), 81–89; "Notes on Nantucket, August 1, 1807," Mass. Hist. Soc., *Colls.*, 2d ser., 3 (1815), 34–35; O. Macy, *Nantucket*, 17.

37. For several instances of the English courts confirming Indian rights within the tract that the English had purchased, see Starbuck, *Nantucket*, 124–29.

38. Mary and Nathaniel Starbuck Account Book, 1662–1757.

39. Ibid.; Nantucket Court of Sessions of the Peace, 1672–1705, in County Records (1661–   ), vol. 2 (1672–1705), Registry of Deeds, Town Hall, Nantucket, Mass.

40. Arthur J. Ray, *Indians in the Fur Trade: Their Role as Trappers, Hunters, and Middlemen in the Lands Southwest of Hudson Bay, 1660–1870* (Toronto, 1974), 137–38, 196.

41. Ibid., 85, 198.

42. Thomas Macy to Gov. Andros, May 9, 1676, quoted in Starbuck, *Nantucket*, 59.

43. Ibid.

44. Petition of Richard Coffin and Abishai Folger to the General Court, 1752, quoted in ibid., 161; Petition of Nantucket Proprietors to the General Court, Apr. 2, 1752, quoted in ibid., 164; O. Macy, *Nantucket*, 44; Z. Macy, "Journal of Nantucket," 158; "Notes on Nantucket," Mass. Hist. Soc., *Colls.*, 2d ser., 3 (1815), 36.

45. Mary and Nathaniel Starbuck Account Book, 1662–1757.

46. Jennings, *Invasion of America*, 102–104.

47. Records of the General Court, Nov. 17, 1718, quoted in Starbuck, *Nantucket*, 143; Silvanus Hussey Account Book, 1724–1734.

48. Quotation from the Petition of Richard Coffin and Abishai Folger to the General Court, 1752, quoted in Starbuck, *Nantucket*, 161.

49. O. Macy, *Nantucket*, 17; "Notes on Nantucket," Mass. Hist. Soc., *Colls.*, 2d Ser., 3 (1815), 35.

50. Earl of Bellomont to the Lords of Trade, Nov. 28, 1700, O'Callaghan et al., eds., *NY Col. Docs.*, 4:787.

51. O. Macy, *Nantucket*, 20, 42; Nantucket Probates, 1:129. Netowa's estate was valued at £23.4 sterling.

52. Nantucket Probates, 1:75.

53. See table 1, and O. Macy, *Nantucket*, 42.

54. Nantucket Probates, 1.

55. Ibid., 1:89.

56. Ibid., 1:121, 2:214.

57. *Journals of the House of Representatives of Massachusetts*, 51 vols. (Boston, 1919–   ), 1:137–38.

58. Ibid., 245–46.

59. Ibid., 2:27; *The Acts and Resolves, Public and Private, of the Province of the Massachusetts-Bay*, 21 vols. (Boston, 1869–1922), 2:104.

60. *Acts and Resolves*, 2:159, 289, 438, 583, 668, 705.

61. Ibid., 363–65.

62. Silvanus Hussey Account Book, 1724–1734.

63. *Clark v. Cooper*, 1 Nantucket Inferior Court of Common Pleas, 35 (1726).

64. Indenture of Robin Mesrick, July 6, 1737, Indenture of Simon Porrage, Apr. 10, 1738, Miscellaneous Bound Papers, Mass. Hist. Soc.

65. Edward Augustus Kendall, *Travels through the Northern Part of the United States . . .* (New York, 1809), 2:196, quoted in Charles E. Banks, *The History of Martha's Vineyard, Dukes County, Massachusetts*, 3 vols. (Edgartown, Mass., 1911–1925), 1:440–41.

66. Petition of Paul Quaab to the General Court, May 6, 1747, quoted in Starbuck, *Nantucket*, 150–51.

67. Petition of Nantucket Selectmen to the General Court, May 27, 1747, quoted in ibid., 152.

68. Petition of Nantucket Indians to the General Court, July 14, 1747, quoted in ibid., 153–54.

69. The boat owners of Long Island manned their craft with their own sons when Indian whalemen grew scarce in the 1670s. See Palmer, "Sag Harbor," 9.

70. Z. Macy, "Journal of Nantucket," 158.

71. "Notes on Nantucket," Mass. Hist. Soc., *Colls.*, 2d ser., 3 (1815), 36.

72. Ibid.

73. Z. Macy, "Journal of Nantucket," 157.

Ruth Wallis Herndon and Ella Wilcox Sekatau

5

The Right to a Name

The Narragansett People and Rhode Island Officials in the Revolutionary Era

In 1675, in the heat of a regional war between native people and English people, New England colonists killed hundreds of the Narragansett (uninvolved in the war at that point) in an unprovoked attack on one of their winter camps located in the Great Swamp in South Kingstown, Rhode Island. Two hundred years later, in 1880, the Rhode Island state legislature, without federal approval, declared the Narragansett people "extinct" and illegally took away the tribal status of people who still called themselves by that name.[1]

In the centuries between these notorious events, generations of the Narragansett faced the choice of staying on their native land, surrounded by non-Indians, or migrating to western land less settled by European Americans. Many of these native people, deeply alienated by the religious beliefs and cultural practices of the Europeans, chose to leave: they moved mainly to Massachusetts, New York, and Wisconsin. Others stayed on ancestral lands; oral history tells us they continued tribal affairs and government, held frequent meetings, kept track of their heritage and lineage, and kept alive the religion, language, and customs of the People.

Preserving Narragansett culture on Narragansett land was an arduous task initially for those who undertook it. Within the first several decades of English colonization, Narragansett leaders realized what were the goals of these newly arrived people. European colonists brought with them attitudes toward land that clashed radically with the practices of native people. Pursuing traditional ways of gardening and hunting proved impossible for the Narragansett after English settlers altered the ecosystem by dividing the land into private tracts for individual use; by prosecuting trespassers; by cutting down forests, constructing fences, and otherwise helping to extinguish wild game; and by introducing free-ranging livestock.[2] When the Rhode Island government officially set apart sixty-four square miles of land as a Narragansett reservation in 1709, this protective act nevertheless signaled that native people could no longer move freely over their ancestral territory and freely exercise cultural practices of having summer residences and permanent residences in different places. This reserved area shrank even more during the eighteenth century, as non-Narragansett people acquired tracts through sales, theft, and gifts.[3]

The Narragansett living on the reservation could not always avoid contact with Rhode Island colonists; some found themselves pulled into the European American world by the economic necessity of working as day laborers in nearby towns.[4] Others of the Narragansett left the reservation and drifted away, physically and spiritually, from the paths of the elders. Some converted to Christianity. Some married non-Indians and merged into the cultures of European Americans and African Americans.[5] Some, prisoners at the end of the 1675–1676 conflict, or later trapped in debt to Rhode Islanders, became bound servants and thus members of European American households.[6] Oral tradition tells us that many native family and clan names disappeared, as local officials attached European names to Narragansett people who were indebted or bound to Europeans.

So things seemed to outsiders. But tribal history passed down orally from generation to generation informs us that hardship and oppression strengthened the resolve of many Narragansett people to maintain traditional ways. The majority of the Narragansett living on or around the reservation did not convert to Christianity, and those who did convert usually moved away from Rhode Island. Many of the native people whom outsiders counted as converts were actually struggling to coexist with European Americans. These Narragansett presented themselves in ways that would win the approval of outside observers and authorities; but in their own confines they continued to practice the cultural ways of the ancients. Not until the illegal detribalization of the 1880s did true conversions begin in some Narragansett families.[7]

Historians have studied this general outline of Narragansett history—although not often from the native point of view—between 1675 and 1880;[8] much less has been written about the details of relationships between native people and European Americans in Rhode Island during those two centuries. This essay attempts to amend this situation by analyzing interactions between Narragansett people and local Rhode Island officials in the latter half of the eighteenth century, a fifty-year period that sits midpoint between the Great Swamp and illegal detribalization. We investigate how European American officials viewed the Narragansett and how the Narragansett viewed those officials.

By "Narragansett" we mean native people who lived on ancestral Narragansett land in what is now called Rhode Island. (In the view of some tribal members, Narragansett territorial boundaries encompassed all of what is now Rhode Island and much more land inhabited by all the subtribal divisions and tribute tribes dwelling in what became parts of Massachusetts, Connecticut, New Hampshire, Vermont, and a small area of southeastern Maine.) Since the written records rarely refer to "the Narragansett"—only to "Indians" or "Mustees"—it is impossible to be sure that every native person in the record was indeed of the Narragansett, except where the name coincides with tribal genealogies. Some of the native people in the documents may have been members of neighboring tribes.[9] But since fourteen of the towns under study were established directly on Narragansett land and the fifteenth (Warren) bordered Narragansett land, we assumed that the majority of native people in the record were of Narragansett heritage.

We also include in this study people described in the record as "Mustees."[10] Rhode Island town records provide ample evidence that local officials used this term to refer to people of native ancestry. Town clerks described as "Mustee" (for example) the children of "Indian" women Elizabeth Broadfoot, Moll Pero, Deborah Anthony, and Lydia Rodman.[11] Contemporaries recognized "Mustee" people as native, at least in part; so do we.

This study focuses on the various interactions between European American officials and individual native people, most of whom lived away from the Narragansett reservation. Native people lived among European Americans in every Rhode Island town in the eighteenth century, when local officials thought of themselves as "fathers of the towns." Just as they ruled over individual households, so these leaders headed a civic "family" as well. Theoretically, *all* the town's inhabitants came under this patriarchal authority, and thus Narragansett people living away from the reservation found themselves dealing with European American leaders from time to time.[12]

Even the Narragansett living on the reservation and under tribal government could not avoid contact with town magistrates. Colonial officials had long tried to have a say in how the Narragansett people would govern themselves, a habit that local officials also adopted. During the latter part of the 1700s, the sachemship was replaced by the Indian council, which had traditionally governed the Narragansett people under the sachem's leadership since time immemorial;[13] during this time, officials from Charlestown, which completely surrounded the shrinking Narragansett reservation (see figure 1), tried to have a say in tribal affairs from time to time. Town records show that tribal council members and town councilmen met and talked on a number of occasions—but always at the convenience of the European American officials.[14]

general area of the reservation

FIGURE 1. Narragansett Reservation in the late 1700s.
(*Source:* John Hutchins Cady, *Rhode Island Boundaries 1636–1936* [Providence, 1936], 18.
Adapted by Ruth Wallis Herndon. *Note:* No map that we know of shows the boundaries of the
tribal territory as they existed during the Revolutionary era. The land set apart for the tribe's exclusive use in 1709 had considerably diminished by 1770. In 1767, two Narragansett men
mourned that "all the land joining to the sea is already sold, that we can't in no one place go to
the salt water without passing through land now in possession of the English" [letter from Samuel
Niles and Tobias Shattock to Matthew Robinson, cited in Simmons and Simmons, eds., *Old
Light on Separate Ways*, 39].)

How did Narragansett people and local officials view each other? On the one hand, we show that town leaders dealt with native people most often as "the poor" in need of official oversight, reinforcing the dispossessed and demeaned status of Indians. Further, and just as hurtful to native people in the long run, town officials stopped identifying native people as "Indian" in the written record and began designating them as "Negro" or "black," thus committing a form of documentary genocide against them. On the other hand, we show that native people often maintained a sense of their own identity, understood that the European American system of government sometimes conflicted with their own interests, and at times manipulated that system to their own advantage.

Our argument rests upon two kinds of sources: the oral history of the Narragansett people and the written records of fifteen Rhode Island towns. Coauthor Ruth Herndon investigated the white archival sources: town meeting minutes, town council minutes, vital statistics, and probate documents for Charlestown, Cumberland, East Greenwich, Exeter, Glocester, Hopkinton, Jamestown, Middletown, New Shoreham, Providence, Richmond, South Kingstown, Tiverton, Warren, and Warwick. The population of these fifteen towns constitutes about half of Rhode Island's population in 1770 and fairly represents the wealth, age, economic orientation, and geographic location of the colony's thirty late-eighteenth-century towns.

Coauthor Ella Sekatau is the source of Narragansett oral history. She has been learning Narragansett history, language, religion, and medicine from her parents, grandparents, and tribal elders since her birth, when she was charged with the responsibility of her people's continuity. Further, she has acted in official capacities for the Narragansett people since the 1970s, when the tribal governing body appointed her as an ethnohistorian and when the tribe approved her as a medicine woman (a responsibility inherited through her father's line). Like the majority of present-day Narragansett people, she can trace her genealogy to the sachems of the tribe in the sixteenth and early seventeenth centuries. Through the intervening centuries, Narragansett elders have been training the young people to maintain the tribe's unwritten history through oral tradition, just as Ella Sekatau was trained.[15] Now in her late sixties, she is presently training young people of the tribe as well as educating outsiders about Narragansett history through presentations in classrooms and other public forums. When we use the terms "oral history" and "oral tradition" in this essay, we are referring to the knowledge that Ella Sekatau embodies—knowledge that was passed down to her over her lifetime and that she is now passing down to others.

Both archival and oral sources have their problems. Narrators have probably introduced some changes in the oral history that has been entrusted from one Narragansett memory to another over two hundred years; but the documentary sources also reflect mediation, since town clerks served as gatekeepers who decided what material should be included in the historical record and in what form. Internal evidence from rough draft and final copies of town records reveal that clerks edited out of the official version any matters and any people they considered "unimportant."[16]

We need both sources in our efforts to reconstruct the situation between Narragansett people and Rhode Island leaders in the eighteenth century, and we find the oral history of the Narragansett people particularly important as a corrective to European American archival sources. Narragansett oral traditional and unwritten laws and lore challenge the records of the official gatekeepers in many respects, and they challenge us to hear voices that have been ignored and suppressed far too long. Since native people were one half of the equation in interactions between Indians and European Americans, we had better take the word of the former as seriously as we have taken the word of the latter.

Narragansett People as "The Poor of the Town"

Narragansett people who lived away from the reserved lands and among European American colonists were legal inhabitants of the towns where they were born. As inhabitants, they had certain obligations (such as paying taxes) and certain rights (such as access to poor relief). But tax revenues were rare, and no native people appear in the probate records as owners of lavish estates. Most of these native people existed on the economic margins of European American society. Stripped of their ancestral lands, they were seen as propertyless people in a society that measured worth by ownership of real estate.

On the whole, Narragansett people of the eighteenth century did not participate in English-style private land ownership. A few wrote wills that disposed of their property in accordance with colonial probate law. In 1781, for example, Narragansett man James Niles left a will that satisfied the Charlestown council acting as a court of probate on his estate.[17] And in 1788, Joseph Cozens, also of Charlestown, left his "Lands" to his daughters Sarah and Mary, stipulating that the property "be Equally Divided between them in Quantity & Quality." But Cozens combined English and Narragansett customs: he appointed a non-Indian as his sole executor, but in his will he appealed to "my indian Brethren" to see that his daughters "have [the Land] & Enjoy it according to our Indian custom."[18]

Where wills were rare, guardianships were nonexistent. In eighteenth-century Rhode Island, local officials routinely placed minor children under guardianship when their fathers died, ensuring that adults experienced in such matters would manage the property until the children reached adulthood. But of 1,504 guardianships enacted by local Rhode Island officials between 1750 and 1800, not one was on behalf of a child identified as an Indian.[19] Apparently local officials did not extend the protections of guardianship to Narragansetts with property.

From the official point of view, this was only logical. Most native people accumulated only meager estates. When Thomas Bartlet of Hopkinton died in 1759, his outstanding debts totaled almost £174; the officials who inventoried his estate valued his goods at (amazing coincidence!) a little over £174, leaving a mere 5½ shillings for the man's heirs.[20] When Betty Sawnos died of smallpox in Exeter in 1760, an inventory of her property revealed only some clothing and a pair of shoes.[21] And when Tent Anthony had a stroke and became helpless in 1767, the Jamestown town leaders inventoried her goods before taking control of her estate; they found that her possessions amounted to less than £24—about $3.00 silver.[22]

What officials saw as a lack of property may simply have been evidence of a traditional native life unencumbered by material objects. Oral tradition tells us that ownership and accumulation of goods were foreign concepts to the Narragansett, in personal property and also in real estate. To this day, members of the tribe have "give-away celebrations" to avoid building up large amounts of material things. Narragansett people who wrote wills very likely did not attach the same significance to those documents that Rhode Island officials did; instead they intended that their children should *enjoy* and *use* an area as long as they treated that area with respect and honor. This was in accordance with traditional Narragansett belief (still adhered to by the tribe) that people have a responsibility to treat the land with care. Human beings do not own the Earth Mother; she owns them.

From the viewpoint of Rhode Island officials, however, lack of property meant vulnerability to debt and bondage. A number of native people appear in the records as someone else's "property" by virtue of bound service. In 1764, Captain Benjamin Sheffield of Jamestown died, leaving behind among his chattels "an Indian Woman Slave called Philis."[23] Five years later, Jamestown officials inventoried Robert Hull's estate, which included "1 Mustee boy named Tavin," a slave valued at £23.[24] And in a not untypical labor contract, Alice Arnold bound herself to Dr. Jabez Bowen of Providence for five years, to work off a debt of £150; she had no property at all to offer in payment.[25]

People without property and separated from the native community of support would need public assistance in times of crisis, and this is how town leaders most frequently interacted with native people. In New England, poor relief was administered on a local basis; town officials arranged for the support of aged, ill, or helpless town inhabitants—including native people. When Hannah Broadfoot of East Greenwich became so old and blind that she could no longer care for herself, her town provided "all Nessarys of Life at the Cheapest Lay."[26] Rose Davids, "a blind squaw," was supported by Tiverton.[27] And when Eunice Yocake was "badly hurt" and "in a helpless Condition,"

South Kingstown councilmen ordered the overseer to "go imediately & take proper Care of sd. Indian in order that She may not suffer."[28]

For native people, poor relief often came too late. When Sarah Fitten became ill and eventually died in Jamestown in 1751, the town paid for her coffin and her burial.[29] In the winter of 1767–1768, the Tiverton councilmen reimbursed inhabitants who cared for two native women in their final illnesses and then buried them.[30] When Dorcas Fry died in East Greenwich in 1780, the town underwrote the cost of burying her "in a Decent Manner."[31]

As the previous examples illustrate, women dominated the records of poor relief granted to native people, garnering official attention far more than men in this respect.[32] This disparity can be explained in part by the fact that local officials encountered more native women than native men. Oral history tells us that native women lived among European Americans more often than native men did, moving more easily between two worlds. Narragansett men, in contrast, were reluctant to be identified by officials; they adopted aliases and took to the woods, unwilling to risk servitude under European Americans. Anecdotal evidence in white archival sources suggests that Indian males suffered higher mortality rates because of their involvement in military and maritime occupations, and Narragansett oral history tells us that women always outnumbered men among the people; until recently, female babies survived more often than male babies.[33] It is not surprising, then, that native women appear in the records more often than native men, especially as they approached old age.

There may be more behind the poor relief figures, however. The overrepresentation of women suggests that native women were more likely than native men to draw official attention. Local leaders, steeped in traditions of male responsibility, probably were more disposed to "see" needy women than needy men. Similarly, women familiar with the conventions of patriarchal hierarchies were probably more apt than men to seek assistance from authorities. In any case, local officials opened the town treasury to native women far more often than to native men.

Native children seldom appear as recipients of poor relief, for a very good reason: most children in needy circumstances were bound out as indentured servants to European American masters. This was a common practice in eighteenth-century New England; town "fathers" acted in the stead of natural parents and placed poor and/or orphaned children of all races in more prosperous households under a contract that obligated the children to live with and work for the master until adulthood. Town officials did not hesitate to remove a child from birth parents and thus break up a family; they considered it better to remove the child from an "improper" situation than to support that family with poor relief. From the viewpoint of the town treasury, the practice made sense: the town saved the cost of raising the child on welfare, and some "respectable" family gained the labor of another household member.

If the master fulfilled the indenture contract, the servant-child would receive more than "suitable" food, clothing, and shelter;[34] at the end of the indenture, the young adult would be equipped with at least a rudimentary education (reading and writing[35]) and training in some marketable skill. Job Smith contracted to teach Peter Norton ("a Poor Mustee Boy") the cooper's trade; but he also promised that Norton would learn to read, write, and "keep common Book Accounts."[36] By such means, town leaders expected indenture to prepare a poor child for an independent adulthood. Whether or not masters always fulfilled their obligations to the children is another question. Oral history tells us that many native people emerged from indenture contracts without literacy skills.

From the child's point of view, indentured servitude was only as good as the master or mistress. There is evidence that bonds of real affection and support formed between the servant and the master's family in some cases. But in other cases, servitude was only slightly disguised slavery; the town records document both servants "absconding" from their masters and masters being charged with abusive treatment of their servants.[37]

Native children appear frequently in the public indentures of the towns under review for the latter half of the eighteenth century: ninety-eight contracts named a child identified as "Indian" or "Mustee."[38] Boys were indentured twice as often as girls, but both boys and girls could expect a dozen or more years of servitude. The children averaged eight years of age at the beginning of the contracts, but some were considerably younger than that. One Indian boy named John entered bound service when he was "4 years 4 months & 6 days old"; another, also named John, was only twenty-one months old.[39] These two youngsters were obligated until they were twenty-four years old, but the average "freedom" age for native children was about twenty-two years for boys and nineteen years for girls—older than would have been case for non-Indian children.[40]

By placing poor children as bound servants and supplying care for helpless adults, local officials met their obligation to care for the needy members of their town family. But public charity did not cover everyone; towns were required to support only their own legal inhabitants.[41] Local officials invested considerable time determining the legal settlement of "transient" residents who actually were inhabitants of another town; if those transient people ever needed public assistance, town leaders would order them, by means of "warnout order" or a "removal order," to return to their home towns, where they were entitled to poor relief. Since transient people often had lived within a town for years, being warned out meant the loss of homes, jobs, and neighbors and the total disruption of their lives. Sarah Greene had lived in Providence "for 24 Years past" and Deborah Church had been there "near Twenty-five Years" when the councilmen ordered these two native women back to the towns where they had been indentured servants in their youth.[42]

For warned-out transients, the trip back to a "home" town emphasized their powerlessness. Those who were too ill or weak to leave on their own were "removed" by the town sergeant or his constables. And at the end of this unwelcome journey, other town officials took over the management of their lives. The Providence town sergeant was ordered to take transient Isabel Hope to South Kingstown "by the most direct way" and put her in the care of the overseers of the poor there.[43] Primus Thompson, a sailor crippled by a wharf accident in Jamestown, was carried by horse and sled across the frozen Rhode Island countryside to Westerly, where the overseer of the poor boarded him out.[44] When Warwick and Jamestown councilmen got into a squabble over which town had responsibility for Mary Pisquish, the poor woman was transported several times between the homes of the overseers in the two towns.[45]

As with poor relief, native women appear in the transient records far more often than native men do: women were the targets in most of the warnout orders issued against native people.[46] Town leaders throughout Rhode Island kept a close eye on transient women unrepresented by men—women who did *not* live in patriarchal households as daughters, wives, and mothers. Women living in nonpatriarchal households seemed "out of place" to the town fathers, not having male heads present to govern them.[47] Native women especially fell into this European "trap," since native traditions of household formation did not emphasize the nuclear unit that English people expected. Native women often migrated between the two worlds they inhabited: oral history tells us they lived for a time in the woods with their mates and other native people; then they moved into European American towns for another space of time. Such independent women stirred fears of disorder in town officials wedded to European custom and prompted their close attention.

Indian men contributed to this "problem" (as the European American leaders saw it) by supporting their families through work as sailors[48] and soldiers[49] and thus being absent for long periods of time. Such jobs fit more easily than others into traditional native cultural patterns of male roles.[50] Unlike most European men, native men were not farmers; anecdotal evidence in white archival sources and tribal oral tradition tells us that many Indian males provided for their families by hunting and fishing, which required travel and separations. Although Narragansett families had flourished under these arrangements for centuries, Rhode Island town leaders believed that absent husbands and fathers left their families vulnerable to poverty and trouble. Consequently, town councilmen stayed alert to what they considered poverty or trouble in these households and were quick to warn out native women to their home towns. The Jamestown councilmen became anxious to move Mary Pisquish because she was "lame & uncapable of supporting herself."[51] And Mary Carder, with two small children but no husband present, stirred the Providence councilmen to action: they ordered this small family removed to Warwick "as soon as may be."[52]

Charlestown town records present a sharp contrast to the usual business of Rhode Island local leaders—ordering transient families out of towns where they had settled, placing grieving children as servants among strangers, supporting elderly people who lived out their last days as boarders in households they did not choose. In Charlestown, councilmen kept their distance from needy Narragansett people, whom they considered the responsibility of the tribal members. Only once did these officials act on behalf of a suffering native person—"a Cripple and unable to support himself"—and their action was limited to identifying this man as "one of the Tribe of Indians called Ninegretts Tribe" and notifying the Indian council to take care of him.[53] One other time the councilmen complained that the Narragansett tribe "doth neglect to Support their Poor," suggesting that these leaders were aware of need among native people but had determined to consider it someone else's responsibility.

This curious lack of official oversight in Charlestown extended to public indentures of native children—there are none in the town records. This leaves the impression that Charlestown had no Indian inhabitants, that all native people belonged to the reservation tribe on adjoining land. But not so. At one council meeting, Charlestown leaders referred to the Narragansett people as the "Tribe of Indians belonging to this Town";[55] and during the 1777 census of men for military fitness, Charlestown officials counted sixty-six "Indians" among the town's adult male inhabitants.[56] Charlestown leaders did not hesitate to claim native men willing to enlist as soldiers;[57] and that sense of possession became pronounced when recruits were hard to find in the last years of the Revolutionary War. Then, Charlestown officials took offense because surrounding towns enlisted "several Indians that were Inhabitants of this Town" and complained that the other towns "had no right to inlist them until this Town had inlisted their full Quota."[58] In times of crisis, it seems, local leaders viewed native men as a labor pool for jobs that European American men would not undertake.

Charlestown records show how town leaders could ignore or recognize native people as official convenience dictated. When native people needed aid, authorities could (and did) become blind to their presence; but when townspeople needed bodies to perform dangerous and tedious manual labor, official vision was miraculously healed. In each case, town leaders solved their problems to their own advantage and to the *dis*advantage of the Narragansett, thus sending a clear message that Indians were disposable people.

Writing the Narragansett Off the Record

In October 1793, a European American physician named John Aldrich brought suit against Narragansett man John Hammer before the Hopkinton justices of the peace. Aldrich wanted payment from Hammer (a matter of three and one-half shillings) for medical care provided the year before. The official warrant for Hammer's arrest described him as a "Black Man" and a "Husbandman," but neither description was accurate. When Hammer appeared before justice David Nichols, he asked for a reduction of the charges because of the error in racial designation: "[Hammer] pleads that he is Not [a black man] But that he is an Indian man." When the judge overruled this objection, Hammer tried again: he pled that the charge should be reduced because "Husbandman" was an incorrect description of his livelihood. The judge overruled this second plea as well, and all subsequent paperwork for the case referred to Hammer as both "Black man" and "Husbandman."[59]

John Hammer's remarkable objections reveal that he understood the judicial system sufficiently well to counter the original suit with complaints about the mechanics of his case. Equally remarkable is the struggle revealed in the court papers between a Narragansett man and a European American man over the right to determine a person's racial designation in official documents. The magistrate did not dispute Hammer's identity as an Indian; Aldrich's book account, presented to the court as evidence, gave details of his professional visit to "John Hammer Indian." But in the eyes of the judicial official, Hammer's identity as an Indian did not clash with his official designation as a "Black man." Abram Coon, who heard Hammer's protests, persisted in retaining justice David Nichols's original description of Hammer in the arrest warrant. To Justice Coon, Narragansett man John Hammer was described adequately by a term that signified non-European skin in a general way.

By registering his protest before a magistrate, John Hammer forced the record-keepers to document evidence of a new weapon of destruction that local leaders wielded against the Narragansett a century after Great Swamp. The number of native people in southern New England had been drastically reduced by war, disease, and outmigration; now those who remained struggled to exist on paper—and to obtain the rights of continued freedom, land ownership, and state revenues that paper documents alone could secure in the European American system.

Abram Coon's decision to describe Hammer as a "black man" was not a fluke; it was part of a pattern that can be traced through the official documents of Rhode Island's towns. Between 1750 and 1800 "Indians" disappeared from these written records. Individual native people were still named in the records, of course; officials simply called them something besides "Indian."

Early on, Rhode Island leaders exhibited reluctance to acknowledge the name of the people who welcomed Europeans to this part of North America: the town records contain only rare references to "Narragansett" people. After the war of 1675–1676, European Americans found even more reason to rely on general terms such as "Indians" and "natives," since surviving Narragansett people sometimes intermarried with other neighboring tribes.[60] But by the latter part of the 1700s, official record-keepers had made an even greater leap in racial designation, and by 1800 the town records contain only scattered references to "Indians"; instead, "Negroes" and "blacks" fill the pages.

This redesignation of subjugated people had its antecedents on the other side of the Atlantic. The first European slave dealers to the west coast of Africa often erased the heritage of the native people they purchased there and sold elsewhere for their labor. Seldom did the European sellers or buyers know what kingdoms, states, tribes, or villages these men, women, and children left behind.[61] Instead, Europeans lumped them all together under the umbrella designation of "Negro," which means "black" in Portuguese and Spanish. In eighteenth-century Rhode Island, local leaders stretched this umbrella designation to cover not only the peoples among them who had been torn from their African homeland but also the Narragansett among them who had been pushed off their native land.

New England officials made liberal use of the term "Mustee" as a first step in transforming "Indians" into "Negroes." In the latter half of the eighteenth century, town clerks used "Mustee" most frequently to describe children being bound out in indenture contracts. Where clerks record the parentage of these "Mustee" children, it is always the *mother* who is identified as Indian.[62] But what of the father? The use of "Mustee" indicates that officials considered the child to have a non-Indian father, even though no details about the father are provided. The implications of this designation are enormous. In the tribes of southern New England, a child was a member of the mother's clan and tribe, regardless of who the father was. But in the world of European Americans, inheritance came through the father. By denying "Mustee" children an "Indian" father, officials prepared the ground to deny these children any rights they might later claim as descendants of Narragansett or other native fathers.[63]

By such means, officials transformed Indians into "Mustees" and transformed both of these into "Negroes" and "blacks." The labels are applied with such a haphazard and casual hand in the record that the changes are easy to overlook. They would have passed undetected if we had assumed that a clerk used the same racial designation each time he referred to a particular individual. This is not so. The East Greenwich town clerk described Benjamin Austin as "Indian" in 1767, but as "a Malatoo Fellow" in 1768.[64] Sarah Hill was an "Indian or Mustee Woman" to the Providence clerk in 1784, but she was recast as a "Negro" by that official in 1791.[65] Harriet (given no last name) was first described as "an Indian" by the Jamestown clerk in 1788; five months later, the clerk identified her as "a Molato girl."[66] Mary Carder appears as an "Indian" in the Warwick town records in 1775 but as a "Negro" in 1784.[67] And from 1780 on, a certain ambiguity appears in the record, as clerks replace their previously clear descriptions of native people with uncertain designations. Thus, in Providence, Susannah Tripp was "a Molatto or Indian Woman," Eber Hopkins "a Mustee or Mulatto Man," and an unnamed stranger was "a

Negro, Indian or Molatto Woman."[68] In East Greenwich, Dorcas Fry was "an Indian or Negro Woman," and in Warwick, three-year-old Lucy Spywood was "a molatto, or Mustee Child."[69]

Although specific examples provide the clearest evidence of the shift in racial designations, there are other ways to document the phenomenon. One is by tracing the racial designation of people warned out of Rhode Island towns over a fifty-year period. Between 1750 and 1800, people identified as "Indians" constituted 2.5 percent of individuals warned out of Rhode Island towns. However, over two-thirds of these particular warnouts occurred *before* 1776. The number of "Indians" dropped off sharply after the outbreak of the Revolutionary War, and only two persons warned out after 1787 were described as "Indian" or "mustee." Warnout statistics for "Negro," "mulatto," and "black" people show the opposite trend. During the entire period, those so identified constituted about 10 percent of all warnout orders; but the great majority of those warnouts occurred *after* 1775.[70]

The same trend occurs in public indentures. Of all indentures binding out minors, 14 percent were for children identified as "Indian" or "Mustee."[71] But the great majority (78 percent) of those contracts were arranged between 1750 and 1775. The number of contracts affecting native children dwindles after the mid 1770s, and there are none recorded after 1795. The opposite is true for children identified as "Negro" or "mulatto" or "black." Only a handful of these contracts are recorded before 1776; after that date, the number surges, reaching a peak in the 1790s.[72]

The uncanny way that "Indians" pepper the town records before the Revolution and "Negroes" and "blacks" dominate afterward strikes us as suspect. Of course there were unusual forces at work during the Revolutionary Era. The increase in African American transients may be due in part to a measurable increase in mobility, thanks to manumission fervor during the Revolutionary War and gradual emancipation laws of the 1780s. And the increase in African American indentures may in part reflect a change in European American tactics of controlling black labor by indentured servitude rather than by slavery.[73] But those dynamics cannot explain the *disappearance* of native people from the ranks of transients and indentured children. The evidence points to a deliberate redesignation of native people as Negro or black, as officials replaced cultural description with physical description.

Narragansett Identity

The Narragansett were keenly aware of these pressures to lose their Indianness. Then, and for generations afterwards, tribal oral history tells us, Narragansett people expressed hatred for the terms "Mulatto" and "Mustee," which implied the loss of tribal distinctiveness. Some grew to hate white people—for grouping Indians and Africans together without concern for heritage; and some grew to hate black people as well—for being the group that the Narragansett were conflated with. That hatred surfaced at "crying rocks" and unmarked gravesites, where some native mothers abandoned babies fathered by non-Indians. Traditionally, the Narragansett had used these sites to abandon imperfect babies born with physical disabilities. After contact with Europeans and Africans, some of the Narragansett stretched "imperfect" to include children fathered by non-Indians, and they rejected these babies instead of incorporating them into the tribe. Other women found a less grim alternative by abandoning children to the care of non-Indians. Now and then European American householders complained that native women had "left" little children and disappeared. Ironically, the complainers were quite willing to take care of the children—as long as officials enacted indenture contracts that bound the youngsters until adulthood.[74] The children that Narragansett mothers grieved over thus became a labor supply for European Americans.

A strong Narragansett identity sometimes surfaced in the town records—occasionally in actual phrases Narragansett people used to describe their native heritage. Delight Robbins informed the Providence councilmen that her father was "one of the Native Inhabitants of the said Charlestown."[75] Mary Fowler told the South Kingstown officials that "her Mother was one of the Tribe of the Indians in Charlestown." She also indicated that she followed native customs: she had lived with James Fowler "for about thirty Years & had Ten Children by him," but she had not married him "in the Manner white People are married in these parts." Similarly, her daughter Mary Champlin told the councilmen that she had lived with John Champlin eleven years and had six children by him "but never was Married to him according to the form Used by the White People in these Parts."[76] (These two women had very likely married their spouses in traditional native wedding ceremonies. Such weddings were and still are accepted as valid under federal law.)

Native people not only identified themselves and each other, they also sought each other's company. Some families stayed together well after the offspring reached maturity. Mary Fowler and her adult daughter Mary Champlin (and their children) were living together in South Kingstown when they were questioned by the councilmen. Sarah Gardner, mother of twelve, kept her family together against formidable odds. In 1762, the South Kingstown town council ordered her to bind out her children to various masters when it seemed to them that Gardner could not support them all. Later, Gardner managed to gather together her scattered offspring; when she left South Kingstown for Providence in 1767, she had six of her children with her. In 1780, when Gardner was warned out of Providence, four of her daughters (now adult) were still living with her; and in 1787, when she was warned out once again, her household included three adult daughters and a grandson.[77]

The Narragansett also took in and cared for other native people in distress. Jack Marsh, an elderly Narragansett man living in Jamestown, housed and tended "an Indian Squaw" who eventually died; he then arranged the details of her burial.[78] In another typical case, an Indian woman named only Freelove received payment from the town of Warren for supplying room and board to Phebe Wood, a native woman who was one of the town's poor.[79] The Jamestown council acknowledged the sense of cohesion among native people when they decided that the best way to care for Mary Mew, an elderly and lame Indian woman, was "to put her into some Indian Family."[80]

The records also suggest that native people sought each other out for times of relaxation and celebration. Homes where the householder had a liquor license often served as gathering places. In 1753, Christopher Fowler was accused of "Entertaining Indeons, Negros &c" in his tavern.[81] In 1760, Joshua Gardner obtained a tavern license only on condition "that he Entertain no Indian or Black people on ye day Calld Fair day at his House on any pretence whatever."[82] The Rhode Island General Assembly had long been distressed at the tendency of native and black servants to head for taverns and had passed legislation in 1704, and again in 1750, restricting their activities. This legislation made it an offense to sell liquor "to any Indian, Mulatto or Negro Servant or Slave" or to entertain such a person in one's home without the master's consent; it also forbade any Indian or black servant to be out and about after 9 P.M., except with the master's consent.[83] Colony and town records together suggest that the Narragansett, both bound and free, knew where they might enjoy the company of other native people and often acted on that knowledge.

As evidence of their cultural heritage, some of the Narragansett living among non-Indians chose traditional native dwellings. South Kingstown's local leaders were aware of "ye wigwam [of] Jo Robinson in Point Judeth"; others caught the attention of town leaders, who feared they would be unable to survive winter weather unless they moved to English style houses.[84]

Given these links to their people and their past, it is not surprising that Narragansett people living among non-Indians did not often think of themselves as "belonging" to a particular Rhode Island town. Oral tradition tells us that the Narragansett customarily moved from winter residence to summer residence and back again, in accordance with the seasons. In addition, they often traveled to home clans and familiar places for celebrations and long-term visits. They moved and lived where they wished; there is little evidence that they felt rooted in the settled, ordered communities that English people valued.

Narragansett habits of travel and long-term visiting clashed with European American concepts of "belonging" to a particular place. Local Rhode Island officials, alert to the presence of "strangers" within their jurisdiction and uneasy about the large numbers who congregated for native celebrations, sometimes tried to break up gatherings by warning out the participants who were not legal inhabitants. When confronted by the town sergeant with order in hand, oral tradition tells us, many of the Narragansett quietly melted into the woods; several days later, they returned and resumed the visit or celebration. Local officials, for their part, complained about transients who returned persistently, despite repeated warnings out. Native people appear regularly in warnout orders,[85] but these orders probably netted only a fraction of the native people actually moving around the region.

To highlight their unconcern about European American regulations that interfered with their traditional customs, native people seldom obtained departure certificates as they traveled from one place to another. The departure certificate was the "passport" that poor people (without real estate) needed to reside for more than a week in a town where they did not have a legal settlement by virtue of birth or bound service; that certificate promised that the bearer's home town would bear any costs of support and transportation if the need arose. Of 919 departure certificates granted by town councils between 1750 and 1800, only 10 (1.1 percent) were issued to people identified as Indians. The warnout orders tell us that native people were moving about in much greater numbers than the departure certificates indicate; but they ignored (or were ignorant of) the regulations associated with legal settlement—a concept that had little resonance for native people adrift on occupied ancestral lands.

Occasionally, town leaders made Narragansett people aware of those regulations in a way that could not be ignored. Cato Gardner moved from South Kingstown to Jamestown without a certificate, and in time the Jamestown council demanded that he leave—or get a certificate. Gardner ignored this first warning, but a second citation some months later was delivered so forcefully that he made the trip back to South Kingstown to get a certificate from the council.[86] Martha Bristol dodged the Jamestown town council for five years, but after receiving her fourth warning out, she obtained a departure certificate from the New Shoreham council to avoid further harrassment in Jamestown.[87] Bristol, Gardner, and other native people complied with regulations only when they could not avoid them. By doing so, they signaled their unconcern about pleasing the non-Indian "fathers" of the patriarchal town family; they had another agenda derived from their own and their families' needs.

Narragansett People Maneuvering through the System

Just as Martha Bristol and Cato Gardner learned how to keep local authorities at bay over the issue of certificates, some of the Narragansett learned how to maneuver through a system heavy with regulations. The record is rich with instances of Indians beating officials at their own game. It is tempting to think of native people relating such "trickster tales" to delighted audiences at homes and in taverns, and thus encouraging those who labored daily to make European Americans even more prosperous.

Old Toby Smith, Young Toby Smith, and Moses (no last name) figured out how to avoid paying taxes. As inhabitants of Rhode Island towns, native people who owned real estate were just as subject to paying taxes as European Americans were. In Middletown, the assessors included these three native men on the rate list for a town tax due in March of 1757. But the men failed to pay the £6 they owed, even after repeated visits from the tax collector and a two-month extension of the deadline. The collector finally reported to the councilmen "that he Cannot get the Rates" from the Indians, and the council covered the sum out of the town treasury.[88] It was not unusual for towns to write off uncollected taxes as "bad rates" from time to time, when the collector advised that certain cases were not worth pursuing.[89] Moses and the Smiths somehow convinced the collector that theirs was such a case; perhaps by pleading, or spinning a tale, or temporarily moving away, they beat the system.

Simeon Matthews got out of a tax assessment and a guardianship both. The Charlestown town council had put Matthews under guardianship "on account of his being a common Drunkard." The idea was to keep him from purchasing liquor by assigning a guardian who would control his ward's money and property. At the same time, perhaps to underscore town authority, the tax assessors levied a tax on him. Matthews promptly petitioned the General Assembly, arguing that he was a member of the Narragansett tribe and therefore not under Charlestown's government. The General Assembly agreed. The tax was canceled and the Charlestown officials dismissed Matthews's guardian, noting for the record that "it is not the Duty of this Council to appoint Guardians to the Indian Tribe."[90]

Marcy Scooner used persistence and a certain skill in hiding to beat the warning out system. In 1759, the Jamestown councilmen warned her out to North Kingstown, the home town where Scooner did not wish to live. But although she was conducted out of town, she soon returned to Jamestown and continued to live there until the council caught wind of her presence and warned her out again in 1763. And again in 1766. Each time, the councilmen ordered the town sergeant to whip Scooner publicly, to deter her from returning. But Scooner was so adept at hiding from authority that the councilmen had to extend the usual time granted to the sergeant to find and whip a miscreant. For seven years, Scooner dodged the council and the sergeant, coming and going as she pleased. After 1766, she disappears from the record. Perhaps she died. Perhaps she changed her name. Perhaps she found a more congenial place to live and moved on. In any case, she provided a fine example of how to frustrate authority.[91]

A young Indian boy (unnamed in the record) figured out how to escape indentured servitude without flight and the dangers of capture and prosecution. In 1780, this young servant of Captain Samuel Babcock enlisted in the Continental Army as part of Hopkinton's quota in the most recent draft. Upset about this defection, Babcock disputed the validity of the enlistment, claiming that his "apprentice" was under sixteen—the lawful age of enlistment—and that Babcock had "a Right to detain him." The town's voters, gathered in a special meeting to resolve this impasse, overruled Babcock's objection and accepted the enlistment of the young man, choosing to believe that he was of legal age. The youth went off to the army. Three weeks later, Babcock found and produced the indenture papers, which "proved" that the Indian apprentice was under age; but it was too late, and Hopkinton's latest soldier had gone to muster. The record contains no explanation of where the indenture contract was three weeks earlier, when Babcock so vigorously objected to his enlistment.[92]

Narragansett people living among European Americans were not helpless against local officials and the systems they constructed to keep order in their towns. Native people understood these systems and could maneuver around them. The evidence is there in the very records kept by the officials who tried to govern their lives. Assuredly, some Indians lived and died among non-Indians without fighting back; but people like John Hammer, Simeon Matthews, and Marcy Scooner dot the record in sufficient numbers to remind us that the war didn't end at the Great Swamp.

Conclusion

At the heart of our study of Indian-European relations in Rhode Island is the phenomenon of local leaders erasing native people from the written record by redesignating them as "Negro." By 1793, when John Hammer argued vainly before a local justice, authorities clearly considered that "Indians'" were "black." A major shift in official thought about native people had occurred in the latter part of the 1700s. Those leaders certainly *knew* the difference between Indian and African peoples; in earlier days they did not hesitate to make distinctions. But as European Americans drew lines between themselves and persons of color, they lumped all non-Europeans together as "the other."[93]

What prompted this particular expression of racism during the Revolutionary era? Social upheaval, economic depression, and political nation-making all offer possible answers. Most obvious, perhaps, are the tensions in race relations occasioned by the end of slavery in New England. Revolutionary fervor galvanized many masters into voluntarily freeing their slaves during the war and soon afterward. Then, in 1784, gradual emancipation became a legal reality in Rhode Island; it signaled the eventual freeing of young adult slaves beginning in the early 1800s.[94] During the Revolution and afterward, a growing number of ex-slaves migrated away from the farms and plantations of southern Rhode Island and swelled the ranks of free African Americans seeking employment on the docks and in domestic service in the commercial centers of the state. One historian has shown that emancipation eroded the carefully ordered world of European Americans in Rhode Island. No longer did all (or even most) people of color fit neatly into the category of "slave," with all the subservience and control that implied. Faced with free black people in growing numbers, European Americans transferred to "blacks" the attitudes they had formerly had toward "slaves." They replaced old regulations designed to control slaves with new ones designed to control free blacks; and racism bloomed in a political environment that encouraged emancipation.[95]

European Americans swept up the Narragansett in this effort to control people of color. Indians had already been associated with people of African descent, by virtue of their shared status as "others" in a world governed by Europeans, of their bondage in European households, and of their unions that produced children who were both Indian and African. In the racially charged atmosphere of the late 1700s, European American bigotry affected the Narragansett just as it did Africans and others of a darker color.[96]

Narragansett land provided another catalyst. The Narragansett had been shorn of most of their land by the 1780s, but even the small remnant looked appealing to European American farmers faced with severe economic depression, exhausted soil, unprofitable harvests, and restless sons ready to migrate westward. But there was a more fundamental problem. Some European Americans must have considered the possibility that Narragansett people might seek to regain what had originally been tribal territory. The way to prevent that problem was to deny the existence of people with any claim to the land. New Shoreham voters tolled that bell in 1780. Noting that "the native Indians [are] extinct in [this] Town," they passed a law taking over the reserved Indian lands, which were to be sold to augment the town treasury.[97] By writing any Indians out of the record in their particular towns, local leaders helped ensure that native people would not regain land in *their* towns in the future.

European American leaders were right to be concerned about possible Narragansett action to regain their land. When the United States was born, native peoples on tribal land came under the authority of Congress, not state legislatures. The Articles of Confederation, ratified in 1781, gave Congress "the sole and exclusive right and power of . . . regulating the trade and managing all affairs with the Indians, not members of any of the States." The Federal Constitution, ratified in 1788 (Rhode Island was the last to ratify—reluctantly—in 1790), granted Congress the right to "regulate Commerce" with all the Indian tribes. Since state and local leaders could not be sure how the federal government would treat native people, it made sense to prevent unwelcome interference by making those people disappear.

We can never know the exact motives that prompted Rhode Island officials to wipe native people from the written record in the late eighteenth century. It was very likely a combination of factors led by a burgeoning racial ideology that would divide the nation into "white" and "nonwhite" peoples. The full answer is probably as complicated as the explanation for the Rhode Island state government's resistance to Narragansett economic development in the late twentieth century. Whatever the reasons, the action was in vain. Narragansett people survived in the flesh, keeping their identity and their history as a tribe intact.

NOTES

Acknowledgments: The authors wish to thank Ann Keppel, Mark Lindall, Joanne Melish, Ann Plane, Paul Robinson, Medicine Man Running Wolf Wilcox, and Cynthia Van Zandt for helping us think through and write this essay.

Abbreviations used in notes: TM = Town Meeting; TMR = Town Meeting Records (located in the respective town clerks' offices); TCM = Town Council Meeting; TCR = Town Council Records (located in the respective town clerks' offices); PTP = Providence Town Papers (located at the Rhode Island Historical Society Library, Providence).

1. No federal law ever took away the tribal status of the Narragansett people. The Rhode Island state legislature's action of 1880, to detribalize the Narragansett people and sell all but a two-acre parcel of their reserved land, violated the provisions of the federal Trade and Intercourse Act of 1790. This was the basis of the Narragansett claim that eventually won them a return of 1,800 acres of land in 1978 and tribal recognition from the federal government in 1983. See Paul A. Robinson, "The Impact of Federal Recognition on the Narragansett Indian Tribe" (paper presented to the Second Mashantucket Pequot History Conference, October 21–23, 1993, Mystic, Connecticut). See also Glenn W. LaFantasie and Paul R. Campbell, "Land Controversies and the Narragansett Indians, 1880–1938" (report lodged in the Office of the Attorney General, State of Rhode Island, February 1978).

2. On the differing attitudes of native and English people in New England toward land ownership and land use, see William Cronon, *Changes in the Land: Indians, Colonists, and the Ecology of New England* (New York: Hill and Wang, 1983), 54–156; Carolyn Merchant, *Ecological Revolutions: Nature, Gender, and Science in New England* (Chapel Hill: University of North Carolina Press, 1989), 69–111; and James Warren Springer, "American Indians and the Law of Real Property in Colonial New England," *The American Journal of Legal History*, 30, no. 1 (January 1986), 25–58. Carl Bridenbaugh, in *Fat Mutton and Liberty of Conscience: Society in Rhode Island, 1636–1690* (Providence: Brown University Press, 1974), argues that the first English settlers of Rhode Island intended to establish large, private estates (like those of the aristocracy in Old England) where they could grow grains and raise livestock on a grand scale.

3. In 1709, Rhode Island leaders negotiated a land deal with then-sachem Ninigret II, who deeded all "vacant" lands (that is, land not yet possessed by whites) to Rhode

Island, except for the reservation in the southwest part of the colony. Ninigret I (father of Ninigret II) had received the sachemship as a reward for assisting the English settlers in Connecticut during their 1675–76 conflict with Pequot, Mohegan, and Niantic people. (This was the same conflict that had spilled over into Narragansett territory and resulted in the massacre at the Great Swamp.) The land that Ninigret II retained for the Narragansett people soon began to shrink, as sachems sold off tracts to pay their creditors, despite vigorous objections and legal maneuvers by members of the tribe.

4. John Sainsbury believes that "the overwhelming majority" of native people in Rhode Island did day labor with, or were bound servants living with, white colonists. John A. Sainsbury, "Indian Labor in Early Rhode Island," *New England Quarterly*, 48, no. 3 (September 1975), 379–80. The practice of living on a reservation but going out to day labor among whites was common also among Indians in Massachusetts during the 1700s. See Yasu Kawashima, "Legal Origins of the Indian Reservation in Colonial Massachusetts," *The American Journal of Legal History*, 13 (1969), 54. We believe that Sainsbury overstates the case. Many of the Narragansett prospered without ever experiencing such bondage; they knew how to survive on the land and continued to do so, out of sight and off the record of European American officials.

5. This intermarriage led to increasing racial complexity among people who still considered themselves Narragansett. See Rhett S. Jones, "Miscegenation and Acculturation in the Narragansett Country of Rhode Island, 1710–1790," *Trotter Institute Review*, 3 (1989), 8–16.

6. Although the Rhode Island General Assembly banned perpetual slavery of Narragansett people in 1676, white Rhode Island colonists continued to put some of the Narragansett in bondage well into the 1700s by means of indentured servitude of children and debt peonage of adults. Pressured by citizens outraged at this latter practice, in 1730 the colony legislature passed an act "to prevent Indians from being abused by designing and ill-minded Persons, in making them Servants." The act deplored the business of whites "draw[ing] Indians into their Debt, by selling them Goods, at extravagant Rates" and then forcing them into bondage to pay off the debt. But this legislation came too late for the considerable number of the Narragansett already trapped in servitude; the act did not free them. *Acts and Laws of The English Colony of Rhode-Island and Providence Plantations, in New-England, in America* (Newport: Samuel Hall, 1767), 150. See also Sainsbury, "Indian Labor," 378–93. Exploitation of native people continued, however, and in 1783 the General Assembly passed "An Act to prevent Impositions upon Indians of the Narragansett Tribe," once again citing the problem of Narragansett people being trapped in enormous and spurious debts. *The Public Laws of the State of Rhode-Island and Providence Plantations* (Providence: Carter and Wilkinson, 1798), 615–16.

7. On illegal detribalization, see note 1.

8. The most thorough discussion of this 200-year period is Paul R. Campbell and Glenn W. LaFantasie, "Scattered to the Winds of Heaven—Narragansett Indians 1676–1880," *Rhode Island History*, 37, no. 3 (August 1978), 67–83. See also Ethel Boissevain, *The Narragansett People* (Phoenix: Indian Tribal Series, 1975); Laura E. Conkey, Ethel Boissevain, and Ives Goddard, "Indians of Southern New England and Long Island: Late Period," in Bruce G. Trigger, ed., *Handbook of North American Indians*, vol. 15: *Northeast* (Washington, D.C.: U.S. Government Printing Office, 1978), 177–89; Sainsbury, "Indian Labor"; and William S. Simmons and Cheryl L. Simmons, eds., *Old Light on Separate Ways: The Narragansett Diary of Joseph Fish 1765–1776* (Hanover, N.H.: University Press of New England, 1982).

9. Campbell and LaFantasie argue that, by 1700, the native population in Rhode Island was "an aggregate of peoples" and that the postcontact Narragansett tribe was considerably reduced and diluted. "Scattered to the Winds," 70. Sainsbury cites evidence that native people from *outside* New England were imported as slaves during the early 1700s by Rhode Islanders frustrated by the ban on enslaving Narragansett people: see Sainsbury, "Indian Labor," 379, 386–88. Campbell and LaFantasie have assumed that non-Indian assessments of tribal identity are correct; but in fact Narragansett oral history tells us that some tribal members have maintained a solely Narragansett lineage since well before the arrival of Europeans.

10. Samuel Johnson's English dictionary contains no definition of the term "mustee." In fact, it contains none of the terms used by New England officials to describe native people. See Samuel Johnson, *A Dictionary of the English Language*, 2 vols. (London: W. Strahan, 1755). This dictionary's importance to town leaders is testified to by its appearance in their probate inventories. See, for example, its inclusion in the possessions of Providence town clerks James Angell (estate inventory, February 14, 1785, Providence *Wills*, 6:460–61) and Daniel Cooke (estate inventory, January 9, 1794, Providence *Wills*, 6:557–60).

Since "Indian," "squaw," and "mustee"—which appear frequently in the local records—do not have official definitions, we have inferred their meaning from the text of the colonial records. This approach is recommended by Jack D. Forbes in *Africans and Native Americans: The Language of Race and the Evolution of Red-Black Peoples*, 2d ed. (Urbana: University of Illinois Press, 1993). Forbes's study of the changing meanings of such terms as "mustee" and "mulatto" between the 1500s and the 1900s emphasizes the necessity of "engag[ing] the primary data" (3). Providing specific geographical and chronological context in this way demonstrates that such terms had different meanings in different times and places. After studying the use of "mustee" in various eighteenth-century documents, Forbes concluded that the term, in its most general sense, was "used for part-American [Indian] persons (usually slaves) who were mixed with either European or African or both" (227).

11. TCM, Aug. 29, 1761, East Greenwich TCR, 3:76; TCM, Mar. 27, 1762, Jamestown TCR, 1:143–44; TCM, Mar. 14, 1764, Warwick TCR, 2:241–42; TCM, May 11, 1769, South Kingstown TCR, 5:215.

12. Sainsbury figures that 35.5 percent of all native people in Rhode Island lived with white families in 1774. "Indian Labor," 379. If this estimate were correct, it would mean that over one-third of the Indians in the colony were legal inhabitants of Rhode Island towns.

13. See Simmons and Simmons, eds., *Old Light on Separate Ways*, xxx–xxxvii. John Wood Sweet has studied the archival material relating to Narragansett leadership in this period and has produced a thorough analysis from that perspective in "Bodies Politic: Colonialism, Race and the Emergence of the American North: Rhode Island, 1730–1830" (Ph.D. diss., Princeton University, 1995), ch. 1.

14. See, for example, the Charlestown town council meeting of Oct. 1, 1772, when the councilmen sent the town sergeant to the "Indian Council" with an order for them to appear at the next council meeting "to Render an accompt of what Blacks their is now amongst them & on their Land, that does Not Belong to their Tribe": Charlestown TCR, 2:210. A few years later, the members of the tribal council with a complaint about a Charlestown inhabitant had to bring their concerns to a regularly convened Charlestown council meeting: TCM, Feb. 6, 1775, Charlestown TCR, 2:256–57.

15. Narragansett elders and parents train young people by having them watch and

repeat verbatim as the elders speak and enact Narragansett history, language, unwritten laws, and ceremonies. Adults watch and guide children through repeated reenactments and retellings. Through this kind of training, for example, Ella Sekatau learned from her parents the Narragansett morning ceremony. She was taught to begin the day by going outside, speaking the words "wunnegan nippaus" (meaning "welcome, sun"), and giving verbal thanks to the creator for the sun, the earth mother, and the four directions from whence all things come. Such ceremonies have been maintained among the Narragansett because elders have overseen the intensive instruction of young people through the generations.

16. Ruth Wallis Herndon, "On and Off the Record: Town Clerks as Interpreters of Rhode Island History," *Rhode Island History*, 50, no. 4 (November 1992), 103–15.

17. TCM, June 18, 1781, Charlestown TCR, 3:66.

18. Will of Joseph Cozens, recorded Jan. 7, 1788, Charlestown TCR, 3:219.

19. The Charlestown town council did try to appoint a guardian over an adult Narragansett—a man named Simeon Matthews—whom they considered a drunkard and thus incapable of managing his own affairs; but they had to cancel the guardianship when the General Assembly ruled that Charlestown had no authority to place a member of the Narragansett tribe under guardianship. See Matthews's story below.

20. Inventory of Thomas Bartlet, June 25, 1759, Hopkinton TCR, 1:33–35. The monetary amounts were expressed in Rhode Island Old Tenor currency. In 1759, £6 in this currency was worth $1.00 in silver, so Bartlet's estate (and debts) totaled about $29.00 in silver. See "Rhode Island Currency Conversion Ratios, 1751–1800," in Ruth Wallis Herndon, "Governing the Affairs of the Town: Continuity and Change in Rhode Island, 1750–1800" (Ph.D. diss., American University, 1992), 364–70.

21. Betty Sawnos Inventory, Mar. 21, 1760, Exeter TCR, 2:112.

22. Tent Anthony was "taken with a Numb Palsey fit," which left her "Bad" on one side, and one of the overseers of the poor supported her at the town's cost: TCM, May 19, May 23, and Aug. 1, 1767, Jamestown TCR, 2:2, 5.) The value of her estate was expressed in Rhode Island Old Tenor currency; in 1767, £8 was the equivalent of $1.00 in silver: see Herndon, "Governing the Affairs of the Town," 364.

23. Inventory of Benjamin Sheffield, Jan. 5, 1764, Jamestown TCR, 1:170–72. Phyllis was not mentioned in this inventory, but she was identified as part of Sheffield's estate when she needed assistance some seven years later. See TM, July 16, 1771, Jamestown TMR, 1:171, and TCM, Nov. 12, 1772, Jamestown TCR, 2:73.

24. Inventory of Robert Hull estate, Mar. 11, 1769, Jamestown TCR, 2:43–45.

25. Indenture contract of "Indian Woman" Alce [sic] Arnold, Apr. 2, 1759, PTP, 1:149. In 1759, £150 Rhode Island Old Tenor would be worth $25.00 silver. See Herndon, "Governing the Affairs of the Town," 364.

26. TCM, Oct. 7, 1758, East Greenwich TCR, 3:45a.

27. TCM, June 5, 1781, Tiverton TCR, vol. 1.

28. TCM, May 11, 1767, South Kingstown TCR, 5:181–82.

29. TCM, July 16, 1751, Jamestown TCR, 1:44.

30. TCM, Oct. 5, 1767, and Feb. 1, 1768, Tiverton TCR, 2:227, 231.

31. TCM, July 14, 1780, East Greenwich TCR, 3:204. "A decent manner" suggests Christian burial but may in fact refer to Native American rituals.

32. The records of the towns under study include thirty-five incidents of native people receiving direct financial assistance; thirty of those incidents involved women and only five involved men.

33. On Indian males in dangerous occupations, see notes 48 and 49, below. The

census records fail to offer a European American perspective on the sex ratio of native peoples. The 1755 census was the only early count that distinguished between non-white men and nonwhite women; but in that census, Indians were counted as Blacks, so we have no reference point for the sex ratio of native people at midcentury. According to that 1755 census, the numbers of "Black" men and women were nearly equal overall, but nonwhite men outnumber nonwhite women in Newport (400 to 341) and South Kingstown (137 to 109).

34. In a typical indenture contract, Widow Esther Tefft promised to provide to Amos Ookus "meet Drink Clothing Lodging and washing Suitible for an apprntice [*sic*]": TCM, Oct. 26, 1778, Richmond TCR, 2:256–57. The word "suitable" or "fit" appears in most contracts, indicating the gulf that separated bound servants from the rest of society. The clothing they wore, the food they ate, and the bed they slept upon all marked them off as servants.

35. Although both boys and girls were taught to read, writing was usually taught only to boys. Hetty Sharp's contract, for example, specified only that her master teach this native girl "to Read Well in the Bible." TCM, Jan. 6, 1777, Warren TCR, 1:455.

36. Indenture of Peter Norton, Mar. 16, 1780, Providence TCR, 5:163–64 and PTP, 5:38.

37. See Ruth Wallis Herndon, "'To live after the manner of an apprentice': Public Indenture as Social Control in 18th Century Rhode Island" (unpublished paper, presented at the American Studies Association, November 1993).

38. Public Indentures of Children in Rhode Island, 1750–1800

	Native American	All Children
Total indentures	98	712
Indentures of girls	30 (30.6%)	227 (31.9%)
Indentures of boys	64 (65.3%)	461 (64.7%)
Child's sex unknown	4 (4.1%)	23 (3.2%)
Average age at contract	8.0	7.6
Average freedom age, male	21.72	21 (whites)
Average freedom age, female	19.1	18 (whites)

39. TCM, July 13, 1767 and Apr. 16, 1760, South Kingstown TCR, 5:184, 90.

40. This extension of servitude time for non-Europeans was quite deliberately acknowledged by the South Kingstown town council after they miscalculated a child's age and arranged a contract for "Peter a mustee boy" that would free him when he was twenty years old. Since their intent was "that he Should be bound until he was Twenty four years oald," they voted to amend the agreement. (TCM, Aug. 20, 1753, South Kingstown TCR, 4:237.

41. In eighteenth-century New England, people were usually legal inhabitants of the town where they were born. Indentured servants had the option of claiming their master's town when their service was completed. And upon marriage, women automatically gained settlement in their husbands' home towns (and lost their own birth settlement). The only other way to change legal settlement was to purchase substantial real estate—a "freehold"—in another town. Because poor people could not make such purchases, they lived as "transients" wherever they moved and were constantly vulnerable to being "warned out" to their home towns. See Josiah Henry Benton, *Warning Out in New England* (Boston: W. B. Clarke, 1911; reprint, Freeport, N.Y., 1970); and

Ruth Wallis Herndon, *Poverty, Perversity, and Public Policy in Early America: Records of Warning Out in Rhode Island, 1750–1800*, work in progress.

42. TCM, Aug. 7 and Oct. 5, 1786 (Sarah Greene) and TCM, Aug. 13, 1787 (Deborah Church), Providence TCR, 5:393, 401, 6:16. On average, transient people lived about five years in a town before being warned out, but ten and twenty years in a community was not unusual, especially for nonwhite female transients. See Ruth Wallis Herndon, "Women of 'no particular home': Town Leaders and Female Transients in Southeastern New England, 1750–1800," in Larry Eldridge, ed., *Women and Freedom in Early America* (New York: New York University Press, 1996).

43. Examination of Isabel Hope, Jan. 7, 1756, and town council judgment of Jan. 14, 1756, PTP, 1:129.

44. TCM, Jan. 20, 1775, Jamestown TCR, 2:117–18; TCM, Jan. 30, 1775, Westerly TCR, 4:250.

45. TCM, July 4, 1759, and Feb. 4 and June 16, 1760, Jamestown TCR, 1:99, 105, 113.

46. The records of the towns under study show forty-eight warnouts of people identified as native; thirty-six of those warnouts were directed at women and only twelve at men.

47. See Carole Shammas, "Anglo-American Household Government in Comparative Perspective," *William and Mary Quarterly*, 3rd ser., 52, no. 1 (January 1995), 104–44, esp. 109–15.

48. See, for example, the story of Aaron Stephenson, a sailor who became gravely ill during one of his many sea voyages under Captain William Read: TCM, Apr. 21, 1752, Jamestown TCR, 1:53. Native men were common seamen in far greater numbers than their share of the general population. See Ruth Wallis Herndon, "The Domestic Cost of Seafaring: Town Leaders and Seamen's Families in 18th Century Rhode Island," in Margaret Creighton and Lisa Norling, eds., *Iron Men, Wooden Women: Gender and Atlantic Seafaring, 1700–1920* (Baltimore: Johns Hopkins University Press, 1996).

49. The record is peppered with evidence of native men enlisting as soldiers. Jack Sawnos, for example, served as a soldier during the Seven Years' War, leaving his wife Betty to manage a household and children without him. Because he unwittingly brought smallpox back from New York and began a small epidemic in Exeter, his story is documented in the town records. Sawnos and his entire family were killed by the infection. TCM, Dec. 26, 1759, to May 13, 1760, Exeter TCR, 2:66–87.

50. See Shammas, "Anglo-American Household Government," 109–11.

51. TCM, July 4, 1759, Jamestown TCR, 1:99.

52. Examination of Mary Carder, Feb. 14, 1775, Providence TCR, 5:18 and PTP, 2:127.

53. TCM, Oct. 7, 1782, Charlestown TCR, 3:115.

54. TCM, Apr. 7, 1783, Charlestown TCR, 3:132.

55. TCM, Feb. 6, 1775, Charlestown TCR, 2:256.

56. *The Rhode Island 1777 Military Census* (Baltimore: Genealogical Publishing Co., 1985), 12–13.

57. See, for example, the payments made to Thomas Sachem and Samuel Niles for their "Six Month's service" in 1781. TCM, Jan. 1, 1781, Charlestown TCR, 3:18a. Most of the "Indian" men who had been classified as "able" to serve in the 1777 military census appear in military papers as evidence that they did in fact serve. Revolutionary War card index, Rhode Island State Archives.

58. TCM, Mar. 25, 1782, Charlestown TCR, 3:27.

59. John Aldrich v. John Hammer, October 8, 1793, Justice of the Peace Documents [1793], Hopkinton Town Clerk's Office. John Hammer eventually gave up

battling the judicial system in Rhode Island. In 1799, he petitioned the Smithfield Friends Meeting to assist him and a number of other Narragansett people who wished to leave the area and relocate in Oneida, New York. At that point, John Hammer was "a prisoner for Debt which arose from his purchasing a horse which he lost by Death"—a matter of $11.00. The Meeting voted to raise $200 to pay off the debts of Hammer and his fellow Narragansett and to fund the expedition for the families to move to New York: Records of the New England Yearly Meeting of Friends, Box 158, 1790 Meeting for Sufferings, Rhode Island Historical Society. I am indebted to Carla Cesario of the University of Wyoming for sharing with me her discovery of John Hammer's petition to the Friends Meeting.

60. See Conkey et al., "Indians of Southern New England," 177–78.

61. There were exceptions to this, of course. The Rhode Island town records occasionally refer to Africans whose names connected them to their previous lives or their place of birth. See, for example, the examination of Solomon Salters of the Mine (TCM, Dec. 17, 1795, Providence TCR, 7:67) and the examination of Titus Guinea (TCM, Mar. 15, 1788, Providence TCR, 6:39–40).

62. See page 116 and note 9.

63. In 1880, the committee appointed by the state to investigate the Indians in Rhode Island reported that no pure-blooded Indians remained: "We learn that there is not a person of pure Indian blood in the tribe, and that characteristic features varying through all the shades of color, from the Caucasian to the Black race, were made manifest at the several meetings of the Committee. Their extinction as a tribe has been accomplished as effectually by nature as an *Act* of the General Assembly will put an end to the name." The state used this report to justify official action to "detribalize" the Narragansett people and appropriate their land: State of Rhode Island and Providence Plantations, *Narragansett Tribe of Indians, Report of the Committee of Investigation . . . Made to the House of Representatives at its January Session, A.D., 1880* (Providence: E. L. Freeman & Co., 1880), quotation from 6. As early as 1852, white officials had claimed that there were "no Indians of whole blood remaining" among the people of the tribe. See State of Rhode Island and Providence Plantations, *Report of the Committee on the Indian Tribe* (Providence, 1852), 4–5; cited in LaFantasie and Campbell, "Land Controversies and the Narragansett Indians," 11.

64. TCM, Aug. 29, 1767, and Nov. 26, 1768, East Greenwich TCR, vol. 3. We have included "Mulatto" along with "Negro" for the same reason we included "Mustee" along with "Indian." Town officials made it clear in the record that they meant "Mulatto" to describe a person with African ancestry. Further, Samuel Johnson's eighteenth-century dictionary—a source consulted by town leaders in the late 1700s—defines "mulatto" as "One begot between a white and a black." See Johnson, *Dictionary* (1755) and note 10 above.

65. TCM, Feb. 3 and 6, 1784, and May 30, 1791, Providence TCR, 5:256–58, 6:163.

66. TCM, Mar. 11, 1788, Jamestown TCR, 2:202; TM, Aug. 26, 1788, Jamestown TMR, 1:325.

67. TCM, Mar. 13, 1775, and June 14, 1784, Warwick TCR, 3:39, 161.

68. TCM, Feb. 16, 1780, Sept. 17, 1787, and Aug. 9, 1784, Providence TCR, 5:162, 6:20, and PTP, 7:159.

69. TCM, July 14, 1780, East Greenwich TCR, 3:204; TCM, Feb. 9, 1784, Warwick TCR, 3:152. Usually town officials could physically observe the person involved, situated as they were on opposite sides of the council table. The indecisiveness of certain descriptions suggests that when white officials were unable to distinguish one race

from the other, they were unwilling or unable to obtain that information from the person who stood before them. Occasionally, officials made decisions about a person who was not present, and in those cases, they relied on the opinion of others about the race of the person involved.

70. Warnouts of Non-European People from Rhode Island Towns, 1750–1800

	Native People	African Americans
Warnouts	48	184
1750–1775	33 (69%)	22 (12%)
1776–1800	15 (31%)	162 (88%)

Note: 1,913 people were warned out between 1750 and 1800. Of that total, 2.5 percent (48) were designated American Indian and 9.6 percent (184) were designated African American.

71. Between 1750 and 1800, the leaders of the towns under study contracted 712 indentures of poor and orphaned children. Of these, 13.8 percent (98 contracts) were for Indian children. This percentage far exceeds the share of the state population designated native at this time — 3.8 percent in 1749; 1 percent in 1783: Evarts B. Greene and Virginia D. Harrington, *American Population Before the Federal Census of 1790* (Gloucester, Mass: Peter Smith, 1966), 66, 69–70. It suggests either that there was an unusually large proportion of poor and orphaned Indian children in the towns, or that white officials were more likely to put native children into indentures than they were to bind out white children.

72. Public Indentures of Non-European Children in Rhode Island, 1750–1800

	Native Children	African American Children
Total contracts	98	74
1750–1775	76 (77.6%)	15 (20.3%)
1776–1800	22 (22.4%)	59 (79.7%)

73. Another factor worth considering here is that, officially, the "Negro" population was falling in Rhode Island during this period — from 6.3 percent of the population in 1790 to 5.3 percent in 1800. U.S. Bureau of the Census, *Negro Population 1790–1915* (Washington, D.C.: U.S. Government Printing Office, 1918), 51.

74. See, for example, the complaint by Joseph Clarke about "Indian Woman" Mary's abandonment of her "mustee" son Jem (TCM, Mar. 27, 1762, Jamestown TCR, 1:143); and the complaint by Jonathan Hazard about "Indian Squaw" Lydia Rodman's "mustee" son London (TCM, May 11, 1769, South Kingstown TCR, 5:215).

75. TCM, Mar. 6, 1798, Providence TCR, 7:226–27.

76. TCM, May 14, 1796, South Kingstown TCR, 6:230. We are assuming that the clerk was using Mary Cummock's words, and not his own, when he included the term "white" in this examination. The local records only rarely use this term, and then only at the very end of the eighteenth century. For most of the eighteenth century, clerks identified by color only those who were *not* European American.

77. TCM, Dec. 13, 1762 and June 14, 1773, Warwick TCR, 2:221–22, 3:25; TCM, Mar. 5, 1770, Feb. 17, 1772, Mar. 20 and Apr. 4, 1780, and Oct. 1, 1787, Providence TCR, 4:299, 322, 5:168–69, 172, 6:23; Warrant for removal of Sarah Gardner, Oct. 1, 1787, PTP, 10:148.

78. TCM, July 16, 1751, Jamestown TCR, 1:44.

79. TCM, Dec. 10, 1764, Warren TMR, 1:87.

80. TCM, Nov. 1, 1758, Jamestown TCR, 1:95.

81. The council eventually dismissed the complaint against Fowler. TCM, Feb. 12 and Mar. 12, 1753, South Kingstown TCR, 4:224, 227.

82. TCM, Sep. 8, 1760, South Kingstown TCR, 5:96.

83. "An Act to prevent all Persons, within this Colony, from entertaining Indian, Negro or Mulatto Servants or Slaves." *Acts and Laws of Rhode Island* [1767], 151–52.

84. Robinson's wigwam is mentioned in TCM, Oct. 10, 1768, South Kingstown TCR, 5:204. White leaders' concerns are evident, for example, in South Kingstown council's decision to rent a house so that Sarah Gardner, a native mother with three young children, would have a place "to live in this Winter." TCM, Nov. 19, 1762, Warwick TCR, 2:218. And the Jamestown council similarly decided to make arrangements for Jack Marsh, who was so "very decrepit" that they feared he would "perish in the Winter Season." TCM, Aug. 27, 1754, Jamestown TCR, 1:76.

85. Of all 1,913 warnout orders, 2.5 percent named a person described as Indian — 47 individual citations. There were probably many more native people named in the record but not described as native. Reuben Suckmug, for example, bears a name with a decidedly Indian ring, but the town clerk who wrote down his transient examination made no mention of his race. TCM, Oct. 13, 1797, Providence TCR, 7:200.

86. TCM, Aug. 28, 1759 and May 24, 1760, Jamestown TCR, 1:100–102; TCM, June 3, 1760, South Kingstown TCR, 5:91. The South Kingstown clerk identified him as "Cato a Mustee Late a Bound Servant to Mr. John Gardner," thus emphasizing this man's former servitude and diluting his Indian heritage. In contrast, the Jamestown clerk identified him as "Cato Gardner" and described him as an "Indian." It is likely that the Jamestown records reflect how Gardner described *himself* to the councilmen who questioned him — fully Indian and with a full name.

87. TCM, May 24, 1763, May 15, 1764, Mar. 23, 1767, and Apr. 30, 1768, Jamestown TCR, vol. 1; TCM, July 18, 1768, New Shoreham TCR, 4:174.

88. TM, Jan. 5 and Apr. 20, 1757, Middletown TMR, 1:60–61; TCM, May 16, 1757, Middletown TCR, 1:332.

89. Herndon, "Governing the Affairs of the Town," 149–54.

90. TCM, Jan. 15, 1781, Charlestown TCR, 3:49–50.

91. TCM, July 4, 1759, Oct. 18, 1763, and Jan. 27, 1766, Jamestown TCR, 1:99, 154, 211.

92. TM, July 16 and Aug. 3, 1780, Hopkinton TMR, 1:291–93. Samuel Babcock was the second wealthiest man assessed in Hopkinton in 1779 and 1780: see state tax lists of Mar. 23, Apr. 6, July 16, and Sept. 10, 1779, and town tax list of Jan. 26, 1780, Hopkinton Town Clerk's Office. Because of Babcock's strong objections to his servant's enlistment, the townspeople promised him that if the boy turned out to be under age, Babcock could claim the boy as his own substitute in the next general town draft. If Babcock had been unable to find the indenture contract among his own records, he would have had to obtain a copy from the town clerk or from the boy's parents or guardians in his home town. This business could easily have taken him three weeks.

93. A number of scholars have argued persuasively that racial ideology developed in the United States during the Revolutionary era when European Americans tried to explain away the unfree status of slaves in the newly free republic. See especially Barbara Jean Fields, "Slavery, Race and Ideology in the United States of America," *New Left Review*, 181 (1990), 95–118. For discussions of the emergence of racial ideology in New England during the Revolutionary era, see Sweet, "Bodies Politic," and Joanne Pope

Melish, "Disowning Slavery: Gradual Emancipation and the Cultural Construction of 'Race' in New England, 1780–1850" (Ph.D. diss., Brown University, 1996).

94. Gradual emancipation provided that all children born to slave mothers after March 1, 1784, would be freed when they reached eighteen (for girls) or twenty-one (for boys). Masters were under no obligation to free anyone born before that date, and it took an act of the state legislature in 1842 to free all remaining slaves.

95. Melish, "Disowning Slavery."

96. Yasu Kawashima has suggested that government officials in colonial Massachusetts expected "the eventual assimilation of the Indians into the whites' society": "Legal Origins of the Indian Reservation," 56, 43. We find it more likely that white leaders expected native people to assimilate into *nonwhite* society that existed on the economic, political, and social margins of white society. In his study, Kawashima discovered that the Indian reservation system in Massachusetts "began to deteriorate rapidly during the Revolutionary period" as whites purchased tracts within the reservations and took up official positions as reservation officials: "Legal Origins of the Indian Reservation," 55. Although Kawashima does not speculate about the reasons for the timing of this white takeover, it is probably due to the same forces that stimulated Rhode Island officials to write native people off the record—the growing population of free blacks provided an opportunity to advance this black-Indian "assimilation."

97. TM, Apr. 22, 1780, New Shoreham TMR, 5:8.

Jean M. O'Brien

6

"Divorced" from the Land

Resistance and Survival of Indian Women in Eighteenth-Century New England

In 1624, Edward Winslow, Governor of Plymouth colony, observed about Native Americans that "[t]he women live a most slavish life; they carry all their burdens, set and dress their corn, gather it in, and seek out for much of their food, beat and make ready the corn to eat and have all household care lying upon them."[1] Winslow's use of the term "slavish" in this passage is instructive. The portrayal of the Native American woman as "squaw drudge" who toiled endlessly for her "lazie husband" was both a common English analysis of Native American division of labor in the northeastern woodlands and a commentary upon English expectations about gender roles.[2] Observers viewed Indian women as "slaves" because, unlike English women, they performed virtually all of the agricultural labor in their societies.[3] In fact, most labor the English would have regarded as male work was performed by Indian women.

The "squaw drudge" permeated early observations of Native Americans in the northeast. Two centuries later, different kinds of images of Indian women could be found in local accounts. Consider the following: "The last Indian here was 'Hannah Shiner,' a full-blood who lived with 'Old Toney,' a noble-souled mulatto man . . . Hannah was kind-hearted, a faithful friend, a sharp enemy, a judge of herbs, a weaver of baskets, and a lover of rum."[4] This description, taken from a nineteenth-century history of Medford, Massachusetts, reflects not just the passage of time but also the extent to which relations, roles, and expectations had changed on both sides of a sustained cultural encounter.

The juxtaposition of these two fundamentally different portrayals reveals crucial changes in the circumstances of Indian women in New England. Four key structural changes differentiate the historical eras from which the images come. First, Indian societies that were "tribal" and politically independent prior to intensive colonization became effectively "detribalized" and politically encompassed by the late seventeenth century. By this time, most Indian individuals and families were incorporated into English communities, mostly in small clusters that rendered Indians virtually invisible within the context of the now-dominant New English society. Second, the prosperity of Indian societies, based on diversified agricultural economies and intensive use of seasonally available plant and game resources, was undermined as the English gained possession of nearly all Indian land by the end of the seventeenth century. The central element of the Indian economy was thus eliminated, requiring fundamental changes that resulted in the recasting of Native gender roles. Third, Indian societies that stressed communal values, sharing, and reciprocity were thrust into a market economy with the advent of colonization. Immersion in the market left Indians at the mercy of English legal institutions and affected the shape of Native social welfare practices. And fourth, Indians were quickly rendered a minority population within their own homelands by the astounding success of the English demographic regime, which was coupled with Indian struggles caused by imported diseases and military encounters. These structural changes compelled Indians to see the landscape in a different way, requiring them to make massive adjustments, and eliciting myriad and contradictory responses.[5]

As they successfully dispossessed and displaced Indians, the heirs of English colonialism seized the power to define the rules governing the social order, and they constructed surviving New England Indians as peculiar and marginal. Local historians underscored the "disappearance" of the Indian population by singling out individuals such as Hannah Shiner as representing the "last survivor" of their "tribe." Even so, historians used their representations of Indians as peculiar and marginal, as hopelessly "other," to continue to constitute and affirm an English identity. They presented Indians such as Hannah Shiner as the complement to "Englishness," thereby reminding themselves of the persistent difference between Indian survivors and themselves. But more than just reinforcing the difference between Indians and themselves, the ways in which they used this binary operated to emphasize English dominance.[6]

The English colonial regime imposed a different landscape, one requiring Indians to transform their relationship to the land. Gender figured prominently in this transformation. The English aimed to "divorce" Indians from their possession of the land in order to establish themselves and English culture in their place. New England Indians' agricultural, hunting, fishing, and gathering economy was interpreted as wasteful, and the sedentary agriculture pursued by English men was seen as the only proper pursuit for Native men. Yet even as they pursued the larger project of English colonialism (replacing Indians and Indian ways of using the land with English people using the land in English ways), colonists also aimed to convert surviving Indians to English culture. As they separated Indians from possession of virtually all their land, colonists also sought to "divorce" Indian women from their role as agriculturalists, replacing them with male Indians working drastically reduced plots of land to the exclusion of hunting and other older economic pursuits. From the perspective of the English, "divorce" from the land would fulfill the biblical directive to "subdue the earth and multiply" by bringing land into agricultural production to sustain a growing English Christian population. And it would also place Indian women and men in a "proper" relationship to the land. In the most crucial sense, however, the English failed to "divorce" either Indian women or Indian men from the land. Although in narrow legal terms, the English succeeded in imposing their own rules for possessing the land, New England Indians did not monolithically embrace English gender ways. They remained crucially connected to the land that sustained their kinship and visiting networks and their own sense of proper place.[7]

In addressing the transformations accompanying the cultural conflicts between Indians and English colonists, I will focus on the issue of "gendered division of labor" rather than on the important problem of lineality in the northeastern woodlands, which also involved different conceptions of how gender ought to operate. Use of the dichotomous construction of matrilineal/patrilineal obscures much diversity in the ordering of families, reckoning of descent, ordering of power relations, and much more. Because of the paucity of early sources that provide detailed information on social organization, combined with the early occurrence of devastating epidemics throughout the region, there is much we will never know about the "precontact" shape of social organization in the northeastern woodlands. Indian peoples in early New England were concerned overwhelmingly with resisting and surviving English incursions, and the disruptions of epidemics that accompanied early contact certainly must have obscured their previous shape at least to some extent. About all that is evident is that, by the eighteenth century, patrilineal naming practices predominated among Indians; whether this was the case because it had always been so, or because the English imposed these forms on Indians in bureaucratic transactions, is not so clear.[8]

About a gendered division of labor, much more seems to be apparent. Most scholars agree that women performed most agricultural labor (except growing tobacco), built and transported bark or mat wigwams from place to place, manufactured baskets and pottery, gathered shellfish and wild foodstuff, processed hides, made clothing, and raised children. Men also made some household tools and were the principal woodworkers, making canoes and fortifications, for example.[9]

By 1700, Native American groups in New England had a long history of encounters with Europeans. Indians reeled from the impact of imported epidemic diseases, with many groups suffering demographic declines on the order of 90 percent. Military conquest followed quickly on the heels of the epidemiological disasters. The last major war in southeastern New England ended in 1676, terminating the political independence of those Native groups who had hitherto avoided encompassment by the English. These events effectively ended the autonomy of Indian groups in that region and rendered many aspects of the aboriginal economy obsolete through massive displacement and dispossession. Under the cumulative impact of the colonial experience, a great many New England Indians found themselves landless, a diasporic population vulnerable to the institutions of English colonialism.[10]

Missionary sponsorship had secured land bases for several Indian groups in the seventeenth century as part of English efforts to transform Indian cultures. Here, the English expected Indians to alter their gender roles in conformity with English cultural prerogatives.[11] Indian groups were allowed to retain small plots of land provided they would express responsiveness to missionary messages about cultural change. The English expected Indians to erect compact, English-style towns in order to fix them in particular places, directed men to forego hunting in favor of agricultural duties, and trained women in "household skills," especially spinning and weaving. Indians were encouraged to adopt English work habits, individual ownership of land, English tastes in material culture, and values structured by a market economy. Some Indians experimented with cultural transformations along these lines, but success in the market economy did not follow so easily. Many Indians were landless at the beginning of the eighteenth century, and, as their land was transformed into a commodity, Indian landowners continued to lose land.[12] Many were encompassed within the flourishing English settlements, finding niches in colonial economies, performing agricultural and nonagricultural labor.

Although some Indians steadfastly resisted English influences on their lifeways, and others struggled within the market economy, still others borrowed extensively from English culture as a means of accommodating to English colonialism. In some senses, Jacob and Leah Chalcom symbolized Indian transformation as conceptualized by the English. Chalcom purchased land, established an English-style farm, and built a frame house in Natick, Massachusetts, an important mission town established seventeen miles southwest of Boston. He was involved actively in the local land market, buying and selling small parcels from time to time as he strove to upgrade his farm. The cultural priorities of this family are visible in their childrearing practices. The Chalcom children were literate, and the daughters were given dowries upon their marriages to local Indian men.[13] After his death, Chalcom's estate included a thirty-acre homelot and "Buildings thereon," plus other lands, an assortment of household goods and husbandry tools, a horse, a cow, and books. After debts against his estate were discharged, fifty-two acres of land remained to be divided among his heirs.[14]

The women in Chalcom's family had made corresponding changes in their lifeways, including their separation from agricultural tasks. Leah Chalcom and her widowed daughters, Esther Sooduck and Hepzibeth Peegun, inherited land from their husband and father respectively. Finding themselves without husbands, they pondered what to do with their inheritance. In 1759 they petitioned the Massachusetts General Court to sell their forty-six acres, arguing that "as your Petitioners [have been] brought up to Household business, [we are] incapable of improving said lands."[15] They requested that their lands be sold and the money be put out to earn interest for their income and support, a strategy adopted by a number of women. The implication here is quite clear: These women were no longer farmers and were thus unable to "improve" the land except insofar as it represented a monetary resource. The mother and daughters recognized that English financial strategies could sustain them and prolong the nurturing functions of land from which they were effectively torn loose. Putting money "at interest" constituted one strategy for women who had maintained clear "legal" connections to the land. Their decision not to use the land for gardening, as English women often did, in part reflected their perception that if they chose to keep the land it would "speedily be exhausted by frequent Law-Suits."[16]

The "Household business" to which Leah Chalcom and her daughters referred reflects the efforts of English missionaries to realign Native American gender roles. Biblical imperatives motivated missionaries who aimed to train Indian women in English skills for structuring a household, and to integrate Indian families into the market economy. In 1648, missionary John Eliot wrote that: "[t]he women are desirous to learn to spin, and I have procured Wheels for sundry of them, and they can spin pretty well. They begin to grow industrious, and find something to sell at Market all the yeer long[.]"[17] Some Indian women continued to pursue these tasks that missionaries had pushed so vigorously in the early years of intensive English-Indian contact. Fifteen percent of inventories of Indian estates from Natick filed between 1741 and 1763 listed spinning wheels.[18] Ruth Thomas, who died in 1758, was described in her probate docket as a weaver; Esther Freeborn and Hannah Lawrence, sisters who both left wills, were described as spinsters.[19]

Esther Sooduck, also a weaver, died in 1778. Her probate documents vividly evoke the kinds of changes Indian women confronted even though very few accumulated and held onto material goods as successfully as Esther had.[20] Her house, described as "much out of repair," nonetheless contained an impressive array of furnishings and sat upon thirty acres of land. Included among her belongings were a bed and bedstead, a chest, a trunk, a rug, a table and two chairs, plus knives, forks, and pewter. She read her two old Bibles with "speti-cals." She owned two spinning wheels, as well as baskets and "Baskets Stuf."[21] Apparently merged in her economic pursuits were English skills (spinning and weaving) and Native American artisanal production (basket-making).

Native American women displayed transformations in their work habits, material life, aesthetic emphases, and even their physical appearance. Han-nah Lawrence owned several articles of clothing when she died in the 1770s, including several gowns and aprons (one of them linen) as well as quilted pet-ticoats and a pair of shoes with buckles.[22] Cloth replaced animal skins, petti-coats and gowns were substituted for skirts and leggings. These accommoda-tions were rooted in more than a century of profound cultural change. And in many ways, they represent an *up*rooting, a broken connection: English-style clothing signified the distance women had moved from their former way of life. Eighteenth-century economic adaptations no longer produced the mate-rials for older ways of clothing production, and adopting English styles proba-bly reflected not just this reality but also newer Indian tastes.

There were many ways in which Native American women in eighteenth-century New England *were* divorced from the land: the colonial experience reoriented their relationship to the land in tangible and not so tangible ways. English ideals for cultural change aimed to realign the Indians' gendered economy and make room for English people to subdue the land in English ways. For Indian women, this meant a stark separation: once the principal producers of the crucial agricultural element of subsistence economies, women were expected to sever the vital connection they had to the soil as its principal cultivators and nurturers. Though the English who wanted to ac-complish these changes may not have noticed, their models for transforma-tion went well beyond a simple shift in the gendered organization of labor. On the practical level, knowledge and skills were altered drastically, and the content of material life was dramatically recast. On the ideological level, less visible reverberations can only be imagined in individual and corporate iden-tity, belief systems, and other deeply rooted cultural values. The tensions ac-companying these transformations can be glimpsed in one possible explana-tion for the ultimate failure of Indian men as farmers in a market economy, which suggests that their reluctance to tend crops stemmed from their view that these "effeminate" pursuits properly remained women's work.[23] In refus-ing English gender ideals, many Indian men resisted this foundational con-cept of English colonialism.

Leah Chalcom, Esther Sooduck, Hannah Lawrence—all of these women came from one kind of Indian community. They all lived in Indian-dominated towns, their land ownership sanctioned by the English, who conferred "posses-sion" of these reduced plots of land according to English legal principals. At least in this nominal sense, they were beneficiaries of missionary endeavors.[24] Although they were relatively successful in emulating English ways, as the eighteenth century unfolded, the slow but steady dispossession of Indian landowners allowed fewer Indians to replicate earlier successes. Other Indians were uprooted utterly almost from the beginning of their contact with the English. They adjusted to English invasion differently, mapping out alternative kinds of lifeways. After the 1660s, for example:

> The remnant of the Pocumtuck Confederacy, adopting in part the English costume, had gathered about the English in the valley towns . . . Here they lived a vagabond life, eking out, as they could, a miserable existence on the outskirts of civilization . . . So hampered, their stock of venison or beaver, with which to traffic for English comforts, was small, and the baskets and birch brooms made by the squaws ill supplied their place.[25]

This is a stark outline of the principal difficulties Indians faced in making the transition to landlessness within a society emphasizing the market. With the possibilities for hunting gone, and no land—what remained? Production of Indian crafts constituted one possibility for women, who remained important in the economy and maintained this earlier economic role, which was possible even when landless. In their artisanal production, women continued to cultivate the specialized knowledge required to gather materials for fashioning baskets and other crafts. Their craftwork represented a revealing accommodation to dispossession: reaping basket stuff did not require "possession" of the land. At the same time, in marketing Indian goods, they earned an income and reinforced their "Indianness" in the popular perception.

Craft production by Indian women constituted one of the crucial threads that ran through the seventeenth, eighteenth, and nineteenth centuries in New England. Indian women in the eighteenth century were engaged especially in basket making as an economic activity, but other artisanal skills were added as well.[26] In 1764, Abigail Moheag attested that she was "64 years of Age and . . . a widow [for] more than fifteen years and hath . . . by her Industery in the business of making Brooms Baskets and horse Collars; Supported her Self till about two years ago She was taken sick."[27] The inventory from Hannah Speen's estate listed "baskets and barkes, brombs and brombsticks."[28] Craftwork, including the production of "new" items like horse collars, moved from the periphery of women's economic activities to the center as Indian women became enmeshed in the market and were no longer engaged in farming. For some women, craft production was fundamentally redefined. No longer one activity in an integrated economy, performed seasonally and for purposes largely internal to the household, artisanal activities became specialized and divorced from seasonal rhythms, and a principal means to get a living.

Wage labor constituted another possibility for Indian women. It remains unclear just what kind of work Indian women were doing, or what it was they received in return. In 1755, the circumstances of some Indian women at

Mattakeset were such that "at present they live among White People, and work with them for a living."[29] The formula in these kinds of situations may have involved the contribution of unskilled and unspecialized labor, perhaps domestic work, in exchange for small wages or even some degree of basic sustenance. The existence of small clusters of Indians in virtually every Massachusetts town suggests that the lives of English colonists and Indians were intertwined in ways we are only beginning to understand.[30]

Disruption of Native societies extended to every sphere, requiring their constant adjustment. Marginal individuals, that is, those with few relatives or friends, Indian or non-Indian, and little in the way of economic resources, suffered the most. Prior to Indian enmeshment in the market, caretaking and nursing constituted central kinship obligations. During the eighteenth century, as kinship networks thinned, families became fractured, and involvement in the market made prosperity precarious at best. Individuals could no longer count on thick networks of relatives to care for them when they were in need of shelter, sustenance, or support. Nursing and caretaking became commodified and unreliable. Even when an intact family was in place, taking on caretaking obligations in this changed context could spell the economic ruin of a precariously established family. These developments represented the cumulative effect of generations of demographic decline, military conquest, economic disruption, and cultural transformation. Abigail Speen reported to the General Court in 1747 that she had

> by Reason of her great age & infirmities . . . been long and still is Unable to do anything to Support herself, & so having cast herself on Mr. Joseph Graves of Sd Natick [an Englishman;] She has been kind entertained & Supported at his House now for near two years, & has nothing to recompense Sd Graves with nor to procure for her the Necessaries of Life for the time present & to come.[31]

This woman had land, and she liquidated the remainder of her estate in order to pay Graves. No doubt he realized that his "investment" was secured by that plot of land she owned in Natick. This replacement of Indian kinship obligations with market-driven social welfare occurred throughout New England and accounted for much dispossession of Indian peoples who might otherwise face legal proceedings for debts they accumulated.[32]

Just as Abigail Speen cast herself on Joseph Graves, Indian women cast themselves upon other Indian women, too. What differed in the eighteenth century was that these women were not necessarily relatives, and that nursing or caretaking was often given in exchange for monetary compensation. The administrators of the estate of Elizabeth Paugenit, for example, allowed nearly two pounds to Hannah Awassamug "for nursing."[33] Sarah Wamsquan was cared for by Eunice Spywood, among others. Englishman John Jones petitioned the General Court in 1770, setting forth Sarah's dire circumstances and begging: "let something be done that Shall Speedily relieve the poor person that has her—or they will perish together."[34] Town authorities did not always countenance such arrangements. In 1765, when "Sarah Short a molatto woman Last from Wrentham [was] Taken in by Esther Sodeck," Natick selectmen feared she would become a town charge and warned her that she should leave the town.[35]

Banding together just to survive, these women struggled within a radically changing world. Often their situation was complicated by the dramatic transformations accompanying their dispossession, which stretched Indian communities thinly across the landscape to form a network of small clusters of families throughout southeastern New England. One response was to move constantly in search of a niche. As landlessness accelerated throughout the eighteenth century, a pattern of Indian vagrancy emerged: this pattern, accepted by the dominant society as natural, was also an accommodation strategy. Indian women, especially, were described as wandering from place to place, a characteristic that was associated in the public mind particularly with Indians. An Englishman of Dorchester petitioned the General Court in 1753 as follows:

> An Indian Woman called Mercy Amerquit, I think Born Somewhere about Cape-Cod, but had no settled Dwellingplace any where, . . . Strolled about from one Town & Place to another, & sometimes she wrought for Persons that wanted her work[. She] came to my House . . . and desired liberty to tarry a little while, and your Petr condescended, expecting that she would go some other place in a little time (as their manner is) and what work she did for your Petr she was paid for as she earned it.[36]

It is clear from this passage that English observers expected Indians to "wander." Their semisedentary lifeways had always been regarded most simplistically as nomadism. In the eighteenth century this translated into constant movement, "from one Town & Place to another . . . as their manner is." In this case, an arrangement seems to have been negotiated that involved Mercy Amerquit performing labor for wages as well as for her temporary residence with the narrator. He expected her to "go [to] some other place in a little time," and the arrangement was regarded as rather unexceptional. The only reason this relationship was documented at all was because Amerquit died while in the petitioner's residence and he sought to recover money he expended for her burial.

The story of Mercy Amerquit was by no means unique. An Englishman from Roxbury reported to the General Court about sixty-year-old Hannah Comsett, who became ill at his house: "She informs that her Mother was born at Barnstable, she at Scituate, and that for 30 years past she has been [strolling] about from Town to Town geting her living where she could but never lived During that time the space of one year at any Town at any time."[37] Though

Hannah Comsett's mobility seems rather astounding, there are so many similar stories available that it is certain it was not an aberration.

The mechanisms behind Indian vagrancy were complex. Prior to the arrival of the English, Indian societies in New England reaped abundance from economies that depended upon knowledge about and extensive use of resources and a semisedentary lifeway. Scheduled mobility lay at the center of this system. In the eighteenth century, Indian migrations may have been scheduled, but if so, they were motivated by very different priorities, since they could no longer rely on movements governed by independently composed Indian communities to and from places that "belonged" to them in the strict legal sense. Probably kinship ties and some knowledge of labor markets entered into movements, but for women like Mercy and Hannah, there seemed to be nothing particularly patterned about their shifting about. Perhaps it was setting about to track the occasional charitable English colonist that spurred on the solitary and needy Indian women, from whom a different kind of resource might be procured. One important element that differentiated earlier migratory practices from new patterns was their largely individual nature; this new "vagrancy" drew upon older patterns and places, but was not necessarily kin-group sponsored movement with planned, deliberate ends in mind. At the heart of the problem lay landlessness, whether it had resulted from military conquest in the seventeenth century or from failure in the market economy in the eighteenth. "Divorced" from the land initially when their economic role was redefined along English lines, a much more literal separation had been accomplished for most by the middle of the eighteenth century.

The situation of these women hints at two recurrent themes regarding Indian women in eighteenth-century New England. First, transiency is graphically described in a manner consistent with the emerging problem of landless poverty in New England more generally. The "wandering Indian" had much in common with the "strolling poor,"[38] although the fact that the English categorically distinguished between the two offers testimony for their separatist views about race. The problem of Indian women seems to have been compounded, however. The extent to which these are stories of women alone, or mostly alone, is the second theme and it is most striking.

Where were the men? The evidence suggests that, despite the missionary model of settled agriculture performed by men within nuclear families on family farms, transiency also remained characteristic even of landowning Indian men. Most Indian landowners lost what they had over time, and the tendency for Indian men to enter service in two areas (military service and the emerging whaling industry) contributed to a grossly distorted sort of transiency.[39] As a result of their participation in these activities, Indian men were absent for extended periods of time, engaged in dangerous pursuits that seriously jeopardized their lives and well-being and compromised their ability to function effectively within the English-dominated society. Whaling, in fact, fostered the same sort of debt peonage that proved so devastating in fur trade relationships.[40] These orientations contributed to uncertainty and instability for Indian families and also reduced the number of Indian men available as desirable spouses. Interpretations of the involvement of Indian men in the military and labor at sea have stressed the continuity in skills and culturally determined priorities they offered them.[41] But some men also abandoned their families to escape their predicaments; evidence may be found in scattered narratives of Indian men "absconding" as difficult circumstances evolved into insurmountable economic and legal problems. Such was the case for Eunice Spywood's husband, who "Some Years Ago Absconded and left her in very distressing Circumstances, and he . . . never returned."[42]

An important cumulative effect of English colonialism was to reconfigure the relationships among Indian mobility, a gendered division of labor, and household structures. The semisedentary Indian economy entailed a gendered mobility that assumed that women and men would be apart for periods of time: Men departed central villages for hunting and fishing, leaving women to tend crops and gather wild plant resources near their villages, for example.[43] But these periods of separation were scheduled, part of the seasonal rhythm of life, and as such they rendered neither women nor men helpless. Newer patterns of male mobility (such as participation in the whaling industry and the military) that drew upon older Indian lifeways frequently left women alone to experience harsher circumstances than before, when kin-based social welfare and flexible marriages had provided them with the means to alleviate their wants.[44] At least for women like Mercy Amerquit and Hannah Comsett, mobility was circumscribed by virtue of their being separated from men. And whereas whaling and military service may have reformulated earlier patterns of Indian male mobility, allowing men to resist the redefinition of gender in economic and social roles, the wives of these men—women like Eunice Spywood—were defined as "responsibilities" in new ways and experienced far greater hardship as a result of their men's flight. The English nuclear family model thus reconfigured kin responsibilities and marriage, leaving Indian women newly vulnerable to "divorce" in dramatically different ways.

Whatever the underlying motivations, Indians of both sexes experienced hardship as a direct result of participation of Indian men in military service, especially. The social and demographic impact of the Seven Years' War on Indian enclaves in New England was enormous. In 1756, a cluster of Indians at Mattakesett in Pembroke, Massachusetts, pleaded to the General Court "that Several of us [have] in the late Warrs, lost our husbands & Sons, & Some of our Sons [are] yet in Sd Service, & that some of us are old, blind, & bed rid & helpless poor Creatures, Many of us [are] old Women & want help."[45] Indians of Eastham and Harwich in Barnstable County, Massachusetts, complained that many of their men "Have Died in ye Service & left their Squa & Children in Distressing Circumstances."[46] In 1761 Ezra Stiles reported that in

Portsmouth, Rhode Island, "4 Ind. Boys [had] enlisted in the service . . . only one Boy more in Town, & he [is] about 10 y. old. I can't find . . . any Ind. Men in Town, . . . but several Squaws, perhaps 8 or 10." At Milford, Connecticut, there were twenty male Indians in 1755, at the beginning of the Seven Years' War, but in 1761 "not one: but 3 or 4 Squaws."[47]

Even when they did return, many Indian men were rendered incapable of working to support themselves or their families as a result of war-related disabilities. Thomas Awassamug complained to the Massachusetts General Court in 1761 that "he having been engaged . . . as a Soldier . . . for more than thirty years past, has indured inexpressible hardships, and fatigues and thereby brought on him the Gout, and many other ailments . . . And [he has] no means of support."[48] Awassamug sought to stir compassion by describing in detail his "deplorable Circumstances," and to clarify his own relationship with the colony by reminding the magistrates that he had "jeopardized his life in so many . . . very dangerous Enterprizes against those of his nation who remain Savage, and in behalf of his friends, the English." The General Court allowed a small sum to be paid out of the public treasury for his temporary relief.

No comprehensive evidence is available to investigate the precise dynamics of demographic change for Indians in eighteenth-century New England. Several censuses gathered by Stiles in his journeys through the region are suggestive, however. In addition to his more random observations, Stiles compiled detailed lists of residents by household from three Indian communities he visited in 1761 and 1762. In these communities, widows constituted heads of households in proportions ranging from 29 percent (Mashantucket Pequot in Groton, Connecticut) to 52 percent (the "Potenummekuk" Indians in Eastham and Nauset, Massachusetts). These figures suggest that the tribulations outlined above were not idle and unconnected complaints.[49]

One solution to the apparently growing problem of unbalanced sex ratios and insufficient numbers of Indian men was for Indian women to find spouses among free or enslaved African Americans, who occupied similarly marginal positions in New England. The dynamics of intermarriage between Indians and African Americans are difficult to map precisely from the surviving documentary record. Impressionistic evidence does exist. Stiles observed in 1761 that "At Grafton [Massachusetts] . . . I saw the Burying place & Graves of 60 or more Indians. Now not a Male Ind. in the Town, & perh. 5 Squaws who marry Negroes." A nineteenth-century history of Needham, Massachusetts, noted that there was "a colony of negroes, with more or less Indian blood, dwelling along the south shore of Bullard's Pond (Lake Waban)."[50] Clearly, intermarriage did occur, as yet another kind of accommodation on the part of Indian women, representing an important demographic shift for Native populations of the northeast.

Equating "Indianness" with "blood quantum" (the perceived importance of "pure" blood lines) in rigid ways, English observers failed to understand the demographic and cultural changes that were reconfiguring "race" in New England. Intermarriage, which blurred the picture for those who looked for racial "purity," helped the Native population of New England to survive the devastating consequences of English colonization. Most colonists who noticed Indians just lamented what they saw as an inevitable process of extinction. Some vaguely grasped the complex process of vagrancy and intermarriage that was so central to eighteenth-century accommodations, even if their cultural blinders rendered them incapable of analyzing the changes. In 1797, the minister at Natick observed that

> It is difficult to ascertain the complete number of those that are now here, or that belong to this place, as they are so frequently shifting their place of residence, and are intermarried with blacks, and some with whites; and the various shades between these, and those that are descended from them, make it almost impossible to come to any determination about them.[51]

Indians became, like other groups displaced by the colonizing impulse of the English, a diasporic population defined by the complex transformations and dislocations brought about by English colonialism. In the end, the migratory pattern and complexities of intermarriage created an erroneous impression in the minds of English observers that the Native population was simply and inevitably melting away.[52]

In truth, monumental Indian adjustments spanned the entire colonial period and stretched into the nineteenth century. Both precontact Native American societies in the northeast and early modern European societies were organized according to particular expectations about gender roles. In New England, Indian women were responsible for most agricultural tasks, for gathering wild foods, building houses, most craft production, and childrearing. Men were warriors, diplomats, hunters, and fishermen, and they aided women in agricultural production by clearing fields. This way of organizing society came into direct conflict with English expectations, and the ability to maintain an economy that perfectly reflected older Native gender roles ran into the hard realities of changing circumstances. The loss of political independence and the massive displacement of Indians within their homelands brought tremendous changes that affected Indian women and men in different ways. Hunting and fishing became marginal, diplomacy became obsolete, and military involvement was transformed into economic activity. Agriculture was enormously altered in technique and organization: it became predominantly if not exclusively a male activity for Indian landowners, and it became a diminishing element of the Indian economy as Indians continued to lose land throughout the eighteenth century.

Although English expectations for change within Indian culture (encapsulated most fully in missionary platforms) called for altering the gendered Indian division of labor, the English did not fully succeed in "divorcing" Indian women (or men) from the land. Even though they quite successfully dispossessed Indians, Indians remained in the homelands that continued to sustain their kin, community, and sense of place. Indian women and men found creative solutions for resisting displacement and surviving as Indian people in a milieu theoretically designed to erase their difference completely.

How does all of this connect to Hannah Shiner? The manner in which she is portrayed in the nineteenth-century account that I began with, compared to how she might have been characterized in the seventeenth century, speaks volumes. This Indian woman is not described generically, as most Indian women were when regarded as members of a tribal unit, but as an individual with an Anglicized name. Her categorization as an Indian is based on the observer's judgment of her (pure) genealogy. And her husband is seen as a "mulatto," a mate who probably could trace some African American heritage. Hannah Shiner was assigned several traits, including two ("judge of herbs" and "weaver of baskets") that were associated in the public imagination with "Indianness," and especially with Indian women. They also suggest trades, or means of support, that had always been female activities. Hannah Shiner symbolizes the tumultuous changes experienced by Native peoples in seventeenth- and eighteenth-century New England. Indian peoples survived the catastrophe of English colonization, and they resisted the erasure of their Indianness. Men and women experienced the fundamental transformations in their lifeways differently. "Divorced" from the land in some respects but, crucially, not in others, many women displayed the characteristics that are visible in this brief description of Hannah Shiner. Apparently accepted and incorporated as an individual member of the community of Medford, Massachusetts, Hannah Shiner represents a particular kind of transformation, though not of the sort English missionaries had in mind. "Marginal" and a bit "exotic," she was portrayed as a bit of "local color," a tangible tie to what seemed to be (but was not) an increasingly distant Indian past. Her configuration by a local historian as such was precisely what Anglo-Americans needed for her to continue to represent the "otherness" necessary for the ongoing construction of their own difference.

NOTES

Acknowledgments: For their valuable suggestions in revising the originally published version of this paper, I wish to thank Lisa Bower, Lisa Disch, and Jennifer Pierce.

1. Quoted in Howard S. Russell, *Indian New England Before the Mayflower* (Hanover, N.H.: University Press of New England, 1980), 96.
2. William Wood, *New England's Prospect* (1634), as quoted in *The Indian Peoples*

of Eastern America: A Documentary History of the Sexes, ed. James Axtell (New York: Oxford University Press, 1981), 119; See Rayna Green, "The Pocahontas Perplex: The Image of Indian Women in American Culture," *The Massachusetts Review*, 16 (1975), 698–714, for an analysis of Pocahontas as literary convention and national symbol, and how Native American women have been conceptualized according to the dichotomy between "princess" and "squaw."

3. Women's labor accounted for well over half of Indian subsistence in most northeastern woodland cultures. Agricultural production alone contributed approximately 65 percent to the diet. See M. K. Bennet, "The Food Economy of the New England Indians, 1605–1675," *The Journal of Political Economy*, 63 (1955), 369–97.

4. Charles Brooks, *History of the Town of Medford, Middlesex County, Massachusetts* (Boston: James M. Usher, 1855), 80–81.

5. William Cronon, *Changes in the Land: Indians, Colonists, and the Ecology of New England* (New York: Hill and Wang, 1983). James H. Merrell has analyzed these massive structural changes in Indian-English relations by looking at the important shift in whose "customs" governed encounters between peoples. James H. Merrell, "'The Customes of Our Countrey': Indians and Colonists in Early America," in *Strangers within the Realm: Cultural Margins of the First British Empire*, ed. Bernard Bailyn and Philip D. Morgan (Chapel Hill: University of North Carolina Press, 1991), 117–56.

6. On Indian dispossession and the negotiation of the social order in colonial New England, see Jean M. O'Brien, *Dispossession by Degrees: Indian Land and Identity in Natick, Massachusetts, 1650–1790* (New York: Cambridge University Press, 1997). On the last survivor trope in New England, see William S. Simmons, *Spirit of the New England Tribes: Indian History and Folklore, 1620–1984* (Hanover, N.H.: University Press of New England, 1986), 3–4. On the forging of distinctive European/colonial identities with reference to Native peoples and imported African slaves, see the studies collected in *Colonial Identity in the Atlantic World, 1500–1800*, ed. Nicholas Canny and Anthony Pagden (Princeton: Princeton University Press, 1987); Roy Harvey Pearce, *Savagism and Civilization: The Study of the Indian in the American Mind* (Baltimore: The Johns Hopkins Press, 1953); and Richard Slotkin, *Regeneration through Violence: The Mythology of the American Frontier* (Middletown, Conn.: Wesleyan University Press, 1973).

7 . On the process of missionization see, for example, James Axtell, *The Invasion Within: The Contest of Cultures in Colonial North America* (New York: Oxford University Press, 1985); and O'Brien, *Dispossession by Degrees* (especially ch. 2).

8. Scholars of this region have argued positions with regard to social organization across a wide spectrum: as matrilineal or patrilineal societies, as bilateral, or as some blend of these general rules. Lewis Henry Morgan, "Systems of Consanguinity and Affinity of the Human Family," *Smithsonian Contributions to Knowledge*, 218 (Washington, D.C.: Smithsonian Institution, 1870), and Lorraine Williams, "A Study of 17th Century Central Community in the Long Island Sound Area" (Ph.D. diss., New York University, 1972), are most often cited by those who argue for the matrilineality of southeastern New England groups. William S. Simmons and George F. Aubin, "Narragansett Kinship," *Man in the Northeast*, 9 (1975), 210–31, argue for the patrilineal reckoning of political leadership and tribal identity, and suggest that exogamous matrilineal clans may have existed to regulate marriage. In general, Kathleen Bragdon has agreed: "'Another Tongue Brought In': An Ethnohistorical Study of Native Writings in Massachusett" (Ph.D. diss., Brown University, 1981). Elise Brenner suggests that a bilateral kinship system was in place: "Strategies for Autonomy: An Analysis of

Ethnic Mobilization in Seventeenth Century Southern New England" (Ph.D. diss., University of Massachusetts, 1984). Those who argue for patrilineal or a bilateral system focus on the lack of evidence for matrilineality from the seventeenth century. Dean R. Snow, *The Archaeology of New England* (New York: Academic Press, 1980), and William A. Starna, "The Pequots in the Early Seventeenth Century," in *The Pequots in Southern New England: The Fall and Rise of an American Indian Nation*, ed. Laurence M. Hauptman and James D. Wherry (Norman: University of Oklahoma Press, 1990), 33–47, have argued that the inconclusive nature of the evidence might signal differences in degree and/or be the result of the chaotic conditions surrounding conquest, which required flexible social responses and at least the periodic appearance of matrilineal or bilateral kinship systems. I am indebted to my research assistant, Margaret Rodgers, for helping me sort out this literature.

9. Robert Steven Grumet, "Sunksquaws, Shamans, and Tradeswomen: Middle Atlantic Coastal Algonkian Women During the 17th and 18th Centuries," in *Women and Colonization: Anthropological Perspectives*, ed. Mona Etienne and Eleanor Leacock (New York: Praeger, 1980), 43–60; Snow, *Archaeology of New England*; Neal Salisbury, *Manitou and Providence: Indians, Europeans, and the Making of New England; 1500–1643* (New York: Oxford University Press, 1982); and William Cronon, *Changes in the Land*. Debate over gender roles in this region centers on the permeability of the boundaries between women's and men's work, and implications of the meaning of gendered division of labor for the relative power and status of women and men in these societies.

10. See especially Francis Jennings, *The Invasion of America: Indians, Colonialism, and the Cant of Conquest* (New York: Norton, 1976); Salisbury, *Manitou and Providence*; Cronon, *Changes in the Land*; and O'Brien, *Dispossession by Degrees*.

11. Axtell, *Invasion Within*; and Theda Perdue, "Southern Indians and the Cult of True Womanhood," in *The Web of Southern Social Relations*, ed. Walter J. Fraser, Jr., R. Frank Saunders, Jr., and Jon L. Wakelyn (Athens: University of Georgia Press, 1985), 35–51.

12. The process of gradual loss of individually owned land in one missionized Indian town is documented in my book *Dispossession by Degrees*.

13. Massachusetts Archives, 31 (1730), doc. 175 (hereafter cited Mass. Arch., vol. (year), doc.); and Mass. Arch., 32 (1753), 417–18.

14. Middlesex County Probate Docket no. 4124, Jacob Chalcom, Admin. (1756) (hereafter cited as Middlesex Probates). For a discussion of the diverse cultural patterns of Indian adjustment to the English, see O'Brien, *Dispossession by Degrees*, especially ch. 5.

15. Mass. Arch., 33 (1759), 106–76.

16. Ibid. On English women and gardening, see Laurel Thatcher Ulrich, *Good Wives: Image and Reality in the Lives of Women in Northern New England, 1650–1750* (New York: Vintage Books, 1980). On the loss of individual, Indian-owned land through legal prosecutions, see O'Brien, *Dispossession by Degrees*.

17. Thomas Shepard, *The Clear Sun-shine of the Gospel Breaking Forth Upon the Indians in New-England* (London: Printed by R. Cotes for John Bellamy, 1648), reprinted in Massachusetts Historical Society, *Collections*, 3d ser., 4 (1834), 59.

18. O'Brien, *Dispossession by Degrees*, ch. 6.

19. Middlesex Probates, 22411, Ruth Thomas, Admin. (1758); Esther Freeborn, Worcester County Probate Docket no. 22322 (1807) (hereafter cited as Worcester Probates); and Hannah Lawrence, Worcester Probates, 36457 (1774).

20. Probate documents for several hundred Indian estates in Massachusetts were filed throughout the eighteenth century and have been preserved in county court records. Probate procedures seem to have followed most vigorously when English creditors to Indian estates sought payment. The majority of Indians died intestate; divisions of Indian estates then almost always followed English estate law quite closely, with provisions made for "widow's thirds," a double share given to the eldest son, and equal shares to other children.

21. Esther Sooduck, Middlesex Probates, 20860, Will (1778).

22. Hannah Lawrence, Worcester Probates, 36457 (1774).

23. This is a common theme. See especially Anthony F. C. Wallace's classic work *The Death and Rebirth of the Seneca* (New York: Alfred A. Knopf, 1970), as well as a critique offered by Diane Rothenberg, "The Mothers of the Nation: Seneca Resistance to Quaker Intervention," in Etienne and Leacock, eds., *Women and Colonization*, 63–87.

24. Indian women could obtain title to land as individuals within the landholding system of Massachusetts, but most Indian women gained access to land as wives and children, as heirs to estates. In the process of dividing land in early eighteenth-century Natick, Massachusetts, nineteen individuals were designated proprietors, with principal rights to all of the land within the town. One of these was a woman, the rest were men. O'Brien, *Dispossession by Degrees*, ch. 4.

25. George Sheldon, *A History of Deerfield, Massachusetts* (Greenfield, Mass.: E. A. Hall & Co., 1895), 1:71.

26. Ann McMullen and Russell G. Handsman, eds., *A Key into the Language of Woodsplint Baskets* (Washington, Conn.: The American Indian Archaeological Institute, 1987).

27. Mass. Arch., 33 (1764), 300.

28. Hannah Speen, Middlesex Probates, 21027, Will (1742).

29. Mass. Arch., 32 (1755), 675–76.

30. See, for example, John A. Sainsbury, "Indian Labor in Early Rhode Island," *New England Quarterly*, 48 (1975), 378–93. Sainsbury found that "35.5 percent of all Indians in [Rhode Island] were living with white families in 1774; and if the Indians still living on the Charlestown reservation are excluded, the figure rises to 54 percent." He suspected they were "rent-paying lodgers." (Quotations are from p. 379.) In examining vital records from all over Massachusetts to identify Indians who were connected to the town of Natick, I located at least one Indian in each of 113 towns. Taking nine very distinctive surnames of Natick Indians, I located individuals with the same surnames in twenty towns. O'Brien, *Dispossession by Degrees*, ch. 6.

31. Mass. Arch., 31 (1747), 529. Speen was petitioning the General Court for permission to sell all of her remaining land so that she could reimburse Graves for caretaking. Massachusetts erected a system of oversight for Indian land that required General Court permission in order for Indian individuals to sell land to non-Indians. O'Brien, *Dispossession by Degrees*, ch. 3.

32. O'Brien, *Dispossession by Degrees*, ch. 6.

33. Middlesex Probates, 17057, Elizabeth Paugenit, Will (1755).

34. Mass. Arch., 33 (1770), 513,

35. Natick Town Records, First Book of Records for the Parish of Natick, 1745–1803, Morse Institute, Natick, Massachusetts.

36. Mass. Arch., 32 (1753), 375–76.

37. Mass. Arch., 32 (1751/2), 230.

38. Douglas Lamar Jones, "The Strolling Poor: Transiency in Eighteenth-Century Massachusetts," *Journal of Social History*, 8 (1975), 28–54; and Jones, "Poverty and Vagabondage: The Process of Survival in Eighteenth-Century Massachusetts," *New England Historical and Genealogical Society Register*, 133 (1979), 243–54.

39. Richard R. Johnson, "The Search for a Usable Indian: An Aspect of the Defense of Colonial New England," *Journal of American History*, 64 (1977), 623–51; Daniel Vickers, "The First Whalemen of Nantucket," ch. 4, this volume; Laurie Weinstein, "'We're Still Living on Our Traditional Homeland': The Wampanoag Legacy in New England," in *Strategies for Survival: American Indians in the Eastern United States*, ed. Frank W. Porter III (Westport, Conn.: Greenwood Press, 1986), 91.

40. Vickers, "The First Whalemen of Nantucket."

41. See especially Johnson, "Search for a Usable Indian"; and Vickers, "First Whalemen of Nantucket."

42. Mass. Arch., 33 (1762), 204.

43. Cronon, *Changes in the Land*.

44. O'Brien, *Dispossession by Degrees*, ch. 6. On English colonialism and the institution of Indian marriage, see Ann Marie Plane, "'The Examination of Sarah Ahaton': The Politics of 'Adultery' in an Indian Town of Seventeenth Century Massachusetts," in *Algonkians of New England: Past and Present*, ed. Peter Benes, The Dublin Seminar for New England Folklife Annual Proceedings, 1991 (Boston: Boston University, 1993), 14–25; and Plane, "Colonizing the Family: Marriage, Household, and Racial Boundaries in Southeastern New England to 1730" (Ph.D. diss., Brandeis University, 1994).

45. Mass. Arch., 32 (1756), 710.

46. Mass. Arch., 33 (1757), 10.

47. Franklin B. Dexter, ed., *Extracts from the Itineraries and Other Miscellanies of Ezra Stiles D.D. LL.D. 1755–1794* (New Haven: Yale University Press, 1916), 117 and 149.

48. Mass. Arch., 33 (1761), 170.

49. Stiles, *Itineraries* ("Potenummekuk"), 170; ("Nyhantic" in Lyme, Connecticut—47 percent widow-headed households), 130; and Stiles, "Memoir of the Pequots," in Mass. Hist. Soc., *Colls.*, 3d ser., 10 (1834), 102–103.

50. Stiles, *Itineraries*, 203; and George Kuhn Clarke, *History of Needham, Massachusetts, 1711–1911* (Cambridge, Mass.: University Press, privately printed, 1912), 558. Determining the degree of intermarriage between Indians, African Americans, and whites is problematic lacking vital records that systematically note the race of the individuals. Even when race is designated in vital records, labels such as "colored" and "mulatto" only indicate that intermarriage had occurred at some time in the past. Clerks did not necessarily use these labels consistently, either. Certainly intermarriage had been occurring between Indians and African Americans over the course of the eighteenth century. Intermarriage with the English was proscribed by legal statute. See Jack D. Forbes, "Mulattoes and People of Color in Anglo-North America: Implications for Black-Indian Relations," *The Journal of Ethnic Studies*, 12 (1984), 317–62.

51. Stephen Badger, "Historical and Characteristic Traits of the American Indians in General, and Those of Natick in Particular, in a Letter from the Rev. Stephen Badger of Natick, to the Corresponding Secretary," Mass. Hist. Soc., *Colls.*, 1st ser., 5 (1790), 43.

52. O'Brien, *Dispossession by Degrees*, ch. 6.

Barry O'Connell

7

"Once More Let Us Consider"

William Apess in the Writing of New England Native American History

For my mother

In what was once the conventional version of New England and much of American history, William Apess was a nobody. Born into poverty in 1798 in a tent in the woods in Colrain, Massachusetts, his parents of mixed Indian, white, and possibly African American "blood," this babe had attached to him nearly every category that defined worthlessness in the new United States. His upbringing would have struck respectable people then, as now, as but a fulfillment of their routine expectations. Beaten badly by his Indian grandmother when he was four, Apess was bound out to a succession of white gentry families in Connecticut until he ran away from the last one in 1813. Then a slight lad, short for his age, he had only six winter terms of education, enough to be barely literate. He had committed no crimes but he had caused trouble in the families who raised him and was already given, in their eyes at least, to lying and to indulging himself in drink.

Enlisting in a New York State militia unit bound for the Canadian front in the war of 1812, Apess soon became as much a heavy drinker as the older enlisted men who plied him with whiskey. After the war he wandered around northern New York and into Canada for awhile, holding down a variety of jobs from farm laborer to galley cook, but never far from being penniless and often going on benders for days. Gradually he worked his way back to his Indian family in southeastern Connecticut, much of the time with only the clothes on his back and nothing for food. In 1821 he married—another person of mixed race, herself raised in poverty by a single mother—and, again as though to fulfill the smug certainties of the respectable, they began having children right away.

Eight short years later Apess published *A Son of the Forest*, which is probably the first published autobiography by a Native American. By 1836 he had written and published four additional and more substantial pieces of work, led the protests of the Mashpees of Massachusetts against their white overseers in what came to be known as the "Mashpee Revolt" (1833–1834), and achieved at least a brief fame in New England and somewhat beyond as an agitator. In him, from a more tempered perspective, might be recognized a masterful polemicist and a canny strategist in leading a small minority to "persuade" a dominant majority to treat the minority with some respect.

Apess's existence and his books were long forgotten in written histories of literature, of New England, and of the United States. His people, the Pequots, were assumed by virtually all white Americans to have been wiped out by the allied Puritan forces in 1637. And, by 1829 when he published his first book, it was a commonplace in most of New England that there were no more Indians there—except for the occasional "half-breed," ruined by too close contact with white civilization. Yet Apess's books and what the autobiographies tell about his life provide more than a little evidence that native peoples persisted in New England and continued to be an important part of its economic and cultural life. As an itinerant preacher Apess ministered to many communities in which his "brethren" lived, the term he regularly used not for his fellow Methodists so much as for his fellow Indians.

At least briefly this accomplished man revealed the narrowness of the prejudices the respectable carry—and in his writing eloquently denounced their viciousness and falsity. To become a writer, arguably an important one in the history of American literature, and a successful preacher and important leader may have required Apess to "overcome" the disadvantages of his birth and economic stations. But his achievements may more reliably call into question not only the conventions by which respectable Americans make judgments about others but much that was once held as historical certainty both in the history of the New England region and in that of the United States itself.

Written history could be no academic subject for William Apess. History mattered too much in the daily lives and prospects of the Pequots, his own people, whose past, whose name, and whose very existence the Puritans sought so deliberately to erase. And he knew well that it was his taking hold of his own personal history—first by testifying to it before his fellow Methodist Christians and then by writing it—that saved him, at least in the world if not assuredly in the world to come (for what can man know of God's ways?). In the short twenty years of his public life Apess extended to an ever widening circle of Indian peoples his concern about the role written history played in his own fate and in that of the Pequots. He became, one could say, an early, possibly one of the first Pan-Indianists, before the term itself existed. From the appendix to *A Son of the Forest* in 1829 (although the bulk of it was lifted wholesale from Elias Boudinot's *A Star in the West*), through *Indian Nullification* in 1835, and culminating in the *Eulogy on King Philip* in 1836, Apess ventured to reframe New England history.

The renewed and sustained attention to his writings, which began no more than a decade ago, has accompanied and sometimes framed new scholarship on New England Native American history after the American Revolution.[1] For a very long time virtually no historian and no written history even troubled to argue that Native Americans were not a part of New England life in the nineteenth century. They were simply gone, "extinct," or if undeniably present, as in Maine or on Martha's Vineyard, were seen as remnants, in effect as shadows and so of no importance. A number of historians and literary scholars, some of them New England Native Americans, have begun to bring light into the great darkness in the written histories about Indians of the last two centuries in the region. There is a noticeable increase in conference papers, in articles in journals, and in books on postcolonial New England Native America. Slowly, within the academy and even without, this body of work has begun to wear at the settled pieties of the established history. Too much remains to be researched, too little is still known by scholars in the academy, to proclaim either an achieved fundamental revision of nineteenth-century New England history or to celebrate the demolition of the old and very powerful ideology that undergirded the basic erasure of native peoples from the written history. So powerful is that ideology that it still affects all who attempt to write about Indians in the region (indeed, it affects writing about Indians in any region of the United States). The "noble savage" can get sentimentally reincarnated in the form of heroic survivors or by overreading the militant presence of someone like Apess. Or there can be gestures of tough-minded realism that diminish the presence of Indians, or mistake its complexity, by too much insistence on their marginality. All of which is only to say that in the written history of New England for the nineteenth century we have yet to recover the inevitable diversity and richness of many individual and communal Indian histories so as to overcome all stereotypes through the sheer variety and particularity of actual Native American lives.

Where might William Apess fit into all of this—as a writer and so an actor in the history and as one individual from whose life we might begin, at the least, to propose new models for New England native histories? One place to begin a response to the question is by turning, once again, to his writings—to think of him not only as an historian, but as a self-consciously critical historian of what was becoming established in the written histories of his own time. And then, one might also examine his life, much of it available of course only through his representations of it in his books, as a body of data.

Apess's endeavors as an historian moved toward a different kind of narrative than the Eurocentric and increasingly nationalistic ones that, though in contest with each other in the 1820s, either regarded Native Americans as a doomed people or simply left them on the margins or altogether out of any meaningful participation in the making of the United States. But like Washington Irving, from whom he liberally borrowed, or Daniel Webster, against whose idealization of the Pilgrims he wrote, Apess worked from the documentary record. He was, of course, attuned to its inherently Anglo-American bias, but he was equally aware of how much it revealed about the history of Euro-American and Native American interaction, that it was neither monolithic nor monotonic if read from different angles of vision. Oral sources and traditions may well have shaped his reading of the documents, but nowhere in his published texts does he unmistakably draw upon or refer to the oral. His aim, from *A Son of the Forest* to the end of his writing life, was to establish the grounds for a cross-cultural written history of the region and by doing so to assert the vital presence of Native Americans. This history would include the shaping effects on American life of all people of color. Were such a written history achieved and absorbed by all Americans then, Apess hoped possibly more than he believed, the ground would exist for the indigenous peoples, African Americans, and Euro-Americans to exist together as Americans:

> Shall we cease crying and say it is all wrong, or shall we bury the hatchet and those unjust laws and Plymouth Rock together and become friends? And will the sons of the Pilgrims aid in putting out the fire and destroying the canker that will ruin all that their fathers left behind them to destroy?

> We want trumpets that sound like thunder, and men to act as though they were going at war with those corrupt and degrading principles that robs [sic] one of all rights, merely because he is ignorant and of a little different color. Let us have principles that will give everyone his due; and then wars shall cease, and the weary find rest. Give the Indian his rights, and you may be assured war will cease.[2]

Here and elsewhere in his writing Apess may be read as demanding that Indians be accorded only their rights as American citizens. Or he may be seen as proceeding simply by inverting conventional Anglo-American versions and valuations, as with this polemical flourish near the end of the *Eulogy for King Philip*: "I shall pronounce him the greatest man that was ever in America; and so it will stand, until he is proved to the contrary, to the everlasting disgrace of the Pilgrim fathers" (308). His witty, and at first glance rhetorical, hodgepodge of "shall we bury the hatchet and those unjust laws and Plymouth Rock together . . . ?" reveals a considerable and different design. Only when

Euro-Americans abandon not just their most self-justifying stereotypes of native peoples (savages wielding "hatchets"), but also their attachment to the fake history embodied and embedded in the enshrinement of Plymouth Rock, may unjust laws be wiped away. For Apess a genuinely cross-cultural history requires the recognition of what Europeans had consistently done to native people in the Americas and of the mythological histories they had shaped that not only legitimated these acts but virtually sanctified them.

The Pilgrims and Plymouth Rock were but an aspect, for Apess, of an entire complex of assumptions, attitudes, and historical understandings in Euro-American culture that variously relegated native peoples to the moral, economic, and historical margins of the United States. White Americans saw themselves as bearers of civilization and the blessings of Christianity to a savage people. Their benevolence was all the greater for the fact, as they believed it, that the Indians were ultimately doomed as an inferior people. Piety and historical inevitability, thus joined, created a rationale that made it impossible for many white people to conceive any wrong in the treatment of native people. And for those who were critics of one or another Indian policy, or of particular acts committed against Indians, the conviction of the superiority of Euro-American culture meant that their critiques were but acts of charity, an almost automatic sign of their virtue. In either instance Indians remained symbolically subordinate and materially at risk. Exposing the falsity of white Americans' Christianity was Apess's most constant strategy in seeking to move all Americans to reencounter and thus to revise the meanings they gave to history:

> Having now given historical facts, and an exposition in relation to ancient times, by which we have been enabled to discover the foundation which destroyed our common fathers in their struggle together; it was indeed nothing more than the spirit of avarice and usurpation of power that has brought people in all ages to hate and devour each other. And I cannot . . . look back upon what is past and call it religion. No, it has not the least appearance like it. Do not then wonder, my dear friends, at my bold and unpolished statements, though I do not believe that truth wants any polishing whatever. And I can assure you that I have no design to tell an untruth, but facts alone. Oft have I been surprised at the conduct of those who pretend to be Christians, to see how they were affected toward those who were of a different cast, professing one faith. Yes, the spirit of degradation has always been exercised toward us poor and untaught people. If we cannot read, we can see and feel; and we find no excuse in the Bible for Christians conducting toward us as they do. (308)

Apess's turn here is not simply, or primarily, to point to the hypocrisy of white Christians. His "ancient times" points at once to the first landings of Europeans in the Americas and to even earlier European history. And what is to be seen, coolly and objectively, in that long history? "Avarice and the usurpation of power." Bluntly, these and nothing else—no great mission, no

divinely ordained messianic colonization—but an old, familiar, and unen-
chanting tale. Nothing, offers Apess matter-of-factly, of religion here, not
even its appearance. These words are less polemical, less startling than the
now better-known indictment in "An Indian's Looking-Glass for the White
Man": "Now suppose these skins were put together, and each skin had its
national crimes written upon it—which skin do you think would have the
greatest?" (157). But it is their very straightforwardness that carries his
point—and very possibly his weariness after seven years of preaching, organizing, and advocating.

Within his own time one might argue that Apess failed. In the northeastern as well as southeastern United States, native peoples continued to lose
land, to be self-righteously elected as the objects of missionary efforts from
the invading barbarians, and in many instances removed altogether. The removal of the Cherokees, though determined upon and though the other "civilized" nations had already begun the long trek, had not yet come to its final
stage. West of the Mississippi the history would play itself out differently in
some respects, but the outcome would be similar. And the triumphal narrative of manifest destiny achieved complete dominance so thoroughly and so
deeply in the psyches of many that not until the 1960s and 1970s, with the
Civil Rights Movement and the still irreconcilable fact of defeat in Vietnam
and civil conflict at home, did it become possible for any substantially different historical narrative to be conceived and heard in the public world. If
many Americans in the 1820s and 1830s listened to Apess's voice or read his
words, few registered them meaningfully. And, as is now well known, his publications became mute witnesses unseen on library shelves for over a century
and a half, known only to a very small number of historians, who regarded
them as minor.

Apess may also have judged himself a failure. He left Mashpee sometime
between 1836 and 1838. It had been the scene of his most substantial tri-
umph—his leadership of the "Mashpee Revolt" and the consequent restora-
tion to the Mashpees of most of their civil rights. But after that achievement
came some estrangement, the outlines of which have yet to be uncovered.
Some of the leaders among the Mashpees seem to have been at some pains
to emphasize their independence of Apess. Possibly he continued to agitate
beyond their willingness to follow. Reverend Phineas Fisk, the Harvard-
appointed minister to the Mashpees, remained in his place until 1840 despite
their firm opposition, and Apess may have persisted with that grievance or
urged new ones. He may have left for personal reasons only. People in Mashpee were poor and, though he had been given a house and some land, he may
well not have been able to support his family there. All that he owned in
Mashpee was sold for debts by court action in 1838. The years between 1836
and 1839 when he died in New York City have yet to be documented. There is
reason to surmise that he had lived in the City from time to time since as early

as 1829, and he may well have returned to it in the expectation of some support or for a particular ministry.[3]

His death was sudden, unexpected.[4] He had been boarding, with his wife, for four months at a lodging house at 31 Washington Street, owned by a William Garlick. The neighborhood was a respectable one though in decline. His wife, another boarder, and Catherine Garlick, the daughter of the owner, all testified to Apess's basic good nature and behavior. But his wife also describes him as "formerly a preacher of the Methodist society." How he and she were supporting themselves is unspecified, though there may be a hint in a reference to his giving lectures on the history of the Indians and selling some of his books. One might suggest from this, at least at this moment in his life, that he literally made his living by history. On a Friday in early April he complained to his wife that he did not feel well. The next day he went to a Doctor Viers and got some medicine, took it, and went to bed at his usual hour, but he seemed to have had an adverse reaction to the medicine and could not get up and dress on Sunday so weak was he. On Sunday night, a Doctor Atkinson, a "botanic physician," came to see Apess, who told him he had a pain in his right side and that he had been purging and vomiting for two days. The doctor gave him medicines to help him purge himself more thoroughly. He died the next day, April 10. The conclusion of the inquest was that he died of apoplexy. Reading the report tempts this reader to another conclusion—that he was killed by the medicines given him by Doctors Viers and Atkinson, evidence not of any plot or of discrimination but only of the woeful state of mid-nineteenth-century medical practice.

The report has other tantalizing information. His wife, who testifies, is identified as Elizabeth and as having been married to him for ten years. What had happened to Mary Apess, his first wife and the mother of all his known children? (He and Elizabeth might have had children. Since the coroner's report makes no mention of any family other than Elizabeth, one can draw no conclusion.) If he and Elizabeth had been married for ten years this would mean that Mary was no longer his wife at the time he published her account of her conversion in *The Experiences of Five Christian Indians* (1833). And who was Elizabeth? Both she and Catherine Garlick testify that they were "affectionate and kind to each other," so it seems to have been an amicable relationship. John Wright, the boarder, testifies that Apess "would some time get on a Frolic and continue a few days and then abstain from liquor altogether." This, by itself, cannot sustain my too conclusive judgment in an earlier essay that he died from alcoholism.[5] Nor does his wife's comment that "he has lately been somewhat intemperate." The notice of his death in the *Greenfield Gazette & Mercury* (May 7, 1839), which reprinted parts of the obituaries from the *New York Sun* and the *New York Observer*, added that "In New York, it appears that for some time past, his conduct had been quite irregular, and he had lost the confidence of the best portions of the community." But this on what authority? It seems that Apess in the last months of his life, possibly the last years, was sporadically going on drunks, but, if his fellow boarders' observations are reliable, that he would then go for periods when he abstained entirely. There is no hint in these new materials that he was impoverished, and nothing that would reliably indicate his demoralization. All that we can so far know is that he no longer had a congregation or any clear role in a community of native people or among reformers.

But to think of Apess as a failure, or to imagine him succumbing to that sense of his own life, is to evoke, yet again, what Thomas Doughton has termed the "discourse of disappearance," a discourse that saturated the consciousnesses of white Americans as it became fully articulated in the 1820s and 1830s.[6] Its tenacity throughout the nineteenth century supported the common idea of the inevitable extinction of Indian people, culturally if not physically. And it remains vital throughout much of American culture into the late twentieth century—in the still commonsense assumption that there are no "real" Indians left in New England and that elsewhere in the country surviving Indians are but pale simulations of "authentic" ones. Whatever its other uses in white American culture, it functioned as an exceptionally blinding legitimation for the taking of Indian lands, artifacts, burials, and the exclusion of any consideration of native peoples' shaping presence in New England and in much of American history. Apess as failure would make of him no more than a figure in a white version of his people—as a "declining" and "doomed" remnant.[7]

How, then, might historians, other scholars, and teachers read Apess and his life for what we might learn both about him and about Native Americans in New England? Unless one makes a case that Apess is an anomaly, the fact of his presence, and of the body of important writing he accomplished, in itself brings into question a whole body of conceptual language used to write about Indians. His books and his life also contradict the long unchallenged assumption by historians that there was no significant presence of Native Americans in most of New England (and elsewhere east of the Mississippi) for much of the nineteenth century. And they at least open the imagination to the possibility of something like a native-centered history of histories—that is, the writing of histories with native peoples at the center and with their various understandings of American society as the controlling perspective.

In part Apess himself answers the question of how we might read him and his life. Both autobiographical accounts indicate the presence of a quite deliberate shaping hand. They assume a primarily white readership and situate that assumption in frequent explicit address, as in this instance from *The Experiences*: "When you read this, ask yourselves if ever you had such trials. If not, begin now to prize your privileges and show pity to those whose fates are wretched and cruel" (119). His writing recurrently reveals a sophisticated understanding of the ideas his white contemporaries thought were reliable truths about Indians. Here, usually, Apess moves less directly, more subtly, in an effort to weaken people's presumptions.

Take the always tangled question of identity. Apess pointedly, in the first sentences of *A Son of the Forest*, identifies himself as biologically of mixed blood: "my grandfather was a white man" (3). But his father, of mixed blood as Apess reiterates, "On attaining a sufficient age to act for himself, . . . joined the Pequot tribe, to which he was maternally connected" (4). Apess's straightforwardness makes it seem natural that culture is a social fact, partly chosen by individuals and partly a matter of acceptance in and by specific families or communities. Personal and kin history and community are the keys, not biology. And there is no apology for being the child of mixed race, which was, for many contemporary whites in New England, certain evidence of degeneration. But Apess complicates the matter of identity much further by what he emphasizes in recounting his own growing up in *A Son of the Forest* (1829) and *The Experiences of Five Christian Indians* (1833).

The story, as he sets it up, is one of progressive alienation from his own family, from his Pequot relatives, and from any community of native people. Beaten terribly when he was four by his Pequot grandmother, who was urged on by his Pequot grandfather, Apess is at pains to dramatize their Indian identity. He also makes vivid their poverty in a fashion that could only confirm whites' prejudices about the degeneration of "remnant" Indians of mixed blood living too close to a world of civilized people:

> Our fare was of the poorest kind, and even of this we had not enough. Our clothing also was of the worst description: Literally speaking, we were clothed with rags, so far only as rags would suffice to cover our nakedness. We were always contented and happy to get a cold potato for our dinners—of this at times we were denied, and many a night have we gone supperless to rest, if stretching our limbs on a bundle of straw, without any covering against the weather, may be called rest. Truly, we were in a most deplorable condition—too young to obtain subsistence for ourselves . . . and our wants almost totally disregarded by those who should have made every exertion to supply them. (5)

Yet "some of our white neighbors . . . took pity" and brought milk in the worst times. That Apess anticipates white readers' responses, articulates them, and turns them around to deny them/us a sense of moral superiority to these "poor Indians," does not by itself explain or exhaust how this detailed tale of degradation and separation from this family works in the narrative.[8] He describes nothing from his brief young life among the Pequots that would suggest some positive ground for his choosing, many years later, to return to them, to identify himself as a Pequot. His attention to his years with the three white families with whom he lived until he was fifteen only adds to our awareness of his cultural distance from the Pequots.

This awareness is not accidental. Central to his version of his time with the

Furmans, the white family who cared for him longest and to whom he felt close, is an almost emblematic vignette of racial and cultural alienation, even of alienation from his own physical self. That it occurs in the woods only suggests some of the ironic play in his choosing to entitle his book *The Son of the Forest*. Apess goes, one day, with several members of the Furman family to pick berries in the woods. He does not say how old he was; it could have been anytime between his sixth and twelfth birthdays. Shortly after entering the woods, they come upon another group of berrypickers, "a company of white females," the adult narrative voice tells us immediately, but to the child's eyes of the character in the story, the second "I" throughout the autobiography:

> their complexion was, to say the least as *dark* as that of the natives. This circumstance filled my mind with terror, and I broke from the party with my utmost speed, and I could not muster courage enough to look behind until I had reached home. By this time my imagination had pictured out a tale of blood, and as soon as I regained breath sufficient to answer the questions which my master asked, I informed him that we had met a body of the natives in the woods . . . Notwithstanding the manifest incredibility of my tale of terror, Mr. Furman was agitated; my very appearance was sufficient to convince that I had been terrified by something. (10–11)[9]

This "tale of terror" moves very complexly within the narrative. Just before he tells it, Apess explicitly names his alienation. As one given "unnatural treatment" by "those who should have loved and protected me," and being nothing more than a "cast-off member of the tribe," he knew he had no reason to expect "favor" or even "mercy" from other Indians. But the vignette is more than a repetition. It can take a reader, momentarily, toward a felt sense of the subject's distance from those who should be nearest and dearest. And it also, as Apess goes on to interpret its meaning, provides a disturbing realization of the depth of white people's racism about Indians. By prefacing the vignette with his rational grounds for being apprehensive of other Indians, Apess makes more powerful our sense of how whites have succeeded in getting him to internalize a yet deeper distrust and something very like the self-hatred that he proposed drove his grandmother to beat him nearly to death. As narrator he takes no chance that his readers will miss this point:

> the great fear I entertained of my brethren was occasioned by the many stories I had heard of their cruelty toward the whites—how they were in the habit of killing and scalping men, women, and children. But the whites did not tell me that they were in a great majority of the instances the aggressors—that they had imbrued their hands in the lifeblood of my brethren, driven them from their once peaceful and happy homes—that they introduced among them the fatal and exterminating diseases of civilized life. (11)

This conclusion, among its other effects, informs a reader that the tellers of these stories cannot be trusted, that their versions of history are not simply selective as, of course, all versions of history must be, but that they are profoundly self-interested and willfully blind about the meanings of their own acts.

The vignette, along with the description of his grandmother's beating, and the sequence of tales about his long wanderings faraway from his Pequot homeland, also make it almost completely mysterious both why and how Apess comes to identify himself as a Pequot—what I have suggested as his further snarling of the always, in the United States, confusing questions of racial and ethnic identity. Apess might be taken here as pointing future historians in several directions, or as alerting us against still regnant simplifications of people's identities and of the nature of that baggy monster of a term—"culture." Set aside, for now, the clarity of his portrait of how a dominant culture produces self-hatred and alienation among those it subjugates—a reminder, if needed, of an ongoing struggle for Indian peoples and individuals that continues to this day. The conditions under which that struggle is conducted vary importantly from American region to American region and across time, but Apess has caught, I think, the central dynamics.

Apess might well not have been able to survive spiritually had he not found some means to realign himself with his fellow Pequots and with other Indians. The alternative, as his autobiographies make palpably real, was to live in complete isolation—despised and mistreated by whites and separated from any who might both understand his experience and have some affirmative sense of identity. "Assimilation," then, for a native person, as arguably for any person of "color," in the prevailing racial codes of white culture, is not only a problematic concept, but it is also not a possibility in any social or cultural reality so far available in the United States. Survival, then, Apess might be read as telling us, requires of Native Americans and other people of color a steady clarity that assimiliation is never being offered, regardless of what various spokesmen for white culture say. Native Americans must, then, be innovators, keeping what they can of inherited but also altered material and spiritual practices, of belief-systems and ways of making meaning. To these they adapt whatever can be of service from the world of the dominant culture. And this process goes on, and will go on, for as long as native people are subjugated. Any concept that assumes some "authentic" Indian culture, recognizably "Indian" ways, and thus identifies who is and is not Indian, can only be imperialistic and ahistorical.

If we return to Apess's narratives, we may find some other pointers, too. Throughout, though these references are never made much of, he mentions seeing his father quite regularly. And further thought brings into relief the fact that the Furmans, with whom he lived some seven years—the most formative—were close neighbors to his Pequot grandparents and his uncles. One can suspect that he may even have seen some of his relatives daily. That the silences and marginalities may be as telling as what is narrated is not the important or surprising matter. Instead I want to suggest the possibility that Apess had considerable and regular contact, at least until he went into the army, with members of his family and with other Pequots. (And, given the number of New England Indians who fought in the War of 1812, during his time in the army he almost certainly had contact with other Indians, if not with other Pequots.) He also never says whether he speaks Pequot, though—given his account of Ann Wampy, who seems barely in possession of English, and of Aunt Sally George, who had only a little English—it seems more than probable that he had some fluency in his first language. All of which is to propose, if not to conclude, that as historians we keep firmly before us in using Apess for historical evidence how artful, indeed literary, and politically self-conscious are his memoirs.

Why might he have remained, if not completely silent, so reticent about such vital matters as his ability to speak Pequot and his persistent ties throughout childhood with his family and with a larger native community? The complexity of his narrative structure and its effects suggests at least one answer. The central drama in his autobiographies is his story of conversion, of his being saved. Not only does he receive the balm of Christ's grace in this narrative, he is also enabled to take control of his life in the world. Unlike the conventional conversion narrative, however, Apess must overcome two ills—his own sinfulness and sense of unworthiness before God, and the racism of white people, a racism that, among its other costs, has brought him to believe in his inferiority to other men and women. So, in effect, one might read Apess as providing us the story of a double conversion, of his becoming a sanctified child of God and a self-affirming member of the Pequot nation, assured of his value among men and women. The power of his indictment of white culture could only be diminished if the drama of all he must overcome were mitigated by the presence of a supportive family, community, and culture. He means, I believe, to direct his readers' eyes not to the actual social structures of native communities in New England but to white society, its structures, its hypocrisies. By taking possession, as well, of Christianity, he not only can turn against Euro-Americans a crucial element in their conviction of their superiority to Indians, he can also attack and, at least rhetorically, undermine all the equations of conversion with moving from savagery to civilization. When Apess converts he becomes simultaneously Christian and Pequot.

Mining his writings carefully as a rich source of many kinds of data, one can draw from them ample evidence for an extensive network throughout southern New England, Long Island and New York City, and up through the Hudson Valley at least as far as Albany, of connected communities of native people, often gathering as Christian congregations, most commonly as Methodists or Baptists, and allied in some measure with other people of color: African Americans, Cape Verdeans, recent immigrants from the Caribbean, and others. And by tracing Apess and members of his family, the collateral relations and the descendants, one can postulate an ongoing New England Native America neither marginal nor precisely "invisible," neither silent nor silenced, however ideologically overlooked by whites and many of their institutions. Among these relatives and descendants are people who were railroad workers, stonecutters, farmers, laborers, and seamen. The networks through which they moved, indeed the cultures they shaped and inhabited, mostly await discovery and documentation by academic historians. The fact that native people did not, for the most part, draw attention to themselves cannot be taken as evidence for their absence. Native Americans, like most Americans, lived their lives with no expectation of particular fame or notice.

What this may mean for the histories yet to be written is a prospect of uncovering the patterns of community, forms of survival, and intellectual traditions of Native Americans, which could bring us closer to a genuine social history of New England in the nineteenth century—not because, in numbers or influence, Native Americans can suddenly be found everywhere, but because by tracing their presence, their movements, their struggles, historians will inevitably find out a great deal more about other groups as well who have been undervalued and underattended—the many, African Americans and white people alike, who economically were in the lower half of the population, allies with Native Americans at times, rivals and tormentors at others. In these uncoverings, historians should expect that there will be great differences, that there will not be any single Native American way or pattern, that not only will the stories of the Mashpees, the Western Abenakis, the Penobscots and the Micmacs, the mainland Wampanoags, the island Wampanoags, and the Narragansetts be significantly distinct, but also that there will be many rich and unexpected individual variations within each of these groups.

Two pieces of Apess's history may illustrate the possibilities. One is as yet undocumented, but its existence seems to me more and more certain as I follow Apess through written records. Tempting as it may be to regard Apess as extraordinary in being such a powerful intellectual and writer, it is impossible for him to have achieved all he did in these realms without some form of community. He was not, it should be remembered, the first New England Native American writer and intellectual. Whether he knew directly about Samson Occom, Joseph Johnson, or David Fowler may never be known. But their achievements, along with his and other Native Americans' in the late eighteenth and early nineteenth centuries, should suggest the existence of something like a tradition. And there may well be figures who belong to it who have left no writing, or whose papers have disappeared. But even if there were not many other writers, I want to argue that Apess comes out of a body of dissent, of critique of Euro-America, of engagement and some continuity, both within New England Native America and beyond it, in alliance with at least some other people of color, and a few white people. There was, this is to propose, a dissenting intellectual culture about which historians yet know little. Neither David Walker among African Americans nor Apess among Native Americans is, if I am right, anomalous, a loner, or altogether exceptional. Who did Apess talk to in Boston, in Albany, in Providence, in Hartford, and in New York City? Who lent him books and to whom did he lend? What newspapers did he read? And who assisted him financially in getting time to write and in publishing his books? Did he have a correspondence? These very basic questions remain unanswered, tantalizing, a promise even if only partially answered, of our achieving a much more sophisticated history of New England Native America, intellectual cultures and all.

The other piece indicates something of how collaborative scholarship must be, and how dependent it can be on accident. Through a set of remarkable coincidences, I learned several years ago that a number of Apes [they have kept the first spelling of the name] were living on the South Island of New Zealand. I was told that at least one of them had made inquiry of some American tourists about his "infamous" American forebear, the "preacher and writer" William Apess. Eventually I heard from Erwin Apes in New Zealand, the great-grandson of William Apess. His grandfather, William Apess's son, was named William Elisha Apes and sometimes used William as his first name and at others Elisha. William Elisha was an American Indian whaler, known in New Zealand, and one imagines in New England as well, for his prodigious strength. On what may have been his first voyage to New Zealand on the ship *Ajax* in 1838, William Elisha mutinied with one other sailor "over the inhumane treatment of the ship's boy. They took charge of the firearms and the ship and ordered it put into Port Otago where they loaded a whaleboat and deserted."[10]

Like his father, William Elisha evidently had little tolerance for injustice. Eventually he married a Maori woman named Mata Punahere but also known as Karoraina/Kataraina (for Caroline) in 1844, and they had seven children. If, as I must assume, he is William and Mary Apess's first child and he was born the year after they were married, he would have been no more than sixteen when he joined in the mutiny.

A contemporary description survives from the memoirs of Thomas Baker Kennard, thought to have been the first white male child born in the Otago District on South Island: "He was said to have American Indian blood in him and when in a passion his eyes were as red as fire. He was a six-footer and powerfully made, but his eldest son was short and broad, although the next son was very tall . . ." William Elisha died in New Zealand on December 28, 1891. If the death certificate is correct in listing his age as eighty, then he could not have been William Apess's son, but would instead have been one of his younger brothers. Against this we have to weigh generations of oral tradition among the New Zealand Apeses including Erwin Apes's direct memories of stories his grandfather told about his own father.

Were this all to the story, one might only conclude that, instead of disappearing, American Indians spread themselves across the globe. But William Elisha Apes, though a resident of New Zealand for fifty-two years, did not forego his life at sea. For at least another decade he shipped on American ships, the home ports of which were in New England. In 1851, for instance, he shipped out of Portland, Maine.[11] Here, as with so much else in William Apess's life and with much of the lives of other nineteenth-century New England Native Americans', there exists so far only a tantalizing outline. But there is enough evidence to support the surmise that William Elisha Apes, whaleman and seaman, kept in connection two different native worlds, stayed in touch with at least some of his American family, and when in port—in cities like Portland and New Bedford—may well have joined other Native Americans, African Americans, and others who elected their company not only in fellowship but in sharing ideas and resistance to those who would seek to exercise illegitimate power.

The legacies and the meanings from any one life can never be finally known. It is a rare life in which even a few get recorded, caught and kept against the losses and revisions of memory and the accidents by which some documents survive and others are forever lost. So it is that historians of every kind, students of others and of other cultures, must be not only provisional about what we think we know but fully alive to the mystery of others lives, the fullness of which will always elude us. No category can contain or explain Native Americans—or the people of any human community.

NOTES

1. Two historians, however, are exceptions to all these generalizations. Kim McQuaid's "William Apes, A Pequot: An Indian Reformer in the Jacksonian Era," *New England Quarterly*, 50 (1977), 605–25, written when he was still a graduate student, argued for Apess's importance, but few scholars heeded and Apess remained essentially unread in the academy. Donald M. Nielsen, eight years later, returned to the subject, focusing on Apess's leadership in the Mashpee Revolt in "The Mashpee Indian Revolt of 1833," *New England Quarterly*, 58 (1985), 400–20. But it took, I believe, the work of Indian peoples in New England to create the climate in which scholars and the public began to reconsider the almost two-century-old orthodoxy about the disappearance of Indians in New England. Both McQuaid and Nielsen were ahead of their times, though each in some measure probably moved the times along.

2. *On Our Own Ground: The Complete Writings of William Apess, A Pequot*, edited and with an introduction by Barry O'Connell (Amherst, Mass.: University of Massachusetts Press, 1992), 306, 307. All subsequent quotations from this edition will be identified simply by the page reference in the text.

3. Apess's first three publications were all printed in New York. And the Methodist

Conference that ordained him and appointed him to preach to his own people was located in New York City. Given his poverty, it seems reasonable to assume that he must have had financial support from others in order to publish his works. There were active reformers in New York City during the 1820s who might well have been his patrons. Lydia Maria Child and her husband, David Child, were in residence part of the time. And there was Lewis Tappan, whose papers I have not yet been able to search for any reference to Apess. But there may well have been other less historically well-known patrons, possibly other Protestant Methodists.

4. The formal inquest report fortunately survives and has been found by Reginald H. Pitts, who generously got in touch with me and sent me both a copy of the original and his transcript of it. All of the factual details in the following two paragraphs are drawn from that report, which is from the Municipal Archives of the City of New York, Department of Records and Information, 31 Chambers Street, Room 101, New York City.

5. See my "William Apess and the Survival of the Pequot People," in *Algonkians of New England: Past and Present* (The Dublin Seminar for New England Folklife Annual Proceedings, 1991), 92 n. 5.

6. See, in this volume, Thomas L. Doughton, "Unseen Neighbors: Native Americans of Central Massachusetts, A People Who Had 'Vanished.'"

7. For an especially vivid playing out of a repeated acknowledgment of the existence of Native Americans, formulated so as to confirm the inevitability of their extinction, see John W. DeForest, *History of the Indians of Connecticut* (1851; Hamden, Conn.: Archon Press, 1964).

8. Those familiar with Apess will remember the moment of his turning back on those who might be these kinds of readers: "In view of this treatment, I presume that the reader will exclaim, 'What savages your grandparents were to treat unoffending, helpless children in this cruel manner.' But this cruel and unnatural conduct was the effect of some cause. I attribute it in a great measure to the whites, inasmuch as they introduced among my countrymen that bane of comfort and happiness ardent spirits . . ." (6–7), and the indictment continues from here.

9. The emphasis on "*dark*" is Apess's.

10. From personal correspondence with Erwin A. Apes and the documents he has collected and sent on to me.

11. Personal correspondence with Reginald H. Pitts, who has been checking ship records.

Ann Marie Plane and Gregory Button

8

The Massachusetts Indian Enfranchisement Act

Ethnic Contest in Historical Context, 1849–1869

> We have too much legislation respecting the Indians. It is always
> dangerous to legislate on subjects we do not understand.
>
> —Leavitt Thaxter, September 1859[1]

When we study Indian affairs in southern New England, we generally think in terms either of the earliest encounters of the English and the Indians or of the most recent struggles for official tribal recognition.[2] Yet the
years between the Pilgrims and the present saw a continuing, complex competition to define the meaning of "Indian" identity. In particular, during the
period from 1849 to 1870, Massachusetts state legislators decided to enfranchise the Indians of their state and to remove restraints on the sale of Indian
lands. Formerly wards of the state, in June of 1869 the legislature declared all
"Indians and people of color, heretofore known and called Indians," within
the Commonwealth to be "citizens of the Commonwealth . . . entitled to all
the rights, privileges, and immunities, and subject to all the duties and liabilities" of citizenship.[3] In this act, they provided that lands would revert to individuals and their heirs in fee simple, opening the door to sales to non-Indians:
"all Indians shall hereafter have the same rights as other citizens to take, hold,
convey and transmit real estate." Lands held in common could, upon application by any member of the tribe, be partitioned among the proprietors (i.e.,

tribal members). The act further ordered the provision of aid to indigent Indians through the regular system of state almshouses rather than by individual appropriations in the legislature. Ironically, the offer of full citizenship carried the price of relinquishing Indian identity—Indian "peculiarity." And, whatever the intentions of the legislators, the result was land sold to non-Indians for debt or other reasons, offering opportunities for graft by the white guardians who oversaw sales of tribal lands.[4] As any student of Indian affairs will see, this act foreshadowed, in several important respects, the more sweeping and disastrous federal legislation of the 1880s.[5]

In order to understand the evolution of this notable piece of legislation, we must explore both the particular historical circumstances (involving issues of racial and class relations), that made tribal termination seem essential to white legislators and to a few residents of the Indian enclave communities, and the ethnic boundaries that defined "Indianness" for various groups of whites, African American "foreigners,"[6] and Indians. These two issues—the cultural context of policy formation and the conflicting definitions of ethnic identity—are of course intertwined. Because whites perceived Massachusetts' Indians as "non-white," they thought it logical to treat them as they did blacks. Legislators believed that the only proper course was to wipe out "all distinctions of race and caste, and [place] all [the state's] people on the broad platform of equality before the law."[7] And precisely because Reconstruction-era federal race policy both offered new opportunities to nonwhites and required new, state-level racial policies, the Indian Enfranchisement Act was adopted. The Indian Enfranchisement Act was also related to both the struggle for women's suffrage and a new attention to the male head of household in nonwhite families of the day. Thus, we conclude with a brief examination of the gendered dimensions of this Indian policy. As we hope to make clear, the evolution and implications of this piece of Indian Policy cannot be divorced from the historical context and ethnic contest of the entire Reconstruction period.

The documents collected during the debate over Indian enfranchisement shed light on the definitions and meanings of Indian identity in the mid-nineteenth century, revealing the beliefs of people from Euro-American, African American, and Indian backgrounds. Our findings show that triracial negotiation was as important, in this period at least, in the north as in the south.[8] As elsewhere, Indians in Massachusetts consistently refused the efforts of many whites to force them into a biracial society, and the markers of their distinctive ethnic identity remained fairly consistent throughout the mid-nineteenth century.[9] We demonstrate some of the specific ways in which Indians maintained a separate identity, and the different perceptions of their black and white neighbors. Sometimes these differences in perception provoked bitter conflicts, not only between Indians and non-Indians, but even within the Indian communities themselves. As among many other eastern Indian groups, Massachusetts Indian communities retained their ethnic distinctiveness, despite outsiders' perceptions of them as settlements of mixed-race nonwhites. Exploration of this pivotal moment in American race relations reveals the delicate balance through which ethnic identity is sustained.[10]

Historical Context

Since the colonial period, Massachusetts Indians had lived in small enclave communities scattered throughout the state. The successors of "praying towns" set up by missionaries such as John Eliot, these Christianized Indian communities functioned in the interstices of the white economy. As with all reservations, there was never enough land of good quality to fulfill the model of self-sufficient agriculture held up to them by Euro-American benefactors.[11] Therefore, Indian families turned to itinerant trading of home-produced goods such as baskets and brooms. They also marketed locally available resources: in Natick, Massachusetts, it was cedar rails; on the island of Martha's Vineyard, clay and cranberries. Some found work in white communities as crewmen on whaling ships, laborers, and domestics.[12]

By 1861, the total population of Indians and Indian descendants was 1,610.[13] The bulk of these (1,241) were members of ten "plantation tribes" (state-recognized groups with land, funds, or state support), although not everyone lived in his or her tribal enclave community. The Gay Head (Martha's Vineyard) and Mashpee[14] (Cape Cod) communities were the largest and, together with other communities near whaling ports, accounted for 928 of the 1,241 total plantation population. Nontribal Indians near port towns accounted for 300 more of the total population, meaning that the overwhelming majority (1,228 out of 1,610 or 76.5 percent) of the state's Indian population resided in communities south of Boston, living close to whaling ports and farming the poorer quality soils of the coastal regions.[15] There was considerable movement between these areas as well as in-migration by Indians from the interior of the Commonwealth and other New England states.

These communities were supported in part by charity, first by missionary societies (such as the Society for the Propagation of the Gospel) and later by the state government. As wards of the state, the Indians' property was nontaxable. Most white observers remarked on the poverty within the enclaves. Often they had no roads, and residents lived in very small houses or even wigwams well into the nineteenth century.[16] Those Indians who did not reside on plantations shifted for themselves as did other "people of color" in many small New England towns or urban, African American neighborhoods. Legislators found that, despite their poverty, the Indians made proportionately few requests for state aid, and total state expenditures for support were low.[17] It was in this condition, as the "few remaining representatives" of an "outlawed people," that the Massachusetts Indians were enfranchised by a vote of the legislators.[18]

Questions about Indians' autonomous status in the years before enfranchisement led to an intense debate on all sides regarding Indian identity. In 1834, residents of Mashpee protested both their legal inability to manage their own affairs and the corruption of their white guardians. Their challenge to guardianship ("the Mashpee Revolt") culminated in the status of that community being changed to allow the Indians control of their own affairs without a white guardian,[19] and it provoked a flurry of discussion regarding Indian rights. With an eye toward systematizing the treatment of all of the state's Indians, the Legislature commissioned investigations in 1849 (led by Francis W. Bird), 1859 (with Commissioner John Milton Earle), and 1869 (a joint special commission led by Rodney French for the House and N. J. Holden for the Senate, which included Francis W. Bird) to investigate the number and circumstances of Indians and Indian descendants in the state. All three inquiries were explicitly charged with determining when and how the Indians could be made full citizens of the Commonwealth.[20] In response to inquiries by Commissioner John Milton Earle, town clerks from across the state wrote letters describing the status of Indians resident in their communities. Indian leaders and white guardians shared their ideas about Indian enclave communities and possible enfranchisement. These documents open a window onto the practices of Massachusetts communities with regard to Indians and people of mixed ancestry.

Earle found that the legal status of the Indians varied tremendously from town to town, based as much on their economic status as their race.[21] For example, the town clerk of Carver, Massachusetts, explained that a family of mixed ancestry did not "enjoy the political rights of citizens" because they were formerly paupers, had no taxable property, and therefore the townsmen believed "the constitution of our Federal government does not recognize such persons as citizens of the United States."[22] On the other hand, Francis Coleman, the town clerk of Pembroke, reported that Indians "do enjoy the political rights as citizens," even though his town had no taxable Indian residents.[23] Leavitt Thaxter, an educator and guardian of some of the Martha's Vineyard Indians, argued that the Indians had the legal status of children: "The Indians have been and are quasi minors and Wards of the State, who [sic] has voluntarily assumed Guardianship over them."[24] As of 1859, two Chappaquiddick Indians who owned taxable property and lived "on the 'white side of the line'" had "the same political rights as other citizens, & frequently vote; . . . they are always at the polls at our fall elections."[25]

Both the 1849 Bird report and the 1861 Earle report strongly recommended against blanket enfranchisement. In the words of Earle: "They have been so long accustomed to a state of pupilage, that they are not prepared for the change."[26] Each of these reports argued that the Indians' inability to exercise the rights and duties of citizens came from environmental and historical factors, including their poverty, lack of education, and the enforced dependency of state guardianship itself. Neither commission saw any reason why Indians would not some day be equal to other people "of their class" in all things. Each recognized the need for continued prohibition of land sales to non-Indians, and each asked that a Commissioner be appointed in order to ensure the continued "improvement"[27] of the Indians toward the day when they could be made citizens. But they mainly emphasized eventual citizenship and self-sufficiency, with individual, alienable landholding an important secondary objective.[28]

Through the 1860s, sentiment among whites for Indian enfranchisement grew. In 1862 all self-supporting Indians dwelling off the plantation communities were made citizens, and those residing on plantations were allowed to petition as individuals for the right of enfranchisement,[29] as John Earle had suggested. But very few accepted this new status.[30] By 1869 many whites had become convinced that the state's Indians possessed "as little of the pure Indian blood as of the traditional characteristics of the race," and lawmakers ended the protected status of the Indians, making them full citizens of the Commonwealth.[31]

Policy-Making in the Reconstruction Period

The attempt by Massachusetts lawmakers to resolve their Indian "question" came at one of the major moments in the history of American race relations.[32] Following the Civil War, the nation faced the task of the political and social reconstruction of the South, including the absorption of newly freed African Americans in former slave states. The post-Civil War years saw tremendous increases in the powers of the federal government to influence state policies on civil rights. Large numbers of moderate and conservative Republicans[33] joined radicals in the belief that the federal government had the right to require that states accept African American residents as citizens. Only under these conditions could the Civil Rights Act of 1866 and the Fourteenth Amendment (guaranteeing citizenship to blacks) be passed. The extension of voting rights to African American men in the Fifteenth Amendment was, however, much more controversial, and the actual amendment ended up relying "on negative injunctions rather than positive obligations to secure Negro suffrage."[34] Of course, African Americans vigorously laid claim to these rights in the wake of the war, appealing to the integrity of white Americans to live up to the rhetoric of both Christianity and democracy. Activists such as Frederick Douglass advocated the extension of all the rights of democracy to the freed people, and African American war veterans clamored for the rights they had fought to win.[35] Unfortunately, the end of the Reconstruction period would bring an end to hopes for racial equity.[36]

Given the long commitment of Massachusetts's white residents to the radical Republican and abolitionist agendas of the antebellum and Civil War eras, it is perhaps surprising to find that the state's own Indian descendants lived in a legal no-man's-land.[37] The men who served on the Indian commissions in the years from 1849 to 1862 had strong links to the abolitionist and radical Republican camp.[38] As early as 1849, the commissioners argued that there was no legal basis for the disfranchisement of Indians and people of color: "The progress of civil and ecclesiastical liberality has released all but the Indian from these disabilities. The African, the Turk, the Japanese, may enjoy, in Massachusetts, all the privileges of American Citizenship. The Indian alone, the descendant of monarchs, is a vassal in the land of his fathers."[39] By the post-Civil War period, with its Civil Rights Act of 1866 and the Thirteenth, Fourteenth, and Fifteenth Amendments to the United States Constitution, legislators feared that Massachusetts would be in violation of federal laws if the state did not enfranchise all her residents.[40] And because of Massachusetts's prominent role in radical reconstruction, it seems to have been embarrassing to some legislators to have enfranchised southern blacks and yet still have disfranchised people of color resident in the state. Governor Claflin noted in his 1869 inaugural address that, although Massachusetts had called upon "the national government to guarantee equal civil and political rights to all citizens within its jurisdiction," and while the state appealed "to our sister States to secure to all citizens the same rights and privileges," it was well to remember the "political anomaly" whereby the state's Indians remained disfranchised. Not only would it be beneficial to the Indians to merge "them in the general community,—with all the rights and privileges, and with all the duties and liabilities of citizens," but it would also be "more creditable to the Commonwealth" to do so.[41] As if to make clear the connection between Indian policy and Reconstruction racial policy, the 1869 commission asserted that the "Slave Power" of the South had formerly dictated the Indian policy of Americans and that such unjust barriers of color must now be removed.[42]

Nor can the Indian Enfranchisement Act be completely divorced from class relations in mid-nineteenth-century America. The current view of the poor (of any race) held that charity "too readily bestowed" only "sapped the morality of the recipient."[43] Many of the same attitudes we find expressed toward Indians were also directed at Irish or, later, French Canadian industrial workers. In the same vein, the editor of the *Boston Daily Advertiser* pronounced that the current Indian policy had "not been a good one, either for the Indians or for the State, and has been continued about fifty years too long": they would remain "a peculiar people as long as they are treated as such." While he agreed with both Commissioner Earle and other sympathetic whites that the state owed a debt to the Indians, he thought it best paid "not by annual grants of money in the way of charity, but by admitting the few remaining representatives of this outlawed people to the free exercise of the rights and duties of citizenship." With a sense of fair play that ignored the fact that the socioeconomic deck was stacked against them, the editor predicted that the Indians would enjoy "as many of its [citizenship's] privileges as their industry and self respect [would] enable them to procure."[44]

Ethnic Contest

The Indians of nineteenth-century Massachusetts did not conform to dominant notions of conventional "Indianness."[45] As we shall see, whites largely assumed that people of the same skin color shared the same status. African Americans and others had sought refuge in Indian enclave communities for decades. Many had become resident "foreigners" by marriage to Indian women. Most whites interpreted this intermarriage to mean that the Indians of Massachusetts were not real Indians, because there were no longer any "pure-blooded" Indians in the state.[46] Longtime Mashpee resident John Brown raised the important issue of mixed-race appearance in his testimony before an 1869 joint legislative committee. Identifying himself as a lifelong Mashpee resident of African descent, Brown thought that the legislators had come to Mashpee itself not only "to see what information they could get from us" but also "to see how we looked, whether we bore the resemblance of Indians, or whether we descended from Africa, Ireland, or France."[47]

The Indians, however, did not adopt outsiders as full proprietors, although, by the mid-nineteenth century, children of mixed African and Indian ancestry were entitled to that status. Solomon Attaquin, a Mashpee native, criticized the common white misunderstanding of the complexities of membership in an Indian community, as exemplified by Governor Claflin's 1869 address on the Indians: "He says if a stranger comes into Marshpee, he transforms himself into an Indian. He can't transform his caste, nor he can't transform his condition into the condition of an Indian."[48] Zaccheus Howwosswee, a member of one of the Gay Head community's leading families, reported that the Gay Head Indians had never given full proprietorship, including rights to shares of land ("pole [sic] right") to the "foreigners and strangers" who married Indian women. Nor did the Indian proprietors "wish for the foreigners to vote if it can be so."[49] Howwosswee later defined the real Indians to be any "native indians of the soil," noting that Indians who "come from another indian settlement we do not call . . . foreigners."[50] While those familiar with the Massachusetts Indians understood this careful definition, the 1869 legislation applied equally to all "non-white" residents, lumping Indian proprietors together with "foreign" spouses.[51] It is these different perceptions of "Indianness" to which we now turn.

Because the scholarly literature on ethnicity, ethnic identity, and ethnic boundaries is vast, various authors have employed the blanket concept of "ethnic identity" in conflicting ways, in order to refer to behavioral, symbolic, or other distinct variables.[52] In this paper, we use two separate concepts: "ethnic identity" and "ethnic boundary." "Ethnic identity" here means the complex of recognizably "Indian" cultural "traits" (e.g., a distinctive folklore), or behaviors (e.g., caring for their own poor) that either Indians themselves or others identified as "Indian." For our purposes, the determination of "ethnic identity" usually resides with the group, as the records necessary to confirm individual perceptions of ethnic identity do not survive. "Ethnic boundary" here means the beliefs or conditions that sustained a distinct group identity—value systems (prejudice or pride) or material conditions (legal status, common land reserves). People at the time may have understood these to be "racial" boundaries. We use "ethnic boundary" because it is more flexible, suggesting the cultural rather than biological origins of the maintenance of group identity. There is some unavoidable overlap between the two related concepts.

Whites' Interpretations: Racial Impurity

White outsiders tended to lump all of the colored residents of these enclaves into one mixed-race amalgam. As the town clerk of Edgartown on Martha's Vineyard explained, many of the vices that he saw as inevitable among the Indian descendants stemmed from "the mixture of blood—that of several races flowing in the same veins."[53] The editor of a Republican newspaper, the *Boston Daily Advertiser*, explained that intermarriages resulted when the Indians' "young men of spirit" refused "to share the degradation into which they have fallen . . . [and] their places have been filled by men of other races, till there is left as little of the pure Indian blood as of the traditional characteristics of the race."[54] Here the concept of "blood" defines an ethnic "racial" boundary. The mixture of "bloods" leaves the mixed-ancestry descendants in an ambiguous position, at least in the eyes of whites.[55]

Whether sympathetic or hostile, whites recognized that the Indian descendants were different from themselves. In short, they recognized a corporate ethnic identity even as they denied that the Indians were a "pure" race. Leavitt Thaxter, an educator on Martha's Vineyard, described the social condition of the Martha's Vineyard Indians thus: "They are kind and considerate one to another, and especially to the poor." He added later, "they are generally moral . . . in regard to temperance and general morals."[56] More common was the prejudice of Luke Lyman of Northampton, who reported that twenty-seven-year-old Josiah Bakeman was "much more steady and industrious than is usual for the colored races about here."[57] Benjamin Marchant, Guardian of the Chappaquiddick Indians of Martha's Vineyard, had a harsher view: "they are all so very selfish";[58] of their "temperance and general morals I cannot say anything in their favor. An Indian will generally drink if he can get the wherewith to buy liquor. The females are licentious & some of them will drink to excess when they can have the opportunity."[59]

Like most people of the day, Massachusetts whites seem to have held racial theories of character. Such racial theories would "legitimize in *biological* terms the causal efficacy of *social* processes" or, in other words, as long as Indians were perceived to be backward because of racial incapacity, then no social action was required to improve their circumstances.[60] Even Commissioner Earle, who was relatively sympathetic to the Indians' position, frequently explained the social conditions of the Indians in racial terms. Thus those who turned to seafaring, one of the only occupations open to men of color, had yielded to "the temptations to a race naturally inclined to a roving and unsettled life."[61] Earle reported that some sea captains paid Indians more than other crewmen because they believed that Indians were racially better-suited as whalers.[62] Whites shared the same beliefs in racial characteristics: they differed only over the degree of the racial infirmity and the most appropriate response to the current situation. They recognized distinctive ethnic boundaries, with the white bourgeois ideals of thrift, industry, and morality standing out in high relief against the (perhaps wrongly) perceived social evils of the enclave communities: intemperance, sexual licentiousness, and poverty.

Many Indian descendants who lived beyond the bounds of an ethnic enclave pursued the dominant ideals of self-sufficiency, industry, and hard work, and they tried to support themselves in spite of prejudice. Some whites grudgingly recognized this.[63] Samuel Hartwell of Southbridge wrote to Commissioner Earle in 1859 that Ephraim Nedson, a forty-five-year-old Pequot/African-descended resident, "is industrious, and, *probably from some ideosyncrasy,* is, and has always been, temperate . . ." [emphasis added].[64] So too could C. L. Whitmore, town clerk of Framingham, write on behalf of Elizabeth Brown, an elderly nurse whose son was "a temperate, industrious, laboring man." He questioned the wisdom of state policies that supported indigent Indians but not those with some initiative. When Brown's son inquired after some money held in trust for the Natick Indians, he found that "if some poor drunken idle Indian came along, they received aid, but when one like Brown was able to support herself, she was not able to draw any of the income of the fund."[65] Despite the attention focused upon Indian descendants, these individuals living away from the enclave communities left no record of how they felt about their Indian identity. Earle noted that they were distinctive only in that they had "the tradition that they are Indian."[66] But from the records that survive, it appears that they attempted to turn the brief moment of white attention to their own practical purposes. Priscilla Jackson wondered if Earle would appear before the legislative committee on claims and put in a good word for her mother's claim for support money during a recent illness.[67]

Others who, like Brown, lived in white communities, wrote to Earle asking for their rightful share of any monies coming to them. They might well ask, as did Gideon Fuller, "if he would ever receive any benefit from it [the tribal membership] except by occupancy?"[68]

Indians' Interpretations: Corporate Identity

For the majority of Indians—those living within the ten tribal enclaves—the Enfranchisement Act attacked some of the most fundamental symbols of Indian ethnic identity. These included the communal holding of land and other resources, and the care of their own sick, elderly, and poor. Those Indians who wanted to remain a distinct people faced the challenge of articulating their distinctive cultural features in opposition to those whites, African Americans, and Indians who claimed, for whatever reason, that ethnic boundaries should no longer be maintained by law. They did this in a single-minded determination to protect their legal status and land tenure from any alteration. While they eventually lost the legal battle, their struggle for cultural survival would continue.[69]

From our reading of the 1849, 1861, and 1869 reports,[70] eight fundamental markers of Indian ethnic identity emerged:

1. A communal fund of land and assets (clay, wood, cranberries, fishing rights), distributed to individuals or families, but governed by tradition and memory, and never alienated permanently from the group, contributing, as Commissioner Earle had observed, to "an equality of right and possessions . . . which is most desirable in such a community as this."[71]

2. Work done together in groups (although the ways in which this differed from similar community efforts in white communities is difficult to state).[72]

3. Resistance to state aid and "public pauperism"; group members cared for by the group; aid is viewed as the rightful compensation owed by the state to the Indians for lands wrongfully taken.[73]

4. A tradition of Indian identity (shared with those outside enclave communities).[74]

5. Shared folklore.[75]

6. Group meetings.[76]

7. Recognized criteria for tribal membership.[77]

8. Distinctive economic pursuits (basketry, seafaring).

Not all of these factors necessarily existed in the same measure at any one time, but their presence is well attested to by careful observers such as Earle. And, just as whites who bordered the ethnic enclaves perceived Indians in negative terms, some Indians also felt strong hostility toward their white neighbors. At Gay Head, for example, the 1849 committee reported that Indians simply wanted to be left alone.[78]

What we see, then, is that outsiders and insiders created competing definitions of Indian identity. Because there was considerable pressure on Indians to assimilate, as well as frequent "intermarriage," many whites seemed to believe that Indians had become "extinct" as a separate social group. Most saw those who remained as "non-whites," created from an amalgam of African and Indian intermarriage. While the white majority looked mainly for racial purity and found it wanting, they overlooked a continuing sense of ethnic corporatism. Others—Indians, resident African Americans, and concerned whites (legislators, guardians, residents of towns near Indian communities)—recognized the existence of distinctively Indian communities. Yet their definitions of the markers and meaning of Indianness often conflicted. The main features of "Indianness" included certain behaviors and beliefs, observed by some outsiders but not accepted as truly "Indian."[79] The possibility of such conflicting "in-group" and "out-group" definitions of ethnic identity has sometimes been noted by other social scientists.[80] But within complex policy dialogues, such as that which surrounded the enfranchisement process, we see the process by which the very existence of an ethnic group (Indians) becomes malleable in the hands of different social segments.[81]

The Mashpee Hearings: The Contest Between Definitions

In Mashpee, and possibly also Gay Head, the threat of enfranchisement inflamed controversy over land tenure between the "foreigners," their spouses, and a few Indian families on the one side, and the bulk of the Indian community on the other.[82] Latent political divisions rose to the surface under the threat of potential enfranchisement. By and large, the century-long tradition of African American/Indian intermarriage, as well as intermarriages with Irish, English, and other Indian groups, seems to have been accommodated with little friction. In some sense, the Indian communities had served as havens for African Americans shunned by the white world. Fugitive slaves had sought refuge at Mashpee and probably elsewhere.[83] But once the possibility of political participation opened up, some African Americans appear to have become less willing to remain both landless and disfranchised in Indian communities. Six months after Zaccheus Howwosswee wrote to Earle with his definitions of "native indians" and "foreigners," Deacon Simon Johnson of Gay Head asked the sympathetic Anglo-American educator Leavitt Thaxter to write to Earle regarding the split between two factions. Johnson feared that some of those foreigners who had no poll rights at Gay Head had written to Earle requesting a division of the land. In opposition, Johnson argued that "a division of the land will not promote the best interest of the people, but will be injurious to them, and this I think, is the opinion of most of the people there who are *not* foreigners."[84] The prospect of a change in status, and the potential elevation of non-Indian community members to the status of landholders alongside Indians with full rights may have exacerbated tensions between Indians and some of those who had married into these communities. For his part, Earle reported that at his public hearing on Gay Head, all the Indians agreed that they desired no change to their legal status, "except a very few, whose bad character and vicious habits have rendered them a nuisance to the place."[85] At Mashpee too, Earle's public hearing exhibited some of the potential for conflict between foreigners and Indians on this issue:

> One of the first speakers, a foreigner, who married a woman of the tribe, and who has resided but a short time in the district, near the border, among the better conditioned and more intelligent portion of the inhabitants, advocated the application to the legislature for the extension of the right to them, but after a full and free discussion, the vote was unanimous in favor of remaining as they are, the individual who had spoken on the other side voting with the rest.[86]

The lines of division became sharper as the Reconstruction years progressed, bringing favorable race legislation. The division into two factions—supporters and opponents of enfranchisement—displays some revealing patterns. It seems to have occurred in both Mashpee and Gay Head, as Indians formed opinions on potential enfranchisement. A Gay Head group headed by Abram G. Rodman asked the Legislature in 1868 for the right of citizenship,[87] as did one family from the Deep Bottom community of Martha's Vineyard (a small group of Indian descendants independent of the three recognized plantations on the Vineyard).[88]

But while whites focused on voting rights as the most important symbol of enfranchisement, the African American and Indian residents of the enclave communities struggled over land tenure. During Earle's investigations, the Indians of New Bedford agitated not for citizenship but for a hearing on unlawful possession of lands in Dartmouth and Westport.[89] And in 1869 the issue that really galvanized the Gay Head community was not the possible granting of voting rights but the potential legitimation of an illegal sale of common lands below Gay Head Cliffs by an individual.[90] This focus on the land-tenure aspects of the Enfranchisement Act supports our conclusion that the plantation Indians associated landholding with group survival.

Only for Mashpee do we have documents that reveal the roots of division within Indian enclaves. In December 1868 a group of Mashpee residents petitioned not for citizenship per se but for an act to allow land tenure in fee simple, lifting any restraint on land sales. Thirty-one Mashpee residents, drawn from an estimated twenty-four households, petitioned the Legislature to remove the entailment upon Mashpee lands (which prevented the sale of lands). Fifty-six residents, drawn from an estimated fifty-four households, opposed them with an official remonstrance (table 1). At the meeting with the Joint Special Commission on Indian Affairs in February of 1869, a vote was taken among those gathered to decide both the issue of removing entailment of lands and the issue of citizenship. Of forty recorded votes on land entailment, the majority opposed removing entailment. The issue of citizenship remained unresolved. Of the thirty-six who voted, eighteen favored the change in status, while the other eighteen remained opposed. However, these votes had little influence on the legislation. Four months later, the Legislature passed the Act to Enfranchise the Indians, lifting land entailment.[91]

The linkage of petition signatures with the census data taken ten years earlier by John Earle reveals some interesting divisions between those who petitioned for a change and those who signed the remonstrance against change (table 1). What we learn from this record linkage is that the group that petitioned to be able to sell their land without protection and, presumably, to divide up common lands as well into individual holdings, represented a segment of the population composed of more intermarried individuals (predominantly wives or widows who had married African American men) than the average, as well as several of the wealthiest people in the community (see table 1).

This coalition between colored foreigners and certain Indians can be seen again in the hearings that were held by the Joint Commission on Indian Affairs to hear both the petitioners and the remonstrants. The testimony of several men at this hearing, apparently recorded verbatim, gives us a rare view of the justifications used by residents within this community for and against the Enfranchisement Act.[92] Of the five speakers who argued for enfranchisement and lifting of the entailment of land, three clearly identified themselves as non-Indians and closely linked their arguments to the atmosphere of racial equity in the Reconstruction movement. The first speaker, a Mr. Sewall, described himself: "Born a freeman; I was never a slave." He went on to link his cause with the larger issue of political enfranchisement of African American freedmen: "I have seen men that were born South in slavery come here [to Massachusetts] and have all the rights and privileges of citizens, while we [non-Indians in Mashpee] are set down" (9). He called those who opposed the petition "Red Jackets," recalling the traditionalist Iroquois leader of the late-eighteenth century. According to Sewall, these people never came "to hear the gospel preached" (6). Playing on post-Civil War sensitivities to race equity, he asked for the establishment of Mashpee as a town like other towns, "so that it can be established that colored men can govern themselves . . . I don't want you to establish a town because they are colored men, but because they are men. I don't care whether he is black or white, Hottentot, African, or where he comes from, if he will be a man, let him take his place among us" (7). Another speaker was Samuel Godfrey, a colored "foreigner" who married an

TABLE 1
Divisions in Mashpee Over Changes in Land Tenure

	Petitioners (support change)	Remonstrants (oppose change)	Significance (t-test)
"Colored foreigners" or intermarried [a]	38% (8 of 21 known)	15.2% (7 of 46 known)	2.123 (significant)
Mean total wealth (1859 $)	$1540.35	$1245.18	0.891 (not significant)
Largest total worth (1859 $)	$4615.00	$3811.00	not applicable
Signers with more than $2500	23.5% (4 of 17 known)	11% (4 of 36 known)	sample too small
Mean age (in 1869)	47.83	49.65	−0.451 (not significant)
Number of female signers	16	11	3.233 (highly significant)
Approximate number of households represented	24	54	not applicable
Number of surnames represented	18	32	not applicable
Total number of signatures	31 [b]	56 [c]	

Compiled from information in: "The Petition of Oaks A. Coombs and others, for the passage of the act changing the tenure of lands in Marshpee," Dec. 1, 1868; and "The Remonstrance of William H. Simon and others, against the petition of Oaks A. Coombs and others," Dec. 1, 1868 (Massachusetts State Archives, Columbia Point, Boston, Massachusetts: unpassed legislation, 1869, #1514).

[a] This figure is not adjusted for couples where both sign. The petitioners were accused of packing their petition with women whose husbands also signed, a practice in violation of the customary practice of one representative (male or female) per household. The significance in the proportion of female signers indicates that there is some justification to this charge.

[b] John Thompson signed both the petition and the remonstrance. His name has not been counted in the 31 total signers to the petition or the 56 signers of the remonstrance.

[c] Young Gouch and Mary Gouch both signed the remonstrance against any change but their names were later crossed out. Those two signatures have not been counted in the total of 56. In the hearings, Young Gouch (a former slave) spoke out *in favor* of change.

Indian woman and had three children who served in the Civil War, one of whom died. Godfrey asked for "a chance to breathe the same atmosphere that the rest of you do. I want to live in a town where I can be recognized as a citizen." A widower, he feared that his right to remain on his lands would be endangered if his children chose to drive him off: "My wife had but a few acres of land, but I have made improvements on it, and now they give me to understand 'You may make all the improvements you may choose; when your children come home they can drive you, because you are a stranger and they are Indians'" (21–22). Young Gouch, a former slave from Missouri who had served in the black 55th Massachusetts Regiment of the Union Army, also spoke. Like his fellows, Gouch appealed to his listeners' sense of fairness and belief in individualism. Noting that he had voted in Boston when he lived there, he asked for "equal rights" in Mashpee: "My wife belongs down here, and if I am capable of paying her taxes, I should think I am capable of holding some land" (25). Of the two Mashpee Indians who spoke in favor of this change, successful entrepreneur Solomon Attaquin also argued that Mashpee's citizens would be greatly improved by ending their dependency: "I want to see the day that I am a citizen and man, as well as other men, and I say we are ready for it today" (33).[93]

The four principal speakers opposing any change in status argued that Indians were still not prepared for unprotected participation in the market. Here we would do well to remember James Clifford's observation that these speakers were not necessarily expressing their own honest views of the capabilities of Mashpee Indians. Rather, they couched their arguments for delay in paternalist rhetoric, in order, they hoped, to appeal to the white legislators.[94] Both William Simons and the old blind preacher Joseph Amos elucidated the attitudes expressed in Earle's report—that the Indians were not yet educated enough to participate fully as citizens. Nevertheless, at least one man directly addressed the integrationist arguments of the petitioners. Nathan S. Pocknet refuted Sewall's race-blind attitudes, reminding his listeners that Mashpee had always been an Indian, not a colored, community. The Indians were entitled to special disposition over the land and community affairs because it "was granted to us,—a grant from King Charles, I believe, it was, in England,—set off for the Indians, and accordingly it has been in reserve to us for [sic] that time" (23). As to the complaints of the foreigners that the Indians unfairly excluded them from citizenship, Pocknet heatedly replied: "If they don't like it, why don't they take up their little alls and go away" (22). Refuting the pleas of Godfrey that he be allowed to own his own land, Pocknet argued that "there is no one of the whole township that can become a legal citizen easier than he can. His children are old enough to look out for themselves. He is not a landholder, and he can take his money and go into another town and purchase there; so it is no hard matter for him to become a citizen of another town" (22). The divisions among Mashpee residents did not follow strictly racial lines. Although 38 percent of the signers of the petition for change were either colored foreigners or Indians married to foreigners, 15.2 percent of the signers of the remonstrance *against* change also fell in the non-Indian or intermarried category. One of these non-Indians, John Brown, explained that he threw in his lot with the Indians because he was concerned about the effects of independence on the community as a whole. He feared that the new landholders would not be able to support the added expenses of taxation, and all would become paupers. Born in Mashpee and, like several others, "brought up at sea" as a crewman on ships, he was not considered an Indian, although he seemed a fully integrated community member in other ways and had married a woman who was "a native of the place, holding some portion of land." Although he signed the remonstrance, he did not fear for his own security. Rather, he wanted to "guard these little ones" — children whose parents might squander their land, leaving them permanent paupers (26–27).

The enclave split, then, over two different views of community. One group, associated with individualists and "foreigners," thought that the best opportunity for the Indian communities lay in seizing the chance to become self-sufficient individuals, freed from governmental restraints. These held that entrance into their community should not be restricted by race. In the words of Sewall, "if he will be a man, let him take his place among us." Certainly, these Indian petitioners did not deny their Indian ethnic identity. One of the prominent petitioners, Solomon Attaquin, refuted Governor Claflin's view of racial amalgamation at Mashpee (see above). Petitioners such as Attaquin were perceived by themselves and others as being either wholly or partially "Indian." Nevertheless, they cast their lot with the individualism of the day, rejecting the historical ethnic boundaries (such as communal land tenure) in favor of the possibilities for increased economic opportunity and the community heterogeneity offered by the American "melting pot" of enfranchisement. On the other side was a group of more cautious or more traditionalist Indians, who may have represented the accepted status quo. These residents saw the Indians as a special group, set off by their historical rights. More cautious about change, this group refused to allow whites to shirk their legitimate contractual obligations to Indians. They believed the best course lay in preserving the customary practices of allowing entitled individuals to take up farmlands from the common holdings, and caring for their own, including the poor, the elderly, or the "intemperate."[95] Thus, we see that the Indian Enfranchisement Act revealed the complex distinctions between white, African American, and Indian definitions of "Indianness" and exposed the differences between in-group and out-group perceptions of Indian ethnic identity; it also divided all three groups over what was the best course. And, like members of each of the other two major racial groups, individual Indians weighed the costs and benefits of legally codified ethnic boundaries.

The Gendered Dimensions of Ethnic Controversy

Unlike the white and Indian communities, little is known about the views and motivations of the African American residents of Indian enclaves such as Mashpee. Some pushed for the Enfranchisement Act as the logical extension of other Reconstruction-era race legislation. Yet the situation of African American foreigners had some obviously gendered aspects, and these gender issues tie into the larger struggle for women's rights, which failed to win broad support in the Reconstruction period. Because their poll rights provided the family's land, Indian women had an unusual position in mixed marriages. As became apparent in the testimony of Mashpee's "foreigner" men, husbands who did not enjoy proprietor's rights in the enclave communities would never achieve the usual role of household head and landowner dominant in American culture. This dependency must have grated on men, part and parcel as it was of the freedman's newfound legitimacy as head of household. At Emancipation, African American families in the former slave states struggled to adopt the gender model of male breadwinner/female housewife in order to protect black women from abuses at the hands of white men as well as to take their place as unified families equal to those of other Americans.[96] We have already seen the deep connections between African American struggles for citizenship, the right to property, and the right to vote. Thus another ingredient of the Reconstruction-era struggle—the reconstruction of the African American family according to a male-dominant gender-role ideology—would also be a sore spot for many people of color in the Indian enclaves.[97]

Indian women stood to lose some rights if enfranchisement on white models went forward. Earle noted in his report that among the Chappaquiddick community, the "rights of women are fully recognized, the females taking the same liberty of speech [in meetings] and, when unmarried, or in the absence of their husbands, enjoying the same right of voting with men."[98] In the end, the enfranchisement of Indians as citizens would extend the vote only to the menfolk; women who had exercised considerable authority in the absence of their husband may have actually lost considerable official power when enclaves such as Chappaquiddick were forced to conform more closely to dominant American models of governance.

In an effort to avoid this, some Indians who favored enfranchisement petitioned the legislature at the same time for the adoption of female suffrage throughout the state. The alliance between the causes of abolition and women's rights had been frayed by the passage of the Fifteenth Amendment guaranteeing the vote to black men.[99] Women who had worked hard for the cause of African Americans felt betrayed by their male colleagues. The New England Women's Suffrage Association determined that they would not allow this opportune moment to slip by and launched a massive petition campaign, swamping state legislators with petitions for female suffrage from across the state. Buried in this packet of petitions were three that first went to the Joint Commission on Indian Affairs.[100] The Freeman family of the Deep Bottom tribe, on Martha's Vineyard, wrote separate petitions seeking "all the rights of citizens" for Indians and "that females in this state be enfranchised.[101] An even more startling find is the petition sent by the women of Mashpee, who asked "that women may be Enfranchised and enjoy all the Privileges and immunities of citizens of the Commonwealth." An analysis of the sixteen signers of the petition reveals that more than half had supported the petition for land reform in Mashpee and its attendant Indian enfranchisement.[102] Such connections between "Indian policy" and gender relations have all too often been overlooked. Yet obviously the women of Mashpee and Indian women elsewhere recognized both the liabilities and the possibilities of full membership in white society.

Conclusion

During the Mashpee hearings, Rodney French of New Bedford, a legislator on the 1869 commission, asked Mashpee resident Nathan Pocknet about his hopes for the young people of Mashpee should they be enfranchised: "You don't know but that there may be some child in this town that will make a president of the United States: Would you not like to have all these young men in the line of promotion, so that . . . they will take their place in the world like other men . . . ?" When Pocknet explained that their children still did not have more than a common school education, French replied that many able governors and legislators never had a high school education either.[103]

This incident illuminates some of the differences in perception between whites and most Indians. Although Indian descendants did exercise their political duties by occasionally serving in the state legislature over the course of the next twenty years,[104] many of the Indian enclaves did not simply become amalgamated "American" communities. Groups of Indians and people of color remained unassimilated, and from that day to this, Massachusetts has seen various resurgences of Indian identity, Indian folklore, and tribal self-awareness.[105] Even today, several of these enclave communities are seeking to win back an official legal identity as members of Indian tribes that might entitle them to federal medical benefits, land or compensation, and other social programs. Far from becoming part of an American melting pot, the children of Mashpee and some of the other enclaves would defeat the hopes of legislators by stubbornly maintaining both their own ethnic identity and their own ethnic boundaries.[106]

We have argued that "Indian policy" can never be divorced from the wider social context in which it was produced. The Massachusetts Indian Enfranchisement Act of 1869 could not have been conceived without Reconstruction-era reforms in civil rights for African Americans. Instead of a simple Indian/white conflict, we find also African American/Indian divisions, mid-nineteenth-century class tensions, and gender conflict. In this brief moment, the attitudes of even ordinary Massachusetts citizens came to the surface of political discourse, revealing the cultural beliefs that underlay local, state, and federal policies.

Yet the significance of these events goes beyond a better understanding of Reconstruction-era race policy. Rather, it lies in the confluence of ethnic identity (understood differently by the participants), ethnic boundaries (or the attempt to erase them), and the formation of policy (which, despite overwhelming opposition by Indians themselves, ultimately was decided by powerful whites). Because white policymakers could see only racial groups, while most Indians saw distinctive local ethnic groups, policymakers managed to dismantle the legal structures supporting Massachusetts Indians. Policy affecting ethnic boundaries was inextricably linked to the perception of ethnic identity. The nineteenth-century Massachusetts debate over how best to handle its Indian minority still resonates in ethnic contests affecting Indians and other American minorities today.

NOTES

1. Leavitt Thaxter to John Milton Earle, Sept. 3, 1859, Edgartown, Mass., Earle Collection, box 2, folder 3; American Antiquarian Society, Worcester, Mass., hereafter cited as Earle Collection. Indian Commissioner Earle described Thaxter, a Martha's Vineyard educator, as a "long and steadfast friend" to the Indians. The tone of Thaxter's correspondence and his several intercessions on behalf of Indians (at their request) seem to bear this out. See John Milton Earle, "Report to the Governor and Council Concerning the Indians of the Commonwealth under the Act of April 6, 1859," Senate Document no. 96, Massachusetts State Library, Special Collections, State House, Boston, Mass. (Boston: William White, 1861), 46; hereafter cited as Earle Report, 1861–62.

2. The authors would like to acknowledge the invaluable assistance of Ruth Wallis Herndon, Jacqueline Jones, Neil Kamil, Morton Keller, Daniel Mandell, and Neal Salisbury; the major portion of the research was carried out with the assistance of the staffs at the American Antiquarian Society, the Massachusetts State Library and Special Collections, and the Massachusetts State Archives; archival materials are quoted with the permission of these institutions.

3. *Private and Special Statutes of the Commonwealth of Massachusetts for the years 1866, 1867, 1868, 1869, 1870* (Boston, 1871), 12:780–82.

4. The Gay Head land sales resulted in a legislative inquiry that produced a document accounting for expenses. Richard L. Pease, "Report of the Commissioner Appointed to Complete the Examination and Determination of All Questions of Title to Land and of all Boundary Lines Between Individual Owners at Gay Head, on the Island of Martha's Vineyard, Under a Resolve of the Legislature of 1866, chap. 67" (Boston, 1871).

5. The parallels to the Dawes Act of 1887 are striking.

6. A period term, in referring to African Americans not considered members of Indian proprietorships. We are aware of the very good reasons for discontinuing the use of such terms as "white." But because the term carried such social significance in the period, and because many Indians and African Americans were also of "Euro-American"

descent, we found no acceptable substitute. Then, as now, it referred to skin color combined with social identification as a member of the dominant racial group. African American has been substituted for "negro" and is used along with such period terms as "colored" and "people of color." "Indian" and "Indian descendants" have been used in favor of "Native American" and "Amerindian," although "native" is sometimes used. Finally, while there are certainly no biological categories of race, nineteenth-century Americans of all racial and ethnic backgrounds applied the term "mulatto" to people whom they recognized to be children of two or more socially separated "racial" groups. We have, therefore, adopted "mixed ancestry" as a less offensive descriptive term, without assuming that this determined the individual's ethnic identification. See Barbara Jeanne Fields, "Slavery, Race and Ideology in the United States of America," *New Left Review*, 181 (1990), 97–98.

7. Joint Special Commission on Indian Affairs, "Report on the Indians of the Commonwealth," 1869 House Document 483, Massachusetts State Library, Special Collections, State House, Boston, Mass., 13; hereafter cited as the Joint Special Commission Report, 1869.

8. See also Ellice B. Gonzalez, "Tri-Racial Isolates in a Bi-Racial Society: Poospatuck Ambiguity and Conflict," in Frank W. Porter, III, ed., *Strategies for Survival: American Indians in the Eastern United States, Contributions in Ethnic Studies*, 15 (New York, 1986); 132–33.

9. Of course, the dynamics of the Reconstruction period differed greatly in intensity between the South and the North. By the time of the Jim Crow segregation laws, southern Indian groups faced severe pressures that encouraged them to distance themselves from African Americans. See Helen C. Rountree, *Pocahontas's People: The Powhatan Indians of Virginia Through Four Centuries* (Norman, Okla., 1990), 198–200.

10. The problems attendant on the Massachusetts Indian Enfranchisement Act continue to bedevil Americans and their policymakers today. For more on the maintenance of Indian identity among Massachusetts Wampanoags, especially from 1869 to the present, see Jack Campisi, *The Mashpee Indians: Tribe on Trial, The Iroquois and Their Neighbors*, ser. ed. Laurence Hauptman (Syracuse, N.Y.: 1991); Gloria Levitas, "No Boundary Is a Boundary: Conflict and Change in a New England Indian Community" (Ph.D. diss., Rutgers University, 1980); and Laurie Weinstein, "'We're Still Living on Our Traditional Homeland': The Wampanoag Legacy in New England," in Porter, ed., *Strategies for Survival*, 85–112.

11. Reservations rarely offer enough access to resources for assimilation to occur: George Pierre Castile, "On the Tarascanness of the Tarascans and the Indianness of the Indians," in *Persistent Peoples: Cultural Enclaves in Perspective*, ed. George Pierre Castile and Gilbert Kushner (Tucson, 1981), 186.

12. See William S. Simmons, *Spirit of the New England Tribes: Indian History and Folklore, 1620–1984* (Hanover, N.H.: 1986); see also Daniel Mandell, "'To Live More Like My Christian English Neighbors': Natick Indians in the Eighteenth Century," *William and Mary Quarterly*, 3d ser., 48 (1991), 552–79; Daniel Mandell, "The Indians' Landscape in Massachusetts, 1790–1860: Change and Continuity" (paper presented at the Research Colloquium, Old Sturbridge Village, Sturbridge, Mass., March 14, 1992); Jean M. O'Brien, "Divorced from the Land," ch. 6 this vol.; James P. Ronda, "'Generations of Faith': The Christian Indians of Martha's Vineyard," *William and Mary Quarterly*, 3d ser., 38 (1981), 369–94; Neal Salisbury, "Red Puritans: The 'Praying Indians' of Massachusetts Bay and John Eliot," *William and Mary Quarterly*, 3d ser., 31 (1974), 27–54.

13. Earle Report, 1861–62: lxxviii.

14. Mashpee was known in the nineteenth century as Marshpee. We have referred to it by its present name to avoid confusion.

15. The larger south shore plantation communities included Herring Pond (Plymouth), Christiantown and Chappaquiddick (Martha's Vineyard), and Fall River (in Fall River). The largest non-plantation communities on the south shore were Dartmouth (near New Bedford) and Yarmouth (on Cape Cod).

16. Rev. James Freeman, "A Description of Duke's County, Aug. 13th, 1807 [1815]," Massachusetts Historical Society, *Collections*, 2d ser., 3 (1968), 93–94; Kevin A. McBride, "The Historical Archaeology of the Mashantucket Pequots, 1637–1900: A Preliminary Analysis," in *The Pequots in Southern New England: The Fall and Rise of an American Indian Nation*, ed. Laurence M. Hauptman and James D. Wherry (Norman, Okla., 1990), 96–116; Kathleen J. Bragdon, "The Material Culture of the Christian Indians in New England, 1650–1775," *Documentary Archaeology in the New World*, ed. Mary C. Beaudry (New York, 1989). Modern authors such as McBride and Bragdon are careful to avoid equating a different material culture with poverty.

17. "Report of the Commissioners Relating to the Condition of the Indians in Massachusetts," 1849 House Document 46 (hereafter referred to as Bird Report, 1849), 48; Earle Report, 1861–62: 13–14.

18. Editorial, *Boston Daily Advertiser*, 113, no. 133 (1869), 2. (The flowery language was typical of the editor's romantic view of a vanished Indian race.)

19. Barry O'Connell, *On Our Own Ground: The Complete Writings of William Apess, a Pequot* (Amherst, Mass., 1992), xxxv–xxxviii.

20. Bird Report, 1849; Earle Report, 1861–62; Joint Special Commission Report, 1869.

21. The social significance of race and ethnicity has tended to mask the underlying similarities based in class relations in American history. See David Brion Davis, "The American Dilemma," *New York Review of Books*, 39 no. 13 (July 16, 1992), 17. This point is elaborated in one of the books reviewed by Davis: Jacqueline Jones, *The Dispossessed: America's Underclasses from the Civil War to the Present* (New York, 1992), esp. 1–10.

22. A. B. Maxim to John Milton Earle, December 28, 1859, Carver, Mass., Earle Collection, box 2, folder 5. Similarly, the Bird Commission found from their examination of the constitution that [male] inhabitants should be citizens, except for paupers, aliens, and persons under guardianship: Bird Report, 1849: 50.

23. Francis Coleman to Earle, December 28, 1859, Pembroke, Mass., Earle Collection, box 2, folder 5.

24. Leavitt Thaxter to John Milton Earle, October 5, 1860, Edgartown, Mass., Earle Collection, box 2, folder 3; Thaxter to Earle, January 28, 1860, n.p., Earle Collection, box 2, folder 3.

25. Benjamin C. Marchant to John Milton Earle, December 31, 1859, Edgartown, Mass., Earle Collection, box 2, folder 3.

26. Earle Report, 1861–62: 43.

27. "Improvement" is a cultural concept worth further exploration. It seems to carry the idea that Indians (and, presumably, other "social inferiors") were capable of rising if properly educated and given opportunity. The concept assumes a model of society that is hierarchically arranged, with certain individuals or groups moving upward, closer to dominant values and behaviors, while others remain stationary. The term was also used in reference to buildings that increased property values. People who "improved" their land also had the chance of improving themselves.

28. The 1869 report expressed this as a distinction between political (denied voting rights) and civil (barred from landholding and jury service) disfranchisement: Joint Special Commission Report, 1869: 8.

29. Massachusetts *Acts and Resolves*, 1862, ch. 184.

30. Joint Special Commission Report, 1869: 8.

31. Editorial, *Boston Daily Advertiser*, 113, no. 133: 2.; present-day petitions for federal recognition and restitution for lost land must now demonstrate continuous group identity back to the 1869 change in legal status, according to personal communication, October 1990, from Jack Campisi, Anthropology Dept., Wellesley College, Wellesley, Mass.

32. The link to Reconstruction-era race legislation as it affected Massachusetts has been briefly mentioned in Paul Brodeur's account of the land claims case of the Mashpee in the 1970s. Paul Brodeur, *Restitution: The Land Claims of the Mashpee, Passamaquoddy, and Penobscot Indians of New England* (Boston, 1985), 19–20. Another important treatment of Mashpee history as it was interpreted during the Mashpee land claims case can be found in James Clifford, *The Predicament of Culture: Twentieth-Century Ethnography, Literature, and Art* (Cambridge, Mass., 1988). Both of these excellent studies discuss the historical act of enfranchisement for its significance in present policy and in understanding Indian history.

Morton Keller has demonstrated connections between Reconstruction-era race legislation and racial attitudes as they affected both African Americans and western Indians. Just as postwar America saw intense antinegro sentiment mixed with progressive civil rights legislation, so too was postwar (western) Indian policy "the product of underlying racial hostility tempered by the ideal of equal national citizenship." Morton Keller, *Affairs of State: Public Life in Late Nineteenth Century America* (Cambridge, Mass., 1977), 153. See also Francis Paul Prucha, *American Indian Policy in Crisis: Christian Reformers and the Indians, 1865–1900* (Norman, Okla., 1976), 4, 25–27. Frederick Hoxie has placed the post-Civil War Indian policies of the west in a broad cultural framework; see Frederick E. Hoxie, *A Final Promise: The Campaign to Assimilate the Indians, 1880–1920* (Lincoln, Neb., 1984).

33. The Republican Party was the more liberal party of this period—Abraham Lincoln was a Republican, as were many of those radicals who pushed for the abolition of slavery.

34. Robert J. Kaczorowski, "To Begin the Nation Anew: Congress, Citizenship, and Civil Rights after the Civil War," *American Historical Review*, 92 (1987), 45–54; quote from Keller, *Affairs of State*, 68; The rights and duties of citizenship could be abrogated because of gender or other mitigating factors. At issue in the reconstruction years, however, was the debate over whether race should still be maintained as just such a mitigating factor.

35. Eric Foner, "Rights and the Constitution in Black Life during the Civil War and Reconstruction," *Journal of American History*, 74 (1987), 864–66.

36. After 1870, the courts slowly stripped the Reconstruction-era civil rights legislation of any real meaning by limiting and narrowing the scope of its application to social problems. See Keller, *Affairs of State*, 149–50.

37. Eric Foner, *A Short History of Reconstruction, 1863–1877* (New York, 1990), 104–105. The new federal Indian policy—the General Allotment Act of 1887—would be drafted by another Massachusetts lawmaker, Henry L. Dawes, who would replace radical Republican Charles Sumner as U.S. Senator after Sumner's death in 1874. The focus of the new federal policy would in many ways be similar to that of

the Massachusetts Indian Enfranchisement Act of 1869—the total assimilation of Western Indians, including the division of their lands into family farmsteads and the promise of eventual citizenship. Supporters of Indian assimilation were drawn from the northeastern middle class, and many of these had been vocal supporters of abolition.

38. Francis W. Bird, the chair of the 1849 commission and a member of the 1869 commission, was an illustrious Massachusetts Republican and a close advisor to the state's radical Republican Senator, Charles Sumner. His 1849 report argued that, until the "unjust and unnatural prejudice against color" was removed in the surrounding society, the Indian communities would only be irretrievably harmed by removal of protections and state support (Bird Report, 1849: 24). Yet, he quoted the famous escaped slave and black abolitionist, Frederick Douglass, in arguing that the poverty and vices of the Indians could be attributed to oppressions imposed by whites: "Take your heels off of our necks [here, Douglass referred to African Americans] and see if we do not rise" (Frederick Douglass, cited in Bird Report, 51). John Milton Earle, whose report offered the most sympathetic and detailed accounting of Massachusetts Indians, was a Quaker, and he served previously as the editor of the antislavery newspaper the *Worcester Spy*. *The National Cyclopaedia of American Biography*, vol. 11 (Ann Arbor: University Microfilms, 1967), 145.

39. Bird Report, 1849: 49.

40. In March 1869 the legislature ratified the Fifteenth Amendment to the United States Constitution, which stated: "The right of citizens of the United States to vote shall not be denied or abridged by the United States or by any state, on account of race, color, or previous condition of servitude": "Resolves relative to an Amendment of the Constitution of the United States," passed by the Senate, March 9, by the House of Representatives, March 12, 1869. *Private and Special Statutes of the Commonwealth of Massachusetts for the years 1866, 1867, 1868, 1869, 1870*, 825.

41. Claflin cited in Joint Special Commission Report, 1869: 1–2.

42. This is just one indication of the links between the Abolitionists and Indian Enfranchisement. They then quoted a long passage from Wendell Phillips, the great abolitionist who, after the Civil War, turned his efforts to improving the treatment of the American Indian: Joint Special Commission Report, 1869: 12–13. See Prucha, *American Indian Policy*, 25–27. Prucha discerns that there were few direct links between abolitionist leaders (including Wendell Phillips) and the new movement for an enlightened Indian policy. Yet, there were much more significant connections between the *ideas* affecting African Americans and those of the new era of Indian reform. These have yet to be explored in any detail for the Eastern Indians, who are in the interesting position of often living alongside African Americans, sometimes appearing (because of past intermarriage) quite African American, being mistaken for African American, and perhaps sometimes choosing to function as African Americans in certain circumstances (outside their enclave communities, for example).

43. Keller, *Affairs of State*, 127.

44. Editorial, *Boston Daily Advertiser*, 113, no. 133: 2.

45. Similarly, today's non-Indians are often taken aback when they find that New England "Indians" range in appearance from "white" to "black." See Connecticut Public Television and the Pequot Nation, "The New Pequots: Mashantucket Pequot Tribe," videotape (Hartford, Conn., 1988).

46. Claflin cited in Joint Special Commission Report, 1869: 2.

47. Massachusetts Legislative Papers, 1869, House Document 502, Massachusetts State Library, Special Collections, State House, Boston, Mass., 26.

48. Ibid., 33.

49. Zaccheus Howwosswee to John Milton Earle, January 27, 1860, Gay Head, Mass., Earle Collection, box 2, folder 3.

50. Ibid., September 12, 1860. The roots of this conflict ran quite deep. Intermarriage—or marriages "across a socially significant line of distinction" (after definition in J. Milton Yinger, "Ethnicity," *Annual Review of Sociology*, 11 (1985), 167)—between Indian women and African American men was a common practice in the eighteenth century, and perhaps increased in frequency after midcentury owing to increasing and complementary demographic imbalances in both populations: Ira Berlin, "Time, Space, and the Evolution of Afro-American Society on British Mainland North America," *American Historical Review*, 85 (1980), 52; Lorenzo J. Greene, *The Negro in Colonial New England*, Studies in History, Economics and Public Law, no. 494 (New York, 1942), 198–201. Intermarriage was already a sore point by the late eighteenth century, when another Gay Head leader, Zachariah Howwosswee, had listed each proprietor at Gayhead, along with the degree of their racial mixture. This information was presumably essential because at this point in time the degree of "racial mixture" determined the number of "rights" each individual could claim, and hence whether they were entitled to aid from the state. Howwosswee noted that there were "but few clear Indian families on s'd Gayhead," yet added defiantly that there was "but one clear negro living among us." Zachariah Howwosswee, "Account of the Indians at Gayhead [March 19]," MS copy of 1792 original, by Edward Winslow, August 25, 1852, Massachusetts Historical Society, Miscellaneous Manuscripts Collection, Boston, Mass. Although its purpose is unclear, his census seems designed to document the survival of Indians entitled to continued state support, perhaps reflecting an increasing tendency among Anglo-Americans to define community members as negro rather than as Indian.

51. For example, Earle apparently adopted the distinctions of the Gay Head Indians in his census categories, carefully separating African American and other non-Indian spouses from those born into the enclave communities.

52. Noted by Susan Emley Keefe, "Ethnic Identity: The Domain of Perceptions of an Attachment to Ethnic Groups and Cultures," *Human Organization*, 51, no. 1 (1992), 35–36.

53. Benjamin C. Marchant to Earle, September 17, 1859, Edgartown, Mass., Earle Collection, box 3, folder 3.

54. Editorial, *Boston Daily Advertiser*, 113, no. 133: 2.

55. Karen Blu's study of the Lumbee Indian community in North Carolina found a similar concern with the mystical powers of "blood." While a few drops of black "blood" makes one black, a few drops of white blood does not make one white: see Karen I. Blu, *The Lumbee Problem: The Making of an American Indian People* (New York, 1980), 24–25. See also Rountree, *Pocahontas's People*, 219–20, and ch. 9 throughout, on the racial categorization controversy faced by Virginia's Indians in the early twentieth century.

56. Thaxter to Earle, February 3, 1860, Edgartown, Mass., Earle Collection, box 2, folder 3.

57. Luke Lyman to Earle, August 4, 1859, Northampton, Mass., Earle Collection, box 2, folder 5.

58. Marchant to Earle, August 27, 1859, Edgartown, Mass., Earle Collection, box 2, folder 3.

59. Ibid., September 17, 1859. Mashpee's treasurer also noted: "The sin of fornication and adultery is very great in Mashpee . . . [I]t is about impossible to regulate the

morals of Mashpee." See also Charles Marston to Earle, December 29, 1860, n.p., Edgartown, Mass., Earle Collection, box 2, folder 2.

60. Such findings fit well with growing "Social Darwinist" theories well suited to a view of democracy as meritocracy (in which the ranking of individuals in society was attributed to their differing abilities, with the wealthiest members of the society apparently the "fittest" individuals); George W. Stocking, Jr., *Race, Culture, and Evolution: Essays in the History of Anthropology*, rev. ed. (Chicago, 1982), 243. The Irish and other members of the lower classes were disparaged in similar ways, perhaps owing to their economic inferiority, and within the nineteenth-century context, they were also understood as a racial minority—not as an ethnic group or as a segment of the lower class group. It is this recasting as racial differences of what we now see as issues of poverty or culture to which Stocking alludes.

61. Earle Report, 1861–62: 6. Similarly, the early anthropologist Lewis Henry Morgan believed that the American Indian's "barbarous" stage of evolution made him unfit for the responsibilities of citizenship: see Lewis Henry Morgan, "Factory System for Indian Reservations," *The Nation*, 23 (1876), 58, cited in Robert E. Bieder, *Science Encounters the Indian, 1820–1880: The Early Years of American Ethnology* (Norman, Okla., 1986), 242.

62. Earle Report, 1861–62: 27.

63. As social psychologists who study ethnic prejudice have theorized, when encountered as individuals, members of a despised minority can sometimes break out of their negative stereotype: Miles Hewstone, "Intergroup Attribution: Some Implications for the Study of Ethnic Prejudice," in Jan Pieter Van Oudenhoven and Tineke M. Willemsen, ed., *Ethnic Minorities: Social Psychological Perspectives* (Berwyn, Penn., 1989), 37.

64. Samuel Hartwell to Earle, September 17, 1859, Southbridge, Mass., MS letter, AAS, Earle Collection, box 2, folder 5.

65. C. L. Whitmore to Earle, December 24, 1859, Framingham, Mass., Earle Collection, box 2, folder 1.

66. Earle Report, 1861–62: 8.

67. Richard L. Pease to Earle, March 2, 1861, Edgartown, Mass., Earle Collection, box 2, folder 3). Priscilla Jackson Freeman became adept at petitioning the Legislature for aid to her mother and compensation for the support of her non-Indian pauper stepfather. Throughout the decade 1860–1869, she also served as the sole support of her aged parents, infirm husband, and dependent children, working her family's land and taking in wash from the white neighbors. Information gleaned from petitions at the State Archives requesting state aid—Massachusetts Resolves, 1861, ch. 60; 1862, ch. 38; 1863, ch. 16; 1864, ch. 29; 1865, ch. 10; 1866, ch. 46; 1867, ch. 17; 1868 ch. 35.

68. James Oliver to Earle, February 9, 1861, Lynn, Mass., Earle Collection, box 2, folder 5. Helen Bakeman of Northampton was more direct; she amused the Dudley, Mass., Indian guardian when she wrote to him, after being told by her town clerk that "she was *one of the* heirs to an estate in this place [Dudley, Massachusetts]." She asked him to send her the money "'this week, for I need it, for you must think it is hard to be poor . . .'": Asher Joslin to Earle, March 23, 1860, Webster, Mass., Earle Collection, box 2, folder 5.

69. The Gay Head Indians of Martha's Vineyard recently won federal tribal recognition.

70. John Earle described a cohesiveness in five of the plantation communities (Gay Head, Herring Pond, Mashpee, Christiantown, and Chappaquiddick). His list accords

in many respects with our own: distinct, isolated communities; nearly all members of tribe live on plantation lands; maintain their own local organizations; provide for their own wants and for those of the paupers among them: Earle Report, 1861–62: 86–87.

71. Earle Report, 1861–62: 42. The Bird commission described the surprising smoothness of the informal system of land allotment as "a primitive system, almost realizing the wildest dreams of the communists": "Report of the Commissioners," 1849, House Document 46: 21.

72. Bird Report, 1849: 21; Earle Report, 1861–62: 32.

73. Ibid., 12–14

74. Ibid., 8.

75. Folklore is identified by William Simmons as one of the only visible aspects of Indianness in New England: Simmons, *Spirit of the New England Tribes*, 261–70.

76. These could be formal or informal town meetings, as Jack Campisi has identified with the Indian church of Mashpee: see Campisi, *The Mashpee Indians*, 137.

77. Another possible marker of identity is kinship ties. Jack Campisi mentions a strong tendency for intragroup marriage at Mashpee: Campisi, *The Mashpee Indians*, 118. But there has been no study to date of the rate of endogamous (within-group) marriage among the Indians of Massachusetts. Nevertheless, our superficial tracking of a few individuals, combined with communication with contemporary genealogists of Indian descent, convinces us of some similarities to the ethnic solidarity forged through multiple kinship ties among the mixed Indian/white/African-descended Ramapo Mountain People of New York and New Jersey: see David Steven Cohen, *The Ramapo Mountain People* (New Brunswick, N.J., 1974), 123.

78. Bird Report, 1849: 23.

79. Many of our findings have been confirmed by Karen Blu's study of ethnic identity among the Lumbee of Robeson County, North Carolina. Blu argues that the Lumbee articulate an "ethnic" rather than a "racial" identity for themselves—while they exhibit a variety of racial phenotypes, they maintain a cohesive group consciousness: Blu, *The Lumbee Problem*, xii–xiii, 5, 30, 36, 63. Blu notes that both Indians and blacks in Robeson Country refer to themselves as distinct "peoples" rather than, as whites do, in terms of "race." What makes the Lumbee case all the more interesting is that they successfully won a distinctive Indian racial classification from the state of North Carolina in 1885, just as the Jim Crow laws of the "apartheid" South began to codify a biracial society. Only fifteen years after the Indians of Massachusetts lost their legal status as Indians, some of North Carolina's "free people of color" successfully forged their own Indian identity before the law. Blu also draws a very useful distinction between the stated "traits" or markers of "Indianness" employed by the Lumbee and the actual unstated behaviors and beliefs that define the true Indian identity. In the absence of distinctive language, customs, religious beliefs, or traditions, the Lumbee Indians have substituted borrowed dances and an origin story of dubious authenticity (their descent from the Roanoke Island colonists and the surrounding Indian peoples). In Blu's formulation, these markers are easily recognized by whites as being appropriately "Indian." The rest of their distinctive identity is, of course, "lost." Yet, culture is much more than a series of traits or quaint traditions that can be retained or given up as Indians mix (racially and culturally) with surrounding blacks and whites. Blu identifies several key behaviors that, whatever their historical role, serve today as the essential features of being a Lumbee Indian. These include an ethnic pride and "meanness" (tough resistance to insults); owning land in Robeson County; and keeping one's word. In this way, Indians can identify other Indians and maintain a boundary between

themselves and others. They also may censure Indians who fail to behave in appropriate ways. Blu argues that these behavioral characteristics have remained remarkably constant, even though such outward Indian symbols as their origin story have changed considerably over the years: Blu, *The Lumbee Problem*, 34, 142–43, 168.

80. Since Barth, scholars have differed over the degree of mutual dependence between objective (outside) and subjective (on-the-ground) ethnic ascription as defining criteria of ethnic identity, as well as in the difference between in-group and out-group perceptions of a particular ethnic identification. A consensus has emerged, however, that ethnic identity can only exist in oppositional relations, whether between groups of equal or inequal power. See Fredrik Barth, "Introduction," *Ethnic Groups and Boundaries*, ed. Barth (Boston, 1969), 9–10. See also Ronald Cohen, "Ethnicity: Problem and Focus in Anthropology," *Annual Review of Anthropology*, 7 (1978), 381–84; Frank A. Salamone and Charles H. Swanson, "Identity and Ethnicity: Ethnic Groups and Interactions in a Multi-Ethnic Society," *Ethnic Groups*, 2 (1979): 168–70; Margarita B. Melville, "Ethnicity: An Analysis of Its Dynamism and Variability Focusing on the Mexican/Anglo/Mexican American Interface," *American Ethnologist*, 10 (1983), 272, 274. Fredrik Barth's more recent work on Bali has demonstrated the importance of multi-ethnicity in the operation of complex societies, exploring the difference in culture depending upon the ethnic group and social class to which one belongs: Fredrik Barth, "The Analysis of Culture in Complex Societies," *Ethnos*, 54, no. 3 (1989), 120–42.

81. Yinger, "Ethnicity," 162–63. The study of such groups as Massachusetts Indians further reveals the malleability and situational nature of ethnic boundaries. See also Gonzalez, "Tri-Racial Isolates," 115.

82. For Gay Head, see Gloria Levitas, "The Burden of Proof: Coercion, Autonomy, and Justice in Gay Head," *The Dukes County Intelligencer*, 19, no. 4 (1978), 123–47. Levitas mentions documents in the state archives to support the notion that Gay Head's Indians protested the incorporation of their district as a town, a part of the enfranchisement process at both Gay Head and Mashpee.

83. Bird Report, 1849: 29.

84. Thaxter to Earle, January 28, 1861, Edgartown, Mass., Earle Collection, box 2, folder 3.

85. Earle Report, 1861–62: 43.

86. Ibid., 64.

87. Journal of the Senate, 1869, May 12, 1869, Massachusetts State Archives, Columbia Point, Boston, 405. The matter was referred to the Indian Commission; unfortunately, the petition could not be located in the state archives.

88. "Petition of Tristram Freeman and others . . . to be restored to citizenship & that Females in this state be enfranchised," March 2, 1869, Senate unpassed legislation, referred to the Committee on Indian Affairs, Massachusetts State Archives, Columbia Point, Boston.

89. See "Order by the Commissioner, John Milton Earle, ordering a hearing for 31 August 1859," dated August 23, 1859, New Bedford, Mass., Earle Collection, box 2, folder 4.

90. "The Petition of Aaron Cooper and others for the protection of certain land rights in Gay Head," March 3, 1869, Massachusetts *Resolves*, 1869, ch. 103, file papers, Massachusetts State Archives, Columbia Point, Boston.

91. Massachusetts Legislative Papers, 1869, House Document 502 (hereafter cited by page only in text). The joint legislative committee also intended to visit Gay Head but was thwarted "by temporary derangement of the means of communication with

the Vineyard," and then legislative duties prevented such a visit. They argued that since the Gay Head Indians were quite prosperous and "intelligent," no inconvenience would be wrought if such an examination (simply to inquire into changing Gay Head's status from "district" to "town") was postponed to the legislative recess, after the Enfranchisement Act was voted on. They saw no need to halt the process of the Enfranchisement Act until testimony could be taken from Gay Head residents, and the act went through without their input: Joint Special Commission Report, 1869: 16. See also Levitas, "The Burden of Proof," 126.

92. The document is recorded as if taken verbatim, in question-and-answer format; the transcription appears to have been fairly good. The manuscript copy available at the Massachusetts State Archives may itself have been a transcription, but brief inspection revealed no disparities between it and the printed version: House unenacted 502, February 9, 1869, Massachusetts State Archives, Columbia Point, Boston.

93. Matthias Amos, bearer of a longtime Indian surname and lifelong resident of Mashpee, also spoke out in favor of change. Given the Mashpee Indians' last experiment with a free market—the sale of wood from land lots under the Act of 1842, in which many received only "one-eighth or one-quarter of the value"—he was convinced that they would "act more cautiously" and get a better price (15).

94. Clifford, *Predicament of Culture*, 308.

95. Earle Report, 1861–62: 12–14.

96. Jacqueline Jones, *Labor of Love, Labor of Sorrow: Black Women, Work, and the Family from Slavery to the Present* (New York, 1985), 58–68.

97. An important caution: during the Mashpee hearing, William Simons, who opposed enfranchisement, protested the petition in favor of enfranchisement on the grounds that it "was got up underhand, in a private house," and he added that the only women who signed the remonstrance, unlike those on the petition, were "widows— the heads of families. We though [sic] we might need their help [in having enough signatures], but if they were not needed, we put them on the bottom, so we could cut them off." The figures in table 1 on the number of women signers bear out this backhanded accusation that the petition was "packed" with "double voting" by including wives as well as husbands. Thus, apparently, petitioners were willing to inflate the number of supporters by violating the dominant society's role for the male household head, and the remonstrants were savvy enough to recognize the power of this procedural violation for aiding their own efforts against the pro-enfranchisement petitioners. See Massachusetts Legislative Papers, 1869, House Document 502: 16.

98. Earle Report, 1861–62: 20.

99. William H. Chafe, *The American Woman: Her Changing Social, Economic, and Political Roles, 1920–1970* (New York, 1972), 3–4, 6, 233; Carl N. Degler, *At Odds: Women and the Family in America From the Revolution to the Present* (New York, 1980), 303–307.

100. A fourth, the "Petition of Rosanna G. Rodman and others" of Gay Head, "to be enfranchised," is listed in the Journal of the House for 1869 but cannot be located at the Massachusetts State Archives.

101. One was signed by Priscilla Freeman, "The petition of Priscilla Freeman for Indian enfranchisement and Female Suffrage (1869)," Rejected bills, Senate 325, unpassed legislation; the other by her husband Tristram Freeman and two sons: "Report of the Committee on Indian Affairs on petition of Tristram Freeman and others (1869)," unpassed legislation; both located at Massachusetts State Archives, Columbia Point, Boston.

102. Seven had signed the petition for land tenure reform, an eighth was the wife of a petition signer, and another was the probable wife of a petition signer. One of the female suffrage petitioners had signed the remonstrance against change in land tenure, and three more were the wives or daughters of remonstrance signers. The remaining three signed only the suffrage petition and could not be identified through the Earle census. Even this slim majority of nine becomes much more significant when compared to the almost two-to-one margin of the community against enfranchisement as a whole. See "Petition of the women of Mashpee (1868–69)," Rejected bills, Senate 325, unpassed legislation, Massachusetts State Archives, Columbia Point, Boston.

103. Massachusetts Legislative Papers, 1869, House Document 502: 25.

104. U.S. Department of the Interior, Census Office, *Report on Indians Taxed and Indians Not Taxed in the United States (except Alaska) at the Eleventh Census, 1890* (Washington, D.C., 1894), 330.

105. Clifford, *Predicament of Culture*, 336; Simmons, *Spirit of the New England Tribes*, 8–9.

106. While the Massachusetts case has certain unique features, including Massachusetts's unusual position in the forefront of both radical Republicanism and later Indian policy, it also shows many parallels to the histories of other Eastern Indians and groups of mixed ancestry. In fact, the Indians of Rhode Island experienced many similar events, leading to the termination of the Narragansett tribe in 1880: Ethel Boissevain, "The Detribalization of the Narragansett Indians: A Case Study," *Ethnohistory*, 3 (1956), 225–45. See also Campisi, *The Mashpee Indians*, 62. And the paths of Indian and mixed-ancestry enclaves diverged in other eastern locations, with some identifying more with African American groups, some with Indian, and others finding a white identity most comfortable: Michael L. Blakey, "Social Policy, Economics, and Demographic Change in Nanticoke-Moor Ethnohistory," *American Journal of Physical Anthropology*, 75 (1988), 493–502. And we may yet find that at the individual level, some individuals of mixed ancestry maintained more than one ethnic identity depending upon the context in which they found themselves: Keefe, "Ethnic Identity," 35–43; Yinger, "Ethnicity," 151–80.

Thomas L. Doughton

9

Unseen Neighbors

Native Americans of Central Massachusetts, A People Who Had "Vanished"

> For every time we make others part of a "reality" that we alone invent, denying their creativity by usurping the right to create, we use those people and their way of life and make them subservient to ourselves.
>
> —Roy Wagner, *The Invention of Culture*

> To elaborate a fact is to construct it . . . All history is choice . . . seeks out and accentuates the facts, the events, and the tendencies in the past that prepare the present, that permit understanding it, and help to live it . . . makes for itself the past that it needs.
>
> —Lucien Febvre, Inaugural Lecture,
> Collège de France, in *Combats pour l'histoire*

A nineteenth-century discourse of the disappearance of Native Americans projects the extinction, dissolution, and vanishing of the Indian peoples of central Massachusetts.[1] In this, it perpetuates almost "canonical" or regulatory distortions and simplifications of Native experience long part of New England history.

An "official story" resonates across the discourse banishing Indian people from our historical consciousness, denying a past of Indian adaptation, removing Natives from the region's present as it erases persisting Indian community. Imagining Native experience only across variations of a "disappearance" model, the "authorized" version of New England history is deaf to the voices of individual Indian men and women, blind to actualities of multiple layers of social and political interactions constituting regional Indian community. A world of dynamic nineteenth-century Native social practice is "unseen." Indians who are part of this community are dismissed as racially mixed; they become "colored" and not Indian. The authorized version alleges that what it calls "traditional" culture is gone. Economically exploited as cheap labor, individual Natives are "marginal," people at the edge, disconnected from the social landscape. Or, as even some contemporary scholarly texts put it, regional Indians are "disappeared," a people who vanished in the wake of Metacomet's Rebellion.

Native American peoples of central New England,[2] however, were part of the nineteenth-century social landscape, pursuing established patterns of persistence and cultural survival, affirming their Indian identity. A minority of area residents, Indians lived unevenly distributed in regional towns, in some instances scattered or isolated, at other locales in clusters or concentrations of small yet marked and visible Native communities. They were not, all of them, creatures of white imagination: intemperate, immoral, drunken, or childlike. On the contrary, many were rooted in area towns, stable residents, some of them property owners, woven into the region's social fabric, seemingly "just like their neighbors," but affirming their "Indianness," and often publicly "recognized" or "seen" as Indian.

The public Native identity they affirmed, as individuals and as a collectivity, can be demonstrated through examination of records of the following events or practices: ongoing corporate, legal relationships in which Natives (as aboriginal tribal or band communities) interacted with municipal, county, and state entities on the basis of treaties and legislative covenants; individual relationships between the state and Indians as "wards of the Commonwealth," an arrangement by which guardians administered the legal affairs of Indians connected to families living on corporate tribal lands; official enumeration as *Indian* for the Commonwealth, in legislative reports and state census returns; documentation as *Indian* in original birth, death, and marriage records; depiction and description as *Indian* in town histories, antiquarian publications, and period newspaper accounts; and, through verification of Indian status in court records, many generated, for example, as part of legal actions for recovery of trust money withheld by the Commonwealth when Bay State Indians became citizens in 1869.

Natives' own sense of themselves as distinct and separate was demonstrated in their social practice. For example, five representative Nipmuc families[3] from the eighteenth century to the present reveal a longstanding pattern of intermarriage with Indian cousins and other relatives in towns along the Massachusetts, Connecticut, and Rhode Island borders. These families remained part of a persistent, centuries-old, and socially complex movement of kinship clusters of Indians within their homelands.

Far from "disappeared," Natives of central Massachusetts in the nineteenth century were farmers, plumbers, washerwomen, mariners, chair bottomers or chair caners, "Indian herb doctors," barbers, shoemakers, domestic servants, baggage masters, itinerant entertainers, day laborers, railroad engineers, mill operatives, specialty bakers, broom and basket makers, housewives, and stage coach drivers. Their number included "well-known" individuals identified as Native in nineteenth-century town histories: Benjamin Wiser, deacon and elder of Auburn's Baptist Church in the first quarter of the century; Polly Johns, of Leicester, one of the many "last of the Nipmucs"; Hannah Dexter, apparently "known to many now living" in 1830 as "a doctress, well skilled in administering medicinal roots and herbs," who, in 1821, burned to death, "a tragical end . . . while endeavouring to quell a riot in her household . . . raised by a set of unwelcome visitants, chiefly of a mixed breed of English, Indian and African blood"; Julia Jaha Dailey, allegedly "the last of the Nipmucks" living at Oxford, according to one town history, while a period chronicle of a second town labeled her sister Mary Jaha "the last survivor of the once powerful tribe of Nipmuck Indians"; Ebenezer Hemenway, a well-known janitor at the Worcester city hall, whose mother was an equally familiar Worcester Indian, celebrated in the 1820s and 1830s for custom-ordered wedding cakes; Jacob Glasgow, a "hunter and fisherman"; and "Old Jim Injun" or James Walmsley, who died, aged seventy-five, in 1865 among Natives of Woodstock, Connecticut, where Nedson and Dorus family members also lived; and other Natives like Peter Stebbins, known by many Paxton residents, or John Field of Worcester, a young ventriloquist and musician who entertained at different regional venues in the 1830s. Numerous Native men from the area who saw military service during the Civil War, especially those who became casualties, are likewise described in various town histories.[4] Moreover, many regional town chronicles, even if they often employ conventional nineteenth-century Indian stereotypes, depict individuals like Polly and Joseph Dorus, with four children, "reduced to begging and asking for a place to sleep" and sometimes "hired out to put splint seats in chairs"; or Aunt Sarah Green, who "often said she was a doctor and carried herbs in her basket"; or the Qaun family, who lived in a "shanty" and "wandered for months at a time"—all of these living in the Sturbridge area in the first quarter of the century.

Before 1869, some of the region's Indian people lived at a reservation in Webster (originally part of Dudley), while many others resided in cities and towns in extended family and clan clusters. The majority of Indians in the area were "Nipmucs"; others belonged to various southern New England tribal groups, including several individuals who were part of families connected to or returned from the Brothertown experiment in New York.[5] Indians from other areas had also moved to the region in the antebellum period or later.[6] Additionally, Natives from northern New England passed through Worcester County, making extended visits; in the late 1830s, a group of Penobscots from Maine[7] made annual summer journeys to Worcester for religious services at the region's first Catholic church.

Other northeastern Natives whose "migrations" into the area are documented include: Narragansett-Niantic individuals and families from Rhode Island[8] migrating to towns along the Blackstone River; people from southern Connecticut;[9] people from New York state;[10] and people from even more distant areas who found their way into Nipmuc homelands. Moreover, in 1900, when New York Indian claims were being resolved in Congress, area Native people connected to Brothertown unsuccessfully filed petitions for their families who had lived at Brothertown to be included in a financial settlement for lands taken in New York State.

The practice of these and other families suggests "unseen" Native American community dynamics. A characteristic extension of Indian families in the area can be sketched across the Vickers family:

> Natives of "Quineshepauge," the Nipmuc homelands of the Blackstone Valley region, members of the Vickers family joined the Natick community in the 1730s, where they remained throughout the century, connected to towns including Mendon, Medway, Medfield, Natick, Grafton, and Upton. Christopher Vickers, a son of Revolutionary War soldier Christopher Vickers, married Mary Curless. In the first half of the nineteenth century, fourteen children of Mary Curless and Christopher Vickers were both at Burrillville, Rhode Island, and Thompson, Connecticut. Of six daughters: one married James Pegan at Thompson, where their family lived; another married a Nipmuc at the reservation at Webster; a third moved to Worcester, where she married, eventually locating to Oxford; and the other three daughters each married Nipmuc men at Worcester. Of their eight sons: five lived and raised families at Oxford; one married a Woodstock Nipmuc, one married a Native from Burrillville; and one married a Native at Hampton, Connecticut.
>
> In the next generation, grandson Edgar Pegan married a Columbia, Connecticut, Native at Thompson; grandson Peleg Browns, Jr., at Woodstock, married Nipmuc sisters Ida Shelley and Hannah Nichols (daughters of Lydia Sprague); grandson Orin Vickers married cousin Emma Vickers, at Oxford; one of their sons, Edwin Vickers, married Nipmuc Amanda Dorus; and another grandson, Charles K. Vickers, married Woodstock-born Nipmuc Polly Dorus, whose children were born at Sturbridge, including Charles Henry Elmer Vickers, 1887–1946, who married Orianna Hewitt, a daughter of Martha Dorus Hewitt; and Samuel Vickers, who married, at Woodstock, Nipmuc Alice Susan Dorus. A more detailed discussion of this single family would demonstrate Native kinship connections to virtually all of the towns of southern Worcester County and northeastern Connecticut.

These examples of extensive Native interactions highlight a diversity of Native persistence and point toward a world of long-term regional Indian interaction on the social and physical landscape of Nipmuc homelands[11]—homelands that Eurocentric cultural imperialism imagines to be purged of Indians.

Despite a droning chorus of regional and national commentators telling them they were "vanishing," the area's nineteenth-century Natives were "living proof" in contradiction of the spurious "extinction" of their peoples. For example, several extended families called by others the "Dudley" or "Pegan Indians," who lived at a "reservation" in Webster up to 1869, maintained a relationship to the town of Webster and the Commonwealth that reflects a measure of continued corporate existence of the region's aboriginal people. Recipients of some $27,059 from the state treasury from 1808 to 1869, they were visited by a legislative committee in 1849 and found to comprise forty-eight individuals in eleven families, some farming on the twenty-six-acre reservation, others employed in surrounding towns.[12] During the 1860s, twenty-seven individuals living at Webster, Spencer, Worcester, Oxford, Gardner, New Bedford, and Thompson, Connecticut, received cash payments or other benefits from the Commonwealth of Massachusetts, through their state-appointed guardian, on the basis of their status as Dudley or Pegan Band Nipmucs.[13] In the year 1863, twelve individuals or families of this community were provided with foodstuffs, clothing, medicines, tools, and firewood, and their medical, burial, and legal expenses were also paid by the Commonwealth.[14]

Natives were seen and identified as Indians when, from 1790 to 1813, twenty-seven individuals received cash payments from guardians of Indians at Grafton. Between 1786 and 1829, guardians at Grafton also sold twenty real estate holdings, on behalf of sixteen individuals considered Native by the Commonwealth, while guardians purchased real estate for Nipmucs at Princeton in 1801, at Royalston in 1803, and at Worcester in 1825, 1844, and 1857.[15] In 1839 the state provided funds to the Worcester County Judge of Probate to be used, for ten years, to meet the needs of some area Indians; in 1849, the provision was extended for an additional ten years.[16] In 1859, another $1000 was allocated to Worcester Probate Court for the needs of Indians at Grafton and Worcester; and in 1865, state funds were paid to the Grafton selectmen for needs of the town's Indian residents.[17] Even after formal "detribalization" in 1869 when the Act of Enfranchisement terminated guardianship and made Nipmucs state citizens, several individuals applied for and received annuities or cash payments, as Indians, from the Commonwealth.[18]

As Massachusetts Indian Commissioner, in 1860, John M. Earle[19] was able to find many Natives, in part through contact with living Native families whose voices he heard. Earle identified 181 men, women, and children, including non-Indian spouses, as connected to the region's Nipmuc peoples:[20] 147 of these individuals resided in area towns (48 in Worcester); another 21 persons lived beyond central Massachusetts borders; 2 young Nipmucs were institutionalized, one at a reform school, the other at an insane asylum; and the whereabouts of another 11 Nipmucs, including among them Mrs. Amey Robinson, a "migratory Indian doctor," could not be ascertained. Earle also reported a Nipmuc among several Bay State Indians moving to California, presumably between 1849 and 1861.[21]

The Massachusetts state census of 1865, on the other hand, claimed there were 99 "Indians" in Worcester County, including 18 persons at Mendon; 13 at Webster, at Dudley, and at Grafton; 10 at Southbridge; and 8 Indian people at Sturbridge.[22]

Both Earle's tallies and the state census returns were probably incomplete, but they do provide clear documentary evidence of a nineteenth-century Indian presence. Natives represented a distinct minority of the region's total population, but the figures suggest a significant clustering or concentrating of Indians at specific locales, homeland towns where Native communities coalesced during the antebellum period.[23]

As early as 1800, Isaac Glasko,[24] a Native from Cumberland, Rhode Island, and his Native wife, Lucy Brayton from Smithfield, Rhode Island, relocated to North Uxbridge, Massachusetts, one of the towns in the Blackstone Valley. Isaac was followed to Massachusetts by his father, Jacob, and brother, George, both of whom lived at Northbridge in southern Worcester County, also in the Blackstone area. In 1807 the three Glasko men moved from Northbridge to Connecticut. Jacob Glasko settled at Preston, where his first wife, Martha, died sometime after the birth of their son, also Jacob, in 1815; at Putnam, he married Native Elizabeth Dailey and died at Griswold in 1824. George Glasko, a shoemaker, settled first at Preston, then at Killingly, and finally at Thompson, his children, including Miss Elsie Glasko, taking up residence in various Connecticut towns. When he moved from Northbridge, Isaac Glasko settled at Griswold, Connecticut, where he operated a forge, manufacturing axes, hoes, harpoons, and other metal tools; his children also settled in various Connecticut towns. Isaac Glasko died, eighty-five years old, in 1861 while visiting a daughter at Norwich.[25]

In the 1830s and 1840s, for example, connections within this area can also be seen through the Cisco family, Natives, moving from Massachusetts/Rhode Island borderlands up the Blackstone River:

> Of the children of Hannah Potter and Edward Cisco or Scisco, several moved into Worcester County from Cumberland or Slatersville, Rhode Island. Brother Francis R. Cisco (1811–1892), relocated to Mendon in 1832, marrying a Medfield-born Native, Lucy Coffee; their children and grandchildren were all born at Mendon. In the early 1840s, sister Harriet Cisco married a Native from Uxbridge, where she established her family. In 1843, at Mendon, another brother, George W. Cisco (1819–1902), married Native Lucretia Coffee, their family living at Mendon and Milford. Their son, George Cisco, Jr., born in 1848, was a teamster resident at Smithfield, Rhode Island, in 1870 when he

married a Native born in Greenwich, Rhode Island. In 1844, at Grafton, another sibling, Samuel C. Cisco, married Sarah Maria Arnold (1818–1891), whose Nipmuc family had been resident at Grafton, Upton, and surrounding towns since the seventeenth century.

In 1850, the federal census recorded 621 persons of color in Worcester County. Of these, 84 were Native Americans representing 16 families living in Blackstone Valley towns. Of the small Native community here, 7 families and an additional 4 persons lived in white households at Uxbridge, one family lived at Douglas, another at Charlton, 4 at Mendon, 1 at Grafton, 1 Native woman lived in a white household at Blackstone, and 1 family lived at Milford. Native families in the Blackstone Valley comprised almost 20 percent of "colored" people in Worcester County's rural towns and 13 percent of all people of color in the County.[26]

Although some Native families were among town poor,[27] many in the area continued working family farms, functioned as day laborers, or, like the family of Mary Vickers, a Burrillville, Rhode Island, Nipmuc, began seeking employment in Blackstone Valley mills. With adult children or other relatives, Mary Vickers and her sons lived, at different times, in several Blackstone Valley towns. Many in her family were shoemakers in Connecticut in 1850 and had returned to work in mills at Uxbridge, Milford, and Oxford by the decade's end. In Connecticut, they had been part of an Indian concentration in the greater Woodstock area, including another thirteen Native households, four of them headed by Indian shoemakers.[28]

In 1860, Worcester County had fifty-four Native households: thirty-eight were in county towns, thirty-three headed by males, five headed by women.[29] There were another sixteen Native households in Worcester. However, most of the area's Natives lived in rural settings. Data indicate a wide clustering of Indians in an arc extending from the Blackstone River Valley along the southern Worcester County and Connecticut border where 85 percent of Native families in county towns and 70 percent of all Worcester County's Indian families, rural and urban combined, were concentrated.[30]

A comparable, almost arcing or radiating movement can be drawn, in silhouette, in the actual world of Nipmuc family extension, from Framingham and Natick, through the Blackstone Valley, to southern Worcester County towns.

David Munnalow, participant in a wartime raid, moved from Grafton and Upton to Westboro and Marlboro; his son Abemelich David married at Grafton, and his wife, Patience Abraham, was known as Patience David. Her father had been an English scout during the war, with connections to Nipmucs at Natick; a daughter of Abemelich, known as Patience Abemelich, grew up at Grafton and married Samuel Pegan at the Nipmuc reservation at Dudley. A daughter of theirs, Patience Pegan, married Julius Ceaser, and they became the parents of Betsey Ceaser. Betsey Ceaser and husband, in turn, raised a family at the reservation, three of their children marrying Nipmucs. One of the daughters, Angenette White Dorus Hazzard, married one Nipmuc at Sturbridge and another at Woodstock where she died. She was mother of eight children born at Sturbridge, Union, Connecticut, or Woodstock named Dorus and two named Hazzard, born at Woodstock. The only son to marry, at Sturbridge, wed a Nipmuc from the reservation. One daughter married another Native at Sturbridge, a second married a Native from Abington, Connecticut, and a third was the mother of eight children from three different marriages. She was married to a Native at Worcester, children born at Dudley; her second marriage was to a Nipmuc at Woodstock, children born at Woodstock and Dudley; and the final marriage was with a Stonington, Connecticut, Native at Webster. A child from the first marriage, Angenette Arkless, born in 1872, chose a husband from another extended Nipmuc family and until recently had living children; she is connected to several hundred contemporary Nipmuc people.

At Shrewsbury, Westborough, and Grafton, Native people clustered. Harriet Forbes, writing in an idiom representing Natives as colorful, amusing characters long remembered and discussed, but debased, drunken, quick to anger, violent, wasteful, and willing to work only until alcohol can be purchased, portrays a squatters' settlement located in the once great cedar swamps along the intersecting borders of these three towns. Here, "degenerate" whites who were emotionally disturbed or mentally ill without family to care for them, Nipmuc Indians who were former slaves left to their own resources when emancipated, and others lived, in Forbes's version, virtually uncivilized lives in swamp "hovels." Her work documented a regional oral tradition among Euro-Americans, retaining information and "quaint" anecdotes about almost twenty-five Nipmuc people resident in the three towns between 1785 and 1840. Additionally, she described in detail a group of "celebrated" tramps "wandering" from Framingham to Grafton and Upton, associated with Sarah Boston or Phillips (her father was named Boston Phillips), who was a "gigantic Indian woman . . . weighing nearly three hundred pounds and . . . very tall" who dressed in garments usually worn by men, wrapped in a blanket, and earned her living working in the fields alongside men.[31] Part of a Nipmuc family at Grafton, Sally Boston has been depicted in several area town histories.

At antebellum Southbridge was a recognized locale called "New Guinea," occupied by members of related Nedson, Dorus, and Dixon Nipmuc families. Dismissed in a 1901 writing as "Negroes, Indians, or half-breeds,"[32] the occupants of this neighborhood were of an Indian heritage so well documented that this small gathering at Southbridge can be seen inscribed within the spheres of the extended regional Native American social community, and thus can be "recovered."

At Woodstock (originally "New Roxbury," a Massachusetts town), on the Connecticut side of a border drawn through specific Nipmuc settlement areas, thirty-eight Indians (including Nedson, Dixon, and Dorus families) constituted a small community during the early nineteenth century. In 1850, for example, eighteen Indian families in the Woodstock area and in adjoining towns represented a continued Native presence in the townships of northeastern Connecticut, created from the precontact Nipmuc settlements Wabaquasset, Senexet, and Quantasset. In the second half of the nineteenth century, the Woodstock Native community continued expanding to become, in 1900, a site to which almost all Nipmucs had social connection. Even Nipmuc craftsmanship was retained here; as recently as the 1920s baskets (now at the Connecticut Historical Society in Hartford) were collected from this community, as "there could be found in many Woodstock homes specimens of this handiwork."[33]

Additionally, there was a Native presence in Worcester County associated with individual family or clan groups, such as those Nipmucs who were associated with Esther Pegan Humphrey in western county towns:

Esther Pegan (1763–1860) was wife of Thomas Humphrey. Born at the reservation at Dudley, Esther married Thomas Humphrey, lived in Sturbridge and then in Barre, where some of their children were born. One of their sons was married twice at Spencer, and raised a family; his first wife was Native. A second son was married three times, also at Spencer. Another son established himself in the Woodstock area, and another settled at Charlton. The only daughter married at Spencer, moving to New Braintree. In the next generation, the daughter's children lived in Barre, Palmer, and New Braintree, two women marrying other Natives in these towns. Of the other grandchildren: two women from Spencer were married at Spencer, one to a Nipmuc from Dudley; one grandson married at Brookfield; and another married a Hopkinton-born Nipmuc, settling at Gardner. A great-grandchild, for example, Mary Etta White (born 1869) married another Nipmuc, James Belden, at Worcester in 1888, and one their daughters, Mary Olive Belden (born 1890), had, in this century, two marriages, each with children, at Putnam, Connecticut, both marriages to men from other Nipmuc families.

While a Native community existed in rural areas of the Worcester County/Connecticut/Rhode Island borderlands, an urban Indian community grew at Worcester, which mushroomed from a village to a major industrial metropolis in the course of the nineteenth century.

In 1840, 144 people of color lived at Worcester, in some 27 households. Seven of these households were Indian families. The 32 people in Native households comprised more than 20 percent of all "colored" people at Worcester.[34]

By 1845, Worcester's total population had grown to 12,000 persons in 2,000 families.[35] Among these residents, as the city directory shows,[36] were 22 "colored" households, 9 of which represented a clustering of Indian families.[37] More friends and relatives of Indians at Worcester made their way to town in the late 1840s.

In 1850, there were fifty-one people in twelve Native households at Worcester. Male Native household heads were five of the fourteen "colored" barbers in town;[38] five were laborers, and one reported no occupation.

Whether African or Native, "colored" people at Worcester in 1850 were in many ways bound to regional landscapes: of the 185 people of color, most had been born in northeastern states and it was a community of more mature adults.[39] Natives were part of a stable "colored" community forming at Worcester in the 1850s: some 8 of 34 household heads owned property; 70 percent of women had been born in the state; 86 percent were born in the Northeast; 92 percent of adults were literate; 60 percent of minors were attending school; and only 7 adult women, 3 adult men, and 2 minors were in white households. Additionally, individuals from Middle Atlantic states were 6 percent and those from southern states 8 percent of the colored population.

In 1855, of fifty adult males in Worcester's "colored" community, sixteen were connected to Native American households: seven of them were barbers (half of the town's "colored" barbers), three were laborers (out of eleven "colored" laborers in town), two were Worcester's only "colored" shoemakers; one was a waiter; one was a farmer; and two males belonging to Indian households reported no occupation.

In the decade from 1845 to 1855, occupations reported by twenty-one male heads of Indian households included: laborer 6, barber or hairdresser 5, shoemaker 5, cook 1, farmer 1, clicker or specialized shoe worker 1, railroad engineer 1, and vault or privy cleaner 1. Eleven Native women were listed in directories as laundresses, one as a "root doctress," and two as wedding cake makers.

In this decade, Native people had anchored themselves at Worcester: of some thirty-three "colored" births during the 1850s, eight were in Native households; and, of forty-five deaths, ten were in these same Indian households.[40] Additionally, at this time, Nipmuc men owned two hairdresser's or barber's shops: Edward B. Gimby owned his place of business, with Native relatives among his employees; the second establishment, where other Nipmucs including the proprietor's cousin Alexander Hemenway and John Morey earned livings, was owned by James J. Johnson.

In 1860, there were 71 Native people at Worcester, comprising 48 percent of the city's 34 "colored" households and 26 percent of the aggregate "colored" population. These figures reflect the arrival in town of many single adults who boarded with families in these 34 family units. In this community adults aged 16 to 39 comprised 70 percent of the "colored" population; 17 percent of the total were born in the South; another 11 percent came from Middle Atlantic states. Native families, however, remained stable, while "colored" Worcester underwent transformation. Among the 13 adult males who were part of Indian families in 1860, 5 were barbers, 4 were day laborers, and 1 was a shoemaker, 1 a farm laborer, 1 a carpet cleaner, and 1 a jobber.[41]

Finally, in 1870, there were 93 Native individuals[42] at Worcester in 22 families. Twenty of these units were headed by males, 2 by women; they were part of a total "colored" population of 524 persons. The 93 Natives represented almost 18 percent of the total population, and the 22 Native families represented 23 percent of the city's "colored" families.[43]

"Colored" Worcester, however, had undergone changes in these decades: for example, in 1870, only 20 percent of the adult population had been born in Massachusetts.[44] In many ways, "colored" Worcester was becoming a southern city — 54 out of 193 adult males and 55 out of 188 adult females were from Virginia, the District of Columbia, or Maryland. However, in this altering environment, Native families persisted.[45]

Movement of Indians into Worcester between 1845 and 1870 reflected the city's development as an administrative, industrial, and commercial center of central Massachusetts. Options for finding mates often were more limited in rural settings, and many Natives had been drawn to the city for social opportunities including marriage. Like their white neighbors in the country, and for many of the same reasons, some Indians left smaller towns and villages in search of employment.

Native families and individuals came to Worcester from Grafton, Westborough, Upton, Charlton, Oxford, Mendon, Uxbridge, Dudley, Webster, Sturbridge, New Braintree, Warren, and Middleborough, all in Massachusetts. Others were drawn from Connecticut towns including Woodstock, Thompson, Ashford, Haddam, Hampton, Union, and Griswold. Several households connected to the Rhode Island Narragansett communities moved to Worcester. Additionally, Wampanoags from the New Bedford and Fall River area settled here, often marrying individuals of Nipmuc heritage.[47] Seeking employment in some instances, marriage in others, and residence with or near relatives in still other cases, Natives — entire families and single individuals — came, incorporating the city into a dense regional web of Native kinship and social structures that extended through Massachusetts, Connecticut, and Rhode Island.

Some of the complexity of Nipmuc social structures can be seen in the marriage of Mary O. Belden, born at Worcester in 1890. She was a great-granddaughter of Esther Pegan Humphrey. She married Ernest Lewis, a great-grandson of Nipmuc Lydia Sprague.

Lydia Sprague had been married four times, at different periods living in Webster, Dudley, Douglas, Sturbridge, Stockbridge, and Woodstock. Of her daughters, one married four times, at Woodstock, Putnam, Conn., and at Webster, with children from each union; three of her husbands were Nipmucs of the greater Woodstock area. Another daughter married Nipmuc Henry Dorus at Sturbridge, where they established their family; and one married, at Sturbridge, a Dudley-born Nipmuc named Peleg Brown, who in second marriage wed another of Lydia's daughters, sister of his late wife. Of the sons of Lydia Sprague, one married and settled at Woodstock; another moved to Sturbridge, where he and his family lived; and a third married a Nipmuc at Putnam, and, in second and third marriages, Nipmucs at Woodstock, confirming continued kinship networks among Nipmucs. Further confirming such networks, a Putnam-born granddaughter married another Nipmuc, and their son, Ernest Clinton Lewis (born 1891), married Nipmuc women: his first wife connected to Webster reservation families, the second was Mary O. Belden from Worcester. Further, a Sturbridge-born grandson (Peleg Brown) was father of Edgar Brown. Edgar Brown married Native Mary E. (maiden name Brown) of Woodstock. They were parents of Maud L. Brown (born 1894), who married three Nipmucs—a cousin, Lemuel Henries, and two Hazzard brothers; several of her thirteen children are still (1996) living in central New England.

Despite the many forms of Native American presence, nineteenth-century Indian people of central New England are "unseen." They have "vanished," according to insinuations of a discourse of disappearing Indians. They did not "behave" as Indians should act, therefore, they were, culturally, less than Indian; they were "disappearing" as a culture. They represented racial and tribal mixtures, therefore, they were, biologically, not Indian; they were "disappearing" as a race. Confronting communities of Natives adapting and adjusting to changes in nineteenth-century New England and still affirming their identity as Indian, the discourse of disappearing Indians employs models, patterns, templates, and paradigms by which it judges and finds deficient the concrete practice of evolving Indian communities. It projects the "Indian" as a social construction, claiming a monopoly in defining the Native American; it transforms a dynamic presence of nineteenth-century Natives to an "absence of Indians." This discourse even postulates an inability to "find" Natives because it assumes they are "hidden." As they will not be "found," there is little necessity to look for them, to try to "see" them; they are a people who have "vanished."

While it is true that Nipmuc Indians had been dispossessed of much of their individual and tribal lands by the last century,[48] the disappearance of the Natives of central Massachusetts is part of a "cant of conquest," repeated uncritically from nineteenth-century writers who told us Indians were "doomed" to disappear.[49] It is part of an appropriation of regional Native American history and an expropriation of Indian identity. In various disguises, notions of the disappearance of Indians limit the historical vision, obliterating the complex social practice of Native communities in their survival as Indians.

The more obvious articulation of disappearance tells us, simply, that Nipmuc Indians "vanished" in the seventeenth century.[50] Disappearance is, however, expressed in the notion of widespread marginality of period Natives, described, for example, by Barry O'Connell. "[I]n an economic order run by people who despised them," Natives had to find a means to survive, according to O'Connell, so they "labored in the lowest occupations when they had employment at all." Unable "to obtain dependable employment," they worked "outside the prosperous parts of the New England economy" and seemed "to have lived in places as out-of-the-way as their occupations . . . or in racially mixed neighborhoods in cities," often "at the far edge of settlements in poor housing," in "economic marginality." For these reasons, many Indians sold baskets and brooms or "worked the lowest rungs as servants in wealthy whites' households."[51] O'Connell acknowledges that this is not the only role nineteenth-century Natives played, and recognizes a need to explore the diversity of Indian survival in the last century, but others advance marginality as if it were the universal condition of regional Natives.[52] Such a view erases the sometimes quiet but ongoing and active participation of Native people in nineteenth-century social and economic spheres.

The development of a kin-based urban community at Worcester and other sites in the region, as suggested here, challenges "marginality." Central Massachusetts Indian families achieved a stability in residence and employment, in comparison to the region's African Americans and European immigrants. Further, "marginality" as an external economic determination tells little about the relationship of the poorest Indian to Native community: for example, Lydia Sprague (1830–1890) married Shelley, married Nichols, married Henries, and her family appears in several regional histories as representative of quintessential derogatory Indian stereotypes. Yet fourteen children, some thirty grandchildren and fifty great-grandchildren, most of whom married other Nipmucs, place Lydia Sprague at the heart of nineteenth-century Nipmuc community—despite the poverty, illiteracy, and mean living circumstances invoked to make her "marginal." Because it anticipates finding "marginal" Natives, the discourse of disappearance can see little other than "marginality."

This discourse also conflates nineteenth-century notions of "people of color" and African American, as if "ethnicity" or "race" and "pigmentation" or "color" are synonymous. It overlooks a certain "fluidity" or ambiguity in ethnic or color labeling in period documents, causing Natives to "vanish" among "colored" people. With families tallied in the Earle Report, for example, individuals of Nipmuc heritage are sometimes recorded as "Indian," but they are also recorded under other designations or attributions including: black, black Indian, yellow Indian, African, colored, Negro, red Indian, mulatto, mulatto part Indian, of Indian descent, and mixed.[53] Ambiguity is also discernible at individual towns like Thompson, Connecticut, where from 1847 to 1868 in fifty-three manuscript records for "people of color," including Natives,[54] one individual is listed as "Indian" once, as "colored" once, as "black" in some twenty-seven instances, and without any color designation in twenty-three of these records. Of the only family recorded as "Indian" at Thompson during this period—the household of James Pegan and his wife, Hannah Vickers—there is still inconsistency: Pegan family members are sometimes "black," sometimes "Indian," and other times "mulatto."

Earle had found forty-eight persons in Indian households at Worcester, a number representing over a third of the Natives he enumerated for Worcester County, but there is a comparable inconsistency, if not uncertainty, in identification of "people of color" in Worcester's vital records. In published vitals from 1714 to 1849,[55] for example, the same individuals, some of whom are Native, are "colored," "black," "negro," as well as "Indian." Additionally, in death records for the period from 1807 to 1831, not included within the town's published vitals, another thirty-seven manuscript death notices use the same color descriptors for former slaves and Natives; here, one even encounters a "black child of Fanny Proctor colored person."[56] Likewise, review of all vital records at Worcester from 1849 to 1890 for an individual Native family confirms the same inconsistency and confusion.

In the nineteenth century, however, regional Natives were often not "seen" because, on the one hand, the meaning of "Indian" was constructed for Euro-Americans in cultural terms advocated by early ethnographers, and, on the other hand, "Indian" was viewed in the biological terms of an emerging Eurocentric "race science." The new "science" codified notions of red, black, and white "races" in such a way that the only real Natives were racially distinct and "clear-blooded," the revealing period designation for "full-blooded." Part of a rising binary racial epistemology, this "science" advocated what Marvin Harris called a "policy of hypodescent,"[57] designating as "black," "African," "negro," or "colored" everyone not imagined "pure white." In this way of conceptualizing identity, "one drop" of African "blood" is antithetical to Indian identity, making a person a "negro." Part of the disappearance paradigm is, thus, the allegation of an emergent biological system of classification that nineteenth-century Natives were not Indian but "degenerate remnants" and "impure mixtures of races." As "Indians," they were not to be "seen."

The hypothesis that seventeenth-century Massachusetts "tribes" became eighteenth-century "enclaves" on the way to becoming nineteenth-century "ethnic groups," is, in a subtle way, part of a discourse of disappearing Indians. In a reading of some of the same sources cited here for confirmation of Indian presence, Daniel Mandell, for example, maintains that Native tribes vanish as "tribes," doomed to become "ethnic groups."[58]

Published texts arguing that within the historical record there is a self-imposed Native "invisibility" and "silence," as it were, "obscuring" the area's Indians, also prolong the discourse of disappearance. From this alleged "invisibility" are postulated "evasion," "hiding," and forms of "covert behaviors," when, in actuality, the region's Native Americans were hardly "hidden" or "invisible" in the last century. Ann McMullen, for example, writes that nineteenth-century New England Natives responded to the "stigmatization of their identity," by "covering . . . recognizable symbols" to give an "impression of assimilation"; they opted for "coversion," hiding languages, ceremonies and symbols "rationalizing invisibility," in part, because of a mixed racial heritage or "the lack of a recognizable Indian phenotype."[59]

Instead of "coversion" and "hiding" of Indian identity, "camouflage" and "disguise," terms used by historian James Merrell,[60] might more accurately describe Native interactions with the dominant culture. Moreover, the concrete practice of this region's Natives challenges Indian "invisibility."[61] Failure to "see" Indians refers only to the "vision" of a Eurocentric observer.

Not only do Native people "disappear" in nineteenth-century New England, according to McMullen, but their "disappearance," through an imagined "silence," was a self-selected strategy for survival. Native "invisibility" here is embraced as if historical fact; it becomes a regulative concept at the core of a "new" interpretation implying Natives cannot be "found" on a historical landscape because they themselves were hiding. This variant of the discourse of disappearance would accept an Indian "absence" but claims that this was because Indians were "hiding."

Other variations of the discourse of disappearance include an overarching assumption that Native people cannot be "found" or identified within the conventional source materials: vital records, census returns, military documents, probate files, real estate transactions, and secondary sources such as town histories. One after another, texts represent an "absence" of documentation required to "prove" Native survival and persistence, a position clearly unsupported by closer study of specific Native individuals and Indian communities in this region.

Nineteenth-century Natives in central Massachusetts persistently affirmed their identity and lived the actuality of their extended kinship-based community. They are "absent" only in a discourse laboring to erase them as part of a dynamic and engaged continued presence of aboriginal people within their traditional homelands. Regional Indians remain a "vanished" people, who are not "seen" because they are assumed already "gone," but this is so only within contemporary prolongation of this discourse.

NOTES

1. The following is a revised chapter from a work in progress titled "Native Americans and the Politics of Representation, Indians in Nineteenth-Century Massachusetts."

2. Taken as "Nipnet," or "Nippienet," the homelands area of the Nipmuc or "Fresh Water People," corresponding to all of contemporary Worcester County, portions of abutting Middlesex, Hampden, Bristol, and Franklin Counties in Massachusetts plus northeastern portions of Connecticut, and northwestern Rhode Island, an extensive territory in the seventeenth century. Cf. this contact-era statement of Thomas Dudley: "About seventy or eighty miles westward from these are seated the Nipnett men, whose sagamore we know not, but we hear their numbers exceed any but the Pecoates and

the Narragansets, and they are the only people we yet hear of in the inland country," in his "Letter to the Countess of Lincoln," Alexander Young, ed., *Chronicles of the First Planters of the Colony of Massachusetts Bay 1623–1636* (Boston: C. C. Little & J. Brown, 1846), 306.

3. Thomas L. Doughton, "Native American Presence and the Politics of Representation: Indians in Nineteenth-Century Central Massachusetts, On Native Americans, Power and the Regional Discourse of their Disappearance" (paper distributed as part of program, March 4, 1996, at Old Sturbridge Village, Sturbridge, Mass., on "Native American Voices in New England, 1600–1995," a workshop series of the Massachusetts Foundation for the Humanities, cosponsored with New England Museum Association and Bay State Historical League), 10–12, cf. idem, "Nineteenth-Century Massachusetts Indians and the Discourse of Disappearance" (paper presented at the annual meeting of the American Historical Association, New York City, January 1997).

4. Some Natives part of Nipmuc families who served in Union troops during the war included: **Hezekiah Dorus**, from Webster, laborer, a casualty at Andersonville, cf. Office of the Adjutant General, *Massachusetts Soldiers, Sailors and Marines in the Civil War*, 9 vol., hereafter MSSMCW (Norwood, Mass.: Norwood Press, 1931), 5:715; **Daniel Gigger**, from Shirley, "A soldier in the Civil War. He never returned," Ethel Stanwood Bolton, *Shirley Uplands and Intervales Annals of a Border Town of Old Middlesex, With Some Genealogical Sketches* (Boston: George Emery Littlefield, 1914), 363; **Benjamin W. Gigger**, MSSMCW, 6:516; **George Rome**, a Narragansett living in Worcester, ibid., 4:713, 730; **Rufus Hazard**, from Mendon, bootmaker, ibid., 6:446; **Alexander Hemenway**, from Worcester, ibid., 4:686; Webster brothers **Joseph E. Bowman**, shoemaker, and **William H. Cady**, a shoemaker, casualty at Andersonville, ibid., 5:713, 6:523; **Joseph H. P. White**, from Webster, ibid., 4:336; **James M. Pegan** of Thompson, who served with Connecticut troops; **Theophilus D. Freeman**, from Webster, barber, ibid., 686; **James E. Belden**, from Worcester, miller, ibid., 7:322; brothers **James Hazzard** and **Lorenzo T. Hazzard**, of Brookfield, both farmers, ibid., 6:495, 528; **Hiram Ransom** from Southbridge, miller; **Charles W. Brown** of Framingham, farmer; **Rufus Hazard**, from Mendon, bootmaker; **Albert E. Esau** from Warren, sailor, ibid., 4:681; **William G. Hector**, born 1824, at Grafton, dying in 1864 at Ft. Jackson, Louisiana, a member of the 14th Battery, U.S. Heavy Artillery, MS Births, Marriages and Deaths, Worcester, Mass., 1849–1890, Deaths: vol. 2:20; **Rufus Vickers**, born 1821, at Burrillville, R.I., shoemaker, married to an Indian from Woodstock, Fanny Thomas, enlisted in 1863, from Oxford, Mass., in the 2nd Massachusetts Heavy Artillery Regiment, was taken prisoner at Plymouth, N.C. in April 1864, and died in the prisoner-of-war camp at Florence, S.C. the same year, MSSMCW, 5:724; **Christopher Vickers**, born 1830, at Thompson, Conn., shoemaker, brother of Rufus Vickers, married an Indian from Hampton, Conn., was mustered in the 2nd Mass Heavy Artillery Regiment, was taken prisoner in April 1864 at Plymouth, N.C., and died at the Andersonville prisoner-of-war camp in November 1864, ibid., 5:724; **James Nedson**, ibid., 4:575; 5:665; **Benjamin Brown**, and **Anstis Dailey**, son of Julia Jaha Dailey mentioned above, both from Woodstock, both serving with Connecticut troops, along with **Lewis Dailey**, **Marcus Lewis**, and **Stephen M. Lewis**, all from Thompson; **John A. Glasgow** from So. Windsor, cf. Office of the Adjutant General, *Catalogue of Connecticut: Infantry, Cavalry and Artillery In the Service of the United States 1861–1865 with Additional Enlistments, Casualties, etc., etc. and Brief Summaries Showing the Operations and Service of the Several Regiments and Batteries* (Hartford, Conn.: Brown and Cross, 1869), 908, 913–14.

5. Brothertown was established in Marshall, Oneida County, New York, on lands

set aside by the Oneida Nation in 1788 for several hundred Natives from southern New England, who lived there in community until 1833, when some of their number were removed to Wisconsin, others returning to their southern New England homes.

6. In the region were also other Natives like Pennsylvania-born Native Susan Walker or Tommy Black Bear from "South America," and some Indians from Vermont, Maine, and Canada: Doughton, "Native American Presence," 44.

7. Ivan Sandrof, *Your Worcester Street* (Worcester, Mass.: Franklin Publishing Co., 1948), 143.

8. For example, Joseph Noka, of a prominent Charlestown political clan, who lived first with the Cisco family at Grafton, years later marrying at Worcester.

9. An eighteenth-century Pequot-Mohegan Nedson whose uncle ran a school at Stonington married Nipmuc Mary Pegan; their daughter, Polly Nedson married Joseph Dorus, a Mahican; nineteenth-century Dorus family members married other Nipmucs in towns at the Massachusetts-Connecticut border.

10. The Burr and Jackson families, living in Holland, West Brookfield, and Sturbridge, were, according to John M. Earle, of a chiefly family at Oneida. See John Milton Earle, "Report to the Governor and Council Concerning the Indians of the Commonwealth under the Act of April 6, 1859," Senate Document no. 96, Massachusetts State Library, Special Collections, State House, Boston, Mass. (Boston: William White, 1961); hereafter cited as Earle Report.

11. Native peoples "moved around homelands according to daily, seasonal and ceremonial calendars, and between homelands to visit kin, they did not abandon or desert these places until forced to," Russell Handsman wrote, and even when Natives moved, "their removal was neither complete nor irreversible": Russell G. Handsman, "Illuminating History's Silences in the 'Pioneer Valley,'" *Artifacts*, 19, no. 2 (1991), 13. A homeland area was a series of interconnecting cores. The core of each was typically five to ten square miles in extent, containing one or two important settlement places, often at long-used fishing sites. Here clan ceremonies and elders' councils were held. Extensive corn fields were near, as were sacred sites such as cemeteries, memory piles, and sweat lodges used for curing. Throughout the core area and surrounding spaces of each homeland were dozens of wigwams, alone, in pairs, or in small hamlets not very different in size from a traditional meeting place. Indians living in each homeland, however, were joined to one another and to their kin in other homelands by enduring social and economic relations, connected by trade, diplomacy, and kinship in ways that mirrored the intricate trails and water routes that traversed the landscape. This description follows a significant discussion of the concept of homelands by Russell G. Handsman and Trudie Lamb Richmond in "Confronting Colonialism: The Mahican and Schaghticoke Peoples and Us" (unpublished paper prepared for "Making Alternative Histories," an advanced seminar at the School of American Research, Santa Fe, N.M., April 1992) 8–9, 18.

12. In 1857, individuals were relocated from their reservation on the outskirts of Webster to a five-family tenement house on an acre of land about half a mile from Webster Center, in order that they may be "better accommodated" and "more directly under the public eye, where a healthy public sentiment could have its sanitary influence, and where the civil authority could have a more direct supervision over them"; *Massachusetts Acts & Resolves*, April 9, 1839.

13. In 1860, recipients of payments and benefits as established through *Public Documents of Massachusetts Being The Annual Reports of Various Public Officers and Institutions . . . For 1860* (no. 41: 1–2); 1861 (no. 36: 1–2); 1862 (no. 36: 1–2); 1864 (no. 36:

1–2); 1867 (no. 31: 1–2); 1868 (no. 31: 1–2); and 1869 (no. 31: 1–2) (Boston: Wright & Potter, 1861–1870).

14. Untitled octavo volume, in MS Webster, Massachusetts Records 1863–1904, American Antiquarian Society, Worcester, Mass., reading on p. 1: "This book was kept by the Town of Webster Authorized with the State of Massachusetts for the Remnant of the Indians of Webster"; cf. Earle Report, 103.

15. Some thirty-one recipients of cash payments from the guardians of Grafton Indians, named in account book of Daniel Heywood, pp. 1–52, from August 1790 through February 1813, in octavo Records of the Proceedings of the Trustees for the Indians of Hassanamiscoe, vol. 2, in MS "John Milton Earle Papers 1652–1863," American Antiquarian Society, Worcester, Mass.; hereafter, Earle Papers; real estate sales on behalf of Nipmucs, all requiring legislative approval in box 1, folder 5, Earle Papers, which contains attested copies of separate resolves of Massachusetts House of Representatives authorizing sales; real estate purchases for Nipmucs, the last in 1857, are in Earle Papers, box 1, folder 1, "Surveys, maps, plots of land, deeds, receipts, documents of Benjamin Heywood . . . ," as unbound individual documents; cf. *Worcester Registry of Deeds*, Worcester County Courthouse, Bk. 144, 554; Bk. 215, 206; Bk. 391, 333; Bk. 575, 335 and Bk. 578, 518.

16. *Massachusetts Acts & Resolves*, April 9, 1839; cf. ibid., 1849: 325, 385.

17. *Massachusetts Acts & Resolves*, 1859, ch. 88: 464–65, allocating $1,000 to Worcester Probate Court; Massachusetts Legislative Papers, 1865, House Document 174, allocating $200 from state treasury to Grafton Selectmen.

18. Some Nipmuc individuals receiving annuities: *Massachusetts Resolves*, 1896, ch. 28; 1895, ch. 96; 1896, ch. 28; 1908, ch. 16; 1909; cf. "Why Annuity Is Paid To Indians," *Gardner News*, March 13, 1909.

19. Author of the Earle Report. Through a Massachusetts legislative act of 1859, Earle, politician and publisher of the Worcester *Spy*, was appointed commissioner, "to examine into the condition of all Indians and the descendants of Indians domiciled in this Commonwealth, and make report to the governor, for the information of the general court," dealing with four issues: (a) "The number of all such persons, their place of abode, their distribution . . ." (b) "The social and political condition of all such persons . . ." (c) "The economic state of all such persons . . ." And (d) "All such facts in the personal or social condition of the Indians of the Commonwealth, as may enable the general court to judge whether they can, compatibly with their own good and that of the other inhabitants of the State, be placed immediately and completely, or only gradually and partially, on the same legal footing as the other inhabitants of the Commonwealth." The actual report, submitted by Earle in 1861, consists of three sections: a 132-page report; a proposed act to enfranchise Bay State Indians; and an appendix of 78 pages, listing Native families, his so-called "census."

20. The appendix of the Earle Report often mistakenly called a census, provides information on some 387 households totaling 1,610 individuals including Natives and non-Native spouses. Under headings "Natick Tribe" (xli); "Hassanamisco Tribe" (li–lv); and "Dudley Tribe" (lv–lix) are enumerated individuals connected to the aboriginal peoples of central Massachusetts. Excluding non-Native spouses, Earle tallied 2 "Natick" households, 25 "Hassanamisco" households, and 26 "Dudley" households for an aggregate population of 131 men, women, and children distributed in the following local townships: totals: Brookfield 1; Douglas 6; Dudley 7; Eastford, Conn. 1; Framingham 5; Grafton 6; Holden 2; Leicester 1; Natick 4; Oxford 3; Putnam, Conn. 1; Shelburn Falls 1; So. Gardner 7; Spencer 4; Stockbridge 7; Templeton 2; Thompson,

Conn. 4; Uxbridge 4; Warren 8; Webster 18; Westboro 2; Worcester 36; insane asylum 1; reform school 1; and Amey Robinson, migratory.

21. On Oct. 20, 1854, James Anthony, a Native from Uxbridge, was left for dead, his father and a child killed, and his wife "massacred" at Monterey, California, after being robbed of some $2,000 and their house set on fire, as reported by the Worcester *Spy*, 82, no. 48, Nov. 29, 1859. The Earle Report, lvi and passim, counts as resident in California, from "Dudley" tribe, 1 miner; from Mashpee, 4 miners and a seaman; from Punkapoag, 2 men; from Herring Pond, a barber and carpenter, and from Dartmouth, 2 men including a sailmaker and his family at San Francisco.

22. Oliver Warner, ed., *Abstract of the Census of Massachusetts 1865; with Remarks of the Same and Supplementary Tables* (Boston: Wright & Potter, 1867), 231–33, 46–55, enumerates for the whole county some 489 blacks, 278 mulattos, and 99 Indians (63 females and 36 males), among 866 "people of color," representing .005 percent of Worcester County's total population of 165,529; however, some Native people could be included in the black and mulatto categories.

23. Earle's numbers can be demonstrated to be low. Two of numerous omissions are the Gimbys of Worcester, mentioned within Earle's text but not included with relatives nor counted in appendix totals; and Samuel White and his extensive family at Sturbridge. White's mother, Betsey Pegan White, sisters Anginette White Dorus and Sally White Sprague, and brother Joseph H. P. White, with families—all resident at the Nipmuc reservation at Webster—are tabulated by Earle but omitted in the report's appendix.

24. An excellent source compiling a variety of types of family documentation for "colored," or African American and Native American, households in southern Connecticut is Barbara Brown and James M. Rose, *Black Roots in Southern Connecticut 1650–1900* (Detroit: Gale Research Co., 1988), 162–63.

25. Another member of this family, Jacob Glasko (1815–1885), was a familiar Native written about in Woodstock, Connecticut, histories; a tintype portrait of him was reproduced by Woodstock historian Clarence Bowen. In May 1870, William A. Glasko, twenty-two years old, an unmarried railroad engineer resident at Worcester, died of consumption, while in September of the same year, possibly visiting relatives or friends, Miss Elsie Glasko, a fifty-five-year-old unmarried aunt of William Glasko, a resident of Putnam, Connecticut, died at Worcester, also of consumption. Jacob Glasgow is described in Bowen, *The History of Woodstock, Connecticut*, 1 (Norwood, Mass.: Plympton Press, 1926), 536; for deaths of William Glasko and Elsie Glasko, MS Worcester Vital Records: Deaths, vol. 2 (1864–1870), 115, 124.

26. Data here extracted from the Returns of the Seventh Census of the United States (1850), Worcester County, Massachusetts, Microcopy no. 432, roll 344: 749 and passim; roll 345: 305 and passim.

27. For example, poorer Indian people at Uxbridge included Marrietta Sisco, aged twenty-eight, who died at the town almshouse of typhus in 1844; Rufus Vickers, a town pauper who died at the almshouse in 1849; and John Wilber, aged twenty-eight, "Indian," from Hampden, Conn., former boot bottomer, a state pauper, who died at the almshouse in 1860. In 1843, the Uxbridge selectmen requested that Douglas overseers of the poor remove from town one "Cyra Jepherson, his wife & three children," all "lawful residents" of Douglas who were "sick and in destitute circumstances"; the Douglas overseers apparently failed to act, since the Uxbridge selectmen's request was renewed. Additionally, Charles Anthony received temporary relief from the town in 1850 following a work injury, and sixty-two-year-old William Anthony died at the

almshouse in 1863. These Native individuals, however, were among another forty-seven persons buried at the town almshouse between 1835 and 1871. See Ricardo I. Elia and Al B. Wesolowsky, eds., *Archaeological Excavations at the Uxbridge Almshouse Burial Ground in Uxbridge, Massachusetts*, OPA Report of Investigations no. 76 (Boston: Boston University, Office of Public Archaeology, 1989), 74 and passim.

28. Mary Curliss Vickers, in 1850, was fifty years old, living at Thompson, Connecticut, with a household including sons Thompson-born Rufus Vickers, a twenty-five-year-old shoemaker; Almon Vickers, a twenty-one-year-old shoemaker; and Christopher Vickers, eighteen, also a shoemaker. Besides daughters Esther and Betsey Vickers, her household contained twenty-five-year-old, Windham-born Indian cousin George Wilber and his Hampton-born eighteen-year-old brother John Wilber, both also shoemakers. Another son of Mary Vickers, thirty-two-year-old Erastus Vickers, was living in Thompson with his wife and four children; he was also a shoemaker. And at Hampton, Connecticut, lived the widow Susan Vickers with her two children and another son of Mary Vickers, the twenty-eight-year-old Samuel Vickers, a laborer, with his wife, Abigail, and four children: Mary Vickers and family, Returns of the Seventh Census of the United States (1850), Microcopy no. 432, roll 51; for Windham County, Connecticut, roll 307: 4–11 and passim. Additionally, there were thirteen other Native households at Thompson or Woodstock, twelve headed by males, four who were shoemakers. Ibid., roll 520: 32–39 and passim.

29. Returns of the Eighth Census of the United States (1860), Worcester County, Massachusetts, Microcopy no. 653; for county towns, rolls 528, 529, 530, 531, 533, and 534; for Worcester, roll 527: 7 and passim, and roll 532: 11 and passim. Among the thirty-three family units headed by males is listed Asa Walker, thirty-five years old, white, at Petersham, with his wife, Susan Walker, born in Pennsylvania, listed as "Indian," along with three Massachusetts-born children recorded as "mulatto"; additionally, of the five female heads, Mary Toney, forty-six, at Fitchburg, and Martha Fiske, twenty-five, at Oxford, were living alone, while fifty-five-year-old Martha Wilbur at Uxbridge, sixty-one-year-old Mary Vickers at Oxford, and fifty-four-year-old Julia A. Daley, also at Oxford, were heads of families.

30. Of these thirty-three Native male household heads, some 20 percent (N or Native household heads = 7) were "day laborers," 20 percent (N = 7) were "farm laborers," 22.85 percent (N = 8) were "laborers," 11.4 percent (N = 4) were involved in shoe manufacture, 5.7 percent (N = 2) had no occupation listed, and their number included a Baptist minister, a barber, and a servant, each representing 2.8 percent of the total. Further, individuals listed as day laborers, farm laborers, and laborers, combined as unskilled laborers, represented a total of twenty-two individuals or some 62.8 percent of male Native household heads.

31. Harriette Merrifield Forbes (1856–1951), was author of several works on Worcester County and Massachusetts history and editor of the diary of Westborough's eighteenth-century minister Ebenezer Parkman. An early photographer, she documented older residences and regional gravestones. She is commemorated in a book-purchasing fund at the American Antiquarian Society at Worcester. She collected local oral histories and "legends" about local Indians, discussing Native people in *The Hundredth Town, Glimpses of Life in Westborough 1717–1817* (Boston: Rockwell & Church, 1889), 172–85. She is, for many, often eclipsed by her daughter, Esther Forbes (1874–1967), author of *Johnny Tremaine* and other works of historical fiction. Cf. biographical notice titled "Mrs. William Trowbridge Forbes," in Worcester Historical Society *Publications*, New ser., vol. 3, no. 6 (April 1952), 29–34.

32. Lucius E. Ammidown, "The Southbridge of Our Ancestors, Its Homes and Its People," in *Quinebaug Historical Society Leaflets*, 3 vols. (1901), 1:18.

33. Oliver A. Hiscox, "The Last of the Wabbaquassets," in Allen B. Lincoln, ed., *A Modern History of Windham County, Connecticut*, 2 vols. (Chicago: S. J. Clarke Publishing Co., 1920), 1:62.

34. Data here are based on the Returns of the Sixth Census of the United States (1840), Worcester County Massachusetts, roll 199: 164 and passim.

35. In the period from May 1844 through May 1845, there were 299 births, 79 marriages, and 227 deaths in a population of 11,566 in 2001 families, *Worcester Almanach Directory and Advertizer for 1846*, hereafter Worcester City Directory for successive years (Worcester, Mass.: Henry J. Howland, 1845), 12.

36. The Worcester City Directory does not record "color" in listings; Natives are identified utilizing the Earle Report federal census returns, state census rosters, MS records of Indian trustees, published town vitals, MS town vital records, military documents, MS legal records including family identification data from suit against Commonwealth, and real estate and probate files, which are fully cited, and some of the data reproduced in endnotes, in Doughton, "Native American Presence," 45–47. The nine Native families were 41 percent of the town's twenty-two "colored" households in 1845.

37. Worcester City Directory, 1846–1850. Six of these nine Indian households were headed by males: four of these household heads were "day laborers," one was a shoemaker, and another two male household heads were barbers, each operating his shop, while a total of eight women in Indian households were listed as laundresses.

38. Barbering, which could be seen as providing a service on the model of eighteenth-century modes of Indian labor, whether bound or free, entailed serving in white households. But in 1850, live-in domestics in Massachusetts earned $1.48 a week and day laborers without board earned $1.09 a week (from 1850 Census Abstract); barbering was better work. It became one of the successful employments in the community of people of color, some becoming wealthy and successful city "colored" men barbers. By 1860, out of thirty-nine adult males in the "colored" community at Worcester reporting employment, some fourteen, or 30 percent, of all these males were barbers, but barbering employed fourteen males while day laboring employed eleven men, and eleven men reported no occupation. At Worcester, as elsewhere, "colored" clergymen were also barbers or hairdressers.

39. Data extracted from Seventh Census of the United States (1850), Microcopy no. 432, roll 342:338 and passim: of 185 people, 68 percent of adults and 80 percent of minors 15 and under were born in the northeast; 12 percent (N=9) were born in the south; minors were 33.5 percent of the total "colored" population; the average age of a "colored" resident was 33.55 years; adults between 16 and 39 years old were 50.2 percent of the population; adults between 16 and 49 years old constituted 60.5 percent of all "coloreds."

40. MS, *Births, Deaths, Marriages, Worcester, Massachusetts 1849–1890*, 1:100 and passim.

41. Worcester 1855, data based on MS State Census of Massachusetts 1855, vol. 43, unnumbered pages, reproduced in Doughton, "Native American Presence," 46; Worcester 1860, from Returns of the Eighth Census of the United States (1860), Worcester County, Massachusetts, roll 527, 11:38–40 and passim; roll 532, 12:1–3 and passim.

42. Data here are from analysis of the 1870 census for Worcester as found in Returns of the Ninth Census of the United States (1870), Worcester County, Massachusetts, roll 658, 7:7–16, and passim; roll 659, 97:24 and passim.

43. In 1870, twenty male heads of Native families reported the following occupations: laborer 5; barber 6; stone worker 2; hardware store worker 1; whitewasher 1; farmer 1; paperhanger 1; truckman 1; waiter 1; and carpenter 1.

44. In 1870, 40 of 193 adult males, and 28 percent (N=52) of 188 adult females, were born in Massachusetts; 13 percent of both men and women were unlettered; some 45 percent (N=87) of men and 36 percent (N=68) of adult women had come from the South. Factoring the 14 percent (N=27) of women and 11 percent (N=21) of males, born in Middle Atlantic states, 56 percent (N=106) of adult males and 50 percent (N=95) of adult women were born outside the Northeast.

45. For example, in a federally funded tribal census of Nipmuc people in 1992, over 33 percent of 1,400 officially enrolled Nipmucs lived at Worcester, many representing Native families who settled at Worcester between 1840 and 1900.

46. What should be emphasized here is not so much absolute numbers, but that regional Native individuals and families *persisted*. Worcester County's population grew from 46,437 in 1776 to 95,313 in 1840. The county's population increased to 159,659 in 1860. Native individuals and families *endured*. Though small, numbers of Natives demonstrate a *survival* or *presence*, not an absence.

47. Extended discussion, with documentation, in Doughton, "Native American Presence," 7–8, 46–48.

48. Dispossession of Nipmuc land and resultant poverty are discussed in Daniel R. Mandell, *Behind the Frontier Indians in Eighteenth-Century Eastern Massachusetts* (Lincoln: University of Nebraska Press, 1996). Jean O'Brien's *Dispossession by Degrees: Indian Land and Identity in Natick, Massachusetts, 1650–1790* (New York: Cambridge University Press, 1997) presents a far more systematic overview of the means by which Nipmucs and other Natives of the eighteenth-century Natick community, at the mercy of state-appointed guardians, were separated from their lands. Nipmuc dispossession is also discussed in Thomas L. Doughton, *The Indian Reservation at Hassanamesit and the People of Hassanamesit, later Grafton, Massachusetts* (Worcester, Mass.: Nipnet Press, 1990), and "'That Justice Be Done Them': Nipmuc Indians and Their Eighteenth-Century Guardians" (unpublished paper); see also idem, "The Pegan Band of Nipmucs and Their Reservation at Dudley, Massachusetts 1665–1890" (pamphlet published by the Nipmuc Tribal Acknowledgment Project, 1992), 2–5.

49. For almost "classic" articulations of Nipmuc disappearance: Stephen Badger, "Historical and Characteristic Traits of the American Indians in General, and Those of Natick in Particular; in a Letter from the Rev. Stephen Badger, of Natick, to the Corresponding Secretary," Mass. Hist. Soc. Colls., 1st ser., 5 (1790), 32–45; Joseph Allen, *Topographical and Historical Sketches of the Town of Northborough* (Worcester, Mass.: W. Lincoln and C. C. Baldwin, 1826), 25; or William Lincoln, *History of Worcester Massachusetts, from Its Earliest Settlement to September 1836 with Various Notices Relating to the History of Worcester County* (Worcester, Mass.: Moses D. Phillips and Co., 1837), 16–17, 27–28.

50. For example, a recent scholarly work claims that, following the 1675–1676 conflict, "Many Nipmucks who survived . . . were captured and sold into slavery. Those avoiding English captivity moved further away to Western Abenaki County, to Maine, or to Hudson Valley Indian towns. Few returned to Nipmuck County after the war ended." And some "Nipmuck people returning to their lands generally camped briefly on old homesites before moving on to new homes farther from English settlers." Robert S. Grumet, *Historic Contact: Indian People and Colonists in*

Today's Northeastern United States in the Sixteenth through Eighteenth Centuries (Norman: University of Oklahoma Press, 1995) 104.

51. Barry O'Connell, ed., *On Our Own Ground: The Complete Writings of William Apess, A Pequot* (Amherst: University of Massachusetts Press, 1988), xiv–lxxvii, 166–80; 180–90; see also idem, "William Apess and the Survival of the Pequot People," in Peter Benes, ed., *Algonkians of New England: Past and Present,* Dublin Seminar for New England Folklore Annual Proceedings for 1991 (Boston: Boston University Press, 1993) 93–95.

52. For example, Ann McMullen, who writes that "native people formed a social and economic subclass," and "remaining communities and individuals were spatially, socially and economically marginalized" in the nineteenth century. For Indians, "life was tough, however, as all groups attempted to eke out a living on dwindling amounts of land. Indians suffered discrimination, poverty and starvation. Indian communities were never economically or politically integrated into mainstream white societies": "What's Wrong with This Picture? Context, Coversion, Survival, and the Development of Regional Native Cultures and Pan-Indianism in Southeastern New England," in Laurie Weinstein, ed., *Enduring Traditions: The Native Peoples of New England,* (Westport, Conn.: Bergin and Garvey, 1994), 54.

53. For example, of some sixty-five manuscript records from various regional towns for the family of Lydia Sprague, in thirteen instances individuals were listed as Indian, while in other instances she and her many family members are colored, mixed, black Indian, African, brown, and mulatto. A comparable review of some thirty-five records for Betsey White and family, from Sutton, Charlton, Webster, and Sturbridge, reveals individuals defined as Indian in some eight records while red, African, colored, black, mulatto, yellow, or white are designations employed in other remaining birth, death, and marriage documents: Doughton, "Native American Presence," 32, 57–60, analyzing comparative manuscript vital records for three Indian families from several towns, at different, successive periods of the nineteenth century.

54. MS, Thompson, Connecticut, Births, Deaths, Marriages, vol. 3 (1847–1868), 14 and passim, Town Clerk's Office, Thompson, Conn.

55. Franklin P. Rice, *Worcester, Massachusetts Vital Records to 1849,* Worcester Society of Antiquity, *Collections,* vol. 12 (1894), throughout. Here, 205 records document "people of color"; in 60 percent (N=123) of citations individuals are identified as "colored," in 8.7 percent (N=18) as "negro," in 4.3 percent (N=9) as "black," and in 3.4 percent (N=7) of the total records individuals are labeled "Indian." Further, in 23.4 percent (N=48) of these records, identifiable "people of color" are listed without any color attribution or other descriptor.

56. From unnumbered MS pages in "Bills of Mortality: Town of Worcester 1807–1831," in box 4, Vital Records 1686–1831, in American Antiquarian Society, Worcester, Mass., *Collections*; cf. Doughton, "Native American Presence," 31, 58–59, for discussion and documentation of unpublished Worcester vitals describing family of Nipmucs John and Susannah Toney Hector.

57. Hypodescent occurs when "racial" heritage governs membership in one or two groups that "stand to each other in a superordinate-subordinate relationship" and when an individual who has a lineal ancestor who is or was a member of the subordinate group is likewise considered a member of that group. In the United States, this means that "all persons with any demonstrable degree of Negro parentage, visible or not, fall into the subordinate caste," in such a way that "anyone who is known to have had a Negro ancestor is a Negro," explained anthropologist Marvin Harris in *Patterns of Race in the Americas* (New York: W. W. Norton, 1964), 37, 56, 108.

58. Mandell, *Behind the Frontier*, 202 and passim.

59. In "What's Wrong," McMullen offers an important discussion of regional Native culture and Pan-Indian political movements of the 1920s and 1930s, but maintains that nineteenth-century Natives "were seldom recognized as native because of the relative invisibility of their covert cultures they maintained and the lack of a recognizable Indian phenotype." Indian identity became "a stigmatized category" in southern New England following Metacomet's armed resistance in 1675, with the result that "Native people reacted to the stigmatization of their identity by covering its recognizable symbols to give the impression of assimilation . . . In trying to manage information about themselves . . . New England's native people restricted use of identifying symbols to avoid recognition and appear, superficially, to be like non-Natives, a process I call 'coversion.'" We're told "native people developed oral traditions and ideologies rationalizing invisibility" and "hid their languages and ceremonies and altered material aspects of culture to appear similar to non-native neighbors." Through this "subversion of visible symbols," in McMullen's opinion, "native people maintained significant covert cultures unrecognizable to non-Natives." In the nineteenth century, then, "native people and their cultures survived despite an ideological system that defined them as a marginal underclass . . . Within this milieu they altered the use of cultural symbols to coexist with non-natives and maintain invisibility of their covert cultures." "What's Wrong," 124, 130, 133, 135–37.

60. "But if neighboring Indians did not prosper, they did survive" in the eighteenth century, writes Merrell, "One secret of their survival was the ability to make themselves inconspicuous." He gives examples of Indian drinking, cursing, and dressing like Europeans at that time, suggesting that "this camouflage, too, was crucial to their survival." Some Braintree Indians had so well "perfected their disguise" that they were often mistaken for English, but just "as important as this mimetic talent was the ability to retain a distinctly Indian identity." James H. Merrell, "'The Customes of Our Countrey': Indians and Colonists in Early America," in Bernard Bailyn and Philip D. Morgan, eds., *Strangers Within The Realm: Cultural Margins of the First British Empire* (Chapel Hill: University of North Carolina Press, 1991), 154.

61. I am aware that some area Natives, for a variety of reasons, would have selected "invisibility," "obscurity," "evasion," or "silence" to protect themselves and resist, much in the manner described by James C. Scott in *Domination and the Arts of Resistance* (New Haven, Conn.: Yale University Press, 1990), and other works; my objection is that it should not be assumed, without specific reference to actual living Indian people, that area Natives in the nineteenth century, universally or generally, employed these and other "weapons of the weak" to survive and resist the racism or class bias of the period's dominant culture.

Harald E. L. Prins

10

Tribal Network and Migrant Labor

Mi'kmaq Indians as Seasonal Workers in Aroostook's Potato Fields, 1870–1980

When we conjure up images of Mi'kmaq tribespeople,[1] we tend to think of woodland trappers, spearfishers in birchbark canoes, or, perhaps, basket makers. Not coming to mind, probably, are rows of potato pickers working on large white-owned farms in the rolling hills of New England or the Canadian Maritimes. Yet almost every Mi'kmaq alive either has worked in the vast potato fields during the fall harvest or has a family member who has.

I first became aware of the importance of seasonal wage labor in Mi'kmaq Indian culture in the fall of 1981 when I began working as a tribal researcher in northern Maine for the Aroostook Band of Micmacs—at the time an impoverished off-reservation Indian community seeking federal recognition of its "tribal" status. Since then I have explored the socioeconomic conditions that gave rise to the wage labor complex in this tribal society, in particular to the Mi'kmaqs' participation as migrant workers on Maine's potato farms. Somewhat to my surprise, I found that, although wage labor often functions in the disintegration of traditional communities (Engels 1972; Redfield 1953, 26–53), migrant work opportunities for widely scattered Mi'kmaq kin groups in northeastern North America have actually contributed to the recent articulation of modern Mi'kmaq nationhood (for more detail see Prins 1996; cf. Meggitt 1962, 333; see also Wolf 1982, 192, 323, 354–83).

Although some Indian communities in this region became involved in wage labor as early as the mid-1600s, this chapter focuses on the period since the 1870s.[2] During this era the Mi'kmaqs, like many other Native groups in North America, turned in considerable numbers to seasonal wage labor — picking potatoes, apples, blueberries, and so on and working as guides, lumberjacks, or river drivers "herding" logs downriver (see, among others, Abler and Tooker 1978, 514; Bock 1978, 119; Boxberger 1988, 169–72; Kelly and Fowler 1986, 387–90; Lurie 1978, 705; Radin 1963, 3–4, 33; Spindler 1978, 709; and Weaver 1978, 531). That the Mi'kmaqs made (and often still make) these temporary work choices in part to retain a measure of their self-ascribed identity as "freedom people" suggests an effort to resist a full commodification of their lives.[3]

Like the Iroquois, the Mi'kmaqs form a large cross-border tribe. Divided in twenty-nine bands, they now number about 25,000. They possess numerous small and scattered reserves located throughout Canada's Atlantic Provinces (Nova Scotia, New Brunswick, Prince Edward Island, and Gaspé Peninsula, Quebec). Focusing on Canadian Mi'kmaq bands living in the Chaleur Bay region (particularly Restigouche) and the nearby Miramichi River area, this chapter examines the social organization of Native labor gangs and their seasonal involvement in the potato-growing agribusiness across the international border in northern Maine. It compares the impact seasonal wage labor had on them with its effect on the off-reservation Aroostook Band of Micmacs in Maine.[4] Reserve-based Mi'kmaqs appear to have been able to withstand complete assimilation into the labor market and persist as a distinct tribal nation on the proletarian edge. In contrast, off-reservation Indians do not have recourse to such economic refuge areas and are thus fully exposed to the pressures of capitalism. In hopes of bringing this picture and analysis to life, I have included recollections and comments made by various Mi'kmaq workers and non-Indian farmers in interviews with Bunny McBride and me.

Historical Background

Traditionally the Mi'kmaq were migratory hunters, fishers, and gatherers. Perhaps numbering 10,000 to 20,000 people immediately before their first encounter with Europeans around 1500, they hunted inland areas during the fall and winter and spent the summer by the seashore (see also Nietfeld 1981, 390–93, 459). Even though their total aboriginal range is uncertain, early seventeenth-century records note their presence throughout a large area stretching from Cape Breton to Gaspé Peninsula to coastal Maine (Prins 1986b, 264–67, 275). The basic social unit among these foragers was the extended family, or kindred. Based on voluntary association, several of these kin groups formed regional bands. Widely varying in size, from less than fifty to over four hundred individuals, these autonomous bands formed large seasonal encampments from spring through summer, dispersing into smaller hunting groups in fall and winter. Usually headed by male chieftains, known as *sagamores*, these widely scattered bands collectively formed the Mi'kmaq—an ethnonym that probably derives from *nikmaq*, their word for "my kin-friends" (Whitehead 1987, 20). As a people the Mi'kmaqs constituted an ethnic group, the social boundaries of which were maintained by a limited set of cultural features that included a distinctive Eastern Algonquian language, as well as certain shared beliefs and practices, but did not comprehend a common political allegiance (Bock 1978; Hoffman 1955; Nietfeld 1981; Prins 1988; Wallis and Wallis 1955).

By the early 1600s when small groups of white settlers first established colonies in Mi'kmaq territory, the Native population had already plummeted to about 3,000, due primarily to alien pathogens introduced by European fishermen, and before the century's end it had reached its nadir of about 2,000 (Nietfeld 1981, 390–35). Survivors became marginally involved in the emerging international political economy as fur trappers. They were gradually drawn into a dependency relationship with European nations—first primarily with the French (until 1759) and then with the English (Upton 1979, 31–78). The most serious blows to Mi'kmaq independence began in the late eighteenth century when the number of colonists settling on Mi'kmaq lands soared to tens of thousands. For instance, in 1782 and 1783, with the American Revolutionary War coming to its conclusion, more than 30,000 British Loyalists resettled in Nova Scotia, tripling its non-Indian population within one year (cf. Upton 1979, 78). By the time of confederation in 1867 the province's population had soared to 400,000. Neighboring New Brunswick province was also inundated by white newcomers, especially Irish refugees, and numbered about 300,000 inhabitants, while Prince Edward Island had become home to about 95,000 inhabitants (Prins 1996). Across the newly established international border Maine also grew rapidly in this time, from about 35,000 to 650,000 (Abbott 1875, 542).

Pushed from traditional fishing sites, driven from hunting grounds, and prohibited from assembling at favorite coastal camping places, the vastly outnumbered Mi'kmaqs faced profound constraints in pursuing their traditional way of life (Prins 1988, 212–22). Divided in numerous small bands usually no larger than a few hundred people each, the Mi'kmaqs represented only a fraction (about 0.4 percent at the most) of the total population.

Meanwhile, beginning in the 1780s, the British colonial government occasionally set aside small tracts of land as Indian reservations (in Canada called reserves), encouraging the dispersed kin groups to settle down and abandon migratory habits (Upton 1979, 81–123). Despite Mi'kmaq military support for the United States' struggle for independence, no protected tracts were provided on the U.S. side of the new border (Kidder 1867, 297–98; Prins 1988,

311–14). The United States and Great Britain, aware that the newly drawn international boundary split the aboriginal range of the Mi'kmaqs and their tribal neighbors, agreed in Article 3 of the 1794 Jay Treaty that these border tribes were free to travel back and forth across the new border for hunting, visiting, and trading purposes (Indian Task Force n.d., 5).

Pauperization of the Mi'kmaqs: The Struggle for Survival

Unable to escape the rapidly expanding political economy controlled by white newcomers, the widely scattered Mi'kmaq communities were soon overwhelmed. Repressed and degraded by the dominant society, these indigenous tribespeople fell on hard times and struggled to survive in a hostile world. Marginalization affected all Mi'kmaq bands, but it was not a uniform process. Moreover, different groups did not always react to these outside pressures in the same way. No matter the particular responses, however, kin groups camping within immediate reach of the newly founded towns were usually the first to be upheaved. In the vicinity of Halifax city, for example, resided large numbers of Mi'kmaqs. Commenting on their squalor, one white settler noted in 1801: "Several of them are employed in the fisheries in different places, and a small number as labourers by the farmers but the greater part choose to follow their ancient mode of living, and make up the deficiency of their hunting by making small baskets and other small articles (which they barter for provisions) and by begging. They are so much addicted to drinking and suffer so much from their own indolence that I think their number must be decreasing" (Smith 1974, 4; see also Plessis 1903, 187).

In the course of the nineteenth century, as it became increasingly impossible to survive on hunting and trapping alone, many Mi'kmaqs turned to crafts such as baskets, brooms, butter tubs, barrels, and porcupine quill work (McBride and Prins 1991, 10–11; Whitehead 1980, 54–58, 66–71). Peddling from door to door, they sold their crafts for cash or bartered them for food, clothing, or other commodities. Those living along the coastal waters speared salmon, eels, and lobsters to sell to the local townspeople. Occasionally the Mi'kmaqs were hired for some odd jobs about the house and yard. In areas such as Restigouche they began to cultivate gardens, growing potatoes, peas, beans, and oats, among other crops. Some even kept cows and horses (Bock 1966, 14–21; Cooney 1896, 216–17). Too often Mi'kmaq families faced periodic starvation, particularly during the winter, and came to depend on government relief in the form of food and clothing.

Meanwhile, the white newcomers ventured deeper into the interior of the Maritime Provinces and New England to exploit the vast timberlands. Soon gangs of lumberjacks reached the wooded borderlands of northern Maine. Initially, economic activities in this extensive region centered almost exclusively on the immense forests, with local farms producing food for home consumption and for the countless scattered *chantiers* (lumber camps) (DuBay 1989b, 154). By the 1860s the white population in northern Maine, which had become organized as Aroostook County in 1844, had grown to 25,000. Still mainly woodland, Aroostook entails an enormous tract of territory measuring 6,453 square miles, larger than the states of Rhode Island and Connecticut combined (Green 1989, 73). In the mid-nineteenth century almost every available man in the area could be found living in the lumber camps during the long winter season—destroying the remnant traditional hunting grounds of the Native peoples in the area. The handful of Indians still pursuing a life based on hunting, fishing, and trapping appeared to be doomed (Nicholas, with Prins 1989, 30–32).

Driven by hunger and despair, the Mi'kmaqs came to understand that they had few survival options left. Increasingly dependent on cash, they faced two major alternatives: selling crafts to white communities or working for them as wage laborers (Canada Dept. of Indian Affairs 1881, 45, 51–52; 1882, 32). In all probability to enhance their success on the white-dominated labor market, they generally abandoned their distinct Indian dress and hairstyle during this period. By the 1880s the Mi'kmaqs were typically dressed in the same way as non-Indian workers, and most had abandoned their traditional birchbark wigwam dwellings for small frame houses or shacks (Gilpin 1878, 111; Canada Dept. of Indian Affairs 1881, 42, 45, 51–52; 1882, 32; 1884, 36–37).

Temporary Wage Labor and Crafts

The completion of Canada's Intercolonial Railway in 1876 linked the Maritime Provinces with the political economies of the rest of Canada and the United States. Trains reinforced and reshaped the migratory traditions of the Mi'kmaqs, facilitating quicker, more far-reaching travel to work opportunities (Canada Dept. of Indian Affairs 1881, 34). Mi'kmaq artisans, producing crafts such as baskets, brooms, and quill boxes, set up camps near railroad stations, hoping for buyers passing by (Canada Dept. of Indian Affairs 1905, 57–58). Mi'kmaq lumberjacks rode the rails to join the booming lumber industry. They were typically hired for temporary labor as loggers and river drivers, dockworkers on the wharves, and woodworkers in the saw mills (Canada Dept. of Indian Affairs 1881, 34; 1897, 50–52; 1925, 21). Others traveled to new tourist centers where sportsmen from the eastern seaboard cities hired them as hunting or fishing guides (Upton 1979, 129–37).

Most Mi'kmaqs pursued a seasonal subsistence strategy, changing activities according to the dictates of environment and labor market (Canada Dept. of Indian Affairs 1897, 50–52; 1912, 66). The seasonal nature of Mi'kmaq economic activity is well documented. For instance, the Indian agent at

Restigouche (population 462) reported in 1883 that in addition to some trapping, fishing, and farming, "the majority of the male portion of the community work for lumbermen during the winter months. Many of these Indians also act as guides to sportsmen . . . during the summer season [making good wages]. Others are employed in the [saw]mills [making reasonable wages]" (Canada Dept. of Indian Affairs 1884, xxix).

In 1890 the agent reported that the Mi'kmaqs of Restigouche "are sought after for the making of logs in the winter. Several camps are composed entirely of Indians under an Indian 'boss' . . . These same Indians, that is to say, all the men who can leave the village, are employed in spring taking rafts down the river, which affords them an important means of livelihood; and . . . they command high wages" (Canada Dept. of Indian Affairs 1895, 33). During the absence of the men the women "employ their time making snowshoes, baskets, and moccasins, and fishing for smelts and tommy-cods." In the summer the women cultivated the gardens and gathered wild berries for sale in the local town, while many men worked in nearby sawmills (Canada Dept. of Indian Affairs 1893, 30).

Commenting on the variety of work Mi'kmaqs were engaged in during this period, one Indian agent noted: "No class of people occupy themselves in more varied ways than the Indians of the Maritime Provinces. Beside work for which they seem naturally adapted such as hunting, trapping, coopering [and other manual labor] . . . in winter and early spring many of them are occupied in lumbering operations; in spring and summer a goodly number are engaged as fishermen; while quite a few work on railroads and in factories year round" (Canada Dept. of Indian Affairs 1912, 66).

Stoop Labor in "Potato Paradise"

Railways first linked the rolling hills of northern Maine to the large population centers in northeastern North America in 1870. Soon thereafter the recently settled fertile lands of Aroostook County, which are primarily located in a squash-shaped area about 120 miles long and from 10 to 30 miles wide, emerged as a prime area for potato cultivation (Wilson 1937, 12; York 1989, 54). The nutritious tuber was in high demand not only as one of the world's major low-cost food commodities but also as a cheap starch source for New England's growing textile and paper industries. During the 1870s dozens of potato starch factories cropped up in Aroostook, and in the next decade the railways were extended considerably, soon giving even remote farming towns in the region access to affordable transportation to the large urban markets of eastern Canada and the United States. Potato production soared from 86,500 bushels in 1860, to 5 million in 1890, to an astounding 80 million in the 1940s. With a total of 220,000 acres in Aroostook dedicated to this crop, the area had become the single largest concentration of potato fields in the entire United States, making up about 10 percent of the total national production (Dubay 1989b, 154–57; 1989c, 146; Rowe 1965; Wilson 1937, 12–13).

With a regional subsistence pattern based primarily on lumbering and potato farming, the economy in Aroostook County was highly seasonal. This is reflected in the fact that less than 15 percent of its farmworkers were employed year round (Fitzpatrick 1982; Goldfarb 1981, 16). Especially during harvest time, a four- to six-week period lasting from mid-September through October, potato farmers needed every available person, including women and children, to bring in the crop. Seeking cheap, unskilled day laborers, farmers turned to, among others, local tribespeople, primarily off-reservation Maliseet and Mi'kmaq Indians living in small clusters on the margins of Aroostook's towns (Prins 1982a, 78–85; Wherry 1979, 62–86).

In the premechanized period, farmers typically divided their potato fields in sections, which were assigned to the harvesting crews. On the average, handpicking a 75–100 acre potato farm required 45 to 50 workers. For their backbreaking work, known as stoop labor, these pickers were paid by the barrel. Even though a strong adult could pick up to 100 barrels in a 10-hour day, the average picker was lucky to fill half as many. For more than a century the primary tool for handpicking has been a big wood-splint basket. These half-bushel containers, usually made by the region's tribespeople, could be filled in about two minutes. Each basketful was emptied into cedar wood barrels placed at regular intervals across the field. Once full, the 165-pound barrels were hoisted onto a wagon, hauled to the potato house, and spilled into huge bins. From there the crop was shipped out by train (see also Bock 1966, 49–50).

The rapid growth in Aroostook's potato production, especially since the 1920s, created a demand for a temporary workforce well beyond local capacity. Consequently, recruitment of migrant laborers became necessary to sustain the region's economic expansion.[5] Too far removed from the southern states, which provided most of the migratory farm labor in the eastern United States, producers in northern Maine recruited workers from across the Canadian border, particularly from the economically depressed Maritime Provinces. Since the turn of the century this region had turned into a backward periphery and thus offered a large reservoir of cheap labor, including widely scattered Mi'kmaq communities that ranged in size from a few families to groups of 500 people.

Although the Indian labor force in Aroostook's potato fields was composed of a variety of regional tribal groups (including hundreds of Maliseets and Passamaquoddies, as well as some Penobscots), the majority was Mi'kmaq, especially from the mid-1940s onward (Bock 1966, 28, 48–52; Prins 1986a, 128–46).[6] The growing need to recruit unskilled farmworkers from the impoverished reserves in Canada is also apparent from the fact that the U.S. federal courts determined in 1927 that "Canadian Indians" could be considered domestic labor for the purpose of agriculture.[7]

By this time the Mi'kmaq people had begun to recover demographically. Their population surged from about 3,400 in 1871 to almost 4,500 in 1889 and nearly quintupled in size during the next one hundred years. This increase is well illustrated by the Mi'kmaq community of Restigouche, which grew from about 300 in 1830 to 481 in 1900, 1,100 in 1962, and more than 2,660 today. Naturally whenever they experienced yet another downturn in their fortunes, the rapidly growing Mi'kmaq communities were forced to disperse, at least periodically, to prevent starvation.

From the beginning, life on the Mi'kmaq reserves was marked by grinding poverty. Local resources were rarely sufficient to sustain the growing number of people surviving on the small tribal enclaves. In an effort to avoid destitution, many tribespeople ventured far beyond their traditional range to find temporary employment as unskilled workers (see also Guillemin 1975, 78–80). Once the railway system was established, they commonly traveled by train. Sometimes they moved about alone, but more typically they journeyed in small cohorts made up of close kinfolk and friends. Although the early Native labor gangs appear to have been made up exclusively of adult males, women and, later, children were included (see also Bock 1966, 52). Anxious to maintain ties to local communities, laborers returned home during periods when there was little or no work available (Braroe 1975). The reserve, as one observer noted, turned into "a place to which one retreats in hard times until opportunity beckons elsewhere" (Guillemin 1975, 82). After several weeks or even a few months on the reserve, spent visiting with family and friends and engaging in such activities as basketry, fishing, clamming, and hunting, migrant Mi'kmaqs would leave once again (Prins 1988, 37–53; Wolf 1982, 307).

Migrating in search of seasonal work opportunities, the Mi'kmaqs sometimes traveled more than two thousand miles. Some, for instance, found temporary employment in the northern plains region, where they participated in the wheat harvests of Alberta, Saskatchewan, Wyoming, and Montana. The majority, however, remained within a closer range; these people went only as far as Aroostook's potato fields and the wild blueberry barrens of neighboring Washington County, where temporary workers were in great demand during the harvesting period. This migratory pattern of seasonal labor is well illustrated by the personal work history of a Restigouche Mi'kmaq named Joe Martin, who first came to pick potatoes in Maine in 1925. He worked in logging camps in Maine and Minnesota during the winter, followed by trout and salmon fishing back at Restigouche River in the spring. Then he worked on the river drives in northern Maine, followed by wheat harvesting in Saskatchewan or Montana during the summer. Like other tribespeople planning to work out west, Martin was entitled to a special "Indian ticket," issued by Canada's federal government, which allowed him to travel by railway for just a few dollars to distant regions. Finally he would return to Maine for potato picking during the fall, before heading back home to Restigouche (Prins 1982b).

Not all the Mi'kmaqs maintained a home base on a Canadian reserve. Bear River chief Richard McEwan (1988, x) writes in his *Memories of a Micmac Life* that he worked more than ten years in New England (1926–1937) before returning to his reserve village in southwest Nova Scotia. His older half-brother Michael, however, moved to Maine and never went back home: "[He] lived up in potato country. He had a little place that belonged to the farmer that he worked for. He worked right through the potato growing operation. He'd be there for planting and looking after gardens or whatever, and then in the fall he would be one of the pickers. Winters, he used to work in the woods."

Although there were many other Mi'kmaqs settling (more or less permanently) in northern Maine, most stayed there only for the harvest before returning to their respective reserves. Especially between 1920 and 1965, picking potatoes in Maine played a vital role in the reserve economies (Prins 1988, 40–53; Wallis and Wallis 1953, 115). For instance, more than 40 percent of the large Mi'kmaq population at Restigouche traveled the almost one hundred miles each September to Aroostook (see also Bock 1966, 48, 52). Many Mi'kmaqs, like other migrants, operated as freelance workers, arriving independently on the potato farms of northern Maine. Others were recruited directly by farmers who personally drove to the reserves to recruit pickers for the coming season (see also Wallis and Wallis 1955, 115). As one farmer remembers: "We'd go up [to the reserves] to pick up the Indians in a truck and bring 'em down to work. And at the end of the harvest we'd take 'em back and drop 'em off. They always got a lot of service" (Fitzpatrick 1982). Another form of migrant labor recruitment involved a special contractor known as a "jobber," who served as a middleman between the farmer and his Indian workers (see also Goldfarb 1981, 19–24). These farm labor contractors, or crew leaders, were commonly Indians with established kinship ties to the local reserves targeted for recruitment. As Philip Bock (1966, 49), who conducted research at Restigouche in the early 1960s, explains:

> Some go individually, but most of them travel in crews recruited by an Indian "jobber" who has agreed to furnish a certain number of pickers, loaders, or drivers for a particular farmer . . . Depending on the size of the farm, the crews may range in size from four or five individuals to twenty or more . . . Kinship, friendship, and locality seem to be the major determinants of crew membership. This is hardly a surprising discovery, but one must note that the potato harvest is presently the only organized activity completely under the control of the Indians.

Indian jobbers not only served in recruiting migrant laborers from the Mi'kmaq communities but also mediated between the farmer and his Indian picking crews during work: "The leader of the crew may work in the harvest or act as coordinator, or both, assigning sections to the pickers, keeping accounts straight, shopping for supplies, and so on" (Bock 1966, 49). As one farmer recalls: "There were crews of 10–30 Indians that came right off the reservation, and one in the group would supervise) . . . The head of the group was the one you talked to. We had buildings for them to stay in. Bedding and utensils they brought. They also brought someone to cook. Never paid 'em till Saturday night" (Fitzpatrick 1982). Generally Mi'kmaq jobbers earned a few cents for each barrel their crews picked (Bock 1966, 51).

The following reminiscence, as told by elderly Mi'kmaq basketmaker Sarah Lund (1987), now residing in northern Maine, is fairly typical:

> How well I remember the harvest season down home in Eel River. Around the fifth of September, everybody was so anxious to come to Maine and pick potatoes. I first came when I was sixteen. We packed up our shacks and packed all our clothes for the trip. Everybody was so excited in anticipation of coming to good old USA and making some money. We boarded a branch train for 10 cents to go the 15 miles to Campbellton to wait for another train to take us to the Maine border. Oh, how we planned for a month just to get here in Maine. It was usually about 36 people . . . going from the reservation. We would board the [train] at 8 A.M. for the 40 cents 95-mile ride to St. Leonard. We had our babies and children, too, and we would all try to stay together. It took us all day to get to the Maine border. The train was so slow . . . When we got to St. Leonard about 7 P.M., the potato farmers would all be waiting for us to take us to wherever they lived. And then began the work. It was a great time for us . . . I picked potatoes for many years after that.

The Mi'kmaqs, like other potato pickers, did their work crawling on their knees or standing square on the ground straddling their baskets, bodies bent in half. When chilly October rains turned the vast fields into dark stretches of cold mud, the work became especially dirty. Further aggravations resulted from the lack of toilet facilities in the fields (see also Thomas-Lycklema à Nÿeholt 1980, 40). Indian migrant workers were usually put up by the farmer who had hired them. They customarily stayed for free in a small picker's shack or camp, several of which were placed in a row behind the farm. These shacks rarely possessed adequate facilities, and the hygienic conditions were usually poor. Occasionally small crews boarded with the farmers themselves (Bock 1966, 49). In other instances, however, they were forced to sleep in the barn. One old Mi'kmaq woman remembers a farmer she worked for who "put everybody up in an old school house, half loaded with straw. There were big hand-made tables there for us to put our stuff on. And there was an old stove. We made tea on it in the morning. For lunch, you just do the best you can" (Doody, in McBride and Prins 1983).

After the fall harvest, where the Mi'kmaqs not only worked but also exchanged information, made new friends, and even found spouses, many headed "back home" to their reserves, where federal relief was barely sufficient for them to scrape through the long winter. Those who could find work often remained in Aroostook, hiring themselves out as lumberjacks; working as day laborers in the local starch factories or dark, dank potato houses; or producing hundreds of sturdy potato baskets for farmers in exchange for very modest housing (shacks or camps), food and clothing, or cash (McBride and Prins 1991). During the summer months from mid-July to late August many Mi'kmaqs picked blueberries on the vast wild barrens of coastal Maine, in Washington and Hancock Counties, situated some 150 miles south of Aroostook's potato fields. Sarah Lund (in McBride and Prins 1983) recalls:

> Abe and I always moved about. From April to June we'd be living on the reserve [period of slack employment], digging clams in Dalhousie. June to July we'd make potato baskets, usually in Maine. August, we'd be in Maine to rake [blue] berries, and during September–October we worked the potato harvest. If we found a good rent after the harvest we'd stay in Maine from November to March [potato house work]. If not, we'd return north to the reserve. But in the winter months we just survived . . . So, we went back and forth, back and forth for years, following seasonal work opportunities and sometimes just following the crazy whims of fate.

Mechanized Harvesting: The End of an Era

In the 1940s, when potato farming reached its peak, a total of 40,000 pickers was needed to bring in the harvest. In addition to local white and Native workers, farmers hired recent Irish immigrants and bonded French Canadians (Wilson 1937). During the war years, when there was a real labor shortage, trainloads of men, too young or too old to be drafted, were shipped in from as far away as Oklahoma. Numbering in this multitude were even 2,000 German prisoners of war (see also DuBay 1989b, 159; 1989c, 167; McBride 1983, 92, 114).

In the mid-1950s farmers started to mechanize harvesting, and the impact on the regional labor market was dramatic. Capable of processing up to 1,200 barrels per day, two-row harvesting machines replaced about 15 to 20 adult pickers each. During the next decade, mechanization of farm labor increased rapidly. By 1968 growers were using more than 1,100 harvesting machines, sharply reducing the need for migrant labor (see also Goldfarb 1981, 12–16). For instance, the number of bonded Canadian workers dropped from 7,800 in the early 1960s to no more than 500 in 1972, while the number of Native Americans migrating from their reserves in Canada to Aroostook's potato fields dropped from perhaps as many as 2,500 to no more than a few hundred (Johnston and Metzger 1974, 3–12).

By the early 1980s barely 10 percent of the crop was still being harvested by hand. The mechanization of farm labor in Aroostook had numerous side effects on the region's social life, including the demise of the more rowdy weekend scenes in town during picking season (see also Bock 1966, 51). Several older Mi'kmaqs living in northern Maine vividly remember the "good old days." An elderly Aroostook Mi'kmaq woman born at Restigouche recalls:

> I first came to Maine in 1934 with [my husband] to pick potatoes. By then there was a lot of people comin' from the reserves down to Maine for the harvest. More men than women came because folks didn't always have money for the train so they had to hitchhike, and men could hitchhike safer than women . . . We met up with all kinds of Indian folks in a beer joint in town. A place called Melissa's—run by a 350-pound woman. Boy was she a bouncer. All kinds of different people, Indians from all over Nova Scotia, New Brunswick and Maine packed into that place every night during harvesting season . . . Some people didn't even have enough money to go home with after picking season. (Doody, in McBride and Prins 1983)

According to another aged Mi'kmaq woman, a basketmaker in Mars Hill: "Maine harvesting—that was supposed to mean having a good time and making money. And there was a kind of freedom . . . in making the money. I could buy nice clothes. That first year, I worked in Presque Isle [Aroostook's potato center]. That was before there were harvesters and we worked with horses. The place was so packed with pickers. We could pick hard all day long and then in the weekend we partied" (Paul, in McBride and Prins 1983).

Mi'kmaq basketmaker Donald Sanipass of Chapman recalls the tail end of Aroostook's potato heydays: "Back in the sixties there were 'bout 20 camps here [in Chapman], because there were all different jobbers around these parts—loggin', potatoes, potato houses. It was a thriving place. Lots of jobs. Like I was tellin' you, during potato season [the city of] Presque Isle was something else—like Dodge City back in the 1800s. No elbow room. There were Indians all over the place here—working . . . for all kinds of farmers. Presque Isle was one wild place on the weekends during harvest time." His wife, Mary, adds, "You bet it was wild. During harvest the jail was full every weekend." Donald continues: "Back then, border police were all around, always checkin' potato fields and potato houses for illegal Canadian workers. Nowadays everything's modern and harvesters have replaced most pickers. So there's only a few [Indians] comin' cross border compared to what it used to be" (Sanipass and Sanipass, in McBride and Prins 1983).

Even though a small number of Mi'kmaqs continue their annual trek from the reserves to work in Maine's potato harvest today (participating in both mechanical and manual harvesting), the introduction of welfare programs on Canada's Indian reserves has also made seasonal farmwork largely unnecessary. Those Indians now working in northern Maine are mostly local off-reservation Mi'kmaqs and Maliseets. According to a 1982 survey of American Indian households in Aroostook County, about half of all resident Mi'kmaqs and Maliseets were still seasonally employed as day laborers in the potato fields and potato houses. Stricken with poverty, often living in shacks or trailers, most of these Indian families depended on food stamps and other welfare programs to supplement their irregular and inadequate wage earnings and income from selling crafts (Prins 1983). Usually hired only as a last resort, these marginalized tribespeople were victimized by anti-Indian racism and suffered from discriminatory labor practices (Cleaves 1980, 1–8; Prins 1988, 51–56; Wherry 1980, 1, 3).

Mechanized harvesting also spelled disaster for the local Indian basketmakers, who witnessed a steep decline in demand for their craft. In contrast to the peak years, when perhaps as many as 25,000 potato baskets were sold each year, demand dropped to a few thousand (see also McBride 1983). Reflecting on this change, one Mi'kmaq basketmaker comments: "Twenty years ago [in 1960], there were more than half a dozen families in [northern Maine] making baskets. Now from Caribou to Fort Kent, there's just Abe and me. All the rest died and their children didn't take up the business, because no one wanted baskets anymore" (Lund, in McBride 1983, 91).

Tribal Network as Communal Survival Strategy

The radical economic transformation among the Mi'kmaqs from a lifestyle based primarily on self-provisioning to one based almost exclusively on wage labor and federal government support (Mingione 1991, 82, 150–51) becomes abundantly clear when we compare demographic information pertaining to nineteenth-century subsistence activities with more recent data. Hunting, fishing, and trapping were still prevalent in the early 1800s, but this was by no means the case later in that century. According to the 1881 Canadian public census, which lists Mi'kmaq adult males by occupation, just 7 percent still subsisted on the basis of hunting and 4 percent on fishing. Most men listed were farmers (29 percent) or coopers (25 percent). Only 10 percent were laborers (Canada 1881).

A 1968 economic profile of the Restigouche band revealed the modern commodification process in one reserve community. By then there were no hunters or fishermen, and only 1 tribesman was still listed as a farmer. In all, 206 men (70 percent) were seasonally employed as day laborers, 24 were millworkers, and 30 were metalworkers. The remainder were on the government payroll as administrative personnel. All told, 88 percent of Restigouche's adult males depended at least in part on wage labor. Since few jobs were available on or near the reserve, an average of only 43 percent of the men aged between 20 and 40 actually resided on the reserve at any given time. In contrast, most women (75 percent) in this age group lived on the reserve year round (Ross and partners 1974, 46– 47).

Restigouche's demographic patterns are fairly representative for Mi'kmaq reserve communities in general. Only on rare occasions were these settlements fully occupied. During much of the year, particularly when there was ample demand for cheap unskilled labor, the reserves were inhabited only by those who were unable to compete for jobs in the labor market, especially mothers, children, and the elderly, as well as the sick or handicapped (Guillemin 1975, 82–92). From the 1950s onward virtually all reserve-based Mi'kmaqs relied in some degree on federal welfare programs: unemployment security, housing subsidies, health care, and/or child welfare support. With the help of such benefits, the reserves continue to function as refuge areas, offering a measure of financial security and social solidarity (Battiste 1977, 3–13).

Obviously the frequently long absences of so many tribespeople have left an indelible mark on the social fabric of the reserve communities. Commenting on the communal strategy for economic survival and the importance of the tribal network among urban Indians, Jeanne Guillemin (1975, 130–31, 136–37, 146) notes in her discussion of Mi'kmaq industrial laborers in Boston:

> The kind of work history which a Micmac Indian accumulates over the course of a lifetime includes an enormous variety of jobs . . . As an outsider the individual Indian is almost immune to the confusion of personal and institutional goals. When routinization threatens to make a machine out of him, he quits his job, even when, from a conventional point of view, he cannot possibly afford to. As more than simply an economic unit, his primary responsibility is to keep himself a viable member of the community . . . The amount of time spent on a job and the interim between one job and another is determined by social imperatives. Kin must be responsible to kin and friend to friend. Socializing, contests and conflicts, and communications must continue. Out of the social activity of the community comes its solution to economic marginality . . . It would be impossible for the Micmac to survive in urban society if money (like information on work, places to stay, and transportation) were not shared. A man or woman can obey the impulse to leave work, shifting attention from earning money to investing time and energy in the community, precisely because the basic economic strategy of the tribe is communal.

By contrast, the Mi'kmaqs who are out of touch with the tribal network and do not have access to reserves may be forced into becoming fully proletarianized. Such is the risk many Aroostook Mi'kmaqs and other tribespeople without such ethnic refuge areas confront. Their predicament is expressed by one old off-reservation Mi'kmaq woman in northern Maine as she sums up her long and difficult life: "You know, I get all mixed up about the dates of things because I moved so many times in my life. I moved around so much through the years that thinking about it makes me dizzy" (Copage, in McBride and Prins 1983). Yet even among these off-reservation Aroostook Mi'kmaqs, there is regular contact with other Mi'kmaq communities. According to a 1983 survey, about two-thirds of Aroostook Mi'kmaq households occasionally visited kinfolk and friends living in Canada's reserve communities

(Prins 1986a, 195–98). By the same token, Mi'kmaq migrant workers from Canada, as well as others passing through, from, or to the Boston area, frequently stop off in northern Maine. One Mi'kmaq elder recalls:

> Came to Aroostook for the first time in 1940 and left in 1948. I've moved so many times, to so many places, in and out of Aroostook. We used to live in Loring Base Street [in Presque Isle, Maine]. A bunch of us all living together, working in the potatoes. One day in 1947, Frank just walked into our place. Him and his brother Simon. They were here for picking, and had come up from Canada. They stayed all winter, then left in the spring to go back to Canada. But Frank came back that summer, and in the second winter he was here with us. He worked in the woods, cutting pulp. Stayed till blueberry time. His father used to come off and on and stay with us, too. (Francis, in McBride and Prins 1983)

Sometimes, of course, this communal economic strategy can turn into a major burden for families residing at major stopping places. Having just been invaded by a party of transient Mi'kmaqs, one Aroostook Mi'kmaq basket-maker complains:

> It's hard to stay ahead because after blue-berrying, people heading back north pass through here [Mars Hill, Maine] need food and a place to stay, and need money to help them get back home. And then there's all the folks who stay on to pick potatoes. Last year we had about a truckload of Indians staying here with us. But many of them we didn't even know. We can't get ahead this way, and we should put an end to it. Our own we would take in. Our friends and family we would take in and help them out. But, you know, even farmers send their pickers over here to pick on us. And we haven't got the money. (Paul, in McBride and Prins 1983)

Conclusion

Forming an internal colony based primarily on small tribal enclaves scattered throughout the Maritime Provinces and northern Maine, the Mi'kmaqs have persisted as a distinct Indian people after nearly five hundred years of direct experience with European power. Theirs is a history of a struggle for survival in which flexibility and adaptability are some of the more salient features. Since the mid-nineteenth century the Mi'kmaqs have found themselves on the proletarian edge. When they could no longer pursue their traditional subsistence strategies of hunting, trapping, fishing, and gathering, they turned to crafts and migrant labor. The seasonal nature of harvesting, in particular blueberry picking at Washington County's wild barrens in the summer, followed by potato digging in Aroostook's fields in the fall, played well into the Mi'kmaqs' traditionally migratory way of life. These temporary wage-earning opportunities within traveling distance from the reserves not only earned them relatively good money (albeit for rather short periods of time) but also allowed them to maintain a vital linkage with their tribal communities (see also Battiste 1977, 3–13).

In this respect the survival of Mi'kmaq bands as federally dependent communities merits consideration. In Canada the government bureaucracy recognizes bands, not tribes, as the corporate groups entitled to the reserved tracts of land and as the administrative units eligible for federal services and funding (Upton 1979, 171–81). Clearly these protected ethnic enclaves have played a critical role in the Mi'kmaq struggle for cultural survival. Serving the Mi'kmaqs as "a haven in hard times and as a focus of sentiments, as a home," the reserves have allowed the mostly unskilled and semiskilled workers to avoid the more dreadful consequences of the cheap labor market (Guillemin 1975, 61).

The impact of migrant labor on the organizational structure of Mi'kmaq tribal society has been threefold. First, it played into the disarticulation of the autonomous bands as self-supporting corporate communities: "Aside from electing band council representatives, people from the same band might never operate as an organized group, though individuals meeting for the first time can use their common band affiliation as an excuse for developing friendship" (Guillemin 1975, 63). In combination with a growing federal dependency, migrant labor also subverted the social, economic, and spiritual authority of the traditional band chiefs (Wallis and Wallis 1953, 120; 1955, 171–75). Second, while economic pressure compelled participation in wage labor, political status as "Indians" entitled Mi'kmaqs to residence on reserve lands and enabled them to resist full proletarianization.

Third, and this is an issue explored further elsewhere (cf. Prins 1996), migrant labor contributed to the process of Mi'kmaq nation formation. Clearly the seasonal demand for large numbers of rural wage laborers, coupled with the availability of mechanized means of transportation, greatly increased the interaction among tribespeople hailing from remote and widely dispersed communities. Periodically associating in Maine's blueberry barrens and potato fields, they not only expanded their knowledge about one another but also shared a common treatment as a low-caste minority group (cf. Hechter 1975, 15–43). Furthermore, these annual occasions provided the Mi'kmaqs with the chance to encounter numerous other Native people, including Maliseets, Passamaquoddies, Penobscots, and Indians belonging to more distant tribes. The outcome has been a growing sense of collective consciousness among the transient Mi'kmaqs clustering in these temporary encampments: "The community is today quite knowledgeable about the extent of its own tribal boundaries. Each member in the course of a lifetime is likely to meet up with many other Micmac who are relatively difficult to place in an immediate kinship network and yet look, speak, and act Micmac and have to be accounted for" (Guillemin 1975, 75).

The issue of migrant labor in modern tribal societies reaches beyond mere economic survival and cannot be understood in terms of one-dimensional categories such as underemployment. Even though Mi'kmaq migrant workers do "sell themselves piecemeal," they do so more or less on their own terms. As members within a diffuse tribal network, with a right to retire to their respective reserve communities, they are not fully "exposed to all the vicissitudes of competition, to all the fluctuations of the market" (Marx 1972, 341). The pursuit of a communal strategy shields them against full-fledged proletarianization and allows them to retain at least a semblance of independence as "freedom people" (see also Guillemin 1975, 146; Mingione 1991, 152, 188–91). Paradoxically, while migrant labor contributed to the waning of traditional band organization, it reinforced the ethnic solidarity among the widely scattered Mi'kmaq people, who increasingly identify themselves as a tribal nation—the Mi'kmaq Nationimow.

NOTES

Acknowledgment: Originally published in Alice Littlefield and Martha C. Knack, eds., *Native Americans and Wage Labor: Ethnohistorical Perspectives* (Norman: University of Oklahoma Press, 1996), pp. 45–66. Copyright © 1996 by the University of Oklahoma Press, Norman, Publishing Division of the University. All Rights Reserved.

1. Historically, the Mi'kmaq have been known by different names. They referred to themselves as L'nu'k (or Ulnoo), meaning "humans." In the early colonial period Europeans used different ethnonyms, including Souriquois, Gaspesiens, Acadian Indians, and Cape Sable Indians. Since the late 1600s the present name began to appear in the records as Micmac, Mikemak, Miquemaque, Mukmack, Muqumawaach, Mic Mac, and Miqmaq. During the past two decades Mi'kmaq has become the preferred indigenous orthography (cf. Dickason 1992, 16), a usage I have also adopted in my case study (Prins 1996). Other spellings are used only when referring to an established name, such as the Aroostook Band of Micmacs, or when the name appears within quotation marks.

2. Although wage labor among North American Indians did not become common until the late 1800s, the practice dates to the early colonial period. For instance, English settlers in Massachusetts employed Nipmucks and other tribespeople, among others, as farmworkers beginning in the mid-1600s. Also, the Narragansett Indians of Rhode Island hired themselves out as stone masons, servants, and laborers beginning in the 1700s (see also Gookin 1806, 162; Simmons 1978, 195).

3. The concept of commodification is based on Polanyi (1944, 73), who observes that labor (like land and money) is a "fictive commodity" (see Mingione 1991, 22, 103). In my discussion of the commodication process in Mi'kmaq culture, I rely on Italian sociologist Mingione (1991, 96–97, 112), who notes that the persistence of various forms of self-provisioning, organized and regulated within reciprocal networks such as kinship, friendship, or local communities or regional and ethnic groupings, poses "limits to the full commodification of social life."

4. The off-reservation Mi'kmaqs and Maliseets in northern Maine organized themselves on a regional basis, forming the Association of Aroostook Indians (AAI) in 1969. In 1980 a group of Maliseets within the AAI gained federal recognition as the Houlton Band of Maliseet. In 1991 the Aroostook Band of Micmacs became federally recognized as a U.S. tribe and received funding to purchase a 5,000-acre tract to serve this 580-member community in northern Maine as a land base (Prins 1994). I served these Mi'kmaqs, who now maintain headquarters in Presque Isle, Maine, as staff anthropologist from 1981 to 1991, conducting in-depth ethnohistorical research on their behalf. For a description of their native rights quest, see, among others, Heald (1987), McBride (1987), and Prins (1988, 1990, 1996).

5. A seasonal worker is commonly defined as someone who works at a job that does not offer continuing, year-round employment, usually involving farmwork, and works 25 to 149 days per year (Goldfarb 1981, 16; Holt 1984, 20).

6. Although it is impossible to accurately estimate the number of seasonal farmworkers, including migrant laborers, a 1974 U.S. Department of Agriculture survey concluded that their number was about 927,000 (Goldfarb 1981, 16). On the east coast the main stream of migratory farmworker movement runs northward in the spring and returns south in the fall and may have involved some 58,000 workers in 1949, most of whom were blacks with a home base in Florida and other southern states. Leaving for the summer to work in the northern states, these black migrant workers were joined by laborers from Puerto Rico, Jamaica, and the Bahamas. In addition, thousands of American Indians and French Canadians could be found in the east coast migratory stream (Thomas Lycklema à Nijeholt 1980, 33–36; see also Friedland and Nelkin 1971).

7. This ruling had the effect of excluding Mi'kmaqs and other "Canadian Indians" from the protections accorded to "bonded" Canadians but denied to domestic farm labor in the United States. A year later the U.S. Congress confirmed the validity of the 1794 Jay Treaty guaranteeing these Indians free border-crossing rights into the United States. This agreement, although challenged repeatedly since that time, continues to be upheld (Buesing 1972, 22–23; Johnston and Metzger 1974, 3–4).

REFERENCES

Abbott, John S. C. 1895. *The History of Maine, from the Earliest Discovery of the Region by the Northmen Until the Present Time.* Boston: B. B. Russell.

Abler, Thomas S., and Elizabeth Tooker. 1978. Seneca. In *Handbook of North American Indians.* Vol. 15, *The Northeast,* ed. Bruce G. Trigger, 505–17. Washington, D.C.: Smithsonian Institution Press.

Battiste, Marie. 1977. Cultural Transmission and Cultural Survival in Contemporary Micmac Society. *The Indian Historian,* 10 (fall), 2–13.

Bock, Philip K. 1966. *The Micmac Indians of Restigouche: History and Contemporary Description.* Bulletin 213, Anthropological Series 77. Ottawa: National Museum of Canada.

———. 1978. Micmac. In *Handbook of North American Indians.* Vol. 15, *The Northeast,* ed. Bruce G. Trigger, 109–22. Washington, D.C.: Smithsonian Institution Press.

Boxberger, Daniel L. 1988. In and Out of the Labor Force: The Lummi Indians and the Development of the Commercial Salmon Fishery of North Puget Sound, 1880–1900. *Ethnohistory*, 35, no. 2: 161–90.

Braroe, Niels W. 1975. *Indian and White: Self-Image and Interaction in a Canadian Plains Community*. Stanford: Stanford University Press.

Buesing, Gregory. 1972. Maliseet and Micmac Rights in the United States. Houlton, Me.: Association of Aroostook Indians. Unpub. ms.

Canada. 1881. *Census of Canada*. Ottawa: Public Archives of Canada. Microfilm.

Canada, Department of Indian Affairs. 1880–1936. *Annual Reports of the Superintendent General*. Ottawa: Government Printing Office.

Cleaves, Robert. 1980. A Betrayal of Trust: The Maine Settlement Act and the Houlton Band of Maliseets. *American Indian Journal* (November), 1–8.

Cooney, Robert. 1896. *A Compendious History of the Northern Part of the Province of New Brunswick and of the District of Gaspe, in Lower Canada*. Chatham, N.B.: D. G. Smith.

Dickason, Olive P. 1992. *Canada's First Nations: A History of Founding Peoples from Earliest Times*. Norman: University of Oklahoma Press.

Dubay, Guy F. 1989a. Aroostook: The Military Impact. In *The County: Land of Promise: A Pictorial History of Aroostook County, Maine*, ed. Anna F. McGrath, 161–70. Norfolk, Va.: Donning.

———. 1989b. The Garden of Maine. In *The County: Land of Promise: A Pictorial History of Aroostook County, Maine*, ed. Anna F. McGrath, 153–60. Norfolk, Va.: Donning.

———. 1989c. The Land: In Common and Undivided. In *The County: Land of Promise: A Pictorial History of Aroostook County, Maine*, ed. Anna F. McGrath, 145–52. Norfolk, Va.: Donning.

Engels, Friedrich. 1972. On Social Relations in Russia. In *The Marx-Engels Reader*, ed. Robert C. Tucker, 589–99. New York: W. W. Norton.

Fitzpatrick, Anthony. 1982. Unpublished interview with Bunny McBride.

Friedland, William H., and Dorothy Nelkin. 1971. *Migrant Agricultural Workers in America's Northeast*. New York: Holt, Rinehart and Winston.

Gilpin, J. Bernard. 1878. Indians of Nova Scotia (1875–1878). In *The Native People of Atlantic Canada*, ed. Harold F. McGee, 102–19. Toronto: McClelland and Stewart.

Goldfarb, Ronald L. 1981. *Migrant Farm Workers: A Caste of Despair*. Ames: Iowa State University Press.

Gookin, Daniel. 1806. Historical Collections of the Indians in New England (1674). *Collections* of the Massachusetts Historical Society. First series, vol. 1: 141–229. Boston.

Green, Jere W. 1989. Aroostook Becomes a County. In *The County: Land of Promise: A Pictorial History of Aroostook County, Maine*, ed. Anna F. McGrath, 63–73. Norfolk, Va.: Donning.

Guillemin, Jeanne. 1975. *Urban Renegades: The Cultural Strategy of American Indians*. New York: Columbia University Press.

Heald, Nan. 1987. The Aroostook Band of Micmacs' Struggle for Tribal Recognition. In *Maine Bar Journal* (Sept.), 272–76.

Hechter, Michael. 1975. *Internal Colonialism: The Celtic Fringe in British National Development*. Berkeley and Los Angeles: University of California Press.

Hoffman, Bernard G. 1955. The Historical Ethnography of the Micmac of the Sixteenth and Seventeenth Centuries. Ph.D. diss., University of California, Berkeley.

Holt, J. S. 1984. Introduction to the Seasonal Farm Labor Problem. In *Seasonal Agricultural Labor Markets in the United States*, ed. Robert D. Emerson, 3–32. Ames: Iowa State University Press.

Indian Task Force. n.d. United States Legal Rights of Native Americans Born in Canada. Boston: Office of the Indian Task Force, Federal Regional Council of New England, with the assistance of the Boston Indian Council.

Johnston, E. W., and H. B. Metzger. 1974. Labor Replacement in Potato Harvesting in Aroostook County. *Research in the Life Sciences*, 22, no. 5: 1–13.

Kelly, Isabel T., and Catherine S. Fowler. 1986. Southern Paiute. In *Handbook of North American Indians*. Vol. XI, *The Great Basin*, ed. Warren L. D'Azevedo, 368–97. Washington, D.C.: Smithsonian Institution Press.

Kidder, Frederic. 1867. *Military Operations in Eastern Maine and Nova Scotia During the Revolution, Chiefly Compiled from the Journals and the Letters of Colonel John Allan, with Notes and a Memoir of Col. John Allan*. Albany: Joel Munsell.

Lund, Sarah. 1987. How I Remember. *Aroostook Micmac Council Newsletter* (November), 3–5.

Lurie, Nancy O. 1978. Winnebago. In *Handbook of North American Indians*. Vol. XV, *The Northeast*, ed. Bruce G. Trigger, 690–707. Washington, D.C.: Smithsonian Institution Press.

Marx, Karl. 1972. Manifesto of the Communist Party. In *The Marx-Engels Reader*, ed. Robert C. Tucker, 331–62. New York: W. W. Norton.

McBride, Bunny. 1983. A Special Kind of Freedom. *Down East: Magazine of Maine*, 29, no. 11: 88–93, 114.

———. 1987. The Micmac of Maine: A Continuing Struggle. In *Rooted Like the Ash Trees: New England Indians and the Land*, ed. Richard G. Carlson, 35–39. Naugatuck, Conn.: Eagle Wing Press.

McBride, Bunny, and Harald E. L. Prins. 1983. In Their Own Words: Oral Histories of Six Contemporary Aroostook Micmac Families. Unpub. ms. on file with the Aroostook Band of Micmacs, Presque Isle, and with authors.

———. 1991. Micmacs and Splint Basketry: Tradition, Adaptation, and Survival. In *Our Lives in Our Hands: Micmac Indian Basketmakers*, ed. Bunny McBride, 3–23. Gardiner, Maine: Tilbury House.

McEwan, J. Richard. 1988. *Memories of a Micmac Life*. Fredericton, N.B.: Micmac-Maliseet Institute, University of New Brunswick.

Meggitt, Mervyn J. 1962. *Desert People: A Study of the Walbiri Aborigines of Central Australia*. Sydney: Angus and Robertson.

Mingione, Enzo. 1991. *Fragmented Societies: The Sociology of Economic Life: Beyond the Market Paradigm*. London: Basil Blackwell.

Nicholas, Andrea B., with contributions by Harald E. L. Prins. 1989. The Spirit in the Land: The Native People of Aroostook. In *The County: Land of Promise: A Pictorial History of Aroostook County, Maine*, ed. Anna F. McGrath, 19–38. Norfolk, Va.: Donning.

Nietfeld, Patricia K. L. 1981. Determinants of Aboriginal Micmac Political Structure. Ph.D. diss., University of New Mexico, Albuquerque.

Plessis, Joseph-Octave. 1903. *Journal des visites pastorales de 1815 et 1816 par Monseigneur Joseph-Octave Plessis Eveque de Quebec*. Quebec: Tetu.

Polanyi, Karl. 1944. *The Great Transformation*. New York: Rinehart.

Prins, Harald E. L. 1982a. Genesis of the Micmac Community in Maine and Its Intricate

Relationship to Micmac Reserves in the Maritimes. Unpub. report on file with the Aroostook Band of Micmacs, Presque Isle, Maine, and with author.

——. 1982b. Unpub. fieldnotes of visit to Micmac Reserves in Canada.

——. 1983. Social and Economic Profile of the Aroostook Micmac Band in Northern Maine, as based on the A.M.C. Census. Unpub. report on file with the Aroostook Band of Micmacs, Presque Isle, Maine, and with author.

——. 1986a. The Aroostook Mimac Band in Maine: An Ethnohistorical View. Document Prepared for the Federal Acknowledgment Petition to the Bureau of Indian Affairs. Unpub. report on file with the Aroostook Band of Micmacs, Presque Isle, Maine; with Pine Tree Legal Assistance, Augusta, Maine; and with author.

——. 1986b. Micmacs and Maliseets in the St. Lawrence River Valley. *Actes du dix-septieme congres des Algonquinistes*, ed. William Cowan, 263–78. Ottawa: Carleton University Press.

——. 1988. Tribulations of a Border Tribe: A Discourse on the Political Ecology of the Aroostook Band of Micmacs (Sixteenth–Twentieth Centuries). Ph.D. diss., New School for Social Research, New York.

——. 1990. The Aroostook Band of Micmacs: An Historical Anthropological Review. In *Hearing Before the Select Committee on Indian Affairs on S. 1413 to Settle All Claims of the Aroostook Band of Micmacs Resulting from the Band's Omission from the Maine Indian Claims Settlement Act of 1980.* 101st Cong., 2d sess. March 28. Washington, D.C.: GPO.

——. 1994. Micmac. In *Native America in the Twentieth Century: An Encyclopedia*, ed. Mary B. Davis, 339–40. New York and London: Garland Publishing.

——. 1996. *The Mi'kmaq: Resistance, Accommodation, and Cultural Survival.* Fort Worth, Texas: Harcourt Brace.

Radin, Paul. 1963. *The Autobiography of a Winnebago Indian.* New York: Dover.

Redfield, Robert. 1953. *The Primitive World and Its Transformations.* Ithaca: Cornell University Press.

Ross, P. S., and partners. 1974. An Economic Development Study for the Restigouche Indian Reserve, Restigouche, 1966. Unpub. report cited in Claude Audet, *Les indiens de Ristigouche*, 46–47. Rimouski, Que.: College de Rimouski.

Rowe, Eugene. 1965. Maine's Potato Empire and How It Grew. *Produce Marketing* (October): n.p.

Simmons, Williams S. 1978. Narragansett. In *Handbook of North American Indians.* Vol. XV, *The Northeast*, ed. Bruce G. Trigger, 190–97. Washington, D.C.: Smithsonian Institution Press.

Smith, Titus. 1974. Extract from 1801–1802 Journal. *Micmac News*, 4, no. 10: 4.

Spindler, Louise S. 1978. Menominee. In *Handbook of North American Indians.* Vol. XV, *The Northeast*, ed. Bruce G. Trigger, 708–24. Washington, D.C.: Smithsonian Institution Press.

Thomas-Lycklema à Nÿeholt, G. 1980. *On the Road for Work: Migratory Workers on the East Coast of the United States.* The Hague: Martinus Nijhoff.

Upton, Leslie F. S. 1979. *Micmacs and Colonists: Indian-White Relations in the Maritimes, 1713–1867.* Vancouver: University of British Columbia Press.

Wallis, Wilson D., and Ruth S. Wallis. 1953. Culture Loss and Culture Change Among the Micmac of the Canadian Maritime Provinces, 1912–1950. Kroeber Anthropological Society Papers, nos. 8–9: 100–129. Berkeley: University of California.

——. 1955. *The Micmac Indians of Eastern Canada.* Minneapolis: University of Minnesota Press.

Weaver, Sally M. 1978. Six Nations of the Grand River, Ontario. In *Handbook of North American Indians*. Vol. XV, *The Northeast*, ed. Bruce G. Trigger, 525–43. Washington, D.C.: Smithsonion Institution Press.

Wherry, James D. 1979. The History of Maliseets and Micmacs in Aroostook County, Maine: Preliminary Report Two. In *Hearings Before the Select Committee on Indian Affairs on S. 2829 to Provide for the Settlement of the Maine Indian Land Claims*. 96th Cong., 2d sess., 506–609. Washington, D.C.: GPO.

———. 1980. Of Maliseets and Micmacs: Maine's Other Indians. *Indian Truth*, no. 231 (April), 1, 3.

Whitehead, Ruth H. 1980. *Eliteky: Micmac Material Culture from 1600 A.D. to the Present*. Halifax: Nova Scotia Museum.

———. 1987. I Have Lived Here Since the World Began: Atlantic Coast Artistic Traditions. In *The Spirit Sings: Artistic Traditions of Canada's First Peoples*, 17–51. Glenbow-Alberta Institute. Toronto: McClelland and Stewart.

Wilson, Charles M. 1937. Potato Race. *Country Gentleman* (January), 12–13, 64–65.

Wolf, Eric R. 1982. *Europe and the People Without History*. Berkeley and Los Angeles: University of California Press.

York, Dena W. 1989. Heading for the Aroostook. In *The County: Land of Promise: A Pictorial History of Aroostook County, Maine*, ed. Anna F. McGrath, 49–58. Norfolk, Va.: Donning.

Contributors

Gregory V. Button is Assistant Professor of Public Health and Anthropology at the University of Michigan in Ann Arbor.

Colin G. Calloway is Professor of History and Native American Studies and John Sloan Dickey Third Century Professor in the Social Sciences at Dartmouth College. His books include: *New Worlds for All: Indians, Europeans, and the Remaking of Early America* (1997), *The American Revolution in Indian Country* (1996), *The Western Abenakis of Vermont, 1600–1800* (1990), and (as editor) *Dawnland Encounters: Indians and Europeans in Northern New England* (1991).

Thomas Doughton, most recently Visiting Assistant Professor of History at the University of Massachusetts, Amherst, and Visiting Assistant Professor in Native American Studies at Dartmouth College, is the former Tribal Historian for the Nipmucs and former Executive Director of the Nipmuc Tribal Acknowledgment Project, Inc. He is involved in several public history projects. Serving as Director of the People's Institute, Worcester, Massachusetts, he is also chair of the Quinsigamond Band of Nipmucs. With Russell G. Handsman, he is working on a critical edition of John Milton Earle's 1861 report and "census" of Massachusetts Indians. His essay in this collection is a revised chapter from a work in progress entitled "Native Americans and the Politics of Representation: Indians in Nineteenth-Century Massachusetts."

Evan Haefeli is completing his Ph.D. in history at Princeton University. He and Kevin Sweeney are working on a full-length study of the Deerfield raid.

David L. Ghere earned his Ph.D. from the University of Maine at Orono, with a dissertation entitled "Abenaki Factionalism, Emigration, and Social Continuity: Indian Society in Northern New England, 1725 to 1765." He has published several articles on Abenaki ethnohistory and is now Associate Professor in the General College at the University of Minnesota.

Ruth Wallis Herndon is Assistant Professor of History at the University of Toledo. She is working on a book entitled "Poverty, Perversity and Public Policy in Early America: Records of Warning Out in Rhode Island, 1750–1800."

Jean M. O'Brien is White Earth Ojibwe from Minnesota. She is Associate Professor of History at the University of Minnesota and author of *Dispossession by Degrees: Indian Land and Identity in Natick, Massachusetts, 1650–1790* (1997).

Barry O'Connell is Professor of English at Amherst College, editor of *On Our Own Ground: The Complete Writings of William Apess, a Pequot* (1992), and coeditor of the series Native Americans of the Northeast, published by the University of Massachusetts Press. He is currently working on a book entitled "Surviving Identities: Native American Writers and Their People's Persistence, 1780–1940."

Ann Marie Plane is Assistant Professor of History at the University of California, Santa Barbara. She has written several articles on issues of gender, race, and ethnicity in New England and is currently writing a book on marriage, households, and racial boundaries in southeastern New England from 1600 to 1730.

Harald E. L. Prins is Professor of Anthropology at Kansas State University. In addition to fieldwork in the Argentine pampas, he worked for a decade with the Mi'kmaq Indians of northern Maine and testified as an expert witness before Congress in the Aroostook Band of Micmacs' successful fight for federal recognition and a land claims settlement. He co-produced a documentary film on Mi'kmaq basketmakers, *Our Lives in Our Hands* (1985), coedited *American Beginnings: Exploration, Culture, and Cartography in the Land of Norumbega* (1995), and is the author of *The Mi'kmaq: Resistance, Accommodation, and Cultural Survival* (1996).

Dr. Ella Wilcox Sekatau is ethnohistorian and medicine woman of the Narragansett tribe.

Kevin Sweeney is Associate Professor of History and American Studies at Amherst College. His 1987 dissertation won the Jamestown Prize for the Institute of Early American History and Culture and will be published as *River Gods and Related Minor Deities: The Williams Family and Eighteenth-Century New England Culture*.

Daniel Vickers is Professor of History at Memorial University of Newfoundland. He is the author of *Farmers and Fishermen: Two Centuries of Work in Essex County, Massachusetts, 1630–1850* (Chapel Hill: University of North Carolina Press, 1994).

Acknowledgments

A number of essays in this volume have been previously published and are reprinted by permission:

Evan Haefeli and Kevin Sweeney, "Revisiting the Redeemed Captive: New Perspectives on the 1704 Attack on Deerfield," *William and Mary Quarterly*, 3d ser., 52 (1995), 3–46.

David L. Ghere, "The 'Disappearance' of the Abenaki in Western Maine: Political Organization and Ethnocentric Assumptions," *American Indian Quarterly*, 17 (1993), 193–207.

Daniel Vickers, "The First Whalemen of Nantucket," *William and Mary Quarterly*, 3d ser., 40 (1983), 560–83.

Ruth Wallis Herndon and Ella Wilcox Sekatau, "The Right to a Name: The Narragansett People and Rhode Island Officials in the Revolutionary Era," *Ethnohistory*, forthcoming, published by the Society for Ethnohistory and reprinted by permission of Duke University Press.

Jean O' Brien, "'Divorced' from the Land: Resistance and Survival of Indian Women in Eighteenth-Century New England," is a revision of an article originally published in Mary Jo Maynes, Ann Waltner, Birgitte Soland, and Ulrike Strasser, eds., *Gender, Kinship, Power: A Comparative and Interdisciplinary History* (New York: Routledge, 1995), 319–33. Copyright © 1996 by Routledge, Inc.

Ann Marie Plane and Gregory Button, "The Massachusetts Indian Enfranchisement Act: Ethnic Contest in Historical Context, 1849–1869," *Ethnohistory*, 40:4 (Fall 1993), 587–618. Copyright 1993, Society for Ethnohistory. Reprinted by permission of Duke University Press.

Harald E. L. Prins, "Tribal Network and Migrant Labor: Mi'kmaq Indians as Seasonal Workers in Aroostook's Potato Fields, 1870–1980," in Martha C. Knack and Alice Littlefield, eds., *Native Americans and Wage Labor: Ethnohistorical Perspectives* (Norman: University of Oklahoma Press, 1996), 45–65.

Index

Abemelich, Patience, 213

Abenaki Indians, 2, 4, 5, 6, 7, 8, 9, 14; conflicts with Iroquois Nation, 50–51, 52; and English/French policy, 62(n32); political organization, 73, 83–84; presence in western Maine, 15, 72–73, 75–84; and tribal labels, 73–74; and tribal status recognition, 11; value of captives, 38, 63(n50). *See also* Androscoggin; Arosaguntacook; Becancour; Cowassuck; Eastern Abenakis; Missisquoi; Odanak; Pennacook; Pigwacket; Saint Francis Abenakis; Sokoki; Western Abenakis

Abolitionists, 183, 200(nn 37, 42)

Abraham, Patience, 213

Adams, John, 8

Adiawando, 77

African Americans: and historical discourse, 219; indentured children, 141(n72); intermarriage with Indians, 7, 135(n5), 155–56, 161(n50); and Massachusetts debate over ethnic identity, 184, 188, 190, 193–95, 201(n50); official population in Rhode Island, 141(n73); and Reconstruction-era race policy, 182; in Rhode Island town records, 126–27, 132–33, 140(n61); in Worcester, Massachusetts, 216–17

Alcohol, 101, 129

Aldrich, John, 124–25

Allen, Ethan, 5

Allen, Ira, 5

American Revolution: development of racial ideology during, 142(n93); Indian participation in, 7, 82, 124, 139(n57); and

New England slave emancipation, 132–33

Amerquit, Mercy, 152

Amesokanti, 44

Amos, Joseph, 192

Amos, Matthias, 205(n93)

Andros, Edmund, 1, 51

Androscoggin Indians, 15, 73–79, 81–84

Anthony, Charles, 225(n27)

Anthony, James, 225(n21)

Anthony, Tent, 120, 137(n22)

Anthony, William, 225(n27)

Apes, Erwin, 175

Apes, William Elisha, 175–76

Apess, Elizabeth, 168

Apess, Mary, 168

Apess, William, 7, 14, 16, 162–75, 176(n3), 177(n8)

Arkless, Angenette, 214

Arnold, Alice, 120

Arnold, Sarah Maria, 213

Aroostook Band (Micmacs), 17, 231, 232, 248(n4)

Arosaguntacook, 74

Arsikantegouks, 37

Ashpalon, 39, 44

Assimilation, 4, 143(n96), 197(n11); Apess on, 172; as federal policy, 199(n37); Massachusetts enfranchisement and belief in, 179, 195; and Narragansetts, 115

Association of Aroostook Indians (AAI), 248(n4)

Attaquin, Solomon, 184, 192, 193

Austin, Benjamin, 126

Awassamug, Hannah, 151

Women (*continued*)
and land ownership, 148, 149, 160(n24); and poor relief/warnouts in Rhode Island, 121, 123, 137(n32), 139(n46); presence in Deerfield raiding party of, 53; and religious piety, 54; role in enfranchisement debate, 193–95, 205(nn 97, 102)

Wood, Phebe, 129

Woodstock, Connecticut, 214–15

Worcester, Massachusetts, 215–18, 219–20, 227(nn 35, 36, 37, 39), 228(n45)

World War II, 241

Wright, John, 168

Written record, 14; Apess challenges to, 163–67, 169–76; and Indians in Massachusetts, 208, 209, 220, 221; and Narragansetts in Rhode Island, 118–19, 124–27, 132–33. *See also* Historical discourse

Yocake, Eunice, 120–21

8167

University Press of New England publishes books under its own imprint and is the publisher for Brandeis University Press, Dartmouth College, Middlebury College Press, University of New Hampshire, Tufts University, and Wesleyan University Press.

Library of Congress Cataloging-in-Publication Data

After King Philip's War : presence and persistence in Indian New England / edited, with an introduction by Colin G. Calloway.

    p.   cm. — (Reencounters with colonialism — new perspectives on the Americas)

    Includes bibliographical references and index.

    ISBN 0–87451–819–9 (pbk. : alk. paper)

    1. Indians of North America — New England — History — 18th century.

2. Indians of North America — New England — History — 19th century.

3. Indians of North America — New England — Social conditions.

4. King Philip's War, 1675–1676.   I. Calloway, Colin G. (Colin Gordon), 1953– . II. Series.

E78.N5A17   1997

974.4'00497 — dc21

                                                 96–51813